THE VICTORY BANNER OVER THE REICHSTAG

RUSSIAN AND EAST EUROPEAN STUDIES

JONATHAN HARRIS, EDITOR

THE VICTORY BANNER OVER THE REICHSTAG

FILM, DOCUMENT, AND RITUAL IN RUSSIA'S CONTESTED MEMORY OF WORLD WAR II

JEREMY HICKS

UNIVERSITY OF PITTSBURGH PRESS

Published by the University of Pittsburgh Press, Pittsburgh, Pa., 15260

Manufactured in the United States of America
Printed on acid-free paper
10 9 8 7 6 5 4 3 2 1

Library of Congress Cataloging-in-Publication Data

Names: Hicks, Jeremy, author.
Title: The victory banner over the Reichstag : film, document, and ritual in Russia's contested memory of World War II / Jeremy Hicks.
Other titles: Film, document and ritual in Russia's contested memory of World War II
Description: Pittsburgh : University of Pittsburgh Press, [2020] | Series: Russian and East European studies | Includes bibliographical references and index.
Identifiers: LCCN 2020034688 | ISBN 9780822946502 (hardcover) | ISBN 9780822987963 (ebook)
Subjects: LCSH: Berlin, Battle of, Berlin, Germany, 1945—Motion pictures and the war. | World War, 1939-1945—Soviet Union—Flags. | Soviet Union. Raboche-Krest'i͡anskai͡a Krasnai͡a Armii͡a—Flags. | Flags—Soviet Union. | Emblems, State—Soviet Union. | Collective memory—Russia—History—20th century. | National characteristics, Russian. | War and society—History—20th century.
Classification: LCC D743.23 .H53 2020 | DDC 940.54/213155—dc23
LC record available at https://lccn.loc.gov/2020034688

Cover art: Evgenii Khaldei, *Victory Banner over the Reichstag*. Courtesy of RGAKFD
Cover design: Melissa Dias-Mandoly

CONTENTS

Acknowledgments
vii
A Note on Transliteration and Document Citation
ix

Introduction
3
1. The Raising of the Victory Banner
20
2. Victory and the Postwar Stalin Cult
51
3. The Death of Stalin and Birth of the Victory Cult
89
4. The Victory Cult in the Age of Television
131
5. Iconoclasm, Resanctification, and the Post-Soviet Victory Cult
170
Conclusion
216

Notes
223
Bibliography
261
Index
277

ACKNOWLEDGMENTS

No intellectual work is conceived in isolation, and *The Victory Banner over the Reichstag* evolved from a study group on iconic images of political violence conceived jointly with my colleagues in film studies: Guy Westwell and Libby Saxton. I owe them an enormous debt, as our conversations helped me to frame this project, develop my ideas, and sharpen my analysis.

This project is also in dialogue with my previous book, *First Films of the Holocaust*. Having written there about *unknown* images of World War II, neglected by Russians and the wider world, I wanted to explore how famous and ubiquitous images serve to shape memory of that conflict, especially in Russia, in such a way as to marginalize or color memory of the Holocaust. This is the result.

There were many other people whose company, ideas, and advice have helped me, in bigger or smaller ways. Too many to mention, these include above all Evgenii Tsymbal, who helped with archival work, advice, friendship, criticism, hospitality, and good humor, and Leonid Terushkin, of the Russian Holocaust Foundation, who has also helped me in so many ways beyond the purely intellectual. My colleagues at NIIK (VGIK), Sergei Kapterev and Nikolai Izvolov, have always provided great companionship and many interesting comments on my ideas. They were joined, in addition to Guy and Libby, by Robert Hariman, John Louis Lucaites, Sylvie Lindeperg, Anja Tippner, Dmitrii Karavaev, and Julian Graffy, among others, in two May 2018 workshops, which helped me to refine my ideas. I am also grateful to my friends in Berlin—Petar Kobilarov, Ava Mirkovic, and Isidor Kobilarov-Mirkovic—for indulging my need to visit some of the sites associated with this narrative.

I am also grateful to those who have facilitated seminars at which I have presented part of this research. These include Claire Knight at Oxford and Philip Bullock (also at Oxford), among others. Likewise, I thank all the contributors who asked questions of me at those events.

I am enormously indebted to the staff at a number of Russian archives, especially Elena Kolikova at RGKAFD (Krasnogorsk), as well as staff at Gosfil'mofond, GARF, RGASPI, RGALI, and RGANI. I am also grateful to the Bundesarchiv-Filmarchiv (namely Beatrix Haußmann) in Berlin, and numerous wonderful libraries without which this research would have been inconceivable, especially the British Library and SSEES-UCL Library, both in London, and the Russian State Public Historical Library and the Russian State Library, both in Moscow.

In addition to the British Academy, whose grant funded three crucial archival research trips and a productive workshop, I thank my colleagues at Queen Mary University of London's School of Languages, Linguistics, and Film for the financial research support and sabbatical leave that made researching and writing this book possible.

Peter Kracht and his team at the University of Pittsburgh Press have been supportive and done a great job on the book in trying circumstances. I thank them for their work and would like to express special gratitude to the two anonymous reviewers of the manuscript, both of whose thoughtful and often in-depth comments, especially the extensive suggestions of the second reviewer, will not be forgotten. These have enabled me to enrich and improve many aspects of the book you are now reading. Any remaining errors or faults are still mine.

Parts of this book appeared in very different, embryonic form as "Appropriating the Presence of History: Raising the Victory Banner over the Reichstag," *Screen* 57, no. 3 (2016): 362–70, and "A Holy Relic of War: The Soviet Victory Banner as Artefact," in *Remembering the Second World War*, edited by Patrick Finney (London: Routledge, 2017), and I am grateful for the opportunity to reprint some of that material in a substantially revised form.

Finally, I thank my wife, Inger, and daughter, Nina, for putting up with me, my absences, and my self-absorption.

I dedicate this book to the memory of my grandparents: Ivor and Sylvia, and Bert and Doreen, who lived in this past and have now passed into it.

A NOTE ON TRANSLITERATION AND DOCUMENT CITATION

I have used the Library of Congress system of transliteration throughout, apart from names widely recognized in English (e.g., Eisenstein rather than Eizenshtein), in the main body of the text.

In the endnotes, Russian archival sources are referenced according to the format 1/2/3, where the first number (e.g., 1) refers to the *fond* (collection) number, the second number (e.g., 2) refers to the *opis′* (description) number, and the third number (e.g., 3) refers to preservation unit or file (*edinitsa khraneniia/delo*). These are followed by the sheet number (in Russian, *list*).

THE VICTORY BANNER OVER THE REICHSTAG

I.1. The Victory Banner. The inscription reads: "the 150th Order of Kutuzov, Second Class Idritsa Division of the Seventy-Ninth Rifle Corps, Third Strike Army, First Belorussian Front."

I.2. The Victory Banner in the 9 May parade, Red Square, Moscow, 2018.

INTRODUCTION

Victory! For most Russians, their country's victory in World War II, referred to almost universally as *Pobeda*, with a capital *P*, proves it is the greatest of all nations, giving it a moral authority that has no expiration date. Victory is the triumph over fascism, symbolized by the capture of Berlin and the raising of a red Soviet flag, the Victory Banner, over the Reichstag. This flag was photographed and filmed, and images of it being raised were disseminated by newsreel and the press in 1945. It exists as a museum artifact, an exact copy of which is paraded annually on Red Square on 9 May, Russia's Victory Day, as well as in facsimiles at parades, demonstrations, and reconstructions around the country. The Victory Banner has also been reproduced in historical and compilation films and referred to in television programs, poems, histories, memoirs, paintings, and even video games ever since.

By contrast, the historic Reichstag building has since 1999 been the seat of the Bundestag, the German Federal Republic's parliament—a symbol of transparency, of democracy and Germany's overcoming of its long and troubled twentieth century, and of its reunification, with Berlin as capital once more, at the heart and head of a European Union.[1] The Soviet capture of it and the raising of the red flag above the building appear as a single episode in a longer history of German democracy overcoming setbacks and challenges to it, a narrative of liberal triumph in World War II that is widely shared in western Europe and the United States.

It is this sharp contrast and mismatch between Russian and Western visions of the Victory Banner that intrigued me when I first encountered a striking photo of it one Sunday afternoon when, as a teenager, I was leafing through *Purnell's History of the Second World War* while listening to

I.3. Evgenii Khaldei, *The Victory Banner over the Reichstag*. Courtesy of RGAKFD.

my brother's collection of obscure punk music (*Fifteen Thoughts of Brinsley Schwarz*?). Although the black-and-white image was sepia-tinted, the implicitly red flag, bearing the hammer and sickle, hoisted from a tall building, fluttered above the ruined, smoldering Berlin cityscape below.

I asked my brother, who usually knows everything, about the image and the building but was not satisfied with the vague answer. The explanation in Earl F. Ziemke's accompanying article was little better: "In the centre of the city, the Russians had driven spearheads through from the north and south to the edges of the government quarter and the Soviet armies were competing for the honor of taking the Reichstag—which to the Russians, even though it had been a charred ruin since 1933, had come to symbolize the Third Reich."[2] The photographic image's dramatic, heroic tenor is not echoed in the chapter devoted to the battle, entitled "Into the Abyss," which focused on the German side and described the battle as "a contested mop up" without naming a single Soviet figure or unit. The scene was described in the text thus: "A quarter of a mile away, the Russians were storming the Reichstag."[3] The image was not attributed (although it was Evgenii Khaldei's famous shot; see chapter 1). The "Russians" were anonymous, inexplicable, and distant; the resonant images of their feats were toned down by anodyne text.

This strange mismatch between text and image was compounded for me years later as I started, already an adult fluent in the Russian language, to experience the way most Russian-language sources and the

Russian media treated this event: it was the holy of holies, a key symbol of the wartime victory, the nation's greatest achievement, which in turn serves an uplifting function, underpinning the national identity.

This vision of the war is partly based on the historical record, such as the fact that the largest and most important land battles of World War II were fought by the Soviets, achieved at the cost of an enormous estimated 27 million Soviet war dead, and the extraordinary transformation from a battle for survival to the conquest of half of Europe up to Berlin and Vienna. However, the conclusions and pride derived from this episode of history do not originate solely in historical fact; for one thing, the dominant historical account underplays other facts, such as the specific fate of Soviet Jews, the Soviets' own alliance with Nazi Germany, and the invasion of their Polish and Baltic neighbors in 1939–1941, and it denies outright the crimes committed during their own drive forward to Berlin. Rather than an objective account, the Russian view of World War II selects and elevates suitably heroic elements from the complex and sometimes contradictory facts of the Soviet contribution to World War II. This requires the selective organization of history, a process that may be described as a construction of *memory*. It is the product of the interaction of a panoply of cultural forms and practices: commemoration in a national holiday, parades, reenactments, museum exhibitions, the wearing of black-and-orange St. George's ribbons, badges, and the waving of flags, through statues and monuments, especially the Tomb of the Unknown Soldier and eternal flame, art, songs, television programs, news stories, memoirs, internet articles, and films of all kinds. There are also serious works of painstakingly researched scholarly history, but the products of mass memorial culture far outweigh them.

The tension between the vast array of often contradictory episodes, some of which make it into the history books, and the selection and organization of these data in popular memory is resolved through the organizing principle of the war as a coherent historical narrative, with a beginning, a middle, and an end. The beginning of the war is highly contentious, involving as it does the joint Nazi-Soviet invasion of Poland in 1939, so, despite recent Russian polemics around this date, in the Soviet case it is important to mark this beginning as occurring on 22 June 1941, with the middle usually seen as the 1942–1943 victory at Stalingrad, and the end is typically framed around the Soviets' storming of Berlin, culminating in the assault on the Reichstag in April and early May 1945. This final defeat of fascism is symbolically completed by the raising of the red flag, the Victory Banner, over it, and the related Victory Parade on Red Square in June that year. These resonant dual images of victory—the conquering of Berlin and the parade on Red

Square—defined the triumph as a Soviet one and fixed the dominant narrative of the war.

In order to ensure that the narrative functions, there is a need to synthesize, as well as to condense facts into symbolically potent scenes. The storming of Berlin, the raising of the Victory Banner, and the Red Square parade are precisely this: a symbolic synthesis of a number of currents relating to the end of the war, to victory, and it is this power to evoke the final victory that is a key reason for the enduring appeal of the Victory Banner.

This is because the war is remembered in Russia and elsewhere not only through a pithy narrative but also through images and symbols. Political scientist Murray Edelman has written that "symbols become a facet of experiencing the material world that gives it a specific meaning. The language, rituals, and objects to which people respond are not abstract ideas."[4] Edelman points especially to the emotional power of what he calls "condensation symbols" that sum up attitudes toward the past.[5] The image of the Victory Banner is such a symbol, and it serves to convey the significant, overarching organizational principle that orders such references to the war: the notion of victory. This is a word that frequently replaces the more official term, Great Patriotic War, itself a rhetorical construction framing the war as one of survival and starting in June 1941, focused on the Soviet Union or Russia. The vernacular way of naming the conflict *Victory* underlines the positive result, the outcome of a complex narrative conferring meaning. Victory helps people to remember what is important and to forget what is not, dismissing the latter as an irrelevance or temporary blip.

The interaction of the notion of victory within an interlocking and overlapping system of symbols across many media can be productively analyzed through the emergent scholarly field of memory studies, which interprets a society's attitude toward its history as analogous to individuals' recollection of their past, a dwelling on favorite memories and reluctant recalling of others, in a way that is socially and culturally constructed, or what has been termed "cultural memory."[6] Alexander Etkind has drawn a distinction between hard and soft memories, where hard memories are the more enduring physical artifacts or monuments and soft memories are the more malleable and negotiable narratives told of them. The more these two modes interact, the more central a memory is: the relative rarity of Gulag monuments and museums suggests how marginal that experience is to Russian self-understanding.[7] By contrast, the Victory Banner raised by the Red Army atop the Reichstag on the night of 30 April 1945 is a key image synonymous with Victory that encompasses both soft and hard cultural forms, across many media, anchored in the

I.4. The Victory Banner on display in the Central Museum of the Armed Forces, Moscow.

symbolic calendar of public holidays. The fact that the recognizably related images of the Victory Banner span reiterations or "remediations" across various different cultural forms enhances the "aura of authenticity" of these images.[8] The "hard" artifact and facsimiles combine with the "soft" images and narratives to strengthen the power of a symbol summing up memory of the war.

ICONIC IMAGE?

We might see the repetition and reproduction of this image as an iconic image in the sense elaborated most compellingly in Robert Hariman and John Louis Lucaites's influential study of iconic photographs in the United States.[9] However, this account is anchored in the specifics of the photographic image that acts as an "object . . . of contemplation."[10] In this account, the singularity of a specific still image is part of the claim that it bears "the aura of history, or humanity, or possibility" and the sacred.[11] By contrast, the Victory Banner is characterized by multiplicity—by the variety of widely recognized photographic and filmic representations of the moment, from a number of angles, and the fact that these are not identical to the actual artifact. This banner, inscribed with an abbreviated form of the name and number of the unit credited with raising it—the 150th Order of Kutuzov, Second Class Idritsa Division of the Seventy-Ninth Rifle Corps, Third Strike Army, First Belorussian Front—is displayed in a glass case, in a special room that evokes the 1945 Victory Parade: it is the centerpiece of Moscow's Central Museum of the Armed Forces. An exact copy of this banner is the one held aloft annually at the 9 May Victory Parade. The multiplicity of this artifact on the one hand and the various film and photographic images on the other, many of which do not bear the famous inscription, undermine notions of the Victory Banner as an icon in the sense described by Hariman and Lucaites, who work from the notion that, like religious icons, other iconic images strictly reproduce their fixed original models.[12] The Victory Banner photographic and filmic imagery purports to record the moment of its raising, but memoirs supplement the verbal narrative of what happened, as well as the actual artifact, itself reproduced in highly controlled facsimile copies. Consequently, there are tensions and differences between the various instances of the iconic images. Yet, despite the multiplicity of the images, the enduring power of the Victory Banner imagery for Russian war memory is difficult to ignore, even if complex and sometimes obscure.

The notion of iconic image also deliberately mobilizes religious connotations to suggest that these images possess a sacred aura of authenticity. Nina Tumarkin's prominent study of what she called the "cult" of the war in the Soviet Union treated the idea of the Victory Banner as a "holy of holies" with skepticism and quoted a 1990s journalist's recollection of his lack of interest in the Victory Banner as a 1970s teenager, dismissing any claim as to its sacred power.[13]

This attitude seems understandable, but misplaced, and it is largely a consequence of when Tumarkin wrote her book—at the beginning of the post-Soviet period, when there was a widespread hostility to Soviet-era symbols. In turn this attitude informed Tumarkin's suggestion that the practice of commemoration of the Great Patriotic War was in terminal decline and would disappear in post-Soviet Russia, as Soviet inconsistencies and silences about the war would result in a post-Soviet shift from collective to individual grieving and the end of the "war cult."[14] A further context that perhaps informs this approach is a tradition in historical scholarship that sees its task as distinguishing between mythical elements, including what we have come to term "memory," and the factual elements of history, which are not only primary but must ultimately be pivotal in shaping societal understanding. A model for this approach is Eric Hobsbawm's attempts to show how "invented traditions," associated, for example, with the English royal family, were actually symbolic practices invented fairly recently with the aim of constructing a spurious continuity. Implicit in this paradigm was an assumption that reason will triumph and that exposing the constructed nature of memory would lead to it becoming less influential.[15]

The emerging field of memory studies has taken a rather different approach to such traditions. Aleida Assmann criticizes Hobsbawm's method, arguing that showing the "inventedness, manufacturedness" of a tradition is not enough and would be unlikely to break its spell anyway. Instead, she suggests scholars analyze their function.[16] This perspective, which sees the Victory Banner as a "mobilizing symbol" within an "affectively charged narrative," informs the present study.[17] This book is an attempt at understanding how the symbol functions, how it has evolved, how it acquired the power it now wields, and what effects this particular "memory construct" has in contemporary Russia.

More broadly, such skeptical attitudes to claims that the Victory Banner is sacred may be seen as a misreading of modernity and its relation to practices that we can understand as religious or as relating to the sacred. Rather than seeing these as backward relics of premodern societies or totalitarianism, the French scholar Danièle Hervieu-Léger develops Emile Durkheim's approach to the sociology of religion and treats religious practices or expressions of the sacred as an important facet of modernity. As well as demystifying religious doctrines, modernity, she argues, also fragments existence and a sense of coherence, opening up spaces that only religious practices can fill. These substitute, secular religions often express themselves in terms of an evocation of tradition.[18] Such a relation to the past is also theorized in Pierre Nora's account of symbols as memory sites (*lieux de mémoire*), which he terms "rituals of a ritualless society; fleeting incursions of the sacred into a disenchanted world."[19] This notion of ritual is particularly important in the Russian and Soviet contexts, where parades and formulaic speech patterns have been seen as central to the ideological edifice.

SOVIET RITUALS

Durkheim made the division of objects into the sacred and profane a key feature of religious belief, arguing that what makes an object sacred is not an intrinsic property but rather the attitudes and social rituals attached to it, as well as the setting of it apart from the profane sphere.[20] This can be seen in the way in which the Victory Banner was presented as sacred and contrasted with the profane sphere through its ritualized use in the Victory Day holiday parade and the narrative constructed around it in its museum home.

While the Victory Banner was invented as a symbol in the Stalin era, at the end of the war, when it was subordinated to the Stalin cult, its ritualized use and references to it as sacred became pronounced in the post-Stalin era, with 1965 marking a key point. This chronology would seem to corroborate Alexei Yurchak's influential account of "late socialism" as one of ritualized participatory performance in which it was important to repeat and cite established norms without analyzing and scrutinizing them.[21]

This perspective has the advantage of explaining the outsider's experience when talking to Russians about World War II to this day: there is often a strange moment when reasoned debate ceases and a strange, hard-wired automation seems to take over. Memory of World War II, the Great Patriotic War, is beyond rational scrutiny; it belongs to a qualitatively different, ritualized, or sacred sphere of discourse, where repetitious formulas must be repeated.

Similarly, the ritualization of the discourse around the Victory Banner, as a key image of the war, is also evident in public debate. There have been book studies and films made that stress the Victory Banner's staged nature, suggesting persuasively that it was not the officially rewarded Mikhail Egorov and Meliton Kantariia who put up the original flag but that those who did so were for many years not credited for it and that the flag in Moscow's Central Museum of the Armed Forces was not the first to be raised over the Reichstag either.[22] Such critical voices, no matter how well substantiated, have done nothing to alter the commentary and claims habitually made in the voice-over for the televised Victory Parade or at occasions such as the April 2017 Storming of Berlin reenactment in Moscow's Patriot Park. Such running commentaries are not only repetitious but they accompany the ritual, repeated performance of the parade or reenactment with a ritual, repeated verbal performance that repeats claims and myths long disputed or disproved as if incontestable, passing over inconvenient truths in silence. The repeated epithets, rituals, and images reinforce each other and serve as a basis for a wider preference for myth (or memory) over history.

The claims made for the Victory Banner may be debunked and disbelieved, but their very repetition throughout a myriad of media implies a need for them. Moreover, to some degree both their constructed nature and enduring presence are inherent in such images, as Susan Sontag points out in a discussion in which she refers to a wide range of iconic photographs, including Khaldei's of the Victory Banner: "What is odd is not that so many iconic news photos of the past, including some of the best remembered pictures from the Second World War, appear to have been staged. It is that we are surprised to learn that they were staged, always disappointed." Sontag sees this as the consequence of an almost primordial desire to be there and capture the event as it unfolded, to be a "spy in the house of love and death."[23] What Sontag seems to be referring to here is a desire that these images be authentic, a need somehow to invest them with aura, a sense of authenticity, despite the fact that they are known to have been staged and constructed.

In the Russian context, however, this desire for the myth rather than the reality takes a particular, state-sponsored form. In March 2016, the director of the Russian State Archive, Sergei Mironenko, resigned from his post, in a move widely seen as connected to his publication of documents showing that the story of the Twenty-Eight Panfilovites, a squad of soldiers from the 216th Rifle Division under the command of General Ivan Panfilov, who supposedly fought to the death to stop the German advance on Moscow, was a myth, made up by wartime journalists.[24] Mironenko's publication had antagonized Russia's then minister of culture, Vladimir Medinskii, who, in a history book devoted to showing that every nation needs its benign "white" myths for their uplifting effects, had, while accepting that the official account was inaccurate in its details, publicly defended the true story of the Twenty-Eight Panfilovites as even more impressive than the long-established version.[25] Needless to say, Medinskii also endorses the long disproved account as to who put the Victory Banner up and where on the Reichstag it was put up, combatively sparring with claims to the contrary, ridiculing the sensationalism of journalistic revelations and the credulity of their readers.[26]

HISTORY, NARRATIVE, AND TRAUMA

In maintaining this uplifting narrative, Russians are also able to exorcise and offset facts about the war that threaten its uplifting tenor, most notably the enormous toll of death and suffering that are inextricably associated with it. In December 1941, the Soviets first narrated the story of Nazi atrocities against their own civilian population, but they did so in a film depicting one of their very first victories, the liberation of Rostov-on-Don, with the recapture depicted in a scene of the raising of the red flag over the city's soviet building. Suffering could be depicted if it was made meaningful as a sacrifice, compensated by victory in a battle dramatically depicted. This followed the logic of established Bolshevik portrayals of death as part of a meaningful, historically redemptive narrative. This may be seen as the insertion of the loss into a narrative, a channeling of grief, leaving little space for mourning in its own right.[27] This logic was subsequently imposed on the war as a whole, through the use of symbols such as the Victory Banner. This process can be understood through Hayden White's reflections on the narrative construction of historical writing.[28] He sees the past as a construct that needs to be organized into a story to be understood as "historical" and thus coherent and meaningful.

A central challenge to such constructions of the wartime experience as meaningful and redemptive was the sheer scale of the suffering and losses, figures for which were revised upward under Nikita Khrushchev in the early 1960s to 20 million.[29] Yet, under Khrushchev this enormous sacrifice was part of a somewhat unstructured reassessment of the war introducing elements that had previously been passed over in near silence, such as the disastrous military reverses of the first months of the German invasion and the direct consequence of this failure to protect the country or the fate of more than 3 million Soviet prisoners of war who died of starvation in German hands. Facts such as these had not yet been incorporated into a positive overall narrative. Fashioning a redemptive narrative that made sense of this scale of loss was an intrinsically difficult task.

In the 1960s there were also attempts to see the enormous suffering caused by the war in terms of trauma, a sense that the experience could not be reconciled with habitual narratives; this is certainly how many people have come to see the mass murder of 6 million Jews—as resistant to all sense-making narratives.[30] A prominent Soviet example of this "trauma" approach was Andrei Tarkovskii's film *Ivan's Childhood* (*Ivanovo detstvo*, 1962), the main character of which is a traumatized boy consumed by revenge and whose grim life and death are, as Jean-Paul Sartre argued controversially, not at all redeemed by victory.[31] However, even if art addressed the after-effects of traumatic experience, the notion itself was taboo, since it originated in the works of Freud, whose works were banned in the Soviet Union.[32]

Overwhelmingly, however, Soviet veterans and Soviet society more widely came to see the war in terms of meaningful sacrifice, suffering, and death redeemed by heroic feats and the ultimate victory.[33] Yet this was the consequence of a deliberate and concerted effort by the Soviet media from the final years of the war right through the Soviet period into present-day Russian society to ensure that war was seen in this way. In particular, the whole thrust of the twentieth-anniversary celebration in 1965 was about regaining control of the image of the war and exciting the whole population with a sense of this as a heroic, holy enterprise that could not be criticized, diminished, or even analyzed dispassionately. Emerging facts such as the Red Army's vengeance against the German population, especially the many rapes committed, was covered in sources from the 1950s in German, including the famous anonymous memoir *A Woman in Berlin*, translated into English in 1955, then in serious scholarly work, and, since the collapse of the Soviet Union, in works published in Russian.[34] However, these claims are very rarely even articulated in Russia, where doing so risks prosecution. For the most part they are obliquely refuted; consider, for example, the famous statue at Berlin's Treptower Park cemetery of a Red Army soldier rescuing a German child, or the references to such acts in numerous memoirs. The social and narrative framework of victory, underpinned by symbols such as the Treptower Park statue or the Victory Banner, largely prevented the claims of rape from being expressed: they made no sense, and there was no place for them in collective memory of the war as victory and of liberation. The campaign of 1965, coming after a period in which Soviet identity and Soviet history, including the war, were reappraised and reassessed, aimed at elevating the cult of Victory beyond such potential criticism in part by working through all conceivable media.

In addition to working the disparate facts of the war into an uplifting narrative, memory of the war also serves to help Russians forget less pleasant and more divisive historical episodes. Michael Rothberg has developed Freud's concept of "screen memory," in which one memory serves to obstruct recollection about another that is more troubling, or more difficult to make sense of, to produce a notion of "multidirectional memory." Rothberg argues that the relation between these two memories is never entirely one of screening, or of a competition in which one remembers either one thing or the other, but that in fact there is an implicit interaction between these two memories, one waiting to be explored by the attentive critic.[35] From this perspective, constructing memory of the war through the prism of victory, as well as the Victory Banner, serves not just to vindicate the sacrifice and price paid as meaningful but also to distract from elements of the war that cannot be assimilated into this paradigm, such as the Holocaust, and that do not fit notions of meaningful sacrifice because those killed did not go to their deaths consciously for a cause but were murdered for their ethnic identity. Moreover, the war also distracts from the crimes of the Soviet state against its own citizens, such as the Gulag and mass arrests of the Great Terror in 1937–1938.

Looking at the war in this way enables us to understand a difficulty with Alexander Etkind's important intervention into the politics of Soviet memory—his wide-ranging and conceptually sophisticated study into repressed memory of the crimes of the Soviet state, *Warped Mourning*. That book unearths and analyzes unsuccessfully repressed expressions of mourning and the parallels between the Soviet and Nazi regimes. However, this task seems to distract the author from the full consequences of the primary mechanism of repression of Stalin's crimes, which he mentions in passing: many Russians believe that victory in the war justifies Stalin's crimes.[36] Thus, whereas Etkind's focus is mourning, he does not even explore the possibility that memory of the Great Patriotic War encourages the expression of a "warped mourning" for which the true object may be a victim of the Soviet state rather than the Nazi state. Here, too, in repetitions of war memories we surely also see the compulsive repetition and reenactment of the past described by Etkind. The difference is that it is the pathological repetition not just of loss but also of the more pleasurable memory of victory, explicitly defined as a dramatic, heroic Soviet victory associated with the state, as a legitimizing force, is one that screens out and dispenses with alternative constructions. The Victory Banner imagery does this in a manner that is both memorable and emotionally powerful.

EVOLUTION OF THE VICTORY BANNER

One of the extraordinary aspects of the Victory Banner is the fact that it has not only migrated across various media but also successfully evolved through numerous changes in the Soviet system. It ultimately outlived the Soviet state that created it, acquiring a more powerful status than ever in post-Soviet Russia. From Stalin's first call for a banner to be raised over Berlin in a speech on 6 November 1944, through its subsequent adoption as a slogan to motivate troops storming Berlin, to the raising of the banner over the Reichstag on the evening of 30 April 1945, it was initially intended to create a powerful symbol of the triumph of the Soviet state and to link that victory with Stalin's leader cult. This endowed the Victory Banner with the sacred, charismatic power of that cult.[37] After Stalin's death, the unstable vacuum left by the absence of an effective leader cult led to a search for powerful, transcendent symbols capable of investing lives with meaning and as "a reference point for a belief system."[38] Ultimately the Victory Banner was selected and promoted as one such symbol, one strong enough to create a continuity that outlasts any single leader. This is its one key advantage over the personality cult: the Victory Banner could assure stability in a way that few symbols could following Stalin's death. In this respect, it was so successful that it became a communist symbol that survived the system that created it, conferring a sacred aura, power, and legitimacy upon the post-Soviet Russian state.

This continuity, however, also functions to redeem the Stalinist mode of charismatic politics, and potentially the package of Stalin's crimes as well, along with other aspects of the Soviet system. In tracing the life of this symbol, across periods and media, my aim is to scrutinize these continuities and discontinuities relating to the end of the war and the late Stalin period. The continuities in historiography, for example, are harder to illustrate and grasp. By following the evolution of a symbol, I hope that readers can more easily grasp this tension. In order to do this, however, I shall be concentrating on moments and texts when we can see the Victory Banner symbol being constructed, contested, and tweaked.

REFLECTIONS ON METHODOLOGY EMPLOYING FILMS AND ARCHIVES

To gain an understanding of the constructed nature of this sacred symbol, talking to people is unlikely to be productive, precisely because the success of the symbol and the narrative of the war it conveys mean that most Russians do not see this as a construct at all: as Yurchak has argued, people reproduce words as performances, the meaning of which they do not fully understand.[39] Moreover, they see the past through the filter of the present.

Instead, this book focuses primarily on representations of the Victory Banner in the mass medium of film and, to a lesser extent, television, as well as on the processes that lay behind the production of these works. Through an examination of unpublished studio debates and decisions, it becomes possible to see how these images were made and constructed, and this approach shows how memory, narrative, and symbols were being selected, debated, and shaped. To trace how effectively these symbols function and are received, I have made extensive use of reviews of those films and television programs, especially reviews from print media. The process of negotiation and shaping is especially clear in documentary and newsreel films, which are a special focus of the book, since their claim to be presenting a factual account and the need in that genre to achieve a quick turnaround to respond to anniversaries and shifting ideological imperatives means that the negotiation of the fixed ideological clichés can be especially clear in the preproduction debates and sometimes even in the actual films. Moreover, for some relevant documentary films there is discarded film footage of the same events, available to the researcher in the archive, and this evidence too grants an insight into the evolution of well-known "iconic" images and their relation to forgotten photographic images of the same events that lay unwatched in the archives.

At the same time, many documentary films tend toward the ritualized repetition described by Yurchak: alongside their quoting of existing verbal formulations and opinions, the filmmakers, especially those producing compilation films, gravitated toward material from already existing movies rather than opting for the more time-consuming and ideologically hazardous path of sifting the discarded footage for a novel angle. This approach reinforced the tendency to reuse the same footage, the "iconic" images, and it also meant the rearticulation of the same interpretations, as the images tended to bring with them their already existing narrative.

The archive of discarded film footage, by contrast, provides the possibility of an alternative narrative, a different account, because it also retains that which was not thought of as significant at the time. Thus, such films oscillate between the repetition of fixed visual formulas and their renegotiation. In this, a symbol such as the Victory Banner is a potential site of contestation, and various films, references in speeches, and uses of the symbol in the media reinflect it and at certain points seek to redefine it.

This account of symbols as a site of contestation echoes Hariman and Lucaites's classic account of the iconic image in US society, where various narratives about ethnicity and the war are played out with regard to the famous image of Marines raising the flag on Iwo Jima. Their account seems to suggest that such a contest can only occur in US society. However, there have been studies since that try to examine the use of popular symbols in other contexts, such as India.[40] In the Russian context too there are a number of conflicts and tensions worked out through the different iterations of the Victory Banner at key moments, even if ritualized repetition of the image dominates.

Of course the Victory Banner is not completely monolithic; there are other frequently repeated and rich symbols of the Soviet victory in World War II. The Twenty-Eight Panfilovites, the Brest Fortress, or Zoia Kosmodem′ianskaia, for instance, would also be interesting subjects for treatment, but they are not as central to the *narrative* of the war as the Victory Banner is and have not shown quite the same mutability as it has, across different media and across the various Soviet and Russian postwar changes of leadership. These other images narrate the story of heroic sacrifice, but the unique role of the Victory Banner is to reassure the public that those sacrifices were ultimately not in vain, that a glorious victory was indeed achieved, ensuring that those sacrifices were indeed meaningful. It remains a crucial symbol to this day, as the current Putin administration (as I write in 2020) has elevated this symbol as one with the power to cohere a society on the brink of fragmentation by evoking the memory of Victory.

The Victory Banner functions as an iconic image inviting repetition. It is a memory meme enabling the fixing and stabilization of a certain view of World War II and affirming the identity of those who recognize the symbol and the interpretation it represents. At the same time, the Victory Banner plays a special role in cementing the continuity of Soviet and Russian memory of the war through periods of profound discontinuity and historical rupture, such as those following the death of Stalin in 1953 and the disintegration of the Soviet Union in 1991. In the Ukraine conflict, facsimiles of the Victory Banner have been widely paraded by the pro-Russian Ukrainians and defiled by the anti-Russians.

This fault line illustrates the ways in which the Victory Banner is paradoxically both a national and a transnational symbol. The red flag itself is a symbol that dates back to the French revolutions of 1832 and 1848, during which radicals used red banners because the Tricolor of the revolution had become compromised by antirevolutionary regimes. It then became an internationally accepted symbol of socialism in the years following the Paris Commune of 1871. From its first use in May Day demonstrations across the Russian Empire in 1900, it subsequently became the state flag of the Russian Soviet Federative Socialist Republic in 1918, prior to its adoption by the Soviet Union in 1922.[41]

Khaldei's 1945 photo itself juxtaposes a conquered Berlin with the triumphant Soviets. It is thus indicative of a stance of conquest, possibly a representation of empire, and certainly Soviet opposition to external enemies. At the same time, the Soviet state flag raised is a variation on the red flag of the international socialist movement—crushed inside Germany by the Nazis but now in ascendance—as well as an emblem of a multiethnic state. The Victory Banner represents the end of World War II, an international conflagration, but its purpose is to stress the Soviet nature of the war and of victory. More recently it has become a uniquely Russian symbol, an alternative state flag, even if Russia can be seen as a never entirely self-contained nation-state but always an empire.[42] This book is about the making of that symbol, the story of its initial inception during the battle of Berlin, and ways in which it has been reused across media, but especially film, since the war.

SUMMARY OF CHAPTER CONTENTS

Chapter 1 charts the initial creation of the Victory Banner as a symbol by analyzing the decision to storm the Reichstag and make it the scene of the Soviets' raising of a red flag over Berlin in 1945 to symbolize victory. The chapter then examines the photojournalism (especially documentary and newsreel films) made about the raising of the Victory Banner and then the organization and filming of the 24 June 1945 Red Square Victory Parade, the absence of the Victory Banner from it, and the way it was displayed at the Central Museum of the Red Army.

Chapter 2 examines the difficulty of integrating victory into the communist symbolic order in the postwar Stalin period, the tensions between the 1 May and new 9 May holidays prior to the abolition of the latter in 1948, and the attempt to subordinate the Victory Banner to the Stalin cult with Petr Krivonogov's 1948 painting *Victory* (in Russian, *Pobeda*) and Mikheil Chiaureli's 1949 film, *The Fall of Berlin* (*Padenie Berlina*). The Victory Banner becomes part of an epic and monumental aesthetic and plays a crucial role insisting on the communist (and Stalinist) nature of victory.

Chapter 3 examines how, following the death of Stalin, memory of the war evolved, culminating in the 1965 Victory Day parade, in which the Victory Banner was central. The chapter begins with an analysis of the films of Stalin's funeral and then discusses the rewriting of the history of the war, which reassessed Stalin's role and also attempted to establish the true story of the raising of the Victory Banner through two secret conferences to determine what happened. After considering this peak of iconoclasm with regard to war memory, the chapter concludes by showing how, with the documentary film *The Great Patriotic* (*Velikaia otechestvennaia*, 1965) and the 1965 Victory Day parade—the first to be covered live on television—the Victory Banner was needed as a symbol associating victory with the communist cause. It was a key part of the emergent Victory cult that emerged following the dismantling of the Stalin cult and was used to confer legitimacy and stability on post-Stalin society.

Chapter 4 examines how commemoration of the Victory cult in the period from 1965 to 1985 was conveyed through a growing variety of forms and how film in particular adapted the narrative of victory to the television age through two epic film series in which the Victory Banner imagery plays a central role: Iurii Ozerov's spectacular five-part *Liberation* (*Osvobozhdenie*, 1970–71), and the television series *The Unknown War* (1978). Analysis of the reception of these films, as well as of the lackluster 1985 Victory Day parade, suggests the decline of the Victory cult among young people in particular.

Chapter 5 surveys the ways in which the Victory Banner and Victory Day commemorations became a site of political contest from the 1990s to the present as the glasnost agenda colored the 1990 Victory Parade and brought revelations as to the staged nature of the images of the raising of the red flag over the Reichstag. This political battle continued through the 1990s, as the communists claimed war memory and the Victory Banner symbolism, which culminated in Vladimir Putin's instituting of the annual Victory Day parade as the central ritual of the Russian symbolic calendar from 2000 onward. The chapter also shows how television coverage of the anniversary parade has become ever more sophisticated and how film and television depictions of the war have evolved in response to the rising popularity of video games among young people. Both the video games and the films that echo them have repeatedly turned to the image of the Victory Banner. The final sections of the chapter examine the growth in uses of the Victory Banner in reenactments and demonstrations across the post-Soviet space and beyond, especially since Russia's annexation of Crimea in 2014.

Needless to say, this book does not aim to provide an exhaustive account of all mentions and uses of the Victory Banner symbolism; rather, it strives to place prominent and indicative examples in film, television, parades, and other media in the context of evolving understandings and interpretations of history.

1

THE RAISING OF THE VICTORY BANNER

A red banner was raised over Berlin's Reichstag on 30 April 1945 at 22:40 in the evening by soldiers from the Third Strike Army of the First Belorussian Front.[1] This triumphal effort came after a brutal frontal assault by thousands of men from at least four regiments (674th and 756th Rifle Regiments of the 150th Rifle Division; 380th and 525th Regiments of the 171st Rifle Division) against the well-defended building.[2] As many as 2,500 German defenders were killed or wounded, with a further 2,604 taken prisoner, and the Red Army's losses were also huge.[3]

While credit for raising what has come to be called the Victory Banner is conventionally attributed to Sergeant Mikhail Egorov and Junior Sergeant Meliton Kantariia of the 150th Rifle Division, the unit credited on the official Victory Banner, there are many conflicting accounts as to exactly who raised the first flag and on what part of the building. It has been now established that in fact the first flag was raised on the roof over the front of the building on an equestrian statue, an allegory of Germania, usually referred to as the Goddess of Victory in Russian accounts. It was followed by others later that night, on 1 May, including Egorov and Kantariia's official banner of the 150th Division, which was moved to the cupola the following day and became known as the Victory Banner (see below, this chapter, and chapters 3 and 5).[4] These disputes are indicative of the chaotic, messy situation of combat, and their resolution into a neat narrative is part of the process of disciplining memory of the war so that it becomes a clear and resonant symbol. Rather than relying on the neat resolutions, we need to understand how this symbol was first constructed and to ask why the Reichstag was chosen as the background for this emotive symbol of victory.

THE DIPLOMATIC BATTLE FOR BERLIN

As the center of Nazi power, Berlin itself had a symbolic significance that outweighed military concerns, even possibly political ones and the desire to capture nuclear scientists and technology.[5] Despite Churchill's desire for the British and American troops to take Berlin, concerns over a regrouping of Nazi forces in a so-called "Bavarian redoubt," as well as the Americans' desire not to antagonize Stalin, led Eisenhower to cable Stalin on 28 March 1945 and propose that the Americans and Soviets link up to the south of Berlin, near Leipzig and Dresden.[6] Yet, although Eisenhower had promised Stalin at a secret one-on-one meeting at Yalta in February 1945 that the Soviets could enter Berlin first, there was room for ambiguity and distrust, so the matter was really only resolved by the Soviets' decisive advance on the German capital in April 1945.[7] Stalin had underscored Berlin's symbolic importance in a widely quoted speech on 6 November 1944, when he stated that Soviet territory (what he called "our earth") had now been entirely liberated from German occupation and that the red flag would fly over Berlin as a symbol of victory.[8]

But the problem was, what building symbolized Berlin? Probably the city's most famous landmark was (and still is) the Brandenburg Gate, and the seat of the Nazis' power was the Reich Chancellery, beneath which Hitler spent his final days in a bunker. It could be argued that the Reichstag was particularly unsuited to serve as a symbol of Nazi power and Soviet conquest, since, as the seat of the German parliament, it was associated with German *democracy* until it was gutted by fire in 1933. Indeed, a number of English-language sources comment on the incongruity of the Soviets' choice of the Reichstag as the symbol of victory, since it was less fitting than the Brandenburg Gate or the Reich Chancellery, and they attribute this misunderstanding to the fact that the Soviets were unaware it had stood empty during the years of the Third Reich.[9]

However, the notion that the Reichstag was chosen as a result of the Soviets' confusion is unlikely and not a little insulting to Red Army intelligence staff; it is belied, for example, by Marshal Georgii Zhukov's memoir.[10] While there is no available definitive document that makes the rationale clear, it is nevertheless possible to surmise a number of reasons why it was chosen as a symbol for the battle and the war, combining as it did both military and symbolic dimensions, as did the battle for Berlin itself. Ultimately, however, one of the sources of confusion is the fact that the elevation of the Reichstag to act as a symbol of victory emerged in the days after its seizure, rather than before, and the symbolic considerations were of greater significance than the military ones. It should be added here that one needs to tread carefully throughout, because many of the memoirs of participants filter their accounts of the past through a contemporary sense of the importance of the storming of the Reichstag.

THE NEED FOR A MILITARY OBJECTIVE

A number of sources claim that the Reichstag was designated a prime or even *the* prime military objective in the battle for Berlin.[11] As one of the tallest buildings in the center of the German capital, it was a candidate to be a military objective because it could be clearly identified. It, along with other prominent buildings, was given a number; the Reichstag was number 105.[12] It was common practice in the Red Army for units to take a red flag into combat and raise it on a prominent building, thus motivating competition between units and boosting the general fighting spirit.[13] This was also part of the political preparation of units for battle; plain red calico "battle flags," typically with no writing or other symbols on them, were usually given by political officers (*politruks*) to Communist Party members in each unit, for whom the act of raising the flag was an honor and responsibility.[14] This was a means of raising fighting spirit that, according to the First Belorussian Front's political directorate, was particularly effective in the battle for Berlin, as, for the soldiers, each flag planted symbolized a step toward the end of the war.[15] It would seem that many soldiers also brought their own unofficial red flags into battle, improvised from whatever material was available.

From a military perspective, there was also the need to have an easily identifiable central objective and to foster rivalry both between the two commanders, Marshal Zhukov and Marshal Ivan Konev, and their competing units, the First Belorussian and First Ukrainian Fronts, so as to ensure that the city was captured swiftly, before the Western Allies could intervene.[16] The Third Strike Army on 22 April 1945 issued nine official Soviet state flags, each bearing a star above the hammer and sickle—one flag to each of its rifle divisions that were to storm the building. The first to be hoisted on the Reichstag was to become the Victory Banner, thus further stimulating the sense of a race between these smaller units as well (the official flag raised was the fifth of these).[17] Although the idea may have come straight from Stalin, as some sources claim, the notion that this was a military objective, singled out not even at the level of the First Belorussian Front but at the lower level of the Third Strike Army, might explain why there were no references to the raising of the flag specifically over the Reichstag in the Soviet press during the battle.[18] The press in fact stressed a general image of Berlin, usually in ruins, with a red flag flying over it: on 24 April the newspaper of the First Ukrainian

1.1. V. Briskin, "Let Us Raise the Victory Banner over Berlin!" *Za chest′ rodiny*, 24 April 1945.

Front, one of the units involved in the battle, had a header calling for the flag to be raised over "Berlin" and did not mention the Reichstag. A cartoon illustrating this shows a Red Army man raising a flag over an unidentified neoclassical structure.[19] Even in the 1 May edition of *Pravda* a cartoon by the famous Kukryniksy triumvirate of cartoonists and verses by the celebrated poet Samuil Marshak do not depict or mention the Reichstag.[20] Likewise, on 1 May 1945 on the front page of the Red Army daily newspaper *Krasnaia zvezda* we see an enormous full-length portrait of Stalin, striking a Napoleonic pose with his hand across his chest. In his address (or "order") summarizing the successes of the Red Army, Stalin refers to them having occupied the main areas of the German capital and "having put up the flag of victory over *Berlin*."[21] The flag

Поверженный Берлин

«...Берлин расположил свою сеть между Эльбой и Одером, как паук, протягивающий паутину между двумя деревьями...»
(Элизе Реклю. «Земля и люди»).

Домов дымящаяся груда...
Отсюда
Гитлер дал приказ
Лавину двинуть против нас.

Берлин... Отсюда в сердце Франции
Направлен был злодейский нож.
Отсюда все радиостанции
В эфир бросали злую ложь.

Отсюда рабство и бесправие,
Как по сплетенным проводам,
Струились в Польшу, Югославию,
На остров Крит и в Роттердам...

Слава тем, кто над Берлином
Водрузил победный флаг.
В самом логове зверином
Сокрушен жестокий враг.

Как стальная паутина,
Протянулась сеть Берлина
Между двух змеистых рек.
Но узор ее паучий
Наш народный меч могучий,
Точно молния, рассек.

В этот грозный час расплаты
Прокатился Майский гром
Торжествующим раскатом
Над разбойничьим гнездом.

С. МАРШАК.

Рис. Кукрыниксы.

1.2. "Defeated Berlin," poem by Samuil Marshak, as printed in *Pravda*, 1 May 1945, 4.

was already up, so there was no need for military secrecy in references to the Reichstag anymore, which suggests it was selected as a symbol after the battle.

Moreover, while there were many published images of the raising of the flag over the Reichstag in early May, they were at first accompanied by images of flags and Red Army men next to the Brandenburg Gate and other symbols of Berlin. Indeed, the photographer whose image of the flag over the Reichstag became the most renowned, Evgenii Khaldei, himself took photographs of the three red flags he had specially prepared in Moscow (supposedly from a tablecloth): one over Tempelhof Airport, one over the Brandenburg Gate, and the third at the Reichstag.[22] Days later, an article in *Pravda* on 9 May had to make it clear that the Reichstag was a symbol of the center of Berlin.[23] Similarly, the original headline above Khaldei's photograph read, "The Victory Banner over Berlin," and only in the smaller text of the caption beneath the image is the Reichstag mentioned: "The crimson flag flies above the Reichstag, in the center of the Fascist capital—Berlin."[24] This suggested that the Soviet reading public would not recognize the Reichstag: the building's symbolic importance was evidently shaped after the 30 April flag raising.

Further evidence that the choice of the Reichstag as a symbol was part of a retrospective, postbattle rationalization can be found in another source, one relying on eyewitness accounts from German participants in the battle. It reflects how strange it was that the building became such a symbol but speculates that this was because fighting had actually taken place there.[25] Certainly, it was very heavily defended and thus had to be stormed in a heroic infantry engagement. Moreover, according to a number of memoirs, the soldiers charged with capturing the structure had no idea what it looked like and did not even recognize it when they first saw it.[26] This was also a point made by a number of participants at the secret 1960 and 1961 special conferences convoked by the History of the Great Patriotic War Section of the Institute of Marxism-Leninism to establish what had happened in the storming of the Reichstag (see below, chapter 3): they state that it had political and symbolic but not military importance.

Whether or not it was a significant military objective, the Reichstag was clearly chosen to become a symbol, probably after 1 May, because it could serve to illustrate key themes in Soviet propaganda's shaping of the meaning of the war for posterity. There were two key explanations for the Reichstag's symbolic potential: its association with the Nazis' rise to power and its capacity to suggest an analogy with the Kremlin.

THE SOVIETS' NEED FOR A SYMBOL OF VICTORY

In seeking a symbol of the glorious, uplifting end of the war, the Soviets were looking for images of the raising of the red flag: drawing on the rich heritage of filmic red flags, most notably the hand-tinted red flag in Sergei Eisenstein's 1926 film *Battleship Potemkin* (*Brononosets Potemkin*), they had celebrated the triumphant raising of the red flag over their own liberated cities, such as Stalingrad, Kalinin, Rostov, and Simferopol, in newspaper articles and photographs and especially in film.[27] Correspondingly, they wanted to turn the battle of Berlin, and the Reichstag, into a broader political symbol.

Since the revolution of 1917, the Bolsheviks had excelled in symbolic politics, which they skillfully employed to legitimize their rule.[28] They had successfully found images evoking insurrection and thus formed those events into a picture. Echoing the French revolutionaries' storming of the Bastille, they had chosen to make the storming of the Winter Palace the embodiment of the culminating point of revolutionary change.[29] It was difficult and somewhat arbitrary to isolate such a moment. As Leon Trotsky put it,

> The final act of the revolution seems . . . too brief, too dry, too business-like—somehow out of correspondence with the historic scope of the events. The reader experiences a kind of disappointment. He is like a mountain climber, who, thinking the main difficulties are still ahead, suddenly discovers that he is already on the summit or almost there. Where is the insurrection? There is no picture of the insurrection. The events do not form themselves into a picture. A series of small operations, calculated and prepared in advance, remain separated one from another both in space and time. A unity of thought and aim unites them, but they do not fuse in the struggle itself. There is no action of great masses. There are no dramatic encounters with the troops. There is nothing of all that which imaginations brought up upon the facts of history associate with the idea of insurrection.[30]

Soviet dramatists such as Nikolai Evreinov, whose 1920 reenactment, *The Storming of the Winter Palace*, "distilled and improved" the historical event on the very site of the Winter Palace, and Sergei Eisenstein, director of the 1927 film *October* (*Oktiabr′*), made the storming of the Winter Palace into a universally recognized symbol of the culmination of the revolution.[31] As film scholar Robert Rosenstone wrote of *October*, the scene of the storming of the Winter Palace fulfilled the need for a conclusive ending, as "a dramatic film must have a pay off . . . a catharsis. On the screen, as in reality: the revolution must have a climax."[32] Indeed, Stalin had even ordered director Mikhail Romm to insert a scene of the storming of the Winter Palace into his 1937 film *Lenin in October* (*Lenin v oktiabre*), arguing that the depiction of the revolution made no sense without it.[33] The images of the storming of the Reichstag thus function as a partial quotation from *October*. This symbolism was made all the more powerful by the building's historical associations.

THE NAZIS' ACQUISITION OF POWER

Despite the Reichstag's associations with German democracy, as the seat of the German Parliament since 1894 it became linked with the Nazis' acquisition of power in 1933. A fire that broke out in the building, an act of arson probably committed by the Nazis themselves but blamed on communists and leading to their persecution, was immediately followed by the Nazis' takeover in dubious elections. The fire also led to the show trial of Georgii Dimitrov, head of the Communist International in western Europe, in Leipzig, where he made a defiant, widely publicized speech, and the Reichstag trial became a cause célèbre, especially in the Soviet Union. This meant that the name of the building was familiar to many in the Soviet Union, even if even the officer in charge of the storming, Colonel Fedor Zinchenko, could not picture what it looked like.[34] The sense that the building's symbolism was based on its association with the Nazis' rise to power is clear from draft plans for Iulii Raizman's 1945 documentary film of the battle for Berlin: he initially wanted to include images of the Reichstag fire in his final film but was unable to locate and acquire the footage within the critical time frame.[35] Making a red flag over the Reichstag the symbol for Victory and the end of the war was a way of completing the narrative that began with the Nazis' seizure of power in 1933, showing the Soviets as the force that destroyed Nazism and reminding the Soviet public of the Nazis' own anticommunism and their doomed bid to conquer the Soviet Union.

THE ANALOGY WITH THE KREMLIN AND STALIN

Iulii Raizman's documentary film about the battle for Berlin also initially envisaged a sequence in which the Victory Banner, taken from the Reichstag, was presented to Stalin in the Kremlin, suggesting that the Reichstag was chosen as the location for the banner's symbolic raising so as to imply an analogy with the Kremlin, the Soviet state, and therefore Stalin.[36] The same connection was suggested by the intention, albeit unfulfilled at the original 24 June 1945 Victory Parade, to display the Victory Banner on Red Square in front of the Kremlin and Stalin.[37] The same association is shared by the curators at Moscow's Central Museum of the Armed Forces, who presented an exhibit devoted to the raising of the Victory Banner. In it, the Victory Banner soars above symbols of the Nazis, such as swastika-emblazoned banners and iron crosses; it is depicted being hoisted on Katiusha rocket launchers against a background showing the 24 June 1945 Victory Parade on Red Square. Alongside this, we see a scale model of the Reichstag and in front of it a piece of the actual graffitied masonry, where a Red Army soldier has written, "You will never set eyes on the Kremlin, but the Reichstag is Kaput."

It appears, then, that the Reichstag was chosen not for its intrinsic associations but above all due to the Soviets' need for a single symbol of the battle, of the culminating battle of the war, and one that could serve as an approved image of the war, cementing it as something uplifting and positive and associating it with the Soviet state, its leader, and its center in Moscow's Kremlin. The way in which the Victory Banner was linked with Stalin during the making of the film about the battle in the immediate days and weeks after the fall of Berlin is indicative of a wider tendency in war memory of the late Stalin period, one beginning with a flurry of coverage in the summer of 1945.[38] In turn, this was part of a deliberate and highly successful downplaying of the notion of a people's army and a people's victory. Thus, while the poet Evgenii Dolmatovskii and others writing at the time describe how everyone wanted to put up a flag over Berlin, over any point of Berlin, the image of the Victory Banner suggested something different.[39] The suggestion was that a highly hierarchical army raised a single banner over Berlin, over the center of power, on Stalin's orders. The notion of many banners, many red flags, detracted from this idea and was thus less frequently expressed in the days that followed. In turn, the Victory Banner could be paraded on Red Square before Stalin and finally placed in the Museum of the Red Army, next to a bust of Stalin, the great architect of the victory.

It is also likely that the choice of a Georgian (or Mingrelian), in the person of Junior Sergeant Meliton Kantariia, along with the Russian sergeant Mikhail Egorov, as those officially credited with raising the Victory Banner was also motivated by the need to echo Stalin's own Georgian ethnicity and close bond with the Russian people.

It is worth briefly considering that these two associations, with the end of Nazism on the one hand and with the Kremlin, Stalin, and the Soviet state on the other, interact in such a way as to emphasize the latter and to downplay the original internationalist socialist (or communist) associations of the red flag and of it being raised on the eve of May Day, even if they are still present in the imagery. For the Soviets, it was vitally important to raise the flag by 1 May, less because it was a holiday associated with workers of the world but rather because it was a symbolic public holiday for the Soviet state. This initiated a tension between the 1 May and 9 May holidays that was ultimately to lead to the abolishing of the former in the post-Soviet period.

REPRESENTATION IN PHOTOJOURNALISM

The claims by most eyewitness accounts that a banner was raised over the cupola of the Reichstag between 22:40 and 22:50 on the evening of 30 April while fighting still continued in the heavily defended building have been viewed with skepticism by the popular British historian Antony Beevor.[40] His reason for doubt is that the date coincides neatly with the Soviets' need to proclaim that the Soviet flag was already in place for the symbolic state holiday of May Day.[41] There are other accounts that also share these doubts over the actual raising of the flag.[42] However, while it has been claimed that the first photographs of a flag over the Reichstag were published on 2 May, or even 3 May, in fact, on 1 May the Soviet daily newspaper *Krasnaia zvezda* described the raising of the "red banner" over the Reichstag as "the symbol of our victory."[43] The same 1 May issue published a photograph, by Roman Karmen, of the flag flying above one of the towers of the Reichstag.[44] While the image looks airbrushed, the archival records of envious reactions from Karmen's colleagues in the newsreel studio confirm its veracity.[45]

Like the many flag raisings on the Reichstag during and immediately following the battle (see below, chapters 3 and 5), there were cameras pointed at and images taken of flags raised over the building. Dozens of Soviet photographers had followed the Red Army's advance into the German capital, and they shot photos from every angle. The most famous photo of the Victory Banner over the Reichstag was by Evgenii Khaldei, who had seen Joe Rosenthal's February 1945 photo, *The Raising of Old Glory on Mount Suribashi, Iwo Jima*, shortly before the battle in Berlin and had decided to do something similar; the image spoke to his own desire to make images that possessed symbolic resonance.[46] He had already made a number of images of red flags raised over various towns captured by the Soviets in their advance.[47] He approached three Red Army men at random on 2 May, though they were not those who actually put up the flag, nor the pair officially recognized as doing so. Nevertheless, Khaldei got them to restage the raising of the flag.[48] He then took at least thirty-six different still images of the flag over the Reichstag.[49] This meant a considerable investment of resources, since photographic film stock was expensive and scarce.[50]

While there are a number of these images in public circulation, the most famous image was published only in the weekly illustrated

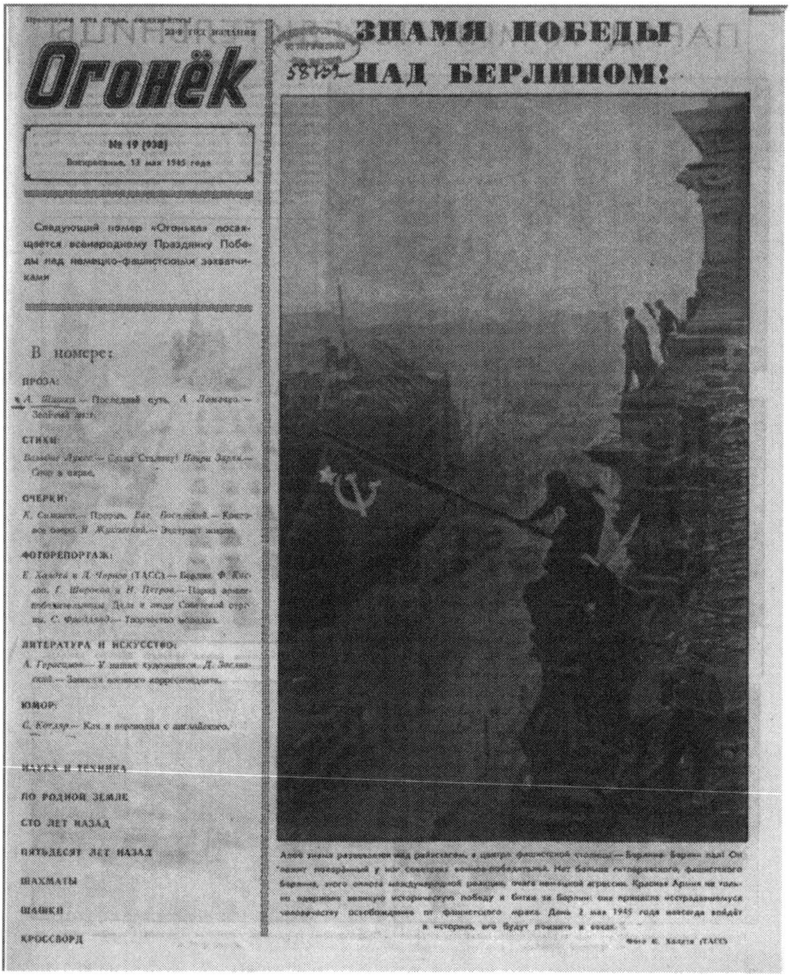

Огонёк

№ 19 (938)

Воскресенье, 13 мая 1945 года

Следующий номер «Огонька» посвящается всенародному Празднику Победы над немецко-фашистскими захватчиками

В номере:

ПРОЗА:

СТИХИ:

ОЧЕРКИ:

ФОТОРЕПОРТАЖ:

ЛИТЕРАТУРА И ИСКУССТВО:

ЮМОР:

НАУКА И ТЕХНИКА

ПО РОДНОЙ ЗЕМЛЕ

СТО ЛЕТ НАЗАД

ПЯТЬДЕСЯТ ЛЕТ НАЗАД

ШАХМАТЫ

ШАШКИ

КРОССВОРД

ЗНАМЯ ПОБЕДЫ НАД БЕРЛИНОМ!

1.3. Khaldei's photograph, as printed in *Ogonek*, 13 May 1945, 3.

magazine *Ogonek*, on 13 May. It is memorable, despite not being the first image published, in showing neither what was to become the official flag nor the official raisers of it, and in not showing the banner being raised over the cupola, as the official Victory Banner supposedly was. I contend that this image's ascent to hegemonic status, to becoming the most widely recognized image, first of the battle for Berlin and then of the wider war on the eastern front, is due to its composition: its qualities as a photograph make it more successful in mobilizing the symbolic potential of its subject than its competitors do.

One of the most arresting dimensions of the image is the fact that it is taken from a high angle, above the soldier raising the flag, thus enabling a view of the street and the ruined city below (the rear of the Reichstag). While less pronounced, Khaldei's image echoes the avant-garde photography of the likes of Aleksandr Rodchenko, who with striking angles and dynamic, diagonal compositions strove to imply a new perspective on the world.[51] Here, too, we look down on a new, utterly transformed world, one in which the Soviet Union has become a dominant world power. The photographer's high angle and the Red Army soldier with banner raised in the foreground stand in contrast to the background of a city in ruins. These ruins generate the habitual association of ruins: they evoke other ruins, such as those of the falling of great empires, the ends or beginnings of epochs.[52] They enhance here a sense of the transformation enacted by Soviet victory, a sense of the new era inaugurated by this momentous conquest. This composition, with its high angle looking down, mobilizes that symbolic content better than the other images, assuring its enduring success.

However, this was all the result of careful calculation and construction. In addition to being staged days after the event that it represents, the image was then subjected to airbrushing, which Khaldei used to add smoke to the scene, implying that it was taken as the battle raged all around. Then, when a keen-eyed editor noticed that the soldier supporting the flag raiser had a watch on each wrist, that detail too was doctored, to cover up evidence of looting.[53] An analogous process of staging occurs with the newsreel and documentary film images of the raising of the Victory Banner, and that process presents an illuminating picture of how Soviet media personnel constructed the representation of the battle for Berlin and the raising of the flag. These go far further than the still photographs in shaping the meaning of that event in particular, as well as the war more widely.

CINEMATIC REPRESENTATION

From the moment it was clear the war was won, after the battles of Stalingrad and Kursk, those in charge of Soviet cinema began thinking about how to reimpose the strict ideological control that had been relaxed in the emergency conditions at the war's outset. In a resolution of 15 May 1944, the Central Committee criticized Soviet newsreels for not showing the war in the right light and appropriate scale. The war did not appear monumental enough: "Cameramen often film insignificant episodes, failing to film the most important military events," the resolution noted. There was a need instead to create newsreels and documentaries that "reflect, in a timely and truthful manner, the military actions of Soviet forces, our soldiers' and officers' sophisticated mastery of the art of war and their heroism, the force of Soviet weaponry and its skillful use in battle, the unanimous support of the workers on the home front for the Red Army."[54]

Events now had to be seen and presented through the filter of their historical importance, in the light of the inevitable victory. Commenting at a 5 February 1945 discussion on the difficulties of adapting to these new demands, one filmmaker at the Central Studio of Documentary Film spoke about the frustrating nature of the time lag with newsreel and documentary. These media present an event some time after the newspapers and radio, which means they have to somehow rekindle people's interest in a subject that ceased to be topical some weeks (or even months) earlier. For camera operators at the front, this entailed a certain orientation toward filming material for the historical record; this new orientation, it was argued, had started to have a negative effect on the newsreels themselves, which were now seen as secondary. As a camera operator named Posel′skii put it, newsreel "has lost its identity."[55] In part this was because some directors had begun to withhold material from the newsreels so as to increase the effect of a subsequent full-length documentary, which had now come to have a great deal more prestige. This was in part because the monumental, epochal tone could be struck more easily in that form. However, in the view of Popov, an influential editor at the studio, there should be no contradiction between filming for newsreel and filming for a full-length documentary, because there was no shame in seeing the earlier material repeated in the later film, where it would take on a new meaning and greater resonance. In practice, however, there was a conflict.

This tension between newsreel and documentary was also described by a number of speakers as a contrast between "reportage" on the one hand and the "complex" method of filming, on the other. In the latter, everything is planned in advance, whereas the former is a reacting to the unfolding of events, to novel, specific details, where there is greater scope for artistic innovation and improvisation. Some of the filmmakers were worried about losing the "originality, freshness, and novelty" of their newsreel reportage if all was subordinated to the need for a complex or, we might say, monumental, predetermined vision.[56] The everyday human dimension of Soviet newsreel footage was now to be sacrificed in favor of the filming of great events in a major key. One consequence of this was that the footage was tending to become more impersonal and stereotypical, with predictable images in each battle, such as the artillery, the tanks, the aviation, the infantry advance, and the moment of victory.[57]

Yet the shift here was not solely about what images would be filmed but also about how decisions would now be made about what to film.

This related to a reimposition in the final part of the war of a strict hierarchy that had sometimes been relaxed for pragmatic reasons earlier on. It was also about initiative: whereas previously the camera operators at the front possessed considerable space in which to make decisions for themselves, now what was filmed was supposed to be organized and controlled from the very top. This was more the case than ever with the Berlin film, since the final film would have so much importance. Nevertheless, this was easier said than done.

To reinforce the new orientation toward the preplanned "complex" method of filming, one of the recommendations of the 15 May 1944 resolution was to get more directors of features into Soviet newsreel and documentary filmmaking; the thinking was that the newsreel camera operators were too oriented toward the recording of news and were not planning sufficiently in advance, nor were their plans ambitious enough in scale or dramatic effect. Feature directors were presumed to plan more in advance of shooting. A prime example was the government's suggestion to involve Iulii Raizman, a famous Stalin Prize–winning fiction film director, in newsreel and documentary production. The 15 May 1944 resolution mentioned him as a director who could shift to that type of work.[58] On 14 March 1945 he was put in charge of the documentary film about the capture of Berlin.[59]

Following this lead, the filmmakers insisted it was possible to predict, control, and predetermine the filming. As the instructions to the Second Belorussian Front film group just prior to the assault on Berlin stated, it was a question of imposing one's will and actively selecting what to film, rather than giving in to "empiricism" and "the resistance of the material."[60] The Berlin film was undoubtedly the Soviets' most extensive and meticulously planned documentary record of a battle in the whole war, with thirty-seven camera operators backed up with on-demand access to airplanes and motorbikes for communications. They shot more than thirty thousand meters (i.e., more than eighteen hours) of film for the project.[61]

With such generous resources, Raizman was expected to create a truly monumental work that presented this key, culminating battle in an appropriately glorious light. The culmination of his effort to do so appears in the final film's crescendo sequence of the storming of the Reichstag, which shows an infantry assault on the building by a small group of soldiers holding a flag, which, in a rapid montage, we then see being erected on the equestrian statue over the building; the occasion is marked by a salute fired into the air.[62] The sequence is accompanied by a frenzied, emotive voice-over:

1.4. Still from Iulii Raizman's 1945 film *Berlin*. Courtesy of RGAKFD.

Raise the Victory Banner over the Reichstag!
Raise the Victory Banner over the Reichstag!
Raise the Victory Banner over the Reichstag!
The Victory Banner over the Reichstag has been raised. Comrade Stalin's order has been carried out!

However, there are many misleading aspects to this sequence. First of all, it suggests that Stalin's order was to raise the Victory Banner specifically over the Reichstag, which, as we have seen, it was not. The military and propagandist purposes of capturing the Reichstag and raising a flag over it are elided in a misleadingly seamless montage, which also suggests that the battle for the Reichstag and Berlin ended soon after the raising of the Victory Banner. With the irrefutably direct presence of film, Raizman's *Berlin* asserts that the historical act of flag raising is occurring in front of our eyes, and it presents a narrative sequence suggesting a plan being carried out unerringly, an unquestionable connection between the narrative of the war and the symbol made to stand for it.

In fact, Raizman's film, like the other media, constructed the Victory Banner over the Reichstag as a symbol in a far from simple process deviating from initial plans and involving an enormous degree of improvisation. A 1962 account of Raizman's *Berlin* could not have been more wrong when it claimed, "The scenario plan for the film was agreed beforehand with the plan of the campaign. During the course of the shooting it hardly changed at all."[63] Indeed, this attempt to impose a belated order on what was in fact often quite chaotic was belied by a later account offered by Raizman himself, as well as by the archival records and the outtakes.[64] Despite the intention to make everything fit a preconceived plan, events, technology, and the material conspired against such prior design, and the design itself evolved during the course of the battle and the editing of the film about it.

Yet there certainly was a great deal of planning of the Berlin film and frequent calls to use the "complex method" of filming, that is, for the camera operators to follow a centrally agreed plan rather than giving in to "empiricism" and just reacting to what they saw. In particular, the idea of having a flag-raising sequence as a culminating moment is prefigured in many wartime films of the liberation of Soviet towns since 1941. Furthermore, in the studio correspondence with the front there are frequent requests to film Soviet flags to create political and historical symbolism: in March 1945, the film group of the Second Belorussian Front was asked to film images of a Pioneers' flag that had been hidden during the occupation as the troops went into battle.[65] In another case, a feature director, Leonid Lukov, who had had his first version of a film (*It Happened in the Donbas* [*Eto bylo v Donbasse*]) rejected because it showed the liberation of Donetsk in too harrowing a way, decided to solve the problem by getting documentary footage of the red flag being raised over a number of different "characteristically Gothic" German buildings, and his request was forwarded by telegram to the First Belorussian Front film group in March: "for fiction film by director Lukov urgently film shots of the raising of the flag on high points and tall buildings in German towns with characteristic gothic stop in background we must see advancing armies and fires stop shoot in medium shots with perspective stop raising of the flag must be at rapid pace."[66] However, the difficulty of executing such plans was clear from the repetition of the request, and it was not until 7 May that the front-line film group was able to confirm that they had fulfilled the order.[67]

Despite this kind of pre-ordering and predetermination of the images, the material the camera operators in Berlin managed to deliver was a great disappointment to those editing the film in Moscow, who were initially annoyed by the poor quality of the footage and the small number of images of combat shot at street level, in yards, in buildings, and from windows. They also bemoaned "the absence of shots of the battle for the key buildings of the city" and the lack of any footage of the battle for the metro.[68] Of the thirty thousand meters of film supposedly shot, only fifteen hundred went into the final film.[69] Many of the discarded images give a more vivid and empathetic sense of the plight

1.5. Roman Karmen's photo of the banner atop the Reichstag, as printed in *Krasnaia zvezda*, 1 May 1945, 4.

of German civilians, in contrast to the triumphant tone and sometimes callous irony of the final film. They also contain many more images of Soviet casualties.

Worst of all, the camera operators completely fouled up the filming of the raising of the Victory Banner over the Reichstag. While this is indicative of a tension between, on the one hand, the desire to stage-manage the image of history and, on the other, the inherent chaos of events, it also suggests that the Soviet media were not fully aware that this was supposed to be the key sequence that would come to represent not just this battle but the war as a whole. Thus, the discarded footage, like the photographs, includes sequences of a banner being raised over various buildings in Berlin, as well as images of a group of soldiers advancing with a banner down different Berlin streets.

Indicative of this confusion was the fact that, rather than filming the raising of the Victory Banner over the Reichstag, star camera operator Roman Karmen ended up publishing his own still photograph in the *Krasnaia zvezda* daily newspaper on 1 May 1945. His colleagues were apoplectic: "appearance of Karmen's photograph in *Krasnaia zvezda* has shocked whole studio stop we cannot finish the special release film about Berlin due to absence of central images of the raising of the flag stop could he not have first thought about his studio."[70] The blow for the newsreel team—that Karmen, one of their own, had prioritized a photographic scoop over his responsibilities to the newsreel studio—was made even harder to take by the fact that the other camera operators had messed up the actual filming of the raising of the flag over the Reichstag, a sequence that retrospectively had come to be so significant.

However, these mistakes and recriminations are not evident from an examination of the memoir accounts. Ivan Panov's memoir gives a dramatic account of how he witnessed the raising of the flag on the evening of 30 April and filmed the already raised flag the next day, on the morning of 1 May.[71]

Moisei (Mikhail) Shneiderov's memoirs, originally a part of but not published in the collection *Their Weapon Is the Film Camera* (*Ikh oruzhie—kinokamera*) due to there supposedly already being too many Jewish-sounding surnames for the antisemitic climate of the 1970s Soviet Union, describes filming the flag being raised on 1 May without mentioning that the first flag had been raised the previous evening.[72]

Raizman's various memoir accounts try to avoid directly discussing who filmed the raising of the Victory Banner. However, possibly with the filming of the Victory Banner in mind, he acknowledged the gap between what the camera operators could see and what they were able to record:

> In the evenings [the camera operators] liked to share their impressions of the day. At first these stories annoyed me: when you listen it's all so interesting, but when you see the material they have filmed, either it's not there or it's a chaotic mess [*kakie-to kontsy bez nachala*]. But, when I gained experience, I grew to understand what frustration they themselves felt at not being able to film a hundredth of what they had seen. And what an extraordinary result it was to have some shots that they had succeeded in snatching from the kaleidoscope of life.[73]

The extent to which the footage was a "chaotic mess" rather than the faultless execution of a wise plan is evident when we compare the final Berlin film with a special-release newsreel film about the raising of the flag over the Reichstag, which was made and released on or just after 14 May: *The Victory Banner over Berlin Has Been Raised* (*Znamia Pobedy nad Berlinom vodruzheno*). Not only did Raizman have to manage an enormous team of camera operators to produce a documentary in record time, but at the same time his team had to produce this special-release newsreel (a ten- to fifteen-minute news film on a single theme for particularly important events, rather than a standard newsreel with four to six items). The tasks of simultaneously making the newsreel and the documentary conflicted since, apart from anything else, this meant following two different plans. Thus, on 3 May the director of the Central Studio of Documentary Film (TsSDF), Sergei Gerasimov, telegraphed

1.6. Still from *The Victory Banner Has Been Raised*, Iulli Raizman's special-release newsreel film, mid-May 1945. Courtesy of RGAKFD.

from Moscow to insist that "the capture of Berlin demands immediate representation on the screen," and the camera operators in Berlin were told that the newsreel had to come out in two or three days, while at the same time they were to prioritize the making of the larger film.[74]

The two films differ, especially as regards the depiction of the storming of the Reichstag. In the newsreel special release, while the raising of the Victory Banner over the Reichstag is central, there are few recognizable shots of the Reichstag itself—nothing like the images of the familiar façade, columns, and the cupola we see in the sequence from the completed documentary film. One could easily doubt that this was the Reichstag at all, so fragmentary is the way in which it is portrayed. Furthermore, its seizure is not presented as the end of the battle and the war, as in the longer film. Moreover, while Stalin's presence is palpable, it is through the less dramatic means of showing the 1 May order being read in newspapers by Red Army men rather than the sense that the Victory Banner was raised to fulfill Stalin's order, as in Raizman's film. As the banner is raised, Stalin's order is not mentioned, and instead we hear this more democratic-sounding statement: "The Victory Banner flew above Berlin. It was raised by Soviet people—soldiers and liberators." Despite the film's title, when the key scene is shown, the commentary repeats the text of Stalin's 6 November 1944 order, rather than attempting to claim that the intention had always been to raise the Victory Banner over the Reichstag in particular, as does Raizman's film.

Crucially, unlike the longer film, the Reichstag in the newsreel is one of a series of images that includes other Berlin landmarks, such as the Brandenburg Gate and Unter den Linden, but still not the Reich Chancellery, which some sources claim the Soviets did not initially realize was so important. Here we see further confirmation that the symbolic value of the Reichstag, the Victory Banner raised above it, and its association with Stalin was something that was elaborated and cemented during the days and weeks that followed and was clearly not something established beforehand. Between the newsreel and the film there is a change in meaning: the newsreel shows the capture of the city, whereas the final film, *Berlin*, already makes the city and the Victory Banner symbolic, as they "signif[y] total and definitive victory over the Reich."[75]

The two films also differ in that some images in the newsreel appear to have been taken inside the Reichstag building, and the image of a flag over one of the building's towers resembles one taken by *Pravda* photojournalist Temin. Moreover, the newsreel film shows a clean, debris-free entrance to the building, and this too is obviously staged, an impression compounded by the fact that it is evidently a composite of images shot by different teams at different times, with no establishing shots to which we might relate the various fragments. For the purposes of worldwide distribution, which Raizman's team were intending for the Berlin film, they needed more homogenous and less obviously confected images.[76]

However, while the later footage was deliberately made in such a way as to ensure that it was clear they were attacking the Reichstag, the documents clearly show that the footage was taken later and, in this sense, was even less authentic than the earlier images.

Thus, on 11 May the studio sent a telegram to the camera operators in Berlin: "material of raising banner over reichstag defective stop urgently film raising long medium shots on background of smoke stop."[77]

The camera operator had messed up possibly the most important moment of the war, one that was now meant to stand as a symbol for victory.[78] In fact it was not until 7 June that Raizman's team in Moscow received the extra footage they required.[79] This meant that the famous film footage was in fact staged more than a month after the actual storming of the Reichstag. It, like the newsreel footage and Khaldei's image, does not show Egorov and Kantariia or anyone else officially credited with raising the Victory Banner, nor is it the recognizable banner with the name of the unit on it, which in any case was also added later. With this footage, the camera operators in Berlin were congratulated and the narrative could be completed.[80]

Yet this too was no simple task, and the various drafts of the script convey the ongoing process of shaping the battle and the raising of the flag into symbols of a glorious victory. The conscious nature of this process is evident in Raizman and co-screenwriter Nikolai Shpikovskii's treatment, dated 28 May 1945, where there is an acute awareness of the symbolic character of the film as possessing "political" and not just "military-strategic" meaning: "Berlin—is the capital of Fascist Germany. The capture of Berlin naturally exceeds the borders of geography. The depiction of Berlin, of fighting for Berlin and the raising of the red flag over the Reichstag, at a certain point acquires a symbolic character [*priobretaet v opredelennyi moment simbolicheskii kharakter*]."[81]

This scenario is the first to stress the raising of the flag as fulfilling Stalin's order. It suggests a glorious finale:

> We can envisage only one possible ending for this film, telling the story of a momentous moment in human history—the fall of Berlin and with it the end of Fascism.
>
> We request the opportunity to film comrade Stalin at the moment where he receives, in the Kremlin, the Victory Banner taken down from the Reichstag.
>
> These images, edited together with images of our country congratulating our leader, should be shown to the whole world.
>
> The Victory Banner, the symbol of victory in the great Stalin's hands.[82]

It is not clear exactly why, but they did not include the planned sequence with Stalin in the Kremlin. Nevertheless, the associations with Stalin and the Kremlin remain an important part of the Victory Banner's symbolism.

The Stalin cult had been downplayed at certain low points in the war, especially in 1941–1942, but it was revived with full force after 1943's victory at Stalingrad, after which the leader's name was closely associated with all war successes.[83] Evidently the film *Berlin* was intended also to satisfy this demand, a key part of which was showing the Victory Banner being raised over the Reichstag as the fulfillment of Stalin's order. Yet this was achieved through the voice-over rather than through any fresh footage, as originally intended. It is likely that this solution was mandated by considerations of time: on 7 June the studio officials declared themselves happy with the footage, and after the editing team worked around the clock in "garrison" conditions, not permitted to leave the studio, the film was approved on 19 June and released a week later.[84] A second consideration was the fact that the Victory Banner was to be part of the 24 June Victory Parade, which was intended to become the subject of a separate film. This would present a new opportunity to link Stalin, the Victory Banner, and the Kremlin in the public consciousness.

THE VICTORY PARADE

The way in which the Victory Banner was immediately associated with Stalin in the scenario for the documentary film of the battle for Berlin is indicative of a wider tendency in the late Stalin period. This tendency began with a flurry of coverage in the summer of 1945 to attribute victory to and associate it as closely as possible with Stalin and the Stalin cult, including his being awarded the title "generalissimus" and two Order of Victory medals.[85] The association of Stalin and victory was also one of the intended functions of the 24 June 1945 Victory Parade on Red Square. But its objectives were also wider: the projection of power, the suggestion of a reimposition of rigid, regimented order as a metaphor for the way the country would now be, a shift from the greater informality and initiative of the war years, and the wild, spontaneous celebrations on 9 May itself.[86] It was to discipline and restrain memory of the war, giving it a ceremonial, "parade-like" character as troops sported immaculately pressed and polished uniforms.[87] The ritual character of a parade was suited to this overall objective, as such displays promote conformity and "an atmosphere of unanimity": the whole country symbolically participates.[88] In turn, this was part of a symbolic echoing of tsarist-era traditions: in 1814 and 1815 Alexander I (1801–1825) had held two enormous reviews of troops in France following the victory over Napoleon—the first, of 80,000 troops on Place de la Concorde, and the second of 150,000, in Champagne. As Richard Wortman comments, "external appearance was indeed the emperor's principal concern, for beauty and symmetry signified order and now the square formed by the armies gave almost mystical confirmation of the divine source of his power."[89] The size of these reviews surpassed those of Napoleon, and the precision of their discipline struck foreign observers, including the duke of Wellington, with awe. Alexander's successor, Nicholas I (1825–1855) further refined such reviews as "spectacles of the monarch's personal authority and the Russian people's gift for obedience."[90]

To project this level of order and symmetry, it would not be appropriate simply to repeat the formula of the 1945 May Day and prewar military parades, since much had changed in Soviet society and culture during the war: the parade had to reflect the Soviet Union's newly acquired "great power," show its "imperial" status, and elevate Stalin still further. Exactly how it would do so was unclear, but it had to be worked out at break-neck pace in the interval between Victory Day and the 24

June parade. The place of the Victory Banner in the story of the Victory Parade was again indicative of these wider tensions.

The parade on 1 May 1945 was the first military parade on Red Square since 7 November 1941, and it gave an indication of what was to come, with careful checks ensuring that the banners and uniforms of the participants were repaired and, if necessary, replaced. The lists of participants were also carefully vetted by "the organs of state security."[91] The route for the May Day parade was meticulously timed, with each part of the parade given a title and timed separately.[92] However, reports on this parade highlighted a lack of discipline: the soldiers had their hands in their pockets and did not salute; they fidgeted, smoked, and ate dried fish, messily leaving the butts and bones where they had been standing.[93] The 1 May troops were primarily from the Moscow garrison and had been troublesome enough, but the front-line soldiers brought to Moscow for the 24 June parade created even more problems, as they bitterly resented being made to march in formation and adopt a rigid, parade-ground bearing.[94] There was much carousing, especially by groups of officers dancing the nights away at the Hotel Moskva restaurant. When the merrymakers were threatened with arrest, some got into gunfights with police. However, order was quickly restored: army drivers, found waiting outside train stations while using their vehicles to make a living as informal taxi drivers, were threatened with having their vehicles confiscated and being themselves sent to penal units.[95]

A further precedent for the 24 June parade was the 4 May Victory Parade in Berlin, which was held jointly with the British and Americans, and some footage of this was included in Raizman's special-release newsreel. Film scholar Dmitrii Karavaev has called this the "first and most sincere" Victory Parade, but it was unsuccessful, in part, he suggests, because it did not serve the cult of Stalin so much as that of Zhukov, who appeared in a white military tunic of the kind favored by Stalin.[96] The fact that Soviet troops shared the glory in this parade with their allies, Great Britain and the United States, was also a shortcoming that the Moscow parade would make good.

From 10 May, the day after victory became official with Germany's surrender in Karlshorst, preparations for the 24 June Victory Parade began.[97] These preparations were highly intensive; the specially selected regiments representing each front were transported to Moscow, where they were all given new gray uniforms made from captured German cloth.[98] They spent five hours a day drilling, training to march, goose-step, and salute in unison. All of these preparations were conducted at Central Airport (in Tushino, then on the outskirts of Moscow). A special observer was sent to report on the way in which the various units were preparing, and this person commented on the marching, on things like the soldiers not lifting their legs high enough when goose-stepping, the lack of perfect synchronization in the swinging of arms, and the way troops carried their weapons.[99]

Alongside preparations for the parade itself, there were almost as many preparations for the recording of it for posterity across all available media, as fourteen documentary filmmakers and numerous writers, journalists, and press photographers were present at the "dress rehearsal" of 19 June and many more at the parade itself.[100] This enabled the media to plan both the film and their reports in advance. In some of the articles written to be published on the day of the parade, there was a sense that the writers already knew what would happen in the parade: the leading article in *Pravda* stressed the centrality of Stalin, which was in any case a plausible and wise strategy and in this respect differed little from the reports published after the parade.[101] Indeed, as Malte Rolf notes, the whole idea of Bolshevik festivities as they had been designed in the Stalin era was to focus on and dramatize the power of the leader.[102] Victory in the war was only serving to increase this tendency, as Stalin had created a precedent to further emphasize his power in the 1 May 1945 parade by walking up to the mausoleum podium alone, before the other members of the Politburo.[103] This practice was to be repeated in subsequent parades, serving to elevate Stalin further and represent his power in dramatic fashion.

A similar intention to celebrate the leader was clearly evident with one of the most notable innovations of the Victory Parade: the choice of Mikhail Glinka's "Glory" (Slav′sia), the triumphant final chorus from his opera *A Life for the Tsar*, known as *Ivan Susanin* in Soviet Russia.[104] The piece of music had been banned from Red Army band repertoires since 1919, because it did not correspond with the spirit of the revolution due to its monarchist, pro-tsarist associations.[105]

The decision to include "Glory" in the parade appears to have been made by Major General Semen Chernetskii, a military band leader who was also a talented composer of marches and who had been in charge of the Red Army's orchestras since 1935. Mikhail Chertok describes this decision as a risky move, since it broke with existing norms, even if the opera *Ivan Susanin* had been revived at the Bolshoi Theater in 1939 and highly acclaimed, with the conductor in the production having been awarded a Stalin Prize in 1941.[106] Indeed, the same production was revived in 1945, and the review of the performance in *Pravda* a month before the Victory Parade may have influenced Chernetskii's request to use it, which was made on 5 June and granted on 9 June:

> The famous "Glory," the inspired hymn that crowns the opera, is an invention of genius by the great master of Russian music that incarnates in a powerful choral sound the strength and immovable might of a great people. It is as if Glinka had encased his heroic tale of Susanin's exploit with a choral introduction and the finale of "Glory" just as Russians enclosed the Kremlins of their ancient cities with a beautiful stone ring of walls. Even without taking into account the other wonderful choral works in the opera, then these elements and the finale are shot through with the music of joy, light, and a victorious nation's confidence in its powers.[107]

The reviewer then comments that he would like the finale to be played out on an even bigger canvas, before a larger public, and reflects on the origins of this desire: "However, it may be that such a wish has just been formed under the impression from seeing the exultant masses of our people on Red Square on the day of that great symphony of human joy, the blessed day of 9 May—day of the celebration of the mighty Red Army's unprecedented victory. That is why I would like that work of genius, Glinka's 'Glory' to ring out on a greater scale over an enormous space."[108]

Chernetskii's decision to use "Glory" in the parade was evidently inspired by a similar desire to transfer the patriotic spirit of Glinka's opera from the theater to Red Square itself. The piece was played as Marshal Zhukov rode to the mausoleum to make the first speech; in Bolshevik parades, the iconic notes of Beethoven's "Ode to Joy" would have been played at that juncture. The playing of "Glory" also may have been motivated by a shift toward more Slavic music (although there were still a number of the marches in the Victory Parade that had been composed by Germans).[109] "Glory," though, played a special role in the parade, functioning to articulate a sense of patriotic gravitas that was similar to that of the national anthem. Indeed, the way in which the shouts of "Hurrah!" punctuate the playing of "Glory" (these are bells in the opera) echoes the way in which the finale to the Soviet national anthem, itself played for the first time on Soviet radio on New Year's Eve 1944, is punctuated by the blasts of an artillery salute when played at military parades, including this one.[110]

While the inclusion of "Glory" was a bold and risky move, it can be considered an overall success; it was praised by Stalin and has become a part of Victory Day parades ever since. However, if it was intended to elevate Stalin and the Stalin cult, it did not work unproblematically, precisely because "Glory" accompanied Marshal Zhukov at the parade, not Stalin.[111] It is this mismatch between the role of Zhukov in "receiving" (i.e., inspecting) the parade on a white horse and the overall intention of associating Stalin with victory that perhaps explains Zhukov's claim that Stalin himself wanted to receive the parade on horseback.

The tradition of receiving the parade on horseback was also something that harked back to the tsarist era, if not before. The choice of a white horse for Zhukov also recalled the legendary Russian generals Suvorov and Kutuzov, who rode white horses before their troops on special ceremonial occasions and thus again evoked the long, prerevolutionary, and indeed antirevolutionary traditions of the Russian army. This kind of detailed attention to such symbolism had not been a feature of previous Soviet military parades.[112]

According to Zhukov's account, when Stalin asked him who should receive the parade, he had suggested Stalin should, but the latter had pronounced himself too old and was in any case not a good enough rider to fulfill the role.[113] Apparently, Vasilii Stalin told Zhukov that Stalin intended to receive the parade himself but had fallen off his horse while practicing and only then decided not to take on the key role in the parade.[114] This account is contradicted by at least two other credible sources: Sergei Shtemenko, who worked at Red Army headquarters managing the parade preparations, and Ivan Bobylev, who worked in the Manège for many years training officers to ride in military parades. Both insist that Stalin never intended to receive the parade and never attempted to train for it, and both suggest that the whole idea of him trying to do so was so obviously doomed as to make it ridiculous.[115] On the other hand, if Stalin had originally intended to receive the parade, then this would have made sense in symbolic terms, since it would have associated him more firmly with victory, suggesting, in the idiom of ritual, that he was its chief architect. The fact that Zhukov became the central focus may thus be connected to the problems that befell Marshal Zhukov following the Victory Parade. However, another possible explanation is that during the war Zhukov had been willing to challenge and contradict Stalin over military matters, and freedom of thought and expression of that sort, albeit limited, was what now had to be curtailed.[116] This anxiety can only have been increased when Stalin saw Zhukov receiving the parade; Stalin would surely have felt anxious as to the marshal's power.

Whether or not the issue of who was to receive the parade worked out as intended, there were many other elements of the parade that had to be canceled at the last minute: the rain caused changes to the schedule and the cancellation of both a fly-over and the traditional parade of workers. Moreover, the Victory Banner was initially intended to head the parade, but it was not actually part of the 24 June 1945 Victory Parade on Red Square.[117]

The official Victory Banner had now been inscribed with the name and number of the unit that had raised it (150th Rifle Division, Seventy-Ninth Rifle Corps, Third Strike Army, First Belorussian Front) in an

1.7. The Victory Banner arriving in Moscow (discarded footage). Courtesy of RGAKFD.

attempt to end any arguments on the matter. It was brought back to Moscow with special military honors on 20 June 1945 and met by a guard of honor from the Moscow garrison. Accompanying the banner were Egorov, Kantariia, Stepan Neustroev (captain of the First Battalion, 356th Regiment, 150th Rifle Division), and Il′ia S′ianov (senior sergeant in charge of the key company of the battalion).[118] Also there to accompany the banner was Senior Lieutenant Konstantin Samsonov, commander of one of the other units involved in the storming of the Reichstag—the 380th Rifle Regiment, 171st Division, Third Strike Army, which was not named on the banner.[119] This episode was photographed and covered in the press, and also filmed, presumably with the intention of including it in the final documentary film of the Victory Parade.[120]

However, the front-line troops who had initially raised the flag and were due to carry it performed poorly at the dress rehearsal the day before the parade.[121] Zhukov instead sent the flag off to the Central Museum of the Red Army. This was a further indication of the difference between what was required of soldiers during the war and what was needed in the postwar period: bravery, initiative, and resourcefulness in combat versus discipline, loyalty, and regimentation in noncombat situations. However, while the banner (since it was not there) was absent from the newsreels and photographs, many memoirs either vaguely imply it was there or even claim that it was seen there.[122] In part this is because it has become an integral part of Victory Day parades since 1965, and memoir writers felt the need to suggest the continuity, consistency, and solidity of tradition. Consequently, its absence in 1945 and the reason for it were only revealed in Neustroev's memoir, published at the end of the Soviet era, when censorship restrictions were breaking down (see chapter 5).

Nevertheless, despite the Victory Banner's physical absence, banners played a key role in the parade. The voice-over for the color version of the commemorative documentary film, entitled *Victory Parade* (*Parad pobedy*, dir. Vasilii Beliaev, Irina Venzher, and Iakov Posel′skii, 1945), identified the representatives of the various "fronts" as they marched past the mausoleum podium with banners for their units. As the First Belorussian Front filed past, the commentary stated that they were carrying thirty-six battle banners: "They took the Reichstag and raised the Victory Banner over Berlin."

Moreover, the Victory Banner was mentioned in Zhukov's speech, as well as by most newspaper reports about the parade.[123] A number of these elevate its status as a sacred object possessing an aura. Thus, on the day of the parade, the colonel whose regiment took the Reichstag, Fedor Zinchenko, who also took part in the parade, wrote in *Trud* stressing how important the banner was as a "relic."[124] The leading article in *Pravda* on the day following the parade, in addition to mentioning the Victory Banner, referred to the participants as "having carried the sacred banner of the fatherland with honor through the hard dangerous roads of war."[125] Had it been a part of the parade, the Victory Banner would have served as a concrete, sacred object standing for all the banners of all the units carried through the war. It was acquiring a holy status already, and its relation to the sacred is important for understanding other key elements of the parade and the Victory cult more widely.

Banners were once again key in the parade's most memorable moment, when the orchestra fell silent and, to the stirring rhythm of eighty drummers, two hundred captured Nazi banners, paraded horizontally with the cloth dragging along the flagstones, were cast down before Lenin's mausoleum, by the Kremlin, the symbolic center of both the Russian and the Soviet state and one of its most holy sites, comparable to the Wailing Wall. The Kremlin Wall, where Lenin's tomb was situated, was also where martyrs to the revolution had been buried since November 1917, conferring gravity and sanctity on Red Square parades.[126] This performance reworked the contest of symbols—the old versus new—that had been key to prewar Soviet parades, only now it was not the church or internal opponents but the Nazis, a vanquished external foe, who were associated with the profane.[127] Their vanquished symbols were contrasted with Lenin's mausoleum and the leaders, including Stalin, standing upon it, but also with the Soviet banners paraded so triumphantly only moments before. Such an opposition of the sacred and profane is said to be a general characteristic of flags.[128] Later, when placed in the Central Museum of the Red Army, the Victory Banner would similarly be contrasted with the Nazi banners, taking on a sacred status from its differential opposition to them.

The parade more generally, as well as the casting down of Nazi banners, was an attempt not just to defile Nazi symbols and emphatically enunciate victory but also to appropriate the Nazis' and fascists' own choreography of power, their talent for the projection of imperial might and the charisma of the leader. There was also a possible Roman model here, evoking "traditional forms of imperial behavior."[129] This perhaps explains the whole idea of casting the banners at the foot of the emperor, which here was the base of Lenin's mausoleum, with Stalin standing on it. Just as the ruins of Berlin suggested the end of an empire, the Victory Parade suggested the birth of a new, Soviet one.

The Victory Parade publicly marked a high-water mark in an ongoing process of reinvention and renegotiation of the Soviet state in which the universal, internationalist aspirations of communist ideology were sidelined in favor of nationalist and imperial overtones. This had already led to the changing of the Soviet national anthem from "The Internationale" (itself composed during the 1871 Paris Commune) to the more russocentric "Hymn of the Soviet Union," which celebrated Russian patriotic heroes and is still used by the Russian Federation, with slightly adapted lyrics. It led also to changes in the structure of the military, such as the abolishing of the political officers' (aka commissars') role in the command structure and the introduction of a more traditional hierarchical system of ranks, reflected in the reintroduction of epaulettes. While the Soviet Union had always been highly militarized, it was at its most militarized yet in 1945.

While the Soviets kept the red flag of revolution, adding their yellow star and hammer and sickle symbols in the "hoist" (the top corner nearest the pole), the raising of this residually internationalist flag over Berlin, atop the Reichstag, transformed it into the Victory Banner, not only symbolizing the end of the Nazis but also serving as a nationalist, military emblem and stressing the victory as a Soviet one, as well as the symbolic enactment of a new Soviet empire stretching over Eastern Europe, to the Elbe. The Victory Banner ambiguously brings together these associations. However, most of all in the early postwar years it was associated with the Stalin cult.

While the Victory Banner was unable to fulfill its function as a cipher for the Stalin cult at the Victory Parade, the error was quickly corrected by the Central Museum of the Red Army. In 1945 the museum display was almost entirely devoted to the Great Patriotic War and contained an enormous number of artifacts, of which the Victory Banner was initially just one among many. It was, however, completely subordinated to the museum's emphasis upon Stalin as the central figure in wartime victory. The museum thus featured "orders issued by Supreme Commander Marshal Stalin during the Great Patriotic War, letters from Red Army soldiers, officers, and workers of the motherland to comrade Stalin, and other documents testifying to the uniting of the Soviet people around the Party of Lenin-Stalin and the government to resist the enemy. Battle plans, genuine relief maps, and documents show the realization of the genius of Stalin's strategic plans for the defeat of the fascist German invaders."[130]

The description of how the Victory Banner was displayed also underlines the overriding importance of this Stalin-centric narrative of infallible foresight and control:

> The Museum display concludes with the Hall of Banners. Here one can find the military banners of the Red Army units who have distinguished themselves in battles for the Motherland. Soviet medals received by the divisions and regiments are attached to the banners, with their medal ribbons. On a high pedestal, lit up by projectors, burns the red flame of the Victory Banner raised on the German Reichstag on 30 April 1945. In the center of the Hall is a bust of the Great Leader, the commander of genius, comrade Stalin, under whose leadership the Soviet people and their armed forces won historical victories in the Great Patriotic War.[131]

Alongside the bust of Stalin, the Victory Banner is already the culminating point of the museum, and it is presented dramatically to highlight its importance and the power of its aura. Yet the Hall of Banners contains flags relating not only to World War II and the Victory Parade but also to the defense of the Soviet state in previous conflicts, such as the Civil War. The Victory Banner did not yet play the preeminent political role it would later assume, just as the war itself was initially subordinated to other Soviet symbols and the mythology of the revolution.

The emphasis upon the Victory Banner reflects the shift during the last months of the war and its immediate aftermath, from its use as a symbol to inspire soldiers in battle to its acquisition of an aura serving to shape memory of the war as uplifting. As we have seen, it was a symbol that could not always be fitted into choreographed and scripted ritual performances, just as the veterans and their experiences and memories could not always be integrated into the narrative of the war and the realities of postwar life. Nevertheless, its path from battlefield to museum was part of the attempt to shape memory of the war as something positive and to distract the population from the bloody, destructive experience of war that dominated soldiers' thoughts in particular during its course.[132] While the transition to peace enabled the brutal realities to recede from view, the country bequeathed to the victors was in a state of ruin. There was an "incongruity between the symbolic triumph of victory for Soviet society and the hard realities of daily life."[133] Rather than permit an honest look at the problems, Stalin forestalled difficult questions as to the price of victory, through the claim that the total of war dead was 7 million, as well as a series of "ideological counterattacks and restrictions in terms of what could be said about the war.[134] A key counterattack was the condemnation of the 1946 film *A Great Life: Part 2* (*Bol′shaia zhizn′*, dir. Leonid Lukov, 1945) for its portrayal of the catastrophic state of the Donbass region: the flooded, ruined pits and barely habitable dwellings, as well as the young adult protagonists' vulgar and rowdy behavior. It had failed to negotiate the tension between the wild spirit of youth and the more severe political imperatives of the new era.[135] Reality had to be portrayed now through the filter of victory, which conferred a heroic aura on all things. Film of the late Stalin era was precisely oriented toward this challenge. The problem for Soviet cinema was how to incorporate the narrative of victory within the cult of Stalin and to do so in a way that had relevance to the contemporary postwar situation. This was a very difficult task, and few films managed it to accomplish it.

2

VICTORY AND THE POSTWAR STALIN CULT

Despite the glorious victory, a major legacy of the war in Soviet society was economic and demographic devastation, leading to a shortage of labor, especially in agriculture. The number of mature and healthy men available to work the land was two and half times less than in 1940. Everything in the countryside was in short supply, including seed, horses, and tools, leading to a 1945 harvest that was only 60 percent of the 1940 level.[1] Two million died of hunger and hunger-related diseases in 1946–1948. The consequent rise in crime, often a result of desperation, was treated extremely harshly by the law; the Gulag population grew to 2.5 million.[2]

Any attempts to reflect upon or portray these difficulties were repressed, as the machinery of the state was deployed to discipline culture and the intellectuals in the famous "Zhdanov retrenchment." Soviet society's attitude toward the war was one of considerable ambiguity in this period: there was tension between a desire to move on and not think about the war and its lingering effects, which loomed over everything. Given that it would be difficult to forget the war entirely, the state was unclear as to what might be the most appropriate and advantageous ways to remember it. The new holiday of 9 May, Victory Day, was a particular problem, as it was hard to integrate it into the existing system of Soviet public holidays. May Day was second in importance only to the commemoration of the October Revolution, and both played an important role in shaping Soviet citizens and reassuring them as to the continuity and stability of the Soviet system.[3]

Initially, Victory Day was linked to May Day. Thus, in contrast to the pomp of the 24 June 1945 military parade, Victory Day 1946 was celebrated in a notably informal way. The run-up to it was dominated by exhortations to the population, disseminated in the press, to work harder to achieve production targets to mark May Day and Victory Day.[4] This is indicative of a sense that Victory Day could be used to mobilize the public. The emphasis here, however, is on 1 May, rather than 9 May. After all, the military parade would still be on May Day, described as "inspection day for the armed forces of the laborers of all countries."[5] There was a sense that the whole country was preparing for this: "The Soviet people are preparing for the inspection."[6]

Nevertheless, the association works both ways at this point, with Victory Day being mentioned on May Day as well as the other way around. So closely associated are the two at this juncture, especially since this May Day was the first anniversary of the raising of the Victory Banner, that Victory Day was mentioned as part of the rhetoric of May Day: "The Soviet people approach the first of May in the glow of unprecedented martial glory. Led by the great Stalin, the warrior-people, the victor-people defeated the enemy, crushed the Fascist beast in its lair. A year ago, almost to the day, the Red Army was storming Berlin—that last fortress of Fascism. The Victory Banner, raised by the miraculous Soviet warriors over the Reichstag, was a symbol of the conclusion of the struggle for the liberation of our motherland from the German-Fascist occupiers."[7]

Similarly, Stalin's 1946 May Day order, or pronouncement, also mentions the Victory Banner.[8] However, the details were unclear and yet to be canonically fixed: the Victory Banner was inconsistently capitalized and there was even uncertainty as to the date on which it was raised. Thus, the 3 May edition of *Pravda* incorrectly cites the date of its raising as 2 May (confusing it with the date of the Berlin garrison's final surrender):

> Among the many memorable dates of the Great Patriotic war there is a special place for 2 May 1945, when the victorious Red Army completed the defeat of Hitlerite Germany and raised the Victory Banner over the prostrate German capital—above Berlin. . . .
>
> A year has passed since the banner of our victory was raised over Berlin. Like a sunrise, heralding the end of night, this victorious banner, run up above the ruins of the Reichstag, heralded the swift end of the Second World War and the return of humanity to peaceful labor.[9]

In turn, on 9 May, May Day was invoked: "Moscow continues to find itself under the enduring impression of the First of May, when the words of comrade Stalin's proclamation rang around the whole country."[10]

Moscow's most prominent squares—Sverdlov (Teatral′naia), Pushkinskaia, Maiakovskaia, and Manezhnaia—and the parks were prepared with red flags, banners, and garlands for the festivities. There were open-air concerts, theatrical performances, clowns, acrobats, and sporting contests. There were also meetings, with political speeches, and a new exhibition of captured Nazi weaponry. As had happened on 24 June 1945, on 9 May 1946 it also rained, but it was clearly quite an occasion. It seemed that no one stayed in, so crowded were Moscow's streets, and the ambiance was somewhat anarchic given the performances, especially the satirical ones. Even the front page of *Pravda* stressed the spontaneity of the joy: "The victory holiday, truly the people's holiday, cheerful, joyous and spontaneous, like the very soul of the people, gripped not only Red Square, not only the main thoroughfare of Moscow—Gorky street, but also squares, streets, and parks as far as the most distant outskirts."[11]

The only 9 May 1946 military parade was one that took place jointly with the other allies in Berlin.[12] Nonetheless, there were many informal meetings of old comrades, establishing a tradition that was to continue for veterans throughout the years and later become a key factor in the evolution of the festival. *Pravda* picked out for symbolic value two old comrades, one who had taken part in the 7 November 1941 parade and one who had taken part in the 24 June 1945 parade. Some veterans danced in the streets, but those who had taken part in the storming of the Reichstag in particular (but not only them) met in the Central Museum of the Red Army by the Victory Banner.[13]

On 9 May, alongside the pronouncement congratulating all on the Victory Day holiday, the presidium of the Supreme Soviet announced the conferment of Hero of the Soviet Union medals, with the Order of Lenin and Golden Star medal on those who had raised the Victory Banner over the Reichstag—Davydov, Egorov, Kantariia, Neustroev, and Samsonov—explicitly for their role in raising the Victory Banner. This was a highly formal, ceremonial, state-controlled move, one that marked a contrast with the largely unstructured public celebrations that characterized this first anniversary, and this act was very prominently featured on the first page of *Pravda*. As Jeffrey Brooks points out, the article on the front page of *Pravda* announcing the awarding of the Victory Banner to those who raised it is overshadowed by a large, full-length portrait photograph of Stalin just above it.[14] This emotive symbol was again deployed, in the rather diffuse and chaotic context of the 1946 commemorations, to associate victory with Stalin and suggest that victory and the storming of the Reichstag had been preordained and preordered by Stalin. However, while the emphasis here was firmly on the great victory, the price paid for it was also mentioned, and atrocities were still referred to, albeit in the context of commemorations: the Red Army was said to have "extinguished the ovens of Majdanek and Auschwitz" and "saved peoples from slavery and extermination."[15]

Alongside the medals, commemorations, and somber reflections, focus was shifting away from the war. An *Izvestiia* editorial on 9 May 1946 stated, "This holiday is not commemorative; it is about our readiness for new feats."[16] Similarly, *Pravda* attempted to link the wartime achievements of the heroes who had raised the Victory Banner over the Reichstag with those who are "heroes of metal and coal":

> The heroes of the new Five-Year Plan are today applying their efforts in the great cause, in the name of which the heroes of the Great Patriotic war accomplished their immortal feats. This great cause is the glory and flourishing of the motherland, the happiness of the Soviet people. Today *Pravda* has published the Decree of the Presidium of the Supreme Soviet of the USSR awarding the title of Hero of the Soviet Union to Captain Davydov, Sergeant Egorov, Junior Sergeant Kantariia, Captain Neustroev, and Senior Lieutenant Samsonov, who raised the Victory Banner over the Reichstag in Berlin. Just as the motherland shall not forget their glorious feat, nor shall it forget today's feats of labor of the heroes of metal, coal, oil and machinery, collective farm fields and science, those who through their selfless toil are turning the new Five-Year Plan into reality.[17]

The sense that the achievements of warriors and workers are linked and equal is one that would be developed in the script for Mikheil Chiaureli's *The Fall of Berlin*, which was first conceived later in 1946, following the 29 June release of his previous film, *The Vow* (*Kliatva*), which marked a new stage in cinema's treatment of the Stalin cult.[18] *The Fall of Berlin*, which will be analyzed in depth below, was something of a continuation of *The Vow*, and it was also conceived in the context of the immediate postwar years, when the subject of victory was more prominent than when it was released in 1950.

Victory Day 1947 was still a public holiday.[19] However, in December 1947, the government declared 9 May would become a normal working day the following year and created the new public holiday of 1 January instead.[20] This shift was anticipated by the way the press paid far less attention to Victory Day in 1947 than it had in 1946. This strengthened the message that there were few rewards due the Soviet population for their wartime achievements; instead, they needed to earn rewards through their efforts. Now, however, there was far less emphasis on the symbolism even of the dates, and rather than calling for promises to fulfill targets by May Day or Victory Day, *Pravda* was full of direct promises to Stalin to fulfill targets, as the Stalin leader cult had become more central to political symbolism.

The 1947 slogans (*prizyvy*) for 1 May mention the Great Patriotic War almost in passing, and the war is no longer anywhere near as central;

there is no attempt to suggest its palpability or relevance. There is also no buildup in the newspapers prior to 9 May; the focus is on the need to fulfill the plans—the main theme is thus the economy. On 9 May 1947 itself, the official pronouncement is made not by Stalin but by Bulganin. There is a far more muted, less festive tone, as well as less description of the carnivalesque activities. Nevertheless, even with such minimal attention paid to Victory Day, *Pravda* does show a 1945 photograph by Iakov Riumkin of soldiers firing a salute as they raise a red flag (said to be the Victory Banner) over the equestrian statue on top of the Reichstag. It is not on the front page but on the second page, and it is not the famous image by Khaldei. Nevertheless, it still mobilizes the symbolism and aura of the Victory Banner, even at this low ebb, for the cult and culture of victory commemoration in the Soviet Union. Subsequently, the main feature of Victory Day from 1948 to 1965 was a fireworks display, with some informal political meetings and veterans' get-togethers, but these, like memory of the war more widely, had to be carefully controlled.

LIMITATIONS ON HISTORY

Many military units adopted the tradition of meeting up on Victory Day every year whether or not it was a public holiday. This was something that was permitted but not officially encouraged, and attempts to lobby for a separate veterans' organization were blocked.[21] Veterans were potentially problematic, because they commanded an authority unvetted by the state; they had learned to talk back to authority and take initiative. Sometimes the sight of them alone was an inconvenience, as with the disabled, in some cases rounded up and kept from view in provincial towns.[22] The appearance in print of veterans' memoirs was no less problematic, and such publications had to be doctored or prevented altogether as part of a wider disciplining of war memory.

It is sometimes said that there were no memoirs and no histories of the war written in the first postwar years under Stalin.[23] This claim needs to be nuanced, however. On the occasion of 9 May 1946 and 1947, one can find one or two pages of usually ghostwritten reminiscences in magazines like the weekly *Ogonek*, the monthly journal *Oktiabr′*, or in military publications. The printing of these pieces stopped for the most part after the cancellation of 9 May as a public holiday at the end of 1947. Memoirs published in book form were very few in number, their content controlled and their distribution often restricted. One example is the 1948 publication *The Storming of Berlin: Memoirs, Letters, and Diaries of Participants of the Fighting for Berlin* (*Shturm Berlina: Vospominaniia, pis′ma, dnevniki uchastnikov boev za Berlin*).[24] While based on memoirs, this work has been entirely rewritten "by a literary team" of six persons, including famous poets Evgenii Dolmatovskii and Aleksei Surkov, so as to create the impression of a single collective voice, as each memoir seems to dovetail with the previous one. The whole is highly orchestrated, such that Zhukov's name is absent, but even then there are discrepancies, with two different times of the raising of the Victory Banner, given as 22:50 in one account and 14:30 in another.[25] The celebrated writer Konstantin Simonov has argued that the conditions were not favorable for the creation of memoirs until after Khrushchev's 1956 "secret speech."[26] He is right in the sense that those published in the Stalin era and its immediate aftermath were not permitted to articulate distinct, individual first-person-voice recollections that might differ from others' statements. However, there was not total silence. The danger of memoirs was clear: in 1947, the Central Committee received a report from the prosecutor's office that questioned all of the Twenty-Eight Panfilovites, the legendary heroes of the battle for Moscow: the journalist Aleksandr Krivitskii and David Ortenberg confessed that they had made the whole thing up.[27] Left unchallenged in this period, the myth became widely accepted. Had such figures been allowed to publish their various accounts, the myth would been stopped there and then. The postwar climate in which proper histories and even memoirs were not available was one that provided fertile conditions for the proliferation of such myths.

Of the few memoirs published, none were by the top military commanders, although fairly senior figures such as Major General Semen Perevertkin, commander of the Third Strike Army's Seventy-Ninth Rifle Corps, troops from which stormed the Reichstag, contributed a few pages to *The Storming of Berlin*. Indeed, Stalin supposedly prevented the publication of two memoirs in the late 1940s, one of which was by a general, with the excuse that it was too soon after the events and attitudes were too colored by passion rather than reason.[28] This stands in contrast to the West, where it was precisely memoirs of the top commanders that dominated the initial years after the war, with Eisenhower publishing his in 1948, closely followed by Churchill's.[29] Similarly, the claim that there were no histories of the war written in the Soviet Union in the postwar Stalin period is true in that, as Sergei Kudryashov notes, there was no serious historical research into the war published in the Soviet Union in the first ten years after the end of the war. There were, however, a number of essays, brochures, and textbooks, as well as a few articles.[30]

V. M. Kulish, in an overview of Soviet historiography of World War II, has stressed that there were attempts to describe the most important military events of the war in the immediate postwar period, but scholars were hampered by the lack of access to archival documents. Instead, the main source of historical knowledge consisted of the speeches, articles, and orders of Stalin, his biography, and publications by others in honor of his seventieth birthday.[31]

The collection of Stalin's wartime speeches from July 1941 to September 1945, *On the Great Patriotic War of the Soviet Union*, constitutes a slim volume (as Robert Service has pointed out, Stalin made only nine substantial wartime speeches, compared to Roosevelt's and Churchill's frequent interventions).[32] The book's bibliography, organized so that Stalin comes first, with other authors then listed alphabetically, stresses the importance of his various speeches and proclamations. Stalin's 6 November 1944 speech, in which he called for the Victory Banner to be raised over Berlin, is recycled repeatedly in this book, sometimes as "over the Reichstag": it appears in the foreword, and then again in the section on the battle for Berlin, where it is quoted verbatim.[33]

These wartime speeches were also reprinted in Stalin's *Short Biography*, which refers to the Victory Banner three times: in the original 6 November 1944 speech, in a comment on the inspirational effect it had on the soldiers storming Berlin, and in the fact that the Victory Banner was raised, on 2 May, the text says, the date of Berlin's surrender: "The Red Army had obeyed Stalin's call: the flag of victory had been hoisted over Berlin."[34] Both books were reissued in enormous print runs. The scarcity of other sources about the war meant that, by virtue of the books' ubiquity alone, Stalin's role in the war was made prominent, underlining a sense of his key role in the conduct of the war and the achievement of victory. This was the only available interpretation of the war.[35] This account was corroborated and amplified in publications authored by members of Stalin's inner circle. These works competed in their sycophantic claims as to his contribution to victory and were presented to Stalin on the occasion of his seventieth birthday. Viacheslav Molotov wrote, "Everyone knows what an inestimable role was played by Stalin in organizing the great victory."[36] As Kliment Voroshilov put it, "the name of Stalin in the minds of Soviet people has always been associated with the notion of victory."[37]

Kulish also draws attention to an anonymous 1948 brochure, *The Falsifiers of History (A Historical Inquiry)* (*Fal′sifikatory istorii* [*Istoricheskaia spravka*]), of which the Soviet Information Bureau printed 5 million copies. This work laid equal blame for the war on Germany, Japan, and Italy, as well as Great Britain, France, and the United States. It also explains the Nazi-Soviet pact as a response to actions of the British and French.[38] This brochure was in turn a response to a US State Department publication on German-Soviet relations from 1939 to 1941, which included German foreign ministry documents and information

2.1. Front cover of *The Berlin Operation of 1945*, published in 1950 by the Soviet military science directorate.

the British and French foreign ministries contributed.[39] This 1948 Soviet response to a foreign government's publication is important context for Soviet depictions of the war. A particularly relevant polemical target of *The Fall of Berlin*, however, is the publication in the same year of the first volume of Winston Churchill's *History of the Second World War.*

A further important dimension of the limited Soviet historiography of the war in this period relates to the military. In the immediate postwar period, much study of the war remained at the level of the military, and the emphasis was on drawing strategic lessons rather than engaging the wider public and considering political and social dimensions of the conflict. This logic is evident from Stalin's proclamation (*prikaz*) on Red Army Day 1946: "The Great Patriotic war introduced a lot that was new into military matters. Combat experience, gained on the field of battle, presents a rich treasure trove for the instruction and training of troops. That is why the army's entire training should be conducted on the basis of effective assimilation of the experience of the recent war. It is also essential to make wide use of this experience for the theoretical education of officer cadres and for the further growth of Soviet military understanding."[40]

Possibly linked to an increasing emphasis on the military as the Cold War intensified, this tendency became more pronounced toward the end of the 1940s, as the 1950 release of *The Berlin Operation of 1945* (*Berlinskaia operatsiia 1945 goda*), by Moscow's military publishing house, suggests. This lavish edition, with a bookmark that resembles a black-and-orange-striped St. George's ribbon (or Order of Glory), states that it is intended for "generals and higher officers of the Soviet army."[41] Indeed, it was not accessible to anyone outside the military, and the rationale for writing it is clearly for military study rather than historical inquiry. Even so, it is still heavily redacted. Thus, while it names lower ranks, such as the participants in the storming of the Reichstag, no one above the rank of captain is mentioned, other than Stalin himself, whose role in the overall victory is said to be central. Marshal Zhukov is absent, with the text referring instead to "the Commander of the 1st Belorussian front," who is not named.[42]

Western publications as well had a focus on military lessons from the war. The US Army drew on the experience of Wehrmacht officers as it prepared internal publications on both the tactics and strategy of the German-Soviet war.[43] These publications were followed by German military memoirs in the 1950s, such as Heinz Guderian's in 1950 and Erich von Manstein's in 1958.[44]

This military rationale in the writing and wider representations of history is one that can be traced throughout most of the Soviet period and arguably right through to present-day Russian society. In the immediate postwar period, however, this was even more pronounced, since the Soviet Union was a highly militarized society in this period in particular.[45]

Nevertheless, while there were memoirs, pamphlets, collections of speeches, hagiographical biographies of Stalin, and some limited attempts at historical interpretation for military ends, none of this really amounted to a serious historical appraisal of the war and its impact, and what was printed lacked a critical or analytical dimension. This gap made the literary and filmic accounts all the more significant. As Kulish puts it, the lack of serious research meant that the fictionalized accounts gained a foothold in this late Stalin period: "Thus, in the first post-war decade Soviet historical scholarship was not enriched by serious research about the events of the Great Patriotic war. But that which was done was enough to establish a conception of the history of the Great Patriotic war in which historical reality and myths, fictions and elementary bragging that had arisen during the war formed into an orderly system."[46]

While describing this pattern as a *system* at this point is premature, it is possible to see the emergence of what might be called "authoritarian repetition": the way in which the memory of the war in this period set a pattern of repetition serving to discipline and silence memory. The seemingly endless repetition of verbal formulas in the Stalin era was intended to dull the memories of participants.[47] Doing so conveyed to veterans that they needed to follow these patterns rather than indulge their own memories, which, if not corresponding with the official formulas, needed to be silenced. The ritualistic, repetitious tendencies identified by Yurchak in the post-Stalin period are already taking shape with the Victory Banner symbol.[48]

In this sense, as we shall see, *The Fall of Berlin* very much reflected the state of Soviet historians' thinking and writing about the war—everything was seen through the prism of Stalin's works and subsumed under the cult of Stalin, with symbols such as that of the Victory Banner serving to hammer home the mythologized account of the war.

WARTIME AND POSTWAR ART

The drift away from historical documents toward loyalty to myth is evident in the evolution of depictions of the war in art both during the war and in its immediate aftermath. While there had been a shift in the tone of depictions of the war in its final year, as the need to depict ongoing, unpredictable events at the front disappeared after victory, the tendency to elevate and memorialize became more marked. The wartime aesthetic, which tended toward the documentary across cinema, graphic arts, and literature, began to contrast with the more monumental forms of postwar film and art more generally. This was especially true of representations of the war. However, the process of transforming the fragmentary, contradictory nature of experience into a coherent, overarching, and uplifting narrative was by no means easy, as an anonymous reviewer of the 1946 All-Union Art Exhibition put it: "If in the prior exhibitions of the war years artistic-documentary material—sketches, life drawing, studies for panels—took up a large amount of space, then at the All-Union Art Exhibition of 1946, the main space belongs to the painting, even if, it is true, one cannot always find in these paintings complete conceptual harmony or its expression. Nowadays simple illustration, description is no longer satisfying: at this exhibition, the main space belongs not to artistic reportage, not to informational representation, but to works in which generalizing images are presented."[49]

In essence, works of art relating to the war now had to depict it as monumental, epochal, uplifting:

> In the exhibition, there are no vivid battle canvases that reveal those grandiose battles, unprecedented in human history, that the Red Army waged with the enemy, that show the nature of contemporary combat, saturated with powerful military machines, the image of the Soviet warrior on the battlefield, at the moment of the greatest test of all his mental and physical strength. We see here only, as it were, isolated fragments, isolated shots, random episodes from the life of the front, that do not raise themselves to the generalizing, grandiose paintings that alone are capable of truthfully recording the events of the Great Patriotic war.[50]

Instead of fragmentary experience, artists needed to mobilize the power of art to synthesize a number of actual historical events into a kind of montage that enables the message to emerge more strongly: "However, our artists, in particular historical painters and specialists in battle scenes, face ever harder tasks: the dynamics of mass scenes, compositions with many figures, clashes of opposing forces, and events that break up into separate episodes. Monumentalists must create synthetic images, generalize a chain of historical phenomena into a single painting or a whole cycle."[51]

This tendency is the very opposite of the tendency toward the factual, the documentary; the reviewer sees these two tendencies—the factual, archival, and the grand narrative sweep—as being in tension. In the postwar Stalin period the factual and documentary tended to be squeezed out by the monumental.

The Victory Banner theme was one way in which the documentary and monumental tension might be resolved and reconciled: the banner had associations with the monumental, with Stalin and the state, but was concrete and palpable, the subject of personal reminiscence. Petr Krivonogov's enormous Stalin Prize–winning painting, *Victory* (*Pobeda*, 1948), which is displayed at the Central Museum of the Armed Forces, was a successful use of this motif and is original in a way that renders the monumental palpable and concrete.

2.2. Petr A. Krivonogov, *Victory*, 1948. This painting was awarded the Stalin Prize.

Nina Tumarkin describes *Victory* as depicting "a vast panorama of the entrance to the Reichstag building at the moment of victory," and she criticizes it for "prettifying" the war.[52] It is of course true that the painting does not depict a harrowing scene of pain or loss, and the defeated Nazis lying dead on the steps of the Reichstag are merely crumpled uniforms without human flesh or substance; their suffering is as irrelevant as it is insubstantial. But what Tumarkin does not say is that the painting portrays the ecstatic experience of the moment of victory rather powerfully and in a rather clever way. The Red Army men are all shown celebrating, waving their arms and guns in the air in a shared moment of joy. They are also looking up, beyond the frame of the painting to the roof of the Reichstag. Presumably they are looking at the raising of the Victory Banner on the Reichstag's cupola (or the equestrian statue of Germania). But we are not shown this, even if three of the soldiers themselves are carrying small red banners or pennants attached to their guns. The fact that we do not see the Victory Banner is intriguing, since we are forced to imagine or picture what they see. This is where another potential association comes into play: in following the soldiers' upward gaze, we may begin to think of Stalin. As Jan Plamper has argued, "looking at Stalin . . . required a celestial, upward gaze."[53] But neither banner nor the great *vozhd′* are actually represented. One implication is that these are unrepresentable, holy sights that cannot be shown. While imparting this sacred aura of the unrepresentable, Krivonogov has also rather neatly resolved dilemmas as to how to represent

2.3. Petr A. Krivonogov, *Capitulation of the Fascist Armies in Berlin 2 May*, 1946.

two difficult subjects: how to represent Stalin, a very difficult but highly important subject for art of that period, and how to represent the Victory Banner, which had not really been a theme in art up to this point but that posed its own problems as to where it was to be shown (over the equestrian statue or the cupola) and whose hands were hoisting it. By leaving all of this to the viewer's imagination, Krivonogov also succeeds in associating the two themes of Stalin and the Victory Banner in a way that Mikheil Chiaureli, an enthusiastic artist and appreciator of art, was to build on as he dared to confront these dilemmas directly. After a protracted three-year scripting process, he was able to overcome these challenges to the satisfaction of all who mattered as he brought *The Fall of Berlin* to fruition.

Krivonogov's painting is without question his greatest achievement, and its receipt of the Stalin Prize evidently is indicative of the importance of the theme for postwar memory. It was preceded by a related painting entitled *The Capitulation of the Fascist Armies in Berlin* (*Kapituliatsiia fashistskikh voisk v Berline*, 1946). Also held by the Central Museum of the Armed Forces, this canvas shows the dispirited Nazi troops filing past the victorious Red Army, gathered in the center of Berlin. In the background we can see the Reichstag, with smoke still rising from it and a red flag flying from its cupola to the left, and to the right the Brandenburg Gate, also sporting a red banner. In the foreground we see Nazi weapons and banners cast to the ground. A study of the artist's work suggests that the composition is too cluttered and that the Nazis are still portrayed with the element of caricature typical of the war years.[54]

The same topic and moment were reworked in *Victory*, over which Krivonogov worked for the next two years. The basis for the painting was a sketch that the artist had made in Berlin in early May 1945. Krivonogov later described the scene he saw:

> The Reichstag was still burning. On it were visible the traces of our troops' protracted battles. The columns were pitted by shrapnel and bullets. The wide steps were strewn with the bodies of the dead, stone panels that had been torn off, lumps of plaster. Everywhere—on the steps, at the bases of columns, on high stone parapets were our soldiers, covered with dust, with the gun smoke of long battles. The soldiers threw their hands into the air, with rifles and submachine guns, steel helmets and forage caps. Here and there you could see little red flags. All heads were raised, all eyes fixed upon one spot, above, over there, where above the cupola, the Red Banner of Victory fluttered in the spring breeze. Beneath the ceiling of the building a mighty Russian "Hurrah!" rang out.[55]

In addition to not showing the object of the soldiers' gaze, a further trick of the composition is that it avoids showing the men as being overshadowed and dwarfed by the scale of the Reichstag building. Instead, they are in the middle and foreground of the composition. Presenting the individual soldiers in this way enabled a presentation of unalloyed joy experienced at the moment of victory. Krivonogov himself elaborated: "In our victorious soldiers, I wanted to convey the joy at the end of the war experienced by those humble foot soldiers of the war who had traveled the hard road from the Volga to Berlin."[56]

The Victory Banner is here once again used to create an emotional image of the meaning of victory. At the same time, it completes a narrative. One critic spells out the symbolism of concentrating on the moment of victory: "Even in the tough times of the battle for Moscow, Krivonogov, as a genuine patriot, started thinking about a painting on this theme. In the days of the hardest trials he believed in victory."[57]

Whether this is true or not, and I find it hard to believe, the claim is nevertheless an interesting one, in that the Victory Banner is the scene of Victory, the image supposedly envisioned at the nadir of the Soviet Union's fortunes. Moreover, the Victory Banner is pictured as completing the narrative of the war. It corroborates the sense that victory was never in doubt, a narrative that Stalin imposed immediately after the war to boost his own prestige. It serves to confer narrative shape and meaning on the chaos of disparate memories and experiences.

THE FALL OF BERLIN AS "FICTIONAL DOCUMENTARY" AND EPIC

Stalin's seventieth birthday, in 1949, has been described as the apogee of the Stalin cult: his portrait was projected onto the night sky above Moscow, suspended from a balloon and lit by searchlights.[58] Mikheil Chiaureli's *The Fall of Berlin* was presented to him on that occasion, though it was not officially released until January 1950.[59] It is tempting to think that this presentation had long been planned, but when we consider that *The Fall of Berlin* was initially conceived in 1946, then evidently there was no original plan to present it to Stalin on his birthday three and a half years later.

This film tells the story of a prize-winning steelworker who falls in love, who meets Stalin, and then faces separation from his lover because of the war. They are reunited when Berlin has been conquered, as Stalin flies in to preside over the jubilant moment of victory. The film underwent a protracted process of script revisions, with nine versions over the course of three years, with the final version of the script accepted in May 1948. This delay was unusually long even for this period, when many officials could have a say in an important production.[60] It is possible to see these changes in the context of censorship—the hand of Stalin. Certainly many of the jettisoned episodes touch upon the film's depiction of Stalin, such as an extended reference to the agronomist Lysenko, as Stalin makes climatically unsuitable plants thrive in his Moscow garden, and an exploration of the fate of his son, Iakov Dzhugashvili, a prisoner of war; the deleted material included a scene in the concentration camp—an uprising intended to save his life.[61] However, while judging the delays to have been a consequence of high-level censorship would be mandated by the "totalitarian" school's view on the Stalin period, which sees Stalin's agency everywhere, it is also possible to see the many revisions as indicative of the difficulty of creating a coherent narrative of the war that is at the same time convincing to those who remember it: one that reaches an account acceptable to a society that remembers these recent events while at the same time assimilating the documentary and historical material into the narrative of the Stalin cult. Critics of the time referred to this task by the misleading and confusing term "artistic documentary" (*khudozhestvenno-dokumental′noe kino*), which might also be translated as "fictional documentary," as I shall be doing here. Certainly, accounts by the production team present the difficulties in terms of the overabundance of material, as a result of the extensive research process, and the difficulty of fitting everything relevant into the final film.[62] The Victory Banner imagery provides an illuminating example of this late Stalinist disciplining of war memory, of the tension between the documentary record, and the epic, monumental myth that Soviet filmmakers were attempting to graft onto it.

Richard Taylor contrasts reviews of the film in the Soviet and other sectors of an as yet undivided Berlin. Whereas the pro-Soviet *Neues Deutschland* stresses that the film is a "fictional documentary," evidently translating the original Russian term, the West Berlin publication *Der Tagesspiel*, by contrast, ridicules the film's claims to documentary status, noting, "What we are being shown here are not documentary photographs, not original pictures. They are posed photographs, grandiose color scenes admittedly, but no more than that."[63] While it is of course true that the film uses no still photojournalism and little newsreel footage, which is itself often "posed," the claims to being a "fictional documentary" are worth considering at a little greater length.

While the term had been used previously in Soviet criticism to refer to significant, "artistic" examples of documentary cinema, such as the work of Vertov or Shub, in the postwar period it began to be used to designate something quite different.[64] The first film to be described as belonging to this supposedly new genre was Chiaureli's previous directorial credit, the 1946 film *The Vow*.[65] Although Soviet criticism did little to elaborate on this category's implicit claim, it is productive to reflect upon it. The Russian term "artistic" is often used to mean fictional, as with *khudozhestvennaia literatura* or *khudozhestvennyi fil′m*, which are how films and literature with fictional plots are designated. There are clearly fictional dimensions to films such as *The Vow* or *The Fall of Berlin*, in that they have fictional characters at their center, but these characters experience historical events alongside historical figures. In this they resemble the tradition of the historical novel, a genre widely practiced in Russia, with notable examples being Lev Tolstoi's *War and Peace* (*Voina i mir*) or Mikhail Sholokhov's *The Quiet Don* (*Tikhii Don*). The historical novel, however, treats events at some chronological distance, such as the period of the previous generation, as with Tolstoi, or ten years earlier, as with Sholokhov. What is documentary about the "fictional documentary" then is the focus on the present or very recent events, which would more commonly be the domain of documentary. Indeed, Denise Youngblood says that the examples of the genre might be termed, in contemporary parlance, "docu-drama."[66]

One way this worked was to take actual speeches, or words close to them, and transfer them to another setting. Chiaureli explains that he came to do this in *The Vow* by taking a speech Stalin gave at the Second Congress of Soviets, held at the Bolshoi Theater on 26 January 1924, and having him make it on Red Square to the whole Soviet people gathered for Lenin's funeral in the same period, in order to strike the correct "epic" and emotive tone.[67]

Thus, rather than simply adhering to historical fact, according to Chiaureli, it was the epic tone of the narrative, mandated by the subject matter of Stalin and the Soviet people, that dictated that he restage historical scenes in accordance with their underlying political meaning, showing their importance and the emotional effect they had on the Soviet public. In other words, a speech given by Stalin can be restaged wherever it may seem appropriate in terms of its content and effect on spectators. This articulation of the basic principle of the "fictional documentary" genre likewise informs *The Fall of Berlin*, especially the scene of Stalin flying to Berlin shortly after the raising of the Victory Banner.

In a 1950 study of the film, Shcherbina stresses that the film organically blends "historical truth" with "broad fictional generalizations": "The unfolding of rich content in this film is achieved with clear and expressive artistic [*khudozhestvennyi*] means."[68] This approach to historical or documentary material is thus also intended to be more accessible, to ensure that spectators are left in no doubt as to the significance of what they are seeing. Implicitly, this was not always the case when a documentary film depicted the war, as, for example, when momentous events end up being represented through underwhelming footage.

Nevertheless, the documentary record had, in a number of places, already created recognizable images—we might even say "iconic images"—depicting the historic events. If they were to be restaged, this had to be done in such a way as to quote and build on the photographic and filmic record, to produce an even more convincing likeness of it.

This can be seen by looking at *The Vow*. In its treatment of scenes from Lenin's sanatorium in Gorki, of the enormous crowds at his funeral on Red Square, or of the battle in Stalingrad, all of which were familiar from newsreels or documentaries, it produces images very close to the photographic documents of nonfiction but introduces fictional characters and episodes on this background that bear a residual trace of documentary authenticity.

The seriousness with which the filmmakers approached their work on the documentary look of *The Fall of Berlin* is evident from correspondence between Antonov, the director of Mosfil′m, and Bol′shakov, the minister of cinematography, in which the former requests that Chiaureli's production team be permitted to watch a whole series of documentary materials. Raizman's *Berlin* film and other documentary footage of the storming of Berlin feature prominently, permitting us to see what footage served as a model for their film:

1. German films and newsreels showing the working activities and private life of Hitler and his entourage
2. German newsreels about the German general staff
3. German films and newsreels with combat footage from 1941 to 1945
4. The film *Berlin*, directed by Raizman
5. Soviet documentary films and newsreel with combat footage from the period of the Great Patriotic War (mostly the Vistula offensive, the route through Oder-Berlin-Seelow Heights, storming of Berlin)
6. Newsreels about the Yalta conference[69]

The request was accepted, with the exception of some of the German materials.[70] Antonov's staff also supplement these requests by one for photographs of the Yalta conference and for documentary footage of the November 1941 Red Square parade, including images of Spasskaia Tower and the viewing stands, as well as long shots of troops, tanks, and artillery parading on Red Square.[71]

The production team then have to cast more than one hundred actors who resemble their actual historical counterparts to some degree and film battle scenes, parades, and so forth, all familiar from newsreel afresh but so as to echo the earlier films, though in color.[72] The intention was "to film so that the spectator would forget that it was a fictional [*khudozhestvennyi*] film and would believe in the reality of the event."[73]

The effect is highly successful, and many of the scenes do indeed resemble enhanced, color versions of the newsreels. This is especially true of the scene of the assault on the Reichstag with the Victory Banner. Richard Taylor sees this scene as Chiaureli's "reversal" of the Odessa Steps sequence in *Battleship Potemkin*: "Whereas in *Potemkin* the victorious Cossacks, representing oppression, descend on the masses from above, in *The Fall of Berlin* the victorious Red Army, representing liberation, ascends against the forces of German reaction from below."[74]

Although Taylor refers to Chiaureli's hostility to Sergei Eisenstein, this should be nuanced by Chiaureli's published praise for *Battleship Potemkin* as conveying the "pathos of the revolution." He reacts to the

Odessa Steps sequence as follows: "those human faces who leave such an impression in the course of a few shots that they remain in your memory for life; you seem to hear the heart-rending scream of the woman with pince-nez glasses in your sleep."[75] A further point of comparison for the sequence is of course Sergei Eisenstein's *October*, as well as Mikhail Romm's *Lenin in October*, both of which stage the storming of the Winter Palace to represent the climactic moment of historical change. The more important point, though, is that Chiaureli is not creating ex nihilo but consciously echoing the already existing newsreel and documentary images created in 1945, which themselves quote the filmic stormings of the Winter Palace and other images of the revolution. *The Fall of Berlin* can be seen as restaging the prewar scenes of revolution but in a far more spectacular manner, in color, with more expressive camera angles and many setups. The Berlin footage likewise quotes the images of Nazi banners being cast to the ground from the 1945 *Victory Parade* film and even Krivonogov's less documentary painting, *Victory*, a resemblance commented upon in studio discussions about the film.[76]

Yet, while important, the look of documentary was not enough in and of itself. The script had to be based on sources, and the filmmakers faced the problem of the relative lack of historical writing or memoirs on the war when they began working on the film. Consequently, they talked to and made extensive use of interviews with veterans of the war more widely and the battle for Berlin in particular: "The authors of *The Fall of Berlin* were faced with a difficult and honored task. The facts of history were concluded, but history had not yet been written. Eyewitnesses and participants of momentous events had also to become its chroniclers. In their work, scientific analysis had to be combined with the artistic reflection of the world, historical research had to conclude with artistic generalization."[77]

Indeed, as Manevich points out, this was a fraught enterprise, given that the film recounted events the Soviet spectators had direct or at least indirect experience of themselves.[78] To assure greater authenticity, Chiaureli and his team flew to Berlin to see the setting for the film and were given a guided tour of the path taken by those assaulting the Reichstag prior to raising the Victory Banner:

> The authors had to work long and hard studying the necessary materials. In doing so it became clear that in order to create a proper and truthful work of art they would themselves have to go and see the fragments of the Fascist empire, walk down the roads of war, talk to the legendary heroes who took Berlin and raised the Victory Banner over the Reichstag. For this purpose,

> in June 1947 the authors of the scenario, the director, the designer, and the future producer of the film traveled to Germany.
>
> The trip lasted one month in all. But we made a detailed study of all the historical places of the momentous battles for Berlin, starting on the Oder, the Seelow Heights, and ending with the vaults of the Reichstag. We met with wonderful Soviet soldiers, with participants of the battle for Berlin. General Shatilov, Heroes of the Soviet Union Colonel Zinchenko and Major Samsonov, with a group of soldiers, led us step by step from the Moltke bridge to the cupola of the Reichstag, recounting to us movingly every detail of this historically unprecedented and never to be repeated battle.[79]

This account, in common with a number of others, insists in particular that the filmmakers consulted widely with veterans of the storming of the Reichstag on the facts of the raising of the Victory Banner. The veterans also talked to the actors, notably the actor playing the main part, Boris Andreev:

> "In this film," wrote Boris Fedorovich, "I was confronted by a very difficult and crucial task; I had to play the role of Aleksei Ivanov so that millions of Soviet people would recognize themselves in this simple man."
>
> In working on the role, Andreev, as always, began to study life. The workers of the Donbas taught him how to work at the furnace, shared their thoughts with him; the valiant warriors of the unit that took the Fascist Reichstag and raised the Victory Banner recounted to him stories about themselves and their comrades and recalled incidents from battle.
>
> When the combat scenes were being filmed in Germany, soldiers and officers from the Soviet occupational forces, who had taken part in the battle for Berlin, watched the footage they had filmed. They commented in detail on Andreev's acting and gave advice as to how to improve certain shortcomings in his performance. This significantly helped the actor in creating the correct image of Aleksei Ivanov.[80]

There is no reason to doubt this account of the extent of documentary research involved in the writing of the film, and its authenticity was apparently sufficient for Vsevolod Vishnevskii, who had reported on the storming of the Reichstag, to proclaim it accurate.[81] However, it is also worth remembering that these public statements by the likes of Andreev help corroborate a sense of the film as being based in fact. This was also one of the effects of the way the film was promoted at its launch, with instructions to cinema directors that they were to invite veterans of the battle for Berlin: "2. On the eve of the general release of the film on the screens of Moscow, to organize at the 'Artistic' [*Khudozhestvennyi*] cinema a screening of the film for activists from the Party, Komsomol,

Soviets, and Trade Unions with speeches by the director of the film, the leading actors and representatives of the Soviet Army—participants in the storming of Berlin."[82]

One veteran of the storming of the Reichstag in particular, Samsonov, was widely invited, in part because he was based in Moscow, unlike Egorov or Kantariia, for example (see chapter 3 for further discussions of his role). The film's release also coincided with the elections for the Supreme Soviet, and using the coincidence, political introductions to the screenings were organized, stressing their immense political importance.[83]

Those insisting upon the film's authenticity emphasize time and again the conversations with those who raised the Victory Banner. The Victory Banner and those who raised it serve as a symbolic guarantee of the truth and reliability of the war narrative.

However, the whole image of the Victory Banner in *The Fall of Berlin* typifies the approach to the factual in this period. Aleksei Ivanov is created as a typical character representative of the Soviet people, through his surname and his having been born on the day of the storming of the Winter Palace. He is exceptional, however, in that not everyone raised the Victory Banner, and he is shown as raising it alongside Egorov and Kantariia, both made Heroes of the Soviet Union for this feat. As one critic puts it, "in not pursuing the petty truth of facts, the authors laid bare the core features of the heroic character of contemporary Soviet man."[84] The factual research and air of documentary enable *The Fall of Berlin* to associate a paradoxically exemplary Soviet everyman with the emotive symbol of the Victory Banner.

Part of this contradiction lay in the pretensions of the film not only to documentary authenticity but also to epic grandeur: *The Fall of Berlin* was characterized on release as a form of "epic," even as a "monumental popular epic."[85] The sense of uplifting narrative closure, of overcoming the pain of loss through the narrative compensations afforded by the ending, and its emphasis upon victory are closely connected to its epic form.

Epic narratives are associated with the classical world, with narratives that stand out in their "range, scope and sheer size" and are produced by communities. They depict heroes that stand for their wider communities, suggesting a harmony between the individual and society. It is as much a function as a set of generic characteristics, and a grand narrative alone is sufficient, in the eyes of many, to qualify something as epic.[86]

However, in the Soviet context there were ideological implications in offering such a description. As we saw above, in discussions about postwar art in 1947, critics identified grandiose epic paintings as the only kind that could truly represent the war, rejecting more fragmentary, documentary sketches. As film director Mark Donskoi put it, "the collective . . . understood that you can forgive an average film about any old theme, but when it's about victory over German Fascism, victory in the Battle of Berlin, you cannot forgive an average film."[87] David Brandenburger argues that the immediate postwar period was defined by attempts to reconcile the war victory with the broader narrative of Russian history, and thus treatments of recent history take on an "epic" character.[88] This is evidently true of *The Fall of Berlin*. Similarly, Soviet analyses of *The Fall of Berlin* not only saw it as possessing an epic form but also saw that form as a reflection of the nature of Soviet society:

> The film *The Fall of Berlin* is a persuasive and highly talented demonstration of the fact that the authentic flourishing of major epic genres in art is possible only in a society that has created the conditions for the socialist solution to the problem of the person and society, the person and the people. Soviet society, driven by the pathos of a socialist reconfiguration of life, has long ago brought our art beyond the bounds of minor, "domestic" chamber themes. Soviet life itself has shown artists that the object of their work should become the movement of millions, the fate of the Motherland, the fate of the people.[89]

More than one critic argued that the film's epic form was proof of the greatness of victory and of the Soviet system and characteristic of Soviet art as a whole.[90]

The interaction between the striving for documentary authenticity and the broad epic sweep was especially clear in the film's treatment of the Victory Banner imagery.

THE FALL OF BERLIN'S USE OF THE VICTORY BANNER

The scene with the Victory Banner was part of the film from its initial conception. Immediately after finishing *The Vow*, Chiaureli supposedly turned to his collaborator on the script, Petr Pavlenko, and summarized his idea for a new film: "Two simple Soviet people love one another. Their happiness is violated by the treacherous Fascist attack. All that is most dear is desecrated—the motherland, his mother, his girl. The hero goes to seek revenge and, in raising the Victory Banner over Hitler's Reichstag, finds his personal happiness."[91]

It is noteworthy that this idea belongs to 1946, when the cult of the Victory Banner was given impetus through the awarding of medals to those who had raised it, and its symbolism was evoked in a number of Stalin's speeches. The depiction of the raising of the Victory Banner in the film stresses that the order to raise it comes directly from Stalin, and it uses the formula from the 1944 speech: "over Berlin" rather than "over the Reichstag." The film thus stresses the symbolism of the Victory Banner as narrative completion, since the raising of the banner fulfilled Stalin's order. This formula helps to create a wider and vaguer sense of Stalin's preordination of the war's conduct and victorious outcome. This is a key element of the postwar Stalinist narrative about the war, summarized by Jeffrey Brooks as follows: "Stalin had foreseen the war, created the economy necessary to defeat Germany, and saved the Soviet Union and the world from tyranny."[92]

Most previous articulations of the war narrative had been in black and white, with few exceptions, such as the film of the 1945 Victory Parade. There was a widely held opinion that the theme of the war did not lend itself to color, because of the dull tones of the grim and monotonous uniforms and weapons.[93] What is more, black-and-white imagery was widely held to be more appropriate for the realist style appropriate in representing the war.

One of Chiaureli's achievements in *The Fall of Berlin* was successfully reimagining the symbol of the Victory Banner, creating its first iteration in color, and integrating it into the aesthetic and narrative system of a color film. In doing so, he develops the symbol of the Victory Banner, harnessing, enhancing, and demonstrating its sacred power, or aura. The importance of using color in such a way as to underscore the narrative was put to Chiaureli when he showed the script to his colleagues at the Mosfil′m studio. One of the points that a number of set designers make to him is that they need to make the storming of the Reichstag and raising of the Victory Banner a dramatic climax that exploits its color: "The break with dramatic cinema is not an achievement. It seems to me that, in order to stop it from being too saccharine, the final film needs to find some striking moments, where you can show that red color (the red banner, for example)."[94]

Vera Stroeva, the well-known director, stressed the link between the red glow of the steel furnace in the first part of the film and that of the Victory Banner:

> I consider that our cinema in the person of Chiaureli in this case is rightly moving into the foreground and raising the theme of the contemporary. . . . The red lines of incandescent bronze will somehow echo between the first part, and the last, with the red banner on the Reichstag building. This color should be laid down as a foundation in the everyday life of the factory. The line of incandescent metal should be approached in such a way that it becomes clear at the end—that it is the beginning of that red flag on the Reichstag. For this reason, the complex of the factory and the complex of the

2.4. Still image of the Victory Banner's first appearance in Chiaureli's *The Fall of Berlin*.

Red Army should be thought through and resolved as the confrontation of two worlds.[95]

The final Victory Banner scene is striking in its use of color, illustrating Chiaureli's use of color in film as a distinct compositional element in its own right, serving the filmmaker's overall vision: "[Color] does not decorate representation, does not color it with a beautiful outfit, but serves as a fundamental element of emotional influence upon the spectator; it has become one of the means aiding the deeper revelation of the authors' conceptual and artistic conceit."[96]

Chiaureli wanted color to reflect content, an approach that belongs to a certain Russian expressionist current in the use of color championed by Eisenstein, for example. By the time the final film was finished, the raising of the Victory Banner had become a key dimension in the film, not just for its above-mentioned associations with authenticity, its place in the narrative of the war as such, but also due to its colorful visuals and emotive dramatic effect, used to convey the broader ideological truth of what Soviet critics called the "generalization": "In the episode of the raising of the Red Banner of Victory on the Reichstag the purpose of the color task consisted in, while retaining all of the concrete nature of the combat sequence, conferring upon it a generalizing, symbolic meaning. The vivid symphony of colors in the representation of rejoicing people on the streets and squares of defeated Berlin was made to underline the totality and joy of victory."[97]

The key thing here is the ecstasy of the moment of victory, and the use of the color red enhances that sense of brightness and rejoicing, while also combining the concrete episode from the battle with deeper and wider symbolism. In the sequences preceding these scenes, the Victory Banner is the only bright spot among the predominantly dark and dismal tones.

In addition to expressing joy, the Victory Banner's red hue is used to express the more somber themes of sacrifice, one of its most common associations throughout the history of the socialist movement more widely and Soviet cinema in particular, dating back, for example, to the earliest Soviet color feature film, *The Nightingale* (*Solovei-solovushka*, dir. Nikolai Ekk, 1936).[98] In *The Fall of Berlin*, Egorov, Kantariia, and the fictional Ivanov are shown kneeling before the Victory Banner, bowing their heads, and kissing it. The officer, identified in the script as the historical figure Colonel Zinchenko, kisses them before the battle. Here the holy aura is brought out. None of the critics of the time commented upon this, but they do discuss the banner's relation to the symbolism of sacrifice. Camera operator Kosmatov emphasizes this use of the color red in the raising the Victory Banner sequence:

> It seems to me that color in the film should be examined in the way it is treated in the course of the whole film.
>
> . . . And here's the episode I want to talk about. A soldier who has come from Stalingrad to Berlin itself falls, cut down by a Fascist bullet on the steps of the Reichstag. With his hand rapidly going cold he pulls from his tunic a handkerchief, which is drenched with blood, and this handkerchief turns into a scarlet flag. We have never seen such an image before in art. With this flag a second soldier, Iusup, ascends toward the Reichstag, but he too falls, cut down. In his already stiffened hand the flag still continues to live. Ivanov says goodbye to him. And it is as if at this moment the scarlet flag appears on Ivanov himself, because at that moment Ivanov is wounded. But, wounded, bloody, he turns his ecstatic gaze to the Reichstag on which the scarlet Soviet flag is actually being raised.[99]

While we might reasonably object that this association of blood sacrifice and the red flag is not without precedent, Kosmatov's point still stands: the red Victory Banner now serves to echo the images of blood spilled in the battle that precedes its raising, articulating the narrative of sacrifice but also echoing earlier, more varied, happier uses of the color red in the narrative. A number of critics draw attention to the scene, commenting on this imagery:

2.5. Still image from Chiaureli's *The Fall of Berlin* showing the Victory Banner on the Reichstag cupola.

2.6. Still image of the unfurled Victory Banner, from Chiaureli's *The Fall of Berlin*.

> The episode of the capture of the Reichstag leaves an enormous impression on you. The brutalized, hardened enemy defenders are fighting the attack off. But the Soviet soldiers climb higher and higher toward the cupola of the building. The scarlet banner of Victory moving from the hands of the wounded to the hands of other soldiers moves ever forward. Cheery Kostia Zaichenko is killed. Ivanov tenderly carries the mortally wounded Iusup. "Look, look where we are, Berlin is ours, Iusup." But Iusup can no longer respond . . . tenderly and grief-struck, Ivanov kisses his dead friend, and along with the other soldiers strives forward. Like the hero of a folk epic [*bylinnyi bogatyr'*] he defeats the enemies. His comrades Kantariia and Egorov clamber up with the banner. Blood flows across Ivanov's face, but he smiles joyfully: the scarlet banner of Victory flies above Berlin. . . . This is a symbol of victory of the great Soviet Union, a symbol of Ivanov's victory, a symbol of the glory of the great Stalin.[100]

This review ends symbolically on the word *Stalin*, stressing the Victory Banner as a symbol of Stalin. The following analysis does the same:

> The scene of the raising of the banner of Victory over the Reichstag is permeated with an elevated beauty. This scene is the apotheosis of Soviet soldiers' glory. Among those storming the Reichstag are the familiar figures of Ivanov, Kantariia, Iusupov, and Egorov. No one can stop them. From the hands of fallen heroes, the banner of Victory is picked up by others, and it ineluctably rises higher and higher, until its radiant light shines above defeated Berlin.
>
> We see the Victory Banner, proudly flying above the Reichstag as a symbol of the triumph of our socialist country, its wonderful people, as a symbol of the greatness of Stalin.[101]

Evidently in this film famous for its panegyric to Stalin, the Victory Banner is very much a part of the promotion of the cult, of associating victory with Stalin and reassuring the Soviet public that the victory had been planned since the very beginning of the war. To get to this point required the participants' memories of the events to be vetted, censored, and systematized.

THE PROCESS OF DISCIPLINING MEMORY IN *THE FALL OF BERLIN*

The Fall of Berlin's Victory Banner sequence had to streamline and systematize the various conflicting memories of those who had raised it, making those memories into a coherent and visually arresting narrative while also attempting to retain a vestige of documentary authenticity. Of course, when viewing the final film, one can see fairly obvious inaccuracies, such as the fact that Stalin did not fly to Berlin at all, let alone within minutes of the moment of victory. Moreover, after the raising of the Victory Banner, fighting went on in Berlin and in the Reichstag for nearly two days, and it was another week before Germany finally surrendered. The broader depiction of the battle, as Taylor points out, omits Zhukov from the final Berlin scenes, even if he appears earlier in the battle, miscalculating and having to be rescued by Stalin.[102]

In examining the many script variants, particularly with a view to seeing how they approach the question of the Victory Banner, we can trace a process of mythologization of the banner, the endowing of it with aura. In the scene where Egorov, Kantariia, and Ivanov receive the banner from Colonel Zinchenko, an early version of the script referred to this as "the red banner." The phrase was then crossed out and replaced with "Victory Banner."[103]

The script variants also bear witness to a process of revision in which the depiction is streamlined and certain themes are tried out before being jettisoned. One version introduces the historical figures of Captain Stepan Neustroev, commander of the battalion that stormed the Reichstag, and Il′ia S′ianov, commander of the company that raised the flag, but they neither appear nor are they named in the final film. Other refinements concern the number of banners: the initial variants of the script followed the historical record by showing many banners being put up on various parts of the Reichstag. One version had Egorov and Kantariia initially tying their banner to a balustrade by the entrance to the building.[104] They then see that there are already a number of such red flags, and it is unclear that theirs is the most prominent, as well as the first:

> Egorov and Kantariia ran outside, to the main steps of the Reichstag, to look at what was happening with their banner. Near to it someone else's was flying. And what's more, from every crack in a wall and column, hundreds of tiny red flags were sticking out. They had suddenly appeared on the gray walls of the Reichstag almost as if they had flowered before our eyes. One bright spark, standing on Egorov's ladder, was already writing with chalk on a column:
>
> "We spat upon Hitler, and then some."
>
> Another was writing with his bayonet:
>
> "For Kiev" . . .
>
> A third was scratching with a stone:
>
> "Left Baku, arrived in Berlin. If I have to, I'll go farther. Arshak Mnatsak′iants."
>
> Thousands of bits of graffiti already covered the stone and walls.
>
> "The Banner should be on top," said Kantariia. "Otherwise you can't see that we were the first."

"That's right," said Egorov.

They ran into the building with the banner.[105]

This is then reworked in a further variant so as to show Egorov and Kantariia putting their banner up on the cupola of the Reichstag. A soldier approaches Egorov and Kantariia, saying,

> "You've put it up wrong," he said, pointing to the banner. "It doesn't look right from below. . . . It's as if the horse is holding it." And he made to take and reposition the banner.
>
> But here Kantariia blocked his way.
>
> "Eh, my friend . . . Don't try and trick us. We put it up, we'll move it."
>
> "I have been sent by the commander," the soldier tried to explain.
>
> "You move your own banner, don't touch ours," Kantariia said severely, and looked around for a place to reposition the banner.
>
> On the crest of the cupola they affixed the banner with its sheath and carefully climbed down.
>
> "Now there can be no competition," said Kantariia.
>
> "Yes, you can't get it any higher," agreed Egorov.
>
> Beneath them lay the conquered city of Berlin.
>
> The red banners on the tall buildings, on the Brandenburg Gate, the Victory column, indicated that the beast's lair was in our side's hands. Egorov looked at his watch, a gift from Melenchuk.
>
> "A quarter past two. What does yours say?"
>
> "Exactly," responded Kantariia, getting out his watch, which was also a gift from Melenchuk.
>
> "Well done." Zinchenko embraced them, [saying,] "You have carried out Stalin's order and immortalized yourselves."[106]

In an earlier script variant, there was no meeting with Zinchenko after the raising of the banner and no reference to Stalin's order.[107] Those details were then inserted in this variant but did not appear in the final film. Evidently the script writers were also unsure about to what extent they needed to associate the Victory Banner verbally and explicitly with the Stalin cult. The final film does this visually, with Stalin's appearance in Berlin. It also does so through an earlier sequence, just before the beginning of the battle for Berlin, in which an unnamed officer gives his troops, including Ivanov, Egorov, and Kantariia, a morale-boosting speech: "Comrade Guardsmen of Stalingrad! The great hour has come, which we have been awaiting for so long, and with us the whole Soviet people have been waiting for it. We will be entering Berlin with the banner of Victory that we have brought from Stalingrad. The Motherland is with us! The spirit of the great Lenin is with us! And comrade Stalin is with us!"[108]

With him is a red flag, the banner he refers to. Evoking at this point the Victory Banner and linking it with Stalin and with Egorov and Kantariia, while not historically accurate, helps assure a sense of the raising of the Victory Banner as the completion of a narrative connected to Stalin.

The above excerpt is also interesting in that Kantariia's comic pugnaciousness and nonstandard Russian (*Shutki ne stroi*) pander to Russian perceptions of Georgians and thus emphasize Kantariia's Georgian ethnicity, while at the same time explaining the contradiction between the various images showing the banner on the equestrian statue and the cupola of the Reichstag.

Kantariia's Georgianness is further emphasized in an earlier script variant, when he uses the Georgian word *genatsvale* (translated as "dear fellow"):

> "Forward?" Egorov asked his comrade.
>
> "Certainly forward" replied the Georgian. "My dear fellow, we can't go back now."
>
> So they kept climbing up.[109]

To complete the picture of Kantariia as Georgian, he then becomes the center of attention in the scenes of jubilation as he performs the *lezginka*, a Georgian dance. The purpose here is to associate the banner with Stalin more clearly through Kantariia's somewhat hyperbolic Georgianness, which is, as mentioned above, probably why Kantariia was chosen as one of those to raise the official Victory Banner. The issue of the extent to which Georgian themes should be brought to the fore was one that Chiaureli grappled with in this film even more so than in his previous two films, *The Vow* and *The Great Glow* (*Velikoe zarevo*, 1938), both of which had been made at studios in Tbilisi. In those films, there are significant and prominent Georgian characters, including Stalin, performed by Georgian actor Mikheil Gelovani, who also plays Stalin in *The Fall of Berlin*. On this occasion, though, Chiaureli had been ordered to shift production of the film, initially entitled *The Great Victory*, from the Tbilisi studio to Moscow, as a telegram of April 1948 to the Ministry of Cinema put it, "on account of the complexity and Union-wide significance of the theme, and the need to hire only Russian actors."[110] As Chiaureli himself stated, "the opinion of the ruling bodies was that this kind of film had to be produced in Moscow, at Mosfil′m."[111] What made "this kind of film" different was perhaps its scale and prestige, and the move meant that in *The Fall of Berlin* the Georgian "color" is more diffuse. Further attempts to reference it come in an early script variant in which one child playing "Russian" war games says he wants to play the part of Bagration, the Georgian general of the Napoleonic era, and another child points out that he is not Russian but Georgian, saying that that is okay—an implicit nod in the direction of Stalin's ethnicity.[112] Moreover, in the garden scene where Aleksei meets Stalin, which is much longer, Stalin's successful adaptation, as someone from the south adapting to the north, is also referenced.[113] None of these elements from earlier scripts made it to the final film, in part because there is no need to emphasize Stalin's Georgian ethnicity more than Gelovani already does through his light accent. Furthermore, Stalin dominates the film to such an extent in any case that associating him with the Victory Banner, and with Victory, through Kantariia, is simply not necessary.

STALIN AND THE VICTORY BANNER IN *THE FALL OF BERLIN*

The association between victory, the Soviets' conquering of Berlin, and Stalin is underlined in the completed film when Stalin flies to Berlin, lands in its center, and is joined by crowds of soldiers who have just stormed the Reichstag, as well as people of all nationalities liberated by the Red Army. As discussed above, this is not historically accurate: Stalin at no point flew to Berlin, nor did he give the dramatized speech in so many words. However, if we recall Chiaureli's earlier programmatic statement with regard to his depiction of Stalin in *The Vow*, then we see that his approach to the "fictional documentary" meant that when the subject matter was Stalin and the Soviet people, then it required an epic tone. Thus, the restaging of historical scenes in this way ensured that the film conveyed the symbolic rather than the literal truth and struck a chord with the audience. The scene is a sort of idealized montage of propaganda motifs, and it makes sense if we cast our minds back to Raizman's documentary film depicting the battle for Berlin, in which filmmakers tried hard to find ways to associate victory with Stalin (see chapter 1). The Victory Banner was one way, because Stalin had called for, or "ordered," it to be put up over Berlin. Showing the sequence of its raising was thus accompanied by the voice-over stating that "Stalin's order has been fulfilled." The filmmakers also envisaged the banner being presented to Stalin, in the Kremlin, a plan never realized. The genre of "fictional documentary" presented no such barriers to filmmakers, and Stalin could be fully associated with victory in the most dramatic, visually compelling, and emotive terms possible. Moreover, Stalin landing in the center of Berlin and receiving idealized tributes from the crowd makes sense in symbolic terms: the center of Berlin echoes, in debased form, the center of the Soviet Union. Stalin is reviewing the Victory Parade in idealized form.

The sequence starts with Stalin arriving in Berlin by plane, a scene that, as Taylor has pointed out, resembles Riefenstahl's *Triumph of the Will*.[114] Just as the 1945 Victory Parade had borrowed and repurposed Nazi innovations in political pageantry through its use of banners, so Chiaureli was not above drawing on a Nazi source to articulate the leader cult. Stepping out of the plane, Stalin then addresses the adoring crowds—this has become a kind of spontaneous political meeting, or Red Square parade, and it all serves to underline the Stalin-victory connection. In a situation in which Stalin appeared in public rarely after the war—indeed, his keynote speeches were mostly left to Malenkov, Molotov, or Bulganin—this projected an image of an idealized parade that compensated for his scarce appearances in the flesh.[115] Indeed, this "monstrously tasteless" scene was inserted at Stalin's own request, according to Konstantin Simonov, with the scripts personally approved by Stalin and corrected for publication, with his signature as the final imprimatur.[116]

The scene is also organic to the film, however, as it makes parades a central feature of the plot and imagery. Hitler is obsessed by capturing Moscow before the October Revolution parade, so when Stalin defiantly speaks at the annual parade, this is a kind of symbolic victory. The Soviet POWs and *Ostarbeiter* (forced laborers drawn from the occupied lands of eastern Europe) are forced to walk past Hitler in the Reich Chancellery in honor of the expected victory, in a humiliating travesty of a parade. Then, when the Soviets are launching their final assault on Berlin, they attempt to capture the Reichstag by 1 May and hang a red flag on it as part of a symbolic appropriation of the German space for the Soviets, a domesticating of it according to the logic observed by Malte Rolf, who argues that the war was in part also "a war over symbolic places and times," including places, flags, and dates.[117]

The final scene also completes the elevation of Stalin to the status of sacred symbol and object of devotion, corroborating Boris Groys's insight that socialist realist art of this period shows "sacred history tak[ing] place among us."[118] Natasha's emotions in particular are used to show an intense, devotional attachment to Stalin: "Aleksei was two paces away from Natasha, but she at that moment was not thinking of him. All her thoughts were now connected to Stalin. To see him and hear him meant to feel her own victory, to become conscious of her own strength and experience a happiness that might only occur once in life."[119]

Natasha then kisses Stalin on the breast (it was on the forehead in one scenario), as one does when venerating icons.[120]

Whether or not Stalin actually demanded the inclusion of this final scene—and we should be cautious as to attempts to suggest that this was for personal or psychological reasons—he presumably did not make stipulations as to the exact form of his representation in the film. Chiaureli's approach to the narrative and ideological use of color was evident in the way in which the Victory Banner is portrayed, and he adopted a similar approach to the depiction of Stalin, consciously employing "all the riches of the color palette" to show him.[121]

Camera operator Kosmatov, who had experience with filming in color, explained how the banners and Stalin are associated with victory through color:

> This color should not be reproduced in an isolated manner, separated off into a single shot or sequence. For example, the use of color in the image of Stalin. This color needs to be examined throughout the whole film.
>
> At the start, comrade Stalin's bright suit, his bright portrait on a cherry background, during the breakfast, and so on. But then war arrives, and all the colors go out, light becomes diffuse and everything acquires a character of austere restraint. Then, gradually, with the coming of victory, the color red appears, flags and banners, on the backdrop of which the image of comrade Stalin is drawn at the end of the film.
>
> So, it seems to me that color in the film should be examined in its treatment through the whole film.[122]

Thus, if we examine the film as a whole, the use of color and the Victory Banner are closely connected with the cultic depiction of Stalin.

BALANCING VICTORY AND THE PRICE PAID IN *THE FALL OF BERLIN*

The Fall of Berlin's emphasis on the joyous, victorious end of the war serves to divert the emphasis of the narrative from the catastrophic reverses suffered by the Soviet Union at the war's start. In the completed version of the film, Alesha is wounded during the initial German advance in summer 1941 and falls into a coma from which he awakens after three months, just as the Germans approach Moscow in the fall. Early script variants, however, devote more space to the representation of the first months of the war, referred to initially by the word "catastrophe" and Alesha's experiences of the occupation: he is in the crowd to whom the Germans read their decree, and he, rather than Natasha, starts to lead the resistance against the Nazis.[123]

The scene in which Alesha returns to his home, now lying in ruins and, not finding his mother, sobs was one that particularly touched viewers: "Remember the scene when Aleksei returns to his ruined town and, on entering the threshold of his ruined home, and when not finding his mother, starts crying. Along with him many spectators also cried. It was done so powerfully, so humanly, so genuinely."[124]

Director Mark Donskoi also said that he cried when watching this scene. However, by the end of the film, these had turned into tears of joy for many, as the composer V. G. Fere described it: "When the film ended I saw many, and not only women, but men too, with tears in their eyes. But these were not the tears that we cried when we watched those hard-to-take films about the Great Patriotic War, these were not the tears of grief and pain for people who had undergone unspeakable suffering, these were the tears of joy for our country, for our victory, for our great human and humanitarian victory."[125]

In order to achieve this sense of the "human and humanitarian victory," the scriptwriters had to carefully moderate the degree to which the film portrayed Nazi atrocities, as well as the Soviets' response to them. In the scene where he sees his ruined home, Alesha tells a captured SS officer that he will inflict the same level of destruction on *his* home in Berlin. In earlier scripts the level of violent revenge promised is much more extreme, with mentions of destroying the German's family and offspring:

> "All I'll leave of Berlin will be dust. I'll destroy your family to the ninth generation, and when you return home, you will start crying, like I was just crying, and you'll cry, you swine, for twenty years in a row." Ivanov's voice was rising to a shout. "And then don't say that I am cruel, do you hear? I am kind, I wouldn't harm a soul. I didn't come to your home. But now I will destroy it, you understand? I will drown you in your own blood, and you, scum, be quiet, don't say a word. Move!"[126]

This rancor was toned down in the final film, as was the depiction of Nazi concentration camps, which had been much more prominent. Indeed, the production team, while preparing, had visited concentration camps in Germany.[127] The scene showing the liberation of a Nazi concentration camp includes an extended sequence depicting the fate of Iakov Dzhugashvili, Stalin's son. His brutal death, with his father's name on his lips, ignites the spark of a revolt in the camp, led by Natasha. It succeeds at the precise moment when the Red Army, with Alesha among their ranks, arrives to liberate the camp, crashing through the barbed wire. The description of the moment of liberation refers to all facets of the Nazi mass murder machine interrupted by the Red Army while in full flow: "They threw the murderers to the ground, opened the doors to isolation cells, pulled the condemned from nooses, threw open gas chambers, and carried the half dead out into the open air."[128]

In a further deleted episode, Heinrich Himmler, chief of the SS, is shown visiting the camp to refine its mass killing operation: "At the same time as looking at some stamps Himmler with almost the same degree of fascination discusses methods for the rapid extermination of people

2.7. Still image of the Victory Banner in the background as Natasha and Alesha are reunited in Chiaureli's film *The Fall of Berlin*.

with one of those present. Maybe there is even a model of a conveyer-belt of death in front of him, with ovens, a guillotine or hangman's scaffold. Himmler considers that they have too low a level of throughput. More, more . . . he demands. And at the same time, he takes great pleasure in examining some stamps through his magnifying glass."[129]

However, it should be noted that, in keeping with many Soviet sources, the concentration and extermination functions are not distinguished, and the *Ostarbeiter* are not distinguished from inmates of the camps, whereas in fact these were different states of suffering, distinguished by murder on the one hand and brutal slavery on the other. The implication is that Soviet people suffered particularly, and there is no mention or wider sense of the separate and particularly terrible fate of the Jews.

As with Alesha's earlier vow to avenge German destruction, there is also a toning down of vengeful curses made by Natasha's friend, a Ukrainian inmate called Oksana: "I curse you forever, land of hangmen! To the end of my life I will not forget and will tell my children to remember your evil and your crimes! . . . Curse you! I hope you never see happiness, that your wives never have children, that the mark of Cain brands you forever!"[130]

The sense in which the final, uplifting scenes of victory and celebration are tempered by loss and suffering is evident in one script variant in which Aleksei, while lying on a stretcher in front of the Reichstag, sees the jubilant dancing. Although he joins in the singing, he is sad: "Aleksei's eyes were filled with tears. He thought about Natasha, and the joy of the great victory was tinged with sadness. *She* is not here, and maybe will never be."[131]

However, Aleksei is finally reunited with Natasha, and the pain of loss is banished by the joy of victory. In this manner, toward the end of the war and following it, the Soviets worked to fix a stable narrative of the war for public consumption. However, memory of the war had to deal with the complex and contradictory nature of what actually happened, with people's memories. At the same time, it faced the difficulty of emplotting them in such a way as to create meaning and subordinate the memories to and associate them with Stalin, with the ultimate victory and a sense of epic grandeur.

This was a precarious process due to the difficulty of negotiating between individual memories and the need for a coherent collective narrative. This meant that the topic of the war had to be limited and controlled, and this itself sometimes meant silencing the theme more generally. In cinema in particular, it was difficult to make successful films that would create a template for others to follow, and it was impossible to follow an already existing template for representation of the war, since the war was unprecedented and constituted something of a break in the Soviet experience.

This is one reason why the Soviets ceased to make war films, apart from documentaries, for some years until Stalin's death. Moreover, there was a fatigue that set in with war films shortly after the release of *The Fall of Berlin*, which followed press calls for a greater focus on the present.[132] Indeed, the theme might have disappeared from Soviet screens earlier had it not been for the fact that there were many films on the subject of the war that had already been initiated even before its end, or immediately following it, and so for reasons of efficiency needed to be completed.[133]

Moreover, by 1950 the war was being overshadowed by the Cold War: any depictions of the wartime alliance had to show its insubstantial nature.[134] *The Fall of Berlin* had done this to a degree, projecting contemporary Cold War politics onto the war, including the implication that Turkey and Spain were German allies.[135] Another of its implications was that the British were supplying the Nazis with steel during the battle for Stalingrad, at precisely the moment when they were sending supplies to the Soviets through the Arctic convoys. However, Denise Youngblood and Tony Shaw argue that the film's contribution to the core themes of Soviet Cold War cinema is negligible. They do not see *The Fall of Berlin* as a Cold War film since it did not contribute to the central characteristics of Soviet Cold War propaganda more narrowly defined.[136]

2.8. The Victory Banner on display in the Central Museum of the Soviet Army, 1950s. From *Tsentral′nyi muzei sovetskoi armii: Kratkii putevoditel′* (Moscow: Voennoe izdatel′stvo Ministerstva Oborony Soiuza SSR, 1955).

The Great Patriotic War is said to serve the cult of Stalin in this period.[137] This is of course true, although it might be added that the war had to fit into the existing system of Soviet symbols. To produce texts and films that did this convincingly was not always easy; it required careful attention. Moreover, there had to be a negotiation with and control of the living memory of veterans, indeed of the whole society. This was a constant battle rather than something that occurred overnight, and its difficulty partially explains why so few films were made on this subject matter in the late Stalin period.

All of this suggests that art and culture function in a more complex way than the claim that, of all the spheres of late Stalinist government, the arts had the least autonomy and the cultural apparatus was simply a tool of the party and the leadership.[138] Rather than illustrating the Stalin-centric totalitarian model, analysis of *The Fall of Berlin* is more illustrative of the bureaucratic account, in which the difficulty of creating a filmic narrative that was both convincing and ideologically correct explains the final results. The Victory Banner illustrates this process of balancing eyewitness accounts and documents with the need for an evocative symbol that could confer Stalin-like charisma and an aura on the moment of victory. Studying it also illustrates how memory of the war could never be entirely Stalinized. However, as a symbol of the war that could be easily repeated, the Victory Banner retained an authoritarian association that it would never lose. Thus, after Stalin's death, when this symbol became even more prominent, it also came to illustrate how memory of the war could not be entirely democratized. Its Stalinist imprimatur and the trace of the totalitarian were never expunged entirely, for fear of undermining its force as a part of a symbolic language, conferring an aura, a sacred power, and unifying the nation.

3

THE DEATH OF STALIN AND THE BIRTH OF THE VICTORY CULT

Throughout the postwar Stalin years, memory of the war had been present across many cultural realms—in literature, film, painting, and sculpture—but it was often marginalized and always overshadowed by the Stalin cult.[1] Victory in the war was presented as Stalin's achievement, and this view obscured a sense of the people as being central to the enemy's defeat.[2] The death of Stalin thus necessarily entailed not only a reexamination of Stalin's legacy and the Stalin cult but also a reassessment of the war, especially the issue of who received credit for victory.

In addition to the historical readjustment, a symbolic one was also required, since, following Stalin's death, the Soviet leadership needed to find a way to transfer the "charismatic legitimation" conferred by the leader cult onto other symbols, especially onto the Communist Party.[3] Ultimately, this legitimation was shifted onto a myth and the cult of the Great Patriotic War, in which the symbolism of the Victory Banner played a crucial role. Yet, before representation of the war could be revisited, Stalin's funeral immediately necessitated a reconsideration of the leader cult, and this process was laid bare dramatically in its filming.

DISMANTLING THE CINEMATIC STALIN CULT IN *THE GREAT FAREWELL*

In her study of representations of Lenin, Victoria Bonnell argues that, like a medieval monarch, Lenin possessed two bodies: the mortal one associated with his earthly existence and the other being that of his immortality, his other body, his "body politic."[4]

While Stalin assiduously managed the cult of Lenin, associating himself with notions of Lenin's infallibility and the immortality of his ideas, before long he had less need of that association and was being widely represented in his own right: "The image of Stalin that developed in the 1930s was highly complex and artists understood that the representation of the leader required vivid depiction of his 'other body' as well. Accordingly, artists searched for new and compelling ways to portray the immortal and infallible Stalin, who was increasingly the object of extravagant verbal praise and whose deification posed challenging artistic problems. How, in essence, to portray a living god?"[5]

Having spent so long striving to represent Stalin's "other body," his immortal one, artists and filmmakers suddenly, in the wake of Stalin's death, had to confront a new challenge: how to represent Stalin's mortal body in death, to show the Soviet public that their god was dead. However they went about it, this was an inherently iconoclastic task, entailing the revision of artistic canons. As Robert C. Tucker puts it, "Stalin's death had to mean de-Stalinization."[6] The newspapers now had to improvise, whereas previously they followed a set template.[7] Everything writers and filmmakers had been doing for the previous twenty years prevented them from preparing for this moment—thinking thoughts of Stalin's death, even if this was the subject of a rich vein of subversive black humor (mined in Armando Iannucci's 2017 film *The Death of Stalin*, banned in Russia).[8] This lack of preparation for the subject of the film of Stalin's funeral was especially true of Mikheil Chiaureli, one of the filmmakers invited to oversee the filming of the funeral due to his success with *The Fall of Berlin*, the cinematic apogee of the Stalin cult. Nevertheless, he was able to draw on his prior experience of representing Stalin, in the days of Stalin's funeral, as he was working on the film:

> One of the demands [of the people] was to see images of Lenin and Stalin re-created on the screen. The top filmmakers strove to respond to this demand of the people, and, as such, I too was honored to contribute to the solution of this creative task. Now with particular clarity I could see in my mind moments from the years of artistic work creating on the screen comrade Stalin in various periods of his life, entirely dedicated to the Party, the people and the cause of building socialism.
>
> . . .
>
> Of Stalin's deeds [*deianiiakh*] one can and should speak in an elevated and poetic way. That approach would reflect the truth of life and the truth of history.[9]

Transposing his "elevated and poetic" approach to films about Stalin from the genre of large-scale epics or "fictional documentaries" to actual documentaries was a challenge for Chiaureli, since he had little or no experience in documentary film, having started out in theater, and had always emphasized the painterly and theatrical elements in his films.[10]

3.1. Stalin lying in state, from *Pravda*, 7 March 1953.

However, it was his experience in using color that he could bring to the project. His approach was once again a synthesis of the ideological and expressionistic, integrating color as a central part of the film's message.[11]

Chiaureli was also experienced in making monumental films whose scale alone was a metaphor for the importance of the message. Like *The Fall of Berlin*, the films of Stalin's funeral were made on an unprecedented scale, not only throughout the Soviet Union, where a hundred thousand meters (i.e., about sixty hours) of material was recorded by a huge number of camera operators, but also ten thousand meters in ten other communist bloc countries, including China, Mongolia, and North Korea. The project was completed extraordinarily quickly, given its enormous scale, with the final cut of a short version, a three-reel newsreel special issue film entitled *Farewell to the Leader* (*Proshchanie s vozhdem*), only covering the funeral itself, predicted to be ready on 22 March, less than three weeks after Stalin's death. The longer color film, *The Great Farewell* (*Velikoe proshchanie*), with a wider remit, including a lot of footage from overseas and from Stalin's life, was due to be ready by 15 April.[12] While ultimately two films were created, with the shorter film narrower in focus, the final version of the longer film, which will be the focus of the following analysis, resembles an amalgam of the two projects, with none of the earlier envisaged flashbacks to Stalin's achievements in life. It is instead a feature-length film devoted entirely to the funeral and memorial meetings held in Stalin's memory, around the Soviet Union and the world. Despite the speed with which the film was made, the political situation in the country was evolving even more quickly, so fast, in fact, that the finished film was shelved without explanation in April 1953.

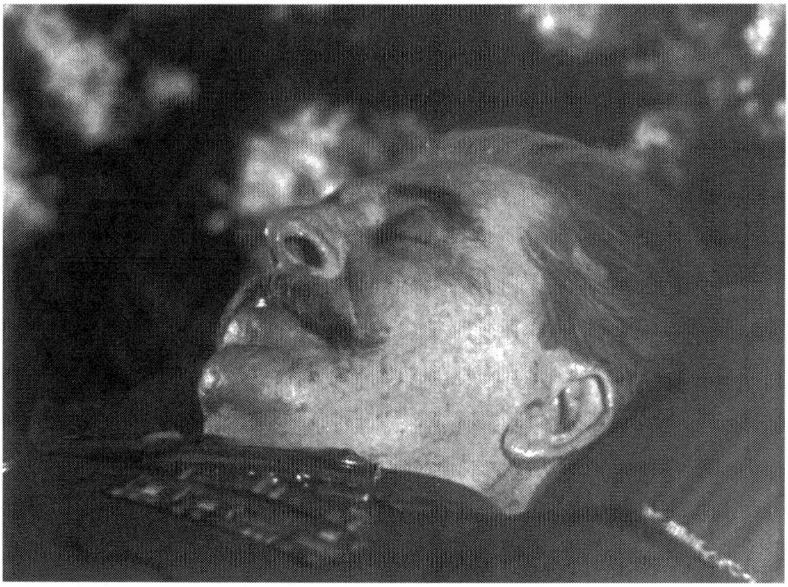

3.2. Close-up of Stalin lying in state, from the film *The Great Farewell*, which memorialized Stalin. Courtesy of RGAKFD.

3.3. Stalin, surrounded by funeral wreaths, from the film *The Great Farewell*. Courtesy of RGAKFD.

The key problems filmmakers faced were how to film Stalin and what narrative to create from the footage. Representations of Stalin's body during his life had been strictly controlled and regulated, with photography and documentary film in particular not allowed to show the pock-marked skin on his face or to focus too closely or revealingly on his slightly irregular left hand.[13] Now filmmakers could film Stalin in death and were faced with a perplexing and unwelcome freedom to break with tried and tested representational formulas. An initial photograph in *Pravda* on 7 March enlarged the image of Stalin in his coffin, so as to dwarf those left behind him.[14]

Such a solution was not available to documentary filmmakers, however, and, when we examine the outtakes from the film, we get an even stronger sense of the difficulties faced in getting the angles right, both figuratively and literally. We find many high-angle shots that make Stalin look like a pitiful fallen idol. He is hard to discern among the flowers surrounding him. Another angle attempts to show Stalin and the other members of the Central Committee from above, but they are unrecognizable and likewise suffer from the high angle's standard suggestion of a belittling and diminishing of power. Stalin's hands and face, as well as his short left arm, are sometimes photographed in such detail that their grotesque associations are brought to the fore.

In addition to the difficulties of representing Stalin's body, there was the problem of how to refer to him and whether to use the verbal clichés of the Stalin cult. The films conveyed a deliberate, stultifying solemnity that had been planned meticulously from the start, with pauses added to the script for Levitan, the iconic voice-over man, and the scenario calling for musical crescendos to heighten the effect of particular verbal clichés, such as "the father of the people's happiness."[15]

At the same time, there is a toning down of some elements of the Stalin cult, in particular the ubiquitous mentions of his name in association with heroic achievements. Thus the *kolkhozniki* are initially said to be "experts [*mastera*] of Stalin harvests," but this is changed to "experts in big harvests."[16] Similarly, the formulation "under the banner of STALIN" is changed to include Lenin: "under the banner of Lenin-STALIN" with the capital letters retained.[17] This suggests a reluctance to employ the full pitch of Stalin-cult rhetoric and a need to hark back to the more reliable Lenin, a tendency that was to dominate the Soviet post-Stalin years. Similarly, in depicting the mausoleum, an early variant of the script draws attention to Stalin's death as unique and points out the addition to the inscription on the mausoleum:

> —There is no death in the world that could have summoned such universal grief and sorrow for hundreds of millions of people, as that of comrade STALIN.
>
> —Burial-vault of the mighty—LENIN's Mausoleum.
>
> Today, alongside the word LENIN, familiar to millions above the entrance to the Mausoleum, the word STALIN has been etched into the granite.[18]

However, all of this text was crossed out and did not appear in either film: while we see Stalin's coffin being taken into the mausoleum in *The Great Farewell*, and his name is visible, there is no attempt to draw special attention to it in the voice-over or to suggest that he is more important than Lenin. Indeed, the seasoned documentary filmmaker Il´ia Kopalin, brought on to the project later than others in a bid to bring coherence to the sprawling mass of material, proposed that the notion of Stalin's death being more important than Lenin's be removed.[19]

In making these changes, Kopalin appears to have been reacting to the evolving situation in which critical voices were being raised regarding Stalin's legacy: already on 10 March, five days after Stalin's death, the interim premier, Georgii Malenkov, said to the Presidium of the Central Committee, "Some major unacceptable things happened here, there was a lot that went on with the cult of personality . . . we believe it is imperative to end the cult of personality."[20]

Another of the film's central problems was how to represent the remaining members of the government present at the funeral: this was evidently going to be seen as a sign of who would be the heir, and this is one aspect of the film to which Sergei Loznitsa's 2019 montage of the footage has drawn attention.[21] While the films of Lenin's funeral had initially been even-handed in showing the candidates for succession (with the exception of Trotskii, who had not been present), subsequent reeditings, such as Dziga Vertov's *Three Songs of Lenin* (*Tri pesni o Lenine*, 1934), had made it clear that Stalin was the anointed successor. Coedited by Elizaveta Svilova, a veteran of the Vertov film, the footage of Stalin's funeral initially included a group of thirteen top officials in the guard of honor:

> In the guard of honor by the coffin—the comrades-in-arms of the great STALIN—the leaders of the Party and government.
>
> Comrades Malenkov, Beriia, Voroshilov, Mikoian, Saburov, Molotov, Bulganin, Khrushchev, Kaganovich, Shvernik, Pervukhin, Suslov, Mikhailov.[22]

However, in the final version of *The Great Farewell*, only eight were named: Malenkov, Beriia, Voroshilov, Molotov, Bulganin, Khrushchev,

Kaganovich, and Mikoian. One draft of the script cut Kaganovich, but he was then restored to the voice-over in a handwritten correction.[23]

These eight were not entirely equal, though: generally speaking, the film sets Beriia and Malenkov apart as the presumed heirs (even if there was indecision as to whether to use the actual term "heirs").[24] They are shown more, and more centrally, and they were the leading pallbearers for Stalin's coffin. This emphasis was one that was toned down in the course of making the film, as is evident from the outtakes, where Malenkov is the only one of the Party Central Committee to be photographed in close-up, posed alone, and reposed with Beriia, and then both in the middle of two others and more prominently at the side, where his name would be the first to be read out in the voice-over. Throughout the newspaper coverage, too, Malenkov was the heir apparent.[25] The final cut of the film(s), however, while making it clear that Malenkov, and to a lesser extent Beriia, are the main contenders for the leadership, presents them much more as part of a group.

This appears to reflect the new line that had started to emerge soon after the funeral, when the Soviet press started talking about the principle of "collective leadership." As Tucker argues, this was initially a negative principle, articulating the implicit message that "there would be no new Stalin."[26] Thus, Malenkov, the initial presumed successor when the footage was filmed, was made to seem more of a partner in a collective when the film was edited.

It was this shifting, increasingly ambivalent attitude toward Stalin and the Stalin cult that led to the film being shelved. As late as 14 March, Chiaureli had been discussing Stalin's legacy and the need for filmmakers to follow it, imagining that there would be many more Stalin cultic films in the days and years to come and stressing Stalin's inspirational leadership during the war.[27] However, as it turned out, *The Great Farewell* was to be the last Stalin cult project even to be initiated for a number of years. Nevertheless, films of the Stalin cult were not removed from distribution, and the first reaction against the "cult of personality" in fact came with regard to Lavrentii Beriia, head of State Security (MVD, i.e., the forerunner to the KGB). Following Beriia's arrest and fall from grace in July 1953, Chiaureli's *The Fall of Berlin* was edited in November 1953 to remove all images of Beriia.[28] So systematically was this done that even today the Russian state film archive, Gosfil′mofond, possesses no unedited copy of the film with Beriia. Germany's Bundesarchiv-Filmarchiv retains the only copy, presumably because the East Germans were more reluctant to make such cuts.

Mentions of Stalin continued in the press and in speeches by party leaders throughout 1954 and 1955, with his seventy-fifth birthday being widely commemorated in December 1954 with articles in *Pravda*, as was the one-year anniversary of his death, observed on 5 March 1954.[29] However, the imagery was more restrained, and the epithets stressed Stalin's role as part of, rather than standing above, the party. The June 1953 plenum of the Central Committee initiated discussion of the "cult of personality" but blamed all negative aspects on Beriia.[30] Yet, criticizing the "cult of the personality" without criticizing Stalin led to strange questions as to what concrete propaganda had exemplified the cult of personality centered on Beriia.[31] In this ambiguous situation of cautious reassessment of the Stalin legacy in the period prior to Khrushchev's 1956 direct denunciation of Stalin, representations of Stalin's part in the Great Patriotic War were central but subtle. Representations of the Victory Banner reflect this convoluted process with a clarity hard to locate elsewhere.

DE-STALINIZING THE HISTORY OF THE WAR

Stalin had centralized and arrested historical thought and the writing of history, from a situation of plurality and flux in the 1920s to one of monolithical stasis. With his death, the situation once more became unstable, and depictions of World War II immediately changed. Even prior to Khrushchev's famous reassessment of the war, as well as his critique of Stalin's role in it in the 1956 "secret speech," there was already a tentative move toward playing down his role in the war, including a 1955 rejection of certain elements of Stalinist military doctrine.[32] There was also a projection of the shift to collective leadership onto the past. Thus, while a 1955 one-volume history of the war still mentioned and quoted Stalin many times, it also stressed the role of the State Committee for Defense and found a number of ways of not mentioning Stalin, by referring to the "High Command" and by quoting a soldier's letter, which itself quoted Stalin's 6 November 1944 speech calling for the raising of a Victory Banner over Berlin, without attribution.[33]

Even if Stalin was not entirely absent from film representations of the war in the Khrushchev era, despite suggestions to the contrary, the same tendency to ration mentions of Stalin can be seen in film of the post-Stalin period.[34] One example is a 1948 documentary film, *In Defense of Peace* (*Na strazhe mira*, dir. Roman Grigor′ev, Mariia Fideleva), which was reedited in 1955 under the same title. Thus, whereas the earlier film stressed Stalin's presence in the Kremlin as a rallying force in the battle of Moscow, the 1955 film shows people listening to Stalin's speech of 7 November 1941, but Stalin's name is not mentioned. The principle of collective leadership is illustrated here, too: rather than show Stalin alone, as in the earlier version of the film, we now see a shot with portraits of members of the State Committee for Defense: Stalin (framed in a tighter close-up than the others), then Bulganin, Voroshilov, Kaganovich, Molotov, Malenkov, and Mikoian. Repeatedly the emphasis is on the party, and while Stalin is mentioned, the film stresses that he was appointed *by the party* to be the head of the State Committee for Defense and of the armed forces.

To illustrate the narrative that it was the Communist Party leaders who everywhere were lending support, instead of just Stalin everywhere, we see Bulganin on the western and Belorussian fronts, Zhdanov in Leningrad, Kaganovich in the Caucasus, Malenkov on the Volga near Stalingrad, and Khrushchev with the troops of Stalingrad and the First Ukrainian Front. Care is taken not to give any one figure undue prominence.

In Defense of Peace also attempts to disassociate Stalin from the battle of Stalingrad. We see soldiers reading a front-line newspaper with an image of Stalin on the front page; there is a reference to "the supreme commander's order" of 7 November 1942, with the quotation from it: "And there will be a celebration on our street too"—but Stalin's name is not mentioned nor do we see him visiting the front. Similarly, the "ten Stalin blows" of 1944, a way of characterizing that year's tremendous battlefield victories, have become the ten "devastating blows" of 1944.

In a telling gesture, Stalin is disassociated from the raising of the Victory Banner over the Reichstag in the 1955 edit of the film. The 1948 version shows a flag being raised over the Reichstag and mentions Egorov and Kantariia but also the often less prominent figures Samsonov and Neustroev. Although Stalin's name is not mentioned, as it had been in the original 1945 documentary films on the battle for Berlin, the camera homes in on a graffito that makes the link. Scrawled on the Reichstag, it reads, "Where Stalin is, there you will find victory." The music reaches a crescendo as we see this. It is swiftly followed by images of the 24 June 1945 Red Square parade, and the voice-over intones, "Victory. Total, mighty victory. It was Stalin who led us to this victory."

The 1955 edit uses most of the same classic newsreel images of the storming of the Reichstag, adding the name of Davydov to those of Egorov, Kantariia, Neustroev, and Samsonov as those who raised the Victory Banner over Berlin. While we see the sequence depicting graffiti on the Reichstag, none of it now mentions Stalin, nor does the Victory Parade mention Stalin, and his image is hard to make out in a long shot of the podium at Lenin's mausoleum. But this tentative de-Stalinization of war memory was soon to be taken a lot further.

THE SECRET SPEECH AND MEMORY OF THE WAR

While Khrushchev's interventions into historical debates have mostly been seen as criticisms of Stalin-era terror and repression, his direct reassessment of the war, in which Stalin's role was either written out of it or his errors made central, was also significant, and this shift began with his 25 February 1956 secret speech (read at all Communist Party and Komsomol cells). This made the crucial claims that Stalin ignored warnings that war was coming, that his 1937 repressions weakened the army, and that he committed a number of strategic errors.[35] While the secret speech was not officially published, it still informed attempts in the arts community to draw attention to the early part of the war and to Stalin's errors, most notably with the publication of the first volumes of Konstantin Simonov's novel *The Living and the Dead* (*Zhivye i mertvye*) in 1955 and 1962 and historian Aleksandr Nekrich's controversial book *22 June 1941* (*22 iiunia 1941-g.*) in 1965, which was banned and the print run destroyed.[36] In cinema, too, this period of the war attracted a number of attempts to change the narrative.

In the Khrushchev years, such rewriting was all about playing down the role of Stalin, dissociating it from the war narrative as much as possible. Moreover, while it never went anywhere near as far as the Stalin cult, there was a greater emphasis on Khrushchev's own contribution to the war effort, as well as a careful sifting of publications to assure a positive construction of his participation, especially in the battle of Stalingrad, which was increasingly known in this period by Khrushchev's preferred (and de-Stalinized) name for it: "The Great Battle on the Volga."[37] Indeed, in a devastating turnaround, at the meeting of the Presidium of the Central Committee that led to Khrushchev's downfall, Secretary of the Central Committee Mikhail Suslov and Khrushchev's soon-to-be successor, Leonid Brezhnev, accused him of promoting a personality cult of his own.[38]

A further dimension of the shift in memory of the war during the post-Stalin period was what has been called "the people's state" (*obshchenarodnoe gosudarstvo*).[39] Secretary to the Central Committee Il′ichev, describing the thrust of the Twenty-First Congress of the Communist Party of the Soviet Union (CPSU), put this in terms of the contrast with the cult of personality: "the main blow was aimed at one of the most dangerous manifestations of the cult of personality—the belittling of the role of the popular masses in the making of history."[40]

In the Khrushchev-era depiction of history, the people's state had an analogue in the orientation toward showing that the war was won through "mass heroism." At the same time, there was resistance to this orientation, in particular from the KGB, which continued to see the state as central not only in the present but also in the past. In this way, debates over World War II history echoed the inherent contradictions between the democratic, participatory tendencies in the Khrushchev state and its retaining of monopolistic, one-party state control.[41]

Another way of thinking about this tension is in terms of the different emphasis in the manner in which the war was depicted. As Polly Jones puts it, the post-Stalin "emphasis on the visual, the corporeal, the personally witnessed and experienced, enacted a break with the spectacular and hierarchical structure of Stalinism."[42]

The personal, witnessed dimension was important in wider Khrushchev-era "thaw" attitudes.[43] For histories of the war, this would mean a greater space for the memoir, the individual's own account of what happened, in contrast with Stalinism. It was also manifested in the highly personal emphasis of thaw-era cinema, sometimes described as melodramatic.[44]

The Victory Banner was a symbol of victory in the war, but one associated with Stalin, the epic, and the monumental and with the Stalin style of elevating selected heroes to stand for the masses. The red flag was at the same time a symbol associated with the party and with the communist cause more broadly. The symbol of the Victory Banner raised over the Reichstag was thus to become an important site where tensions between symbolic meanings were played out, and a concerted effort was made to demonstrate that, like the red banner throughout socialist history, the Victory Banner of 1945 had also been raised by numerous heroes, by the masses, and not one or two individuals acting as surrogates for Stalin. This meant that history became a key ideological battleground.

WRITING *HISTORY OF THE GREAT PATRIOTIC WAR OF THE SOVIET UNION*

The social sciences and humanities became an important tool for the analysis and denunciation of the cult of personality, striving to peel away the thick layers of falsification that had gummed up Stalin-era thought and to write histories of the Soviet period without covering up mistakes and attributing all successes to Stalin.[45] This led to an enormous expansion in the number of historical publications. As the July 1956 issue of the journal *Voprosy istorii* (Questions of history) put it, "It is essential to extend the criticism of erroneous, simplifying, antihistorical views to overcome the cult of personality when illuminating historical events of all kinds."[46]

Of all the works of history generated in this new wave of scholarship, the most prominent was the multivolume (initially five-volume) *History of the Great Patriotic War of the Soviet Union*, commissioned at the 12 September 1957 Presidium of the Central Committee of the CPSU and initially scheduled to be published between 1957 and 1960 in a print run of two hundred thousand.[47] This was accompanied by an unprecedented openness of archives: whereas in 1947 slightly more than four thousand people gained access to state archives, in 1957 this figure was more than twenty-three thousand.[48] In this context, the striving to write well-referenced, factually rich history and to publish archival materials was a politically motivated decision.

In reconsidering Stalin's place in the history of the war period, the editorial team's task was not simply to mention Stalin less and avoid overstating his role but also a question of emphasizing other factors contributing to victory, especially the masses and the party. As Colonel S. I. Roshchin, one of the editors of *History of the Great Patriotic War of the Soviet Union*, said of a draft of the fifth volume, produced before the 1961 Twenty-Second Congress of the CPSU, the editorial board would redouble their efforts to overcome the personality cult and bring the work into line with the resolutions on overcoming the cult of personality: "We do not think that the solution of this matter can be achieved mechanically, by crossing out the name of Stalin. The main thing is to strengthen the depiction of the people as the creator of history, the depiction of mass heroism at the front and on the home front, paying particular attention to the activities of our Party. At the same time, we have to avoid any exaggeration whatsoever in evaluating Stalin's activities as a military leader and his personal role in leading operations."[49]

This striving to show the war as having been won through mass heroism led to the widespread publication of the memoirs of veterans. This tendency has been referred to as a "privatization" of war memory in the 1960s.[50] While these memoirs often filled in blanks in official histories, they necessarily suffered from the limitations of autobiography in typically lacking a sense of the bigger picture and focusing on the unavoidably limited episodes directly experienced by the author. These shortcomings were compounded by the specific Soviet context in which the memoirs were written: they had to have the support of a certain authority, usually higher-ranking officers in the same unit, so that undesired themes were removed, but they also led to a decrease in distinctiveness and quality as the accounts effectively became homogenized and collectively authored.[51]

Nevertheless, in a context in which history and memoirs were valorized, they could also be used as part of a demonumentalizing tendency in which "rich empirical evidence" and "debate about historical details became a legitimate way of voicing doubt and starting a socially charged discussion."[52] This strategy, however, was always kept within limits by the vetting process outlined above, and also through the control of archives, which, as Leonid Maksimenkov has pointed out, selectively restricted access to documents in order to both underpin official commemoration of the war with an authority that could not be challenged and at the same time to manipulate the direction of debate.[53] One example of a thaw-era reassessment that went too far was the questioning of some of the strategic decisions, such as that in the liberal journal *Novyi mir* in 1963 by General A. B. Gorbatov, commander of the Third Strike Army, about the need even to storm Berlin, arguing that had it been besieged, the garrison would soon have surrendered.[54] Given the enormous loss of life in the battle, this view bordered on the heretical in suggesting that the sacrifices were in vain and in rendering the Victory Banner symbolism irrelevant. Such heterodox reinterpretations would be met with not only skepticism but accusations of falsification, since there was an expectation that the document must be produced in order to substantiate the claim, and key documents lay in closed archives controlled by a state keen to block radical reinterpretations of the war.

THE VICTORY BANNER CONFERENCES

The fraught interaction between memoirs, the archive, and history was compellingly illustrated by the two special conferences called by the History of the Great Patriotic War section of the Institute of Marxism-Leninism. These gatherings involved participants in the storming of the Reichstag, so as to inform the writing of the fifth volume of *History of the Great Patriotic War*. After the first conference, held on 8 April 1960, was inconclusive, a second conference was called for 15–16 November 1961 to discuss a draft of the key chapter depicting the storming of the Reichstag. While the conferences were full and frank, their transcripts remained in a closed party archive, and although the debates and conclusions were sometimes later mentioned in memoirs, they were never cited properly or at length. The discussions, however, were used to inform the much more measured account given in the official history.

The fifth volume of *History of the Great Patriotic War*, like the others, was written by a collective from the History of the Great Patriotic War section. Specially commissioned authors who were not members of the editorial committee wrote the text, referring to many documents for the first time. One member of the editing team, Colonel Roshchin, in discussing the fifth volume, says that the Berlin chapter was the most complex, demanding the largest number of rewrites.[55] A large part of the reason for this was the difficulty of writing about the storming of the Reichstag and the Victory Banner episode. The published version of the fifth volume comprised 17 chapters, and the seventh chapter, entitled "The Fall of Berlin," comprised 4 parts, one of which was devoted to the battle of Berlin. The storming of the Reichstag took up 4 pages of the 650-page volume. Despite taking up relatively few pages in the volume, the Victory Banner and Reichstag occupied a special place in the book due to the inclusion of five black-and-white images, two of the small number of the book's color plates, and a special place in the historiography of the war, because this wartime episode, despite being small in scale (involving thousands rather than tens or hundreds of thousands of participants), could stand for the wider battle. Those elements ultimately make the overall narrative of the war coherent and narratable for the reading public by endowing the sacrifice with an uplifting, meaningful ending.

In an attempt to base this narrative on testimony and fact, chief editors Evgenii Boltin and Petr Pospelov wrote to the Central Committee on 29 October 1962 to see if they were permitted to publish the full figures on the number of Soviet troops killed and wounded in the battle for Berlin: "Should we show the high price paid in blood for victory by the Soviet people?" They gave numbers here of 61,454 killed and 234,935 wounded on all three fronts. In the final version, the figures are mentioned, but the text attempts to counterweigh these by emphasizing the fact that these soldiers died "on the altar of victory."[56] The wider honesty as to the price paid could be organized and rendered acceptable if the narrative ended with a redemptive vision of victory, making sense of those deaths as a sacrifice. However, in order for it to function effectively in the new post-Stalin ideological climate, the Victory Banner had to be stripped of its associations with the cult of personality. This entailed a thorough reexamination of what happened and its symbolic importance.

Reflecting on what it was about the storming of the Reichstag that attracted such interest, Boltin, head of the History of the Great Patriotic War section of the Institute of Marxism-Leninism and one of the chief editors of the tome, addressed the veterans of the storming of the Reichstag on 15 November 1961:

> Why was it necessary to call such a meeting? Above all, this event in itself—the storming of the Reichstag—is a very significant episode in the war, of great military and, most importantly, political meaning. In the mind of every Soviet patriot, every Soviet person, the Storming of the Reichstag is the greatest expression of the heroism of our Soviet Army, our soldiers.
>
> The Storming of the Reichstag has entered world history as the triumphant concluding act of the war. It is natural therefore that we should want the Storming of the Reichstag to be preserved in the minds of present and fu-

> ture generations for many decades to come. This is why we have set ourselves the goal of describing this greatest of historical events in the most exacting ideological and historical manner [*na vysokom ideinom i istoricheskom urovne*]. This would be difficult to do without inviting the direct participants in the Storming of the Reichstag.[57]

Yet even some of these claims are disputed by the veterans. Thus, V. D. Shatalin, former commander of the 380th Rifle Regiment (171st Rifle Division, Third Strike Army), says that when he first saw the Reichstag he did not pay it any attention because he was evaluating the building exclusively from a military point of view. Consequently, he concludes that the raising of the Victory Banner was not a wartime action but a symbolic postwar one.[58] This stance seems to have been affirmed earlier, at the 1960 conference, where Boltin says that the Reichstag was politically important, suggesting its military significance was a consequence of that: "The Reichstag was of great political significance. The British and Americans also wanted to capture it, and that is why a lot of importance was accorded to this matter[;] at the highest level this matter was accorded great importance, and we set ourselves the combat mission of taking the Reichstag."[59]

The prominence accorded to the storming of Berlin was not acceptable to all members of the editorial board from a military point of view, however. One member pointed out that it was never a war aim to capture Berlin and that Japan was defeated after the fall of Berlin.[60] Clearly, the special emphasis on Berlin was ultimately political and symbolic, since the fall of the German capital was not in fact the final moment of the war. Its salience was due to the Soviets' greater focus on Europe, on presenting their country as the enemy of fascism and the storming of the Reichstag as a symbol of the end of the war. This symbol was made all the more poignant by the fact that the volume was being written while the Berlin Wall was being built, a low point in the former wartime allies' relationship. Indeed, writer Boris Polevoi, a member of the editorial committee, returned from Berlin and enthused to colleagues about the sight of the recently built wall.[61]

Nevertheless, for all its symbolic importance, this prominence could only go so far. Thus, responding to the requests voiced at the 1961 conference that there be a whole chapter devoted to the storming of the Reichstag, Roshchin says that surely that event is not on the same level as the liberation of Belorussia, the liberation of Poland, or the Berlin operation as a whole, each of which receives a whole chapter.[62] The fact that there is a demand to devote disproportionate space to it, though, suggests that many veterans saw the storming of the Reichstag as equal in importance to enormous, militarily decisive campaigns.

The conferences were ostensibly motivated by the need to establish what had happened and who really put up the flag, and Boltin says that he received a number of letters complaining about the way the Soviet press depicted the storming of the Reichstag.[63] While he and others exhort participants to be objective and stress their need to find out the truth, at the same time, however, the underlying purpose was to reinterpret the whole episode in a way that reflected the Khrushchev-era approach to the war—to reclaim the symbol of the Victory Banner. Thus, Klimov, the editor in charge of volume 5, gave a brief survey of earlier publications, noting that one of the only published sources, *The Berlin Operation* (1950), was a secret book accessible only to military and party people with a need to know and not to the general public (see above, chapter 2).[64] Although Klimov praises this text, he mentions its "weak" portrayal of people's heroism as one of its chief shortcomings. Clearly, the conferences were intended from the outset to redress this imbalance and substantiate the Khrushchev-era reassessment of wartime history and of victory as the product of mass mobilization:

> The mass character of the heroism shown by soldiers in the storming of the Reichstag has not been shown enough. This is not about taking the laurels away from anyone and giving them to someone else. That's not what we are trying to do. What we are actually trying to do is to show the political enthusiasm surrounding the storming of the Reichstag, the mass participation in this act by our soldiers and officers. That's what we are trying to do. We should not forget that this is not a matter of individuals, of mentioning the names of every hero, even if it is important to show the separate units, separate battalions, regiments, divisions, formations so that the reader understands that this was not an act of isolated heroism, the personal heroism of one, two, or three people, but an act of mass heroism orchestrated by our Party, the Political Departments of the Army, and the High Command.[65]

Although Klimov says that he is not intending to take any "laurels" away from anyone (evidently referring to Egorov and Kantariia, who, though present at the 1960 conference, were not present at the second of these conferences, when he said this), his purpose is to present the flag raising as the achievement of a wider group of combatants while at the same time permitting the Egorov and Kantariia version to stand. This approach is indicative of the way in which memory of the war could not be fully de-Stalinized without stripping the power of aura from its symbols.

In shifting the emphasis from the narrow circle of named heroes, the conferences both address the existing problem of conflicting, self-aggrandizing accounts and attempt to make use of them, arguing as

Boltin does at the first conference that reducing the achievement to that of one or two named people is to belittle it.[66] Roshchin's report to the editorial board describes the problem:

> In the literature that has come out since the war, in memoirs of participants, and in speeches, the actions of units capturing the Reichstag have been tendentiously represented. The former commander of the 150th Rifle Division, Lieutenant-General V. M. Shatilov, in his public talks and in a brochure prepared for publication by the Museum of the Soviet Army, asserts that the 150th division alone stormed the Reichstag. Other divisions supposedly took no part in the assault. It is also well known that the raising of the "Victory Banner" over the Reichstag was linked with the names of Egorov and Kantariia alone. The participants of the storming of the Reichstag themselves have been conducting a protracted and heated argument as to who entered the Reichstag first, and who was first on its cupola. There has been no shortage of letters written to the Central Committee of the Party on this question.
>
> The editors of the fifth volume and the directors of the Section [of History of the Great Patriotic War] had to sort out this matter, to produce an objective survey of this most important of historical events. First of all, we studied the archive documents. On the 8th April 1960 we met 11 active participants of the storming of the Reichstag headed by the former commander of the 79th Rifle Corps, Colonel-General Perevertkin. From conversations with them it became clear that the storming of the Reichstag was the heroic achievement of many units and formations, that Soviet soldiers here displayed truly mass heroism, and that what we had here was mass competition to put up flags and banners on the Reichstag. That is how we have tried to describe this in the seventh chapter. . . . Here the actions of many units and formations are portrayed. Flags and banners were put up by many people.
>
> We sent this part of the chapter to many participants of the storming of the Reichstag and, when we received critical comments on the text, decided to talk to the participants of the storming once more. On 15 and 16 of November this year at the History of the Great Patriotic War Section, we held a second conference at which 24 active participants of the storming of the Reichstag were present—from former commander of the 3rd Strike Army, Colonel-General V. I. Kuznetsov, down to a number of sergeants and privates. They recounted many interesting and important details, once more insisting that the storming of the Reichstag and raising of the "Victory Banner" was a feat achieved by a large number of units and groups, that it was an expression of mass heroism, and you cannot reduce the taking of the Reichstag solely to the actions of Neustroev, Davydov, or Samsonov's battalion or attribute the honor of raising the banner over the Reichstag to Egorov and Kantariia alone. In our work, it is essential to depict the whole battle of Berlin and the

> Storming of the Reichstag in depth, truthfully and objectively. The editors now possess enough materials to produce such a depiction of this event.[67]

While Roshchin presents the revision in terms of simply adding to the cast of heroes, at the 1961 meeting in particular there is an iconoclastic mood in which previous representations of the flag raising are criticized. Aleksei Berest, the *politruk* (army political instructor) who was with Egorov and Kantariia but did not receive a Hero of the Soviet Union medal in 1946, possibly because he was a politruk and Marshal Zhukov did not care for them, was not even invited to the first conference in April 1960. At the 1961 conference he asks whether there are any representatives of film studios or of *Pravda* in attendance, because they write whatever suits them.[68] Boltin responds, "We have produced an edition on which we would like to consult with the participants of the Storming. When everything is correct in our book, then it will be a guide for all." He later adds, "The way it is in this book will be the interpretation in films and in the press and so on."[69]

A number of speakers criticize Konstantin Samsonov, author of one of the first memoirs of the raising of the flag, *The Storming of the Reichstag* (*Shturm reikhstaga*).[70] Klimov is the first of a number of speakers to mention it, condemning its making up of conversations between the author and General Perevertkin.[71] General-Lieutenant Firsov tries to explain Samsonov's unmerited prominence, pointing to his becoming a deputy in the Supreme Soviet of the RSFSR and being based in Moscow, whereas the other veterans of the storming of the Reichstag all lived in the provinces. Firsov even goes so far as to suggest not only venal self-interest but even similarities between Samsonov's rise and the cult of personality.[72]

Samsonov insists that these memoirs that bear his name were not written by him; indeed, he claims not to be able to write at all.[73] However, this line does not placate his critics, who find that their own achievements have been questioned by the public because Samsonov has already claimed the credit (he had introduced screenings of *The Fall of Berlin*, for example; see chapter 2). As Neustroev says, he overheard visitors at the Central Museum of the Soviet Army in 1957 being told that the Victory Banner had been raised by a group under Samsonov (and at the incorrect time of 14:25).[74] Neustroev even claims that Samsonov had distorted the archival record at the Ministry of Defense archives in Podol′sk.[75] Samsonov's prominence is such that even Kantariia suggests that the fact that he and Egorov live a long way from Moscow means that they have been forgotten about and Samsonov thus receives all the attention, which is clearly an exaggeration.[76]

Samsonov's and other memoirs exaggerate the role not only of particular participants (invariably the author) but also of their units and imply that they alone took the building and no other individuals or units took part. This story is belied by other, equally biased accounts and by the documentary record, such as the military orders. One participant at the conference, Liadov, tries to assert his own presumably oft-repeated but entirely mythologized, self-aggrandizing account and is shouted down.[77] Another participant, Lisimenko, even claims that he sees traces of the cult of personality in everyone's attempts to say they got to the Reichstag first.[78] While this is not a persuasive claim, the fact that the symbol and debates about it are being used to denounce the cult of personality is noteworthy. Indeed, the discussion at the second conference had to be stopped by the chair, Boltin, from descending into the chaos of claim and counterclaim as to who put a banner on the building first. Attempting to reconcile these competing claims, Neustroev finds an effective formulation:

> The Reichstag was stormed by hundreds and hundreds of people. Many flags of all sizes were put up—Zherbina, Kantariia, the artillerymen, and soldiers from other units, including tankmen. . . . But what is the result? We read *The History of the Party*, and of course I am not criticizing *The History of the Party*[;] it has been approved and adopted and so on. But it's written there that the Victory Banner was raised by Egorov and Kantariia. Someone's found a convenient hero [*Vot Susanina nashli*]! . . . I would say that Egorov and Kantariia carried out a certain historical mission. As the best men of our regiment they were given the banner, and they put up that banner, recording the fact that our people took the Reichstag. That's how you should put it. The Victory Banner was raised over the Reichstag by hundreds and thousands of people. It was raised on the 30th and on 1st May, 2nd May, it was raised for a whole month after the war.[79]

This account corresponds to the factual record regarding film and photographic images, which were taken over the course of days and weeks after the storming of the building. However, Neustroev does not deny that Egorov and Kantariia put up the Victory Banner but stresses that it was one of many, and while it was what might be called "the flag of record," effectively they should not be separated out so dramatically. Klimov makes it clear that there were many flags, not just a single Victory Banner, raised on the building, and this in turn is part of his emphasis on the "mass character" of the assault. Klimov further nuances this:

> We should discuss the issue of the raising of the banner over the Reichstag separately. In the historical literature, it is linked solely with the names of

> Egorov and Kantariia. This is not acceptable. The fact is that the raising of the Victory Banner was not a monumental act but a rather protracted process. The road of the "Victory Banner" was cleared by many soldiers, especially by Communists, many of whom laid down their lives. . . .
>
> We are not calling for the role played by Egorov and Kantariia to be diminished. The idea is that alongside their names there should also be other names, the names of genuine heroes.[80]

Despite these repeated protestations, Klimov evidently is attempting to diminish the role of Egorov and Kantariia, since their selection as the exclusive, "monumental" heroes was at best being questioned and qualified, and at worst their mention was being tolerated alongside the "genuine" heroes, with the clear implication that they were inauthentic. Indeed, he also claims that their names were added to the account of what had happened later, but that despite this, they would not be stripped of their medals and honors. Participants in the conference repeatedly say that Egorov and Kantariia did not put up the banner, with General-Lieutenant Firsov (commander of the Twenty-Sixth Guards Rifle Corps of the Fifth Strike Army, who were now also said to be participants in the storming of the Reichstag) recalling that he had accompanied them on a trip to Berlin during which he had to correct their account of the storming of the Reichstag and raising of the banner because they had no idea what really happened.[81]

However, Klimov too is seen as going too far and striking too iconoclastic a note, as an unidentified "voice from the presidium" corrected his reference to "genuine heroes," thus rejecting the implied distinction between genuine and inauthentic heroes and demanding that he compromise: "name other heroes as well as these."[82] Questioning the residually Stalinist cult around the monumental heroism of Egorov and Kantariia had to be controlled. Instead, we see here very clearly a logic that is "cumulative rather than subtractive"; the new discourse of mass heroism is added without revising the Stalinist myth.[83]

This dissenting mood also affects Roshchin. When attempting to sum up the second conference and stressing that this is entirely his own opinion, he even questions the whole notion of the Victory Banner as a symbol:

> It is now completely clear to me that what we are used to calling the Victory Banner cannot be called the Victory Banner[;] it doesn't make sense. Here's why: first of all, victory is too big a word. We are talking about victory in the war. Are we seriously meant to accept that the raising of the Victory Banner concluded the war? Surely people died at the battles of Stalingrad, Moscow,

> and so on for the raising of this banner. In my view to call this the Victory Banner is unjustified. The Victory Banner is the banner of Lenin, the banner of the Party. Under this banner our people fought and triumphed.[84]

Roshchin then goes on to state that Egorov and Kantariia did not put the first flag up. The iconoclastic mood went even further, when A. I. Negoda, former commander of the 171st Rifle Division, called for the banner in the Central Museum of the Soviet Army to be taken down, although he later qualifies this to say that it should be altered so that it mentions not only the 150th (whose name appears on the Victory Banner) but also the 171st Division of the Third Strike Army.[85] Firsov claims that the banner in the museum is a smaller copy of a bigger one that was taken down earlier.[86] Such accounts were undermining the heroic status not just of Egorov and Kantariia but of the Victory Banner itself, with the risk of diminishing its aura.

One group determined to restrain this iconoclasm and insist upon the established, published version comprised senior officers such as Shatilov. Mikhail Bondar′ (former adjutant to the commander of the Seventy-Ninth Rifle Corps, that is, one level up from the division and Shatilov but part of a special assault group of Samsonov's 171st Division) describes the dichotomy: the conference participants are either dissatisfied, alienated veterans with little authority but intent on getting their story across or they are commanders and political instructors—authority figures with responsibility—who want the account to change very little.[87]

Thus, at the first conference, Shatilov is the first person to speak, apparently because he is the highest-ranking officer (his superior, Perevertkin, arrives late). Shatilov essentially confirms the official version, very little of which he saw firsthand. When he speaks, Perevertkin attempts to subvert the whole purpose of the conference by saying to the conference participants, "I would really not particularly recommend comrades rely on their memory after 15 years."[88] The implication is that the participants trying to correct the record on the basis of their memory are on thin ice.

While Perevertkin had passed away by 1961, what Shatilov says at the second conference is similar, but the eyewitnesses have already gained greater power and influence. Due to the rising tide of Khrushchev-era iconoclasm, those in authority are more willing to listen to such alternative accounts, even to incorporate certain elements from them, but they are not willing to endorse them entirely or to risk stripping the aura of authority from the Victory Banner itself, and thus from Egorov and Kantariia, for fear of diminishing the political power of this symbol and ultimately the Soviet system. Having expressed and listened to the very frank eyewitness accounts, the participants are then told in no uncertain terms to keep everything to themselves and not publicize what they have heard or said. As one of the directors of the section, Boris Tel′pukhovskii, tells them, "There is a last matter that we would like to address the conference about: everything that we have talked about here must remain between us, do not tell anyone about this until our volume comes out. 'I was at a conference and straight off to the press . . .' You are not allowed to publish this. We warn you that there will be consequences. We are banning you from doing this until these questions are resolved."[89]

In the text of the fifth volume that was finally published, there was both a sense of the multitude of flags and a prominence given to the Victory Banner raised by Egorov and Kantariia.[90] The Stalinist myth had been tempered, but not discarded, revised but still retained.

THEY RAISED THE VICTORY BANNER

The tendency to engage with and consult the actual veterans, who were becoming a vocal force in post-Stalin society, was increasingly apparent in this period.[91] This is reflected in documentary films and newsreels, a number of which depict or refer to the way in which veterans would gather in Moscow on Victory Day, even before it had become an official holiday in 1965. Probably the most famous treatment of this theme can be found in the final scenes of Marlen Khutsiev's celebrated 1966 film, *July Rain* (*Iiul′skii dozhd′*), which ends with documentary footage of the elaborate set for the 1965 Victory Day parade on Red Square being assembled: gigantic letters of the slogans are carried past the heroine. These are then contrasted with the informal, spontaneous, and joyful chaos of the veterans' gatherings throughout the capital. The juxtaposition of these two kinds of war commemoration seems to function in the film as a comment on the heroine, Lena, and her own rejection of the formal and conventional expectations for love, in the guise of marriage. She opts for the informal and unconventional and in doing so seems to feel at home among the boisterous veterans' unscripted jubilations.

The newsreel films in the period chart a similar tension between the formal and informal commemorations. Thus, a May 1959 edition of the *Novosti dnia* newsreel (number 19) contained an item referring to Victory Day and showing veterans gathering in front of the Bolshoi Theater in Moscow. The narration states that this had been a tradition on the eve of 9 May every year since 1945. The following year, in 1960, issue number 19 of the same newsreel contains a similar item, albeit with an additional focus on memorial activities around the country. Both of these items are preceded by newsreel footage of the raising of the flag over the

Reichstag (from Raizman's 1945 documentary) as the visual symbol of victory.

However, the following edition that year, *Novosti dnia* number 20, covers the more formal state occasion of a memorial held in Moscow's Palace of Sport at which Khrushchev and the minister of defense, Rodion Malinovskii, spoke. Mikhail Egorov, unaccompanied by Meliton Kantariia and wearing a suit rather than being in uniform, is shown carrying the Victory Banner into the hall. By 1961, as depicted in *Novosti dnia* number 25, the meeting was being addressed by Khrushchev, who is wearing a military uniform and has a Hero of Socialist Labor medal bestowed on him by Leonid Brezhnev. The meeting was attended by other top party officials and now was being held in the Great Hall of the Kremlin. The Victory Banner was brought in ceremonially by Egorov, Kantariia, and Samsonov, with only the last of them in uniform. A similar meeting took place on 22 June, also held in the Great Hall of the Kremlin, and was recorded in *Novosti dnia* number 26, from July 1961. By 1962, the Victory Day commemoration meeting was taking place in the Columned Hall of the House of the Unions, one of Moscow's most impressive buildings and the place where both Lenin and Stalin had lain in state.[92] These more formal proceedings are all attempts to contain, channel, and formalize Victory Day gatherings and events and their driving force: the veterans.

A 1960 short film entitled *They Raised the Victory Banner* (*Oni vodruzili Znamia Pobedy*, dir. L. Danilov) deliberately attempts to engage with the soldiers involved in the raising of the flag and does not limit itself to Egorov and Kantariia. As director Danilov put it on 6 May 1960, "Film documents of the Great Patriotic War have given us the opportunity to show the capture of the Reichstag not as an isolated episode in the war but as one of the culminating events of the war, a victory that was achieved by our entire people."[93] The emphasis on a wider sweep of participants was again part of the Khrushchev-era orientation toward showing victory as having been won by mass heroism and the whole Soviet people.

The finished film starts with a frame narrative in which Mikhail Egorov begins to tell a group of other soldiers on a train about the storming of the Reichstag. After the film illustrates the storming with the 1945 footage, he mentions those who took part in raising the flag: Kantariia, S′ianov, Neustroev, Davydov, Samsonov, Zinchenko, Shatilov, Perevertkin, Kuznetsov. The film commentary then asks, "Where are they now?" and sets off to various parts of the Soviet Union to find the men and show what they are doing now. They are then all shown coming to Moscow, where they go to dinner with Colonel Zinchenko (who lives in the capital), before visiting Red Square and then the Central Museum of the Soviet Army. There they gather by the Victory Banner, which is then once again shown in flashback to the 1945 footage from Raizman's Berlin film.

Yet here, as with the conferences, this fresh emphasis on a larger number of participants ran the danger of getting out of hand. Thus, after the Soviet Army publication *Krasnaia zvezda* published a brief item about the film on 5 April 1960, the filmmakers received a spate of letters, ten of which have been preserved in the film's archive file. These letters are all from veterans saying that they too were participants in the storming of the Reichstag. The most serious and most interesting of these letters comes from a man named Kozhevnikov and is addressed to one-time Stalin associate Kliment Voroshilov, with a copy to *Krasnaia zvezda*, and is signed by a total of twenty people.[94] The primary complaint was that politruk Aleksei Berest's name was going to be left out of the proposed film (just as he was left out of the 1960 conference).

Whereas in answering the other letters, Danilov simply replied that it was too late or that the film already spoke to their concerns, Danilov's reply here is rather different. Here he stresses that since they cannot include everyone, they concentrate on Egorov and Kantariia, who in any case have been made Heroes of the Soviet Union. The most important point, however, is that the whole approach had been prearranged with the Chief Political Directorate of the Soviet Army.[95] As with the conferences, the attempt to reconcile the voices of the veterans and the need for unifying symbols clashed. This may be seen as revealing of a tension inherent in Khrushchev's reign: an attempt to democratize ended in the invocation of the power of the state to stop it from going too far, thus laying bare the contradictions between the democratic, participatory tendencies in the Khrushchev state and its retaining of monopolistic, one-party state control.[96]

THE GREAT PATRIOTIC

While the post-Stalin period saw attempts to revisit the imagery of the Victory Banner by disassociating it from Stalin and by widening the circle of those credited with its raising, it remained a crucial symbol of the war. It succinctly told the war story in such a way as to emphasize victory. It was to play an even more salient role in the period following Khrushchev's fall from power, when the war narrative was rethought once again and the Victory Banner gained greater prominence as an image that associated victory with the state and the party and that could be safely repeated.

In 1964, the legendary Soviet filmmaker Roman Karmen, whose achievements included filming the Spanish Civil War and the siege of Leningrad and releasing the first documentary film about the Nuremberg International Military Tribunal, began work on a compilation documentary about World War II. His collaborator on this project was Sergei Smirnov, a writer and television presenter who had spent ten years tracing the survivors of the defense of the Brest Fortress. Hard as it is to imagine today, when the defenders of the Brest Fortress are celebrated as heroes, in the Stalin era the story of the fortress was told exclusively through objects, and there were said to be virtually no survivors. Thus, when Smirnov began researching the defenders' fates it turned out that most of them had undergone Nazi captivity and therefore been marginalized; they were definitely not seen as heroes by society.[97] Smirnov's efforts in documentary prose, in his television program *Tales of Heroism* (*Rasskazy o geroizme*, airing from 1962), and film scripts such as *Katiusha* (dir. Viktor Lisakovich, 1964) led to precisely the kind of eyewitness account that uniquely meshed with the Khrushchev-era promotion of "mass heroism" and personalized attitudes toward the war. Such documentary accounts were perfectly suited for the intimate and informal nature of television.[98]

The desire to tell the story of individual fates was key to the way the film set out to tell the story of the first part of the war, as the early setbacks, especially the defense of the Brest Fortress, were going to be represented through the accounts of survivors, presumably in interviews: "Those who took part in these battles are alive. The heroes of the Brest Fortress, of Lopatin's border post, of the Khanko Peninsula are all alive. We intend to convey their stories in an organic fusion with newsreel chronicles from those days. This is probably one of the most serious tasks of our film—a truthful, historically accurate documentary account of the first part of the war."[99]

With its determination to offer a narrative that encompassed the first months of the war, Karmen's *The Great Patriotic* was said—both at the time in studio documents and in later reviews in the film press—to be the first Soviet documentary film to cover the whole narrative of the war.[100] While it articulated the whole Soviet narrative, including a detailed account of the start of the war, albeit still with predictable ellipses such as the 1944 Warsaw Uprising, that narrative was actually changing while the film was still in production.

Thus, initially *The Great Patriotic* was conceived as an attempt to articulate an anti-Stalinist vision of the war with a strong emphasis on the disastrous first six months following the invasion, attributing blame for these setbacks to Stalin. An initial treatment is very outspoken:

"However, at this time, the Stalin personality cult was taking on ever more monstrous and cruel forms. Everything that had been created by the people and the Party was attributed to ONE person. The mass arrests under Beriia that had struck down honest people who were devoted to the revolution, struck down outstanding figures from the ranks of the people, the Party, the army, and the economy. And this could not but have an effect on the future mortal combat with Fascism, into which our people and our armed forces were soon to enter."[101]

This treatment likewise draws attention to Stalin's failure to see the buildup of German troops and to anticipate the German attack: "I think that it makes sense for the spectator to be told about Stalin's major errors (oversight in the evaluation of the military-political situation on the eve of war, groundless repressions of Party cadres, including in the military, high-handedness and disdain for the opinion of specialists and others). Without recounting all this, it will be hard to explain the reasons for our major setbacks at the front in the initial period of the war."[102]

Here, in these initial plans for *The Great Patriotic*, we see the renegotiation of the wartime narrative, of the framework of cultural memory, to emphasize the first years of the war much more than had previously been done in popular narratives. The radicalism of this gesture again threatened to unbalance and undermine the overall narrative of the war. Some commentators objected to this emphasis in script meetings, demanding a sense that the party was always in control, even at the start of the war:

> It strikes me that first of all you would want, even in part one of the film, to convey more clearly and distinctly the character of the war as waged by the whole people, the struggle of the people and the army organized by one center—the Central Committee of our Party. This does not come across. You do not want to commit the common mistake of people who, in fighting against the cult of personality, adopt an incorrect position in showing this period as some kind of chaotic period. There is an element of that here.[103]

A number of commentators, in studio reviews of treatments, argued that there was a need for something to compensate for the defeats and criticism of Stalin. The negative dimensions, and Stalin's shortcomings, needed ultimately to be redeemed by an uplifting ending emphasizing victory:

> The Battle of Berlin will be an important and shock episode in our film. The pathos of victory, the triumph of Soviet arms, achieving its apotheosis in the raising of banners over the Reichstag should sound here with particular force!

> Victory! The Victory Parade in Moscow. Fascist standards at the foot of the mausoleum. Soviet people rejoicing. In this very short proposal we will not be deciding in advance on the device that will help us to highlight with the greatest dramatic force this culminating episode of the film, the episode of the Soviet people's great Victory.
>
> The solution to this episode will be born in the process of work on the scenario.[104]

At the discussion of the initial scenario in March 1964, one speaker urges caution over criticism of Stalin:

> The exposing of the Stalin personality cult is a very complex and delicate question, and in cinema it has probably become more sensational than in print. When addressing this question, it should not become an end in itself. In this film, everything serves to reveal how much effort and labor the Soviet people and Party had to expend in overcoming the aftereffects of the cult of personality. Therefore, the cult of personality needs to be shown in such a way as to emphasize the significance of our victory in the circumstances. Stalin attributed all the achievements of the Great Patriotic war only to himself. We need to show the whole pantheon of military commanders of this period in full. This will look much more convincing than if we simply say about this that Stalin attributed all the achievements of the Great Patriotic war only to himself. We should, I repeat, show the military council and its participants. In this document, the accent should be on the role of the Party as an organizer of victory in this great battle of the Soviet people.[105]

The anxiety concerns whether the emphasis on showing, and criticizing, Stalin might undermine the overall narrative of victory. To compensate, the suggestion is that the generals and the party be shown more. Similarly, a review by an unnamed historical consultant representing the Institute of Marxism-Leninism, dated 5 January 1965, points out that Hitler is very prominent in the plans for the film but that no equivalent figure opposes him:

> *A necessary sense of proportion should be maintained in the screen* depiction of Hitler, and other leaders of the fascist bloc *on the one hand, and the Soviet leaders, and also the heads of the government of anti-Fascist coalition countries on the other hand.* In reading the scenario one gets an impression of the "demonic force" of Hitler's personality: his will determines the fate of the German people and other peoples of Europe; he is the head of state and the armed forces, single-handedly making the most important political and strategic decisions; he incarnates the whole evil and loathsome nature of Fascism, and his name appears throughout the pages of the scenario. No one

> is counterposed to him—there is no equally *powerful positive figure either in the Soviet Union or in the other countries of the anti-Fascist coalition* (apart from a few compliments the author pays to Roosevelt).
>
> The "personification" of events in Hitler needs to be toned down, Hitler *mentioned* less, and more mention made of Fascism and of *the true rulers of the Third Reich who stood behind Hitler.* At the same time, you should not be afraid of naming the leaders of the Soviet state and the Soviet armed forces. Without in any way renouncing the critique of Stalin's personality cult, you *need to show Stalin in 1941 at the 6 November meeting, at the 7 November parade* (in the scenario Stalin first appears at the Tehran conference in December 1943). If I am not mistaken, the scenario does not identify the Supreme Commander, Chair of the State Committee for Defense. The scenario *does not mention* head of the Soviet state *M. I. Kalinin* either. It does not mention that Marshal *G. K. Zhukov* was Supreme Commander, and the names of commanders of the General Staff B. M. *Shaposhnikov*, A. M. *Vasil'evskii*, and A. I. *Antonov* are not mentioned once. In a word, it is as if the Soviet people and its armed forces fight and wage war with no leaders.
>
> This impression can be weakened if there are fewer mentions of Hitler, his ministers, and generals, and if all events in Germany are not associated with the name of Hitler, while at the same time depicting Soviet leaders in a reasonable manner.
>
> There is also little attention paid in the scenario to *the leadership of the Communist Party. It is hard to do this with cinema, but in the text the leading role of the Party needs to be reflected more clearly.*
>
> . . . In the scenario, the episodes of our military setbacks and retreats are more vivid than the episodes of advances and victories.[106]

In seeking a powerful symbolic counterweight to the figure of Hitler, and to the defeats of the early part of the war, the filmmakers are being asked to place greater emphasis on victory, leaders, and the party. Depiction of the war could not be permitted to be negative or to undermine the basic hierarchy of Soviet society. It was possible now, after the October 1964 fall of Khrushchev, to mention Stalin more, and at a 22 March 1965 internal studio discussion of the film, director Lia Derbysheva proposes that more emphasis be placed on him:

> I realize that the question of Stalin is rather complex. But a quarter of a century has passed. How long does it have to be before we can honestly and coherently talk about this? We have to find some kind of limits. We know that Stalin did not see the start of the war coming due to his despotism, but we also know that people achieved victory in Stalin's name, because they had the banner of the Party, the banner of the Soviet Union. It is no secret, after

> all, that the overall decisions were made under Stalin's leadership. We can't attribute all problems to him in the way that all victories were previously attributed to him.
>
> Can we possibly talk in a coherent and philosophical way about our tragedy, our faith, and our victory, because faith in Stalin in many ways helped us to achieve victory. How can we not talk about this at all?[107]

Another suggestion is to show Stalin but with him as part of a group of leaders or in conversation with others (as with the earlier *In Defense of Peace*).[108] However, this was a strategy the filmmakers did not want to indulge too much, given the de-Stalinizing emphasis of the original film, even if the outspokenly anti-Stalinist Smirnov was taken off the project after Brezhnev came to power. Nevertheless, there was still ongoing uncertainty and controversy as to depictions of Stalin in the early Brezhnev years. Legendary director Aleksandr Medvedkin describes the problem as "a tough nut to crack," one requiring a clever solution:

> The roles of the Party and of Stalin are not presented in this film as they should be. I understand that it's a tough nut to crack, that you can't just show Stalin and Khrushchev all over the place. This is a question of great tact and a big part of the line of our propaganda today. Many, in searching for literal truthfulness, end up making political mistakes, but you can't avoid this question. You're not making a film just for distribution tomorrow but for future generations.
>
> I think what's needed is a very clever, responsible, and courageous solution, and I don't see that here.[109]

As well as making Stalin and the party more prominent, the writers were told to show the first part of the war in a more positive manner:

> There could be objections against the somewhat minor tone of the first part in which there are motifs of the losses and impossible odds faced by our troops resisting the rabid offensive of the Fascist hordes.
>
> It seems to me that when showing the first part of the Great Patriotic War, which was so hard for the country of the Soviets, the authors should stress that the foundation for our victory was already being laid.[110]

Effectively, the beginning of the war could still be shown, but it now needed to be seen through the prism of victory, with the party and Stalin in control. Nevertheless, a "clever and courageous solution" was found regarding this "tough nut to crack"—the Victory Banner. A script was now produced with a sequence of the Victory Banner at the start of the film:

> *Victory*
> The raising of Banners over the Reichstag
> Victory Parade on Red Square in Moscow
> The face of the country after the war
> Ruins of buildings, factories
> Reconstruction of the economy
> Return of demobilized troops.[111]

In a subsequent variant, immediately after a prologue, the familiar scenes from Raizman's film of the battle of Berlin appear. The narrator intones, "The storm of the last citadel of German fascism—the Reichstag, and the memorable image—the raising of the Victory Banner by Soviet soldiers on the roof of the Reichstag."[112]

This later version also underlined the Reichstag's symbolism, by showing the 1945 fires in Berlin as a means of narrative closure and by reminding viewers that the Nazis set the Reichstag on fire in 1933:

> The last fires in Berlin were burning.
>
> In Berlin itself, here, twelve years earlier, in 1933, one night another fire broke out.
>
> The Reichstag burned, burned by Hitler's storm troopers.
>
> This nighttime fire was the portent of the future fires of the Second World War, of all the misfortunes that humanity was destined to undergo.
>
> This fire meant that Hitler gained total power in Germany.[113]

As the film evolved, the symbol of the Victory Banner came to take on still greater prominence, as a way of representing the party, underscoring the symbolic and emotional importance of victory, the aura and sacred power of the moment of victory. As well as completing the narrative that conferred meaning upon the war, it was an attractive, visually arresting, and inspirational way of showing the Soviet cause and continuity of party control without mentioning Stalin, Khrushchev, or any of the potentially contentious figures. The way in which the film re-creates a narrative with familiar, visually striking symbols is evident in the contradictory praise it received. Some acclaimed its efforts to discover and use unusual, fresh, previously "unseen" material; as one member of the studio's artistic council, Fortuchnyi, says, "Everything is underpinned by authentic material, unlike normal scripts."[114] By contrast, however, other documentary studio people argue that the images it uses images are too familiar. Thus, S. D. Bubrik says, "It's true that there are also shots that pass like a boomerang from one film into another. In Stalingrad, for example, the shot with the pioneers' fountain is already unwatchable [i.e., too clichéd], but there are a great many such shots."[115] The right of

3.4. The Pioneers' Fountain in Stalingrad, in an image from the film *Stalingrad* (dir. Leonid Varlamov, 1943).

the film to repeat images, such as that of the Young Pioneers statue in Stalingrad, is defended by another filmmaker from the studio, A. G. Semin, who asserts that this same shot of the fountain is important as a "historical landmark":

> I think that some shots that we have already seen should stay in the film. I think that the Pioneers' Fountain in Stalingrad should stay. But the soldier in the ruins of Mozdok who walks past a burning building does not add anything, because looking at him, you know that you've seen all this before. I saw this soldier and remembered that I had seen this many times. Therefore, we should avoid those shots that are not vitally important [*ne imeiut printsipial'nogo znacheniia*], that have not entered into the history of cinematography as historical landmarks, and most likely that is what will be done.[116]

In response to this defense of the film, and on seeing the silent variant of the finished film in April 1965, Bubrik revises his earlier criticisms:

> As for well known and less well known shots. When we discussed the first part of the film, I spoke about the image of Stalingrad, where we see Young Pioneers dancing, and that this shot figures in all films about the war. Now I know that I am wrong. This shot is a symbol. Then I said that we do not need to show shots that everybody knows, but now I would say that we do because these are symbol shots [*plany-simvoly*]. They symbolize the whole episode.

> And hasn't the Reichstag become a symbol? Consequently, we should not be afraid of such symbol shots, even if they run through dozens of films.[117]

These "symbol shots," like those of the children's statue in Stalingrad and of the Reichstag, by which he presumably means the Victory Banner, are film versions of what we know as "iconic images," and the Stalingrad and Reichstag images, standing for crucial junctures in the Soviet war narrative, are seen as crucial to the articulation of the war narrative in this groundbreaking film. Unlike Hariman and Lucaites's account of photographic "iconic images" in the US context, they are becoming less a site of contest and more an expression of a stable, authoritarian interpretation of the war as victorious, serving to foreclose the difficult debate as to the reasons why the war started and cost so many lives.[118] Continuing the discussion, Semin further defends the need to repeat these images but argues that it is not their repetition per se that is important but rather the way in which they enable the articulation of a powerful, emotionally engaging narrative:

> In such a film there should be, and what we expect are profoundly exciting episodes, that are not created chronologically, but with the very methods of documentary cinematography, the methods of art, so that the future spectator gets a lump in their throat. That's precisely the kind of film that should be made. No chronology, no matter how detailed the exposition, is capable of doing that because historically it is all more or less familiar to us: that we won the battle of Stalingrad, Kursk, forded the Dniepr, took Kiev, reached Berlin, and raised the Victory Banner over the Reichstag. And the power of these documents should not lie in the fact that we repeat them in the film[;] after all we've seen them in various films, but their strength should lie in the way the authors tell the story as artists, with an air of excitement, so the spectator gets excited along with us.[119]

Nevertheless, the repetition of "iconic" images was clearly critical to the success of this film and the way in which the compilation film in general works. In post-Stalin culture, repetition plays a special role, as Alexei Yurchak has shown, with ritualized formulas taking the place of genuine debate and the possibility of reassessment.[120] The Victory Banner becomes a visual version of this ritualized discourse of authoritarian repetition.

The completed film makes the raising of the Victory Banner over the Reichstag central and makes the link with the red flag raised over Stalingrad, stressing that this was the banner that Soviet troops had brought from Stalingrad. This then enables a flashback to the Reichstag fire and a juxtaposition of Nazi red flags and communist ones (though all of this is black-and-white footage). The flashback to the Reichstag fire is specifically praised in the artistic council; at the final screening, on 23 April 1965, one director, Fedor Kiselev, says, "The episode with the Reichstag and the fire is wonderfully done, where there is a digression and the team say what happened."[121] Curiously, this flashback to the Reichstag fire is the one that, as we have seen in chapter 1, Raizman had planned for the original 1945 film.

At its release, *The Great Patriotic* was shown in the prestigious Rossiia cinema on Pushkin Square on 8 May.[122] Reviewers commented on the narrative power of the film, and critic Konstantin Slavin was quick to identify its narrative turning points—Brest, Stalingrad, Berlin: "The film is dedicated to those to whom it fell to restore hope for salvation to the world—the Soviet soldier who bore the first blows of Hitler's armies in June 1941, who resisted at Stalingrad, who raised the Victory Banner over the Reichstag. In the film, nothing is forgotten. . . . In the film, the heroes of Brest and heroes of Berlin are praised."[123]

The imagery of the Victory Banner was crucial in the articulation of this reconstructed narrative of the war. However, it is worth reflecting on how *The Great Patriotic* achieves this narrative coherence and symbolic power by playing down other narratives. One of those is that of Stalin's crimes, the significance of which is diminished by the renewed emphasis on victory, as well as the Victory Banner, seen at both the beginning and end of the narrative of the war. A further dimension of the war muted by the final film was that of the Nazis' murder of Jews. After earlier versions of the scripts were rejected for showing too much "terror" and for containing clear references to "Jewish ghettos" and the Nazis' specific attempt to annihilate Jews, the final film places its references to the Nazis' crimes in a long list of victims, including the Jews, imparting a certain vagueness and universality.[124] Moreover, the episode is placed in the middle of the Stalingrad narrative. This ensures that the battle comes across not simply as a battle for national survival, in the framing of the "patriotic" war, but also as a struggle on behalf of the various peoples of Europe, in their liberation from a generalized Nazi exploitation. Moreover, the meaning of the Holocaust, as well as wider Nazi policies of forced labor, is subordinated to that of the battle of Stalingrad, to the overall narrative of Victory.

For trenchant anti-Stalinist critics, the film was not a coherent whole. This was because the highly unusual images depicting the early period of the war and the Nazis' crimes could not be made part of the glorious story of redemptive victory, since they stood in stark contrast to the familiar images of the end—of the Victory Banner and Victory Parade, as well as the all-too-familiar voice of God commentary by

Leonid Khmara, familiar to many as one of the narrators of wartime newsreels.[125]

While *The Great Patriotic* ultimately succeeded in packing the whole war into a short but engaging narrative span, in large part due to its use of "symbol shots" or iconic footage, during the course of its production there were many debates about the appropriate size for the planned film. At a final internal studio screening, veteran documentary studio director Roman Grigor′ev argued that the film was insufficiently concise and concentrated in its message.[126] At earlier script meetings too, there were concerns about the film's length, with someone saying that it would require four films (not two); there were deliberations as to whether to release both parts immediately or to release the first part and then delay the second.[127] This approach was quickly rejected because, it was suggested, people simply would not go back to the cinema four times, as they would for the widely screened Western film *Tarzan*; they do not know what's coming in the *Tarzan* films, but they do know what happened after the battle of Stalingrad. It would be a different matter if the documentary were being shown on television:

> If the film was intended for television, then you could have 26 episodes or maybe even 39 30-minute episodes.
>
> But this is a work of art and everything needs to be presented in a rather compressed way. . . .
>
> Two parts is probably the maximum for a documentary film. . . . You have to think about the spectator and not about the enormous quantity of material.[128]

The mention of television is important, however, since the compilation genre was to find its true home in that broadcast medium, where documentary series of "26 30-minute episodes" were already being produced in the United States (e.g., NBC's *Victory at Sea* in 1952–1953). The Soviets too, indeed Karmen himself, returned to the same topic, even under the same title (for the Soviet release of *The Unknown War*), a little more than a decade later, to produce a twenty-part television series. Once again the focus would end up on the overall narrative rather than on the intimate, the personal experience, or individual fates, a dimension of *The Great Patriotic* that was ultimately sidelined along with its champion, Smirnov. Indeed, one commentator criticizes *The Great Patriotic* for lack of human material and compares it negatively with Andrei Tarkovskii's 1962 film about the war, *Ivan's Childhood*, for its personal perspective on the tragic losses of the war.[129] Instead, *The Great Patriotic* insisted on the meaningful nature of sacrifice, and the Victory Banner was key to the articulation of that narrative.

3.5. The Victory Banner being carried in the 1965 Victory Day parade in Moscow. From *Twentieth Anniversary of the Great Feat* (*20-letie velikogo podviga*, dir. Irina Setkina and Elena Vermisheva, 1965).

THE GREAT TURNING POINT, 1965

The way in which *The Great Patriotic* ended up articulating and drawing on the aura of the Victory Banner as a symbol for the Soviet victory and the Soviet state was a logic that was to be repeated on a grander scale but in different media, in the reorganized Central Museum of the Armed Forces, which opened in new premises, and in the Victory Day commemorations of 9 May 1965, where it took pride of place at the reinvented ceremony. Indeed, in the specially commissioned film of the parade, *20th Anniversary of the Great Feat* (*20-letie velikogo podviga*, dir. Irina Setkina and Elena Vermisheva, 1965), there were an enormous number of close-ups of the Victory Banner. It is likewise referred to as a "holy relic of war" in the voice-over commentary. The cultivation of the holy associations of the Victory Banner was a key means of generating symbolic authority in the absence of the Stalin cult or a new leader cult.

This need for symbols conferring legitimacy became especially apparent as the foundational myth of the revolution that had taken place more than forty years earlier grew ever more distant, so that its power to legitimize Brezhnev's sudden power grab was limited. Moreover, Brezhnev's unexceptional personality was unsuited to becoming the center of a new personality cult.[130] Thus, Brezhnev's launching of the cult of Victory within months of assuming control was about creating a way of shoring up support for the Soviet state that would not require the creation of a charismatic leader cult around him. The years since Stalin's death had seen a half-hearted attempt to denounce the Stalin cult, contradicted by the ongoing and reinvigorated veneration of the Lenin cult and tentative efforts to create a Khrushchev leader cult (such as emphasizing him in the rewritten history of the party).[131] Brezhnev, however, could not be the main force bolstering the power of the state, despite unsuccessful efforts from the mid-1970s. The Great Patriotic War cult not only had tremendous legitimizing force, it was also an enormously stabilizing factor—stability was the underlying watchword of the Brezhnev apparatus.[132] Thus, it was capable of functioning irrespective of the personal intervention of a given leader; it continued to work when Brezhnev was incapacitated by ill health in the 1970s and ultimately, despite almost becoming defunct in the 1980s and 1990s, was able to regenerate and spring back to life, functioning beyond his lifetime and the life of the Soviet political system it was built to serve.

The politicized use of history was a strategy Khrushchev effectively employed by denouncing the crimes of Stalin. It was a way of surprising and unsettling his opponents within the party and bolstering his own authority.[133] What Brezhnev was doing, in elevating the importance of the Great Patriotic War, was also boosting his own authority. However, rather than surprising and unsettling his opponents, his strategy was more like the creation of a comfort blanket of memory, one that the opposition and the wider country could all agree was a good thing.

Brezhnev's brother told an anecdote in which he asked Leonid Il′ich whether communism would ever be achieved. The general secretary replied, "'What do you mean[,] Communism? We killed the Tsar, destroyed the churches. The people need something to cling on to. . . . Superstition is better,' commented the General Secretary with conviction[;] 'it's better to have something stupid and ignorant, but with a faith in tomorrow.'"[134]

Analogously, in place of the previous, albeit very cautiously iconoclastic mood under Khrushchev, we witness here a process of re-creating and encouraging an atmosphere of veneration and recharging of the Victory Banner with the aura of the sacred.[135] In addition to serving as a symbol representing the final, most triumphant moment of the Soviet victory, articulating an "affectively charged" narrative, it is also a museum object, a "palpable relic" housed in a museum with an ostensibly educational function. Finally, it has played and continues to play a role in "commemoration rites" with an increasingly wide dimension of "collective participation," most notably in Victory Day commemorations.

A striking example of the abandonment of the iconoclastic mood is the renewed veneration of Egorov and Kantariia, who, the conferences in the Institute of Marxism-Leninism had demonstrated unanimously, had not actually put up the original flag over the Reichstag. In addition to them there is Konstantin Samsonov, widely seen to have had nothing to do with raising the Victory Banner but simply to have had the influence to get his very self-serving account accepted.

Thus, while Brezhnev's wildly applauded 8 May 1965 speech was famous for its positive mention of Stalin, it also referred to the Victory Banner and the men credited with raising it over the Reichstag, marking a sharp contrast with the Khrushchev era.[136] The men who raised the banner are listed among a pantheon of heroes:

> Seven million Soviet soldiers have been decorated with medals by the Soviet Union for their bravery and heroism displayed in battle with the Fascists, 11 thousand people have been awarded the title Hero of the Soviet Union.
>
> Who can forget the immortal feats of Aleksandr Matrosov, Nikolai Gastello, Iurii Smirnov, Vasilii Zaitsev, Aleksandr Pokryshkin, Ivan Kozhedub, Aleksei Mares′ev, and many others. Who does not know the glorious names of Mikhail Egorov, Meliton Kantariia, and Konstantin Samsonov, who raised the Victory Banner over the Reichstag. (Applause).[137]

Commemoration of victory was a way of furthering the restoration of the Stalin cult, or certain dimensions of it, as Roi Medvedev has argued, but it is not widely acknowledged that the Victory Banner now began to fill the vacuum vacated by Stalin, conferring charismatic aura and legitimacy on the Soviet system, just as the leader cult had.[138]

Nevertheless, this was not such a carefully planned business as might be thought. Maksimenkov describes the organization of the 9 May 1965 Victory Day parade as an extemporization due to the unexpected change in leadership but one that turned out to be successful.[139] This is corroborated by the archival documents, which show that the arrangements were rather last minute and gained momentum very quickly. Thus, the resolutions declaring that 9 May should become a public holiday (as it had been prior to 1948) were only agreed to on 27–31 March, a little more than a month beforehand.[140] Moreover, the shifting of the traditional military parade from 1 to 9 May was only agreed to on 15 April:

> XVI—On the conducting of a military parade on Victory Day 9 May 1965 (Comrades Brezhnev, Podgornyi, Mikoian, Kosygin).
>
> To conduct a military parade on Red Square on 9 May 1965 on the day of the 20th anniversary of the victory of the Soviet people in the Great Patriotic War of the Soviet Union 1941–1945. Not to conduct a military parade on 1 May.[141]

Despite their somewhat improvised nature, however, these preparations were incredibly ambitious and aimed to engage every possible level of society in some dimension of the commemorations. Thus, in addition to the new building of the Central Museum of the Armed Forces, to be opened prior to Victory Day, there was a press campaign at all levels.[142] This media effort included a distribution of photographic materials and a ceremonial meeting in the Kremlin Palace of Congresses on 8 May, which was attended by selected Moscow workers and representatives of the armed forces. There were detailed plans for the publication of memoirs and books and articles of all kinds. Novosti Press Agency (whose focus was overseas distribution) was to prepare articles, and members of the Soviet Council of Ministers' State Committee for Cinema were to work with the Chief Political Directorate of the Soviet Army and the Navy to release two films on Victory Day: *Story of a Great Feat* (*Povest′ o velikom podvige*), which was a feature-length documentary, and the short film *A Relic of Military Glory* (*Relikviia boevoi slavy*). There was likewise to be a film festival organized in every cinema and film club in the land, showing "the best feature and documentary films about the Great Patriotic War and the contemporary life of the fleet."[143] Television and radio were similarly to have programs on the theme of victory. The task of organizing all of this was given to Nikolai Mesiatsev, who was appointed chair of Gostelradio immediately following Khrushchev's removal, in October 1964. With his wartime past and service under Stalin, his career might be compared to that of Brezhnev himself, and he was able to impart the required tone to Soviet television's focus on the war.[144] There were many facets to this, including the first Soviet television drama series, *We Call Fire on Ourselves* (*Vyzyvaem ogon′ na sebia*), itself on the war theme, but two programs stand out in particular: the 9 May televised broadcasts of the *Minute of Silence* (*Minuta molchaniia*) and the coverage of the Victory Day parade.

While there had been television coverage of Red Square parades previously, as well as newsreel film of the 1945 parade, the unprecedented fact of a military parade on Red Square on 9 May required improvisation and reinvention, and television coverage was central to the diffusion of this, becoming at this moment a key part of the tradition of Soviet war commemoration.

The 1965 television coverage of the Victory Day parade in fact did not begin on 9 May but built up to it steadily during late April and early May, with the storming of the Reichstag as one focus: television programs, including news bulletins, referred to 1 May as the moment of the storming of the Reichstag, as well as May Day.[145] The Victory Banner in particular can be seen as symbolizing the deep connection between Victory Day and May Day. Thus, the text, carefully scripted in advance but televised live, was put through a number of revisions and vetted by a military censor. It starts,

> Attention! This is Moscow calling and broadcasting!
>
> Live from Red Square!
>
> We are a few minutes from the start of the military parade in honor of the 20th anniversary of the day of Victory of the Soviet People in the Great Patriotic War.
>
> Today the traditional date of the May Day parade has been changed and it will be held on Victory Day.[146]

The sense in which this is a break from convention is further emphasized by the commentary, which instructs the viewer as to the importance and distinguishing features of the Victory Banner:

> The usual ritual of the military parade has been changed today. The parade will start with the dearest military relic, the Victory Banner.
>
> (Commands)
>
> The Victory Banner on Red Square. It is being carried by Hero of the Soviet Union Colonel Samsonov. Twenty years ago he was a First Lieutenant and commander of the battalion that stormed the Reichstag. The assistants to the Victory Banner are Heroes of the Soviet Union Mikhail EGOROV and Meliton KANTARIIA . . .
>
> The Victory Banner . . . a red calico flag. On it are written the name and number of the division, the soldiers of which carried out the final assault on Hitler's citadel.
>
> The Victory Banner. It is accompanied by a guard of honor from the Army, Navy, and Air Force. Young soldiers of our army. They are following those whose hands held the flagstaff of that banner at the heroic moments of the storming of the Reichstag.[147]

The repetition of constructions that start paragraphs with the words "the Victory Banner" serves as a very insistent way of underlining its importance. The audience members throughout the Soviet Union who received the live broadcast through the groundbreaking technology of simultaneous satellite transmission were being instructed as to the banner's importance, its sacred character. A tradition was being invented, setting a template for parades to this day.

Even then, however, for all the explicitly acknowledged novelty of the parade, it simultaneously harked back to the June 1945 parade, starting at the same time of 10:00 a.m. and even more directly, through references in the voice-over text to the throwing of Nazi banners to the ground in front of the mausoleum.[148]

The commentary also stressed the continuity between generations, as those marching in 1965 were taking up the baton of tradition passed from those who had paraded in 1945. In this way, it articulated an important subtext to the Victory Parade from this point onward: the banner embodies societal and intergenerational unity.

Letters to the broadcast agency showed that there was an incredible appetite for this public, ritualized commemoration of the war: the authorities were responding to grassroots demand.[149] The other tradition birthed by television that was at least as successful was the introduction of a minute of silence, first broadcast on television and radio at 6:50 p.m. on 9 May 1965, a time and date that it has occupied ever since. Mesiatsev took a personal hand in the combined effort of writing the text that was broadcast prior to the silent minute itself. This was a kind of prayer that focused and attuned viewers to the solemnity of the actual silence, suggesting what they think about.[150] When first broadcast, it was so powerful and unusual that neither Mesiatsev nor the other members of his team could stop themselves from crying.[151]

Assuring the correct emphasis on heroism was key: this was to be achieved not only through the narrative and rituals stressing victory but also through the bestowing of medals, which was to become a notable obsession for Brezhnev himself. A group of heroes of the Soviet Union, from various Union republics, would be invited to Moscow.[152] New medals were awarded: "20 Years of the Victory in the Great Patriotic War 1941–1945" and "For Victory over Germany in the Great Patriotic War 1941–1945."[153] The release of special commemorative coins resembled and thus recalled these medals. There were also many monuments being built around the country, overwhelmingly with a heroic message rather than one of mourning.[154]

The watchword in Brezhnev-era propaganda was "stability," sometimes rendered as "stable orthodoxy."[155] In a conference of party propagandists, the invitees insisted on this, stressing that the recent period had seen an expansion of the party but that training had lacked continuity and thoroughness.[156] One speaker, from Vladimir Oblast′ Committee of the Party (*obkom*), complained of the zigzags in histories of the war, first exaggerating the role of Stalin and then that of Khrushchev. "Where is the truth?" he asked.[157] Insisting on the memory of the war, as well as on highly rigid, ritualized formulas, was a way of assuring stability and continuity. In visual terms—indeed even in verbal terms—the Victory Banner was a fixed symbol, one that could be used to assure and signify stability and continuity. But at the same time, it possessed an aura, a sacred charge that could supply some of the charismatic legitimacy now missing from Soviet political discourse.

Mark Edele comments on the ways in which this was much more than a state-sponsored cult. But while the reinstatement of Victory Day commemorations was popular, it was also closely monitored.[158] Brezhnev's partial rehabilitation of Stalin went together with the silencing of complex, ambiguous, "Remarquist" representations of the war that suffered from "abstract humanism and pacifism."[159] Edele, however, also notes that the thaw-era emphasis on ordinary people's contributions to the war, referred to by the formula coined in the Khrushchev period of "mass heroism," a facet muted under Stalin, continued to play an important role in the Brezhnev era.[160] This slightly nuances the claim, articulated by sociologist Boris Dubin, that following 9 May 1965 the state became the monopolistic keeper of memory and constructor of history.[161] Rather, the state made a concerted attempt to co-opt and control all grassroots initiatives, such as memorial meetings of veterans and the writing of memoirs.

Edele argues that the notion of the war as "a living religion" is a productive way of approaching the mixture of top-down and grassroots commemorative practices. He argues that "this quasi-metaphysical system of memory of and communion with the dead now flowered not only into a whole pantheon of heroes, saints, and villains but also a fully-fledged set of rituals, large and small, of symbols and gestures suffusing everyday life and punctuating the year."[162]

The physical artifact of the Victory Banner had a special capacity to bridge these different kinds of visions of the war: it was a material, visually striking object that could be situated within a network of personal testimony in memoirs, as well as in photographs and newsreel film records of it supposedly being raised and flying over the Reichstag.[163] But at the same time, its singularity and display at Moscow's Central Museum of the Soviet Army and on Red Square on Victory Day gave it a spectacular and hierarchical charge that was redolent of and still residually associated with the leader cult: it could be mobilized to prevent the "war cult" from becoming too horizontal and democratic. Indeed, the Khrushchev-era attempt to de-Stalinize the war had established, at the two specially convened conferences attended by the participants in the storming of the Reichstag, that the raising of the flag was a process in which a large number of individuals took part and that the elevation of Egorov and Kantariia as the sole raisers of the flag was an error connected to the "cult of personality," that is, of the Stalin cult, and needed to be reassessed in favor of a notion of "mass heroism."[164] This version did not make it to the final published edition of the *History of the Great Patriotic War*, as such inconvenient, iconoclastic complexities had been decisively banished by the 1965 Victory Day parade and the appearance of Egorov and Kantariia as flag bearers. Henceforth, access to archives was strictly controlled for fear documents might be found that would support an alternative view.[165] Memoirs were still more tightly controlled and vetted by the author's comrades and commanders, ensuring that undesired themes were edited out.[166]

Despite an emphasis on history and true historical knowledge, the efforts of serious historians to debunk and demythologize were ultimately undermined in this period in favor of a mythologized, ritualized account that still owes most of its imagery and its overall narrative to the Stalin era.

After Brezhnev came to power there were rumors that Stalin would be restored to the mausoleum.[167] While this never happened, and even references and representations of Stalin remained fairly rare, symbols associated with him were revived, nowhere more so than with representations of the war, which could hardly be made plausible without depictions of Stalin. It is in this period, when the fully fledged war cult first starts to coalesce, that the Victory Banner as cinematic "symbol shot" or "iconic image," one enabling a complex narrative to be conveyed succinctly, as photographic icon and as museum and ritual artifact, comes to play a particularly important role. It fulfills the need for new symbols to confer stability through ritualized, authoritarian repetition, something that is particularly important in difficult times and in times of transition.[168] It projects a charismatic and mystical aura on the state, helping to fill the vacuum left by the critique and collapse of the Stalin cult. At the same time, it could be taken as a cipher for the Stalin cult and the victory in war that was won under his leadership. This curious mutability, not infinite but within a spectrum of rigid, ritualized, meanings, was to be key to the longevity and enduring appeal of the Victory Banner to the end of the Soviet era and beyond.

4

THE VICTORY CULT IN THE AGE OF TELEVISION

Paradoxically, despite the conservatism of the Brezhnev years, the 1965 Victory Day parade presented a marked break with the patterns of commemoration of the war over the preceding twenty years. That year the government reinstituted Victory Day as a public holiday and conferred an unprecedented importance on Victory as a memory uniting the Soviet nation. It also reinvented the Victory Parade, now hoisting the Victory Banner for television cameras. However, after 1965 there were no more military parades on 9 May until 1985, after Leonid Brezhnev's death, and public commemorations generally reverted to the informal, spontaneous traditions instituted by veterans immediately following the war. These traditions typically involved reunions in Moscow, often in front of the Bolshoi Theater, on Red Square, in Gorky Park, and of course by the Victory Banner display in the Central Museum of the Soviet Army. In part, as we shall see, this pattern of commemorative practice was probably connected to the rise of Brezhnev's own personality cult, unlikely and unconvincing as it was, and it may also have been because the 1965 parade was conceived as a one-time exercise, undertaken in exceptional circumstances of political instability.

In this period the narrative and cult of Victory, with the Victory Banner playing a crucial part, was adapted to more diverse media, especially television and cinematic forms reacting to the rise of television. It was also one in which the Soviet Union made a concerted effort to get across its interpretation to the wider world through the export of its films. At the same time, however, there remained a certain fluidity to the commemorations, with many of the elements of the cult of Victory still in flux. In addition to the informal gatherings and concerts, which paradoxically were themselves still usually planned meticulously, despite their appearance,

4.1. Tomb of the Unknown Soldier, at the Kremlin Wall in Moscow. Courtesy of kultura.ru.

there were also more formal features of the festivities that were not just mandated but also performed by the state, such as an artillery salute in the evening, usually at 22:00 local time, in the capitals of Soviet republics and Hero cities, and formal greetings offered by the leaders of other communist states to the Soviet leaders, with the German Democratic Republic usually most prominent among these. The GDR leaders were in turn usually greeted prominently in the press, on the front pages of *Pravda* and *Izvestiia*, by the Soviet communist leadership. The implication was that the GDR's commitment to peace and socialism was one of the war's and the Soviet bloc's great achievements. Sometimes this pattern was altered slightly to convey a not-so-subtle topical subtext, as with the 9 May 1968 greetings sent to Alexander Dubček and the leaders of Czechoslovakia on the anniversary of the liberation of Czechoslovakia, which stressed the importance of Soviet-Czechoslovak friendship and the certainty that it would continue to the benefit of both peoples and "in the interests of socialism and communism."[1] In August, Prague saw another kind of military parade, as the Warsaw Pact sent in its tanks to overthrow Dubček.

Instead of a 9 May military parade, the key focus of commemorations of the war in this period was on grief: the observing of a minute's silence on the evening of 9 May and the public, often ceremonial laying of wreaths on tombs, usually performed by the country's leaders on 8 May, the eve of Victory Day. An important development for such rituals was the official opening, in 1967, of the Tomb of the Unknown Soldier, by the Kremlin Wall. In addition to being located by the Kremlin Wall, the resting place of martyrs to the revolutionary cause, the tomb's connection to the revolutionary traditions was underlined by the way in which the flame was brought from Leningrad, from the fire that burned above the Field of Mars memorial to those who had died in the February and October 1917 revolutions and the Civil War. It also included "holy" earth from common graves of the wartime dead from various sites around the country.[2] References to the "eternal" and the "sacred" were frequent when referring to the war and became more so with the dedication of the Tomb of the Unknown Soldier.

From the moment of its opening for public visits, the tomb would become an important focus for war commemorations, although, unlike the Victory Banner, it did not emphasize the narrative of victory directly. The Tomb of the Unknown Soldier was also important in this period for televised representations of the commemorations. For example, the twenty-five-minute-long program *A Minute's Silence* built up to the silence while showing a picture of the eternal flame. Television played a crucial role in shaping viewers' responses to the new rituals, directing thoughts and prompting emotions. This even preceded the creation of the Tomb of the Unknown Soldier in Moscow: a 1965 viewers' survey stressed the emotional power of the minute's silence and detailed some special remembrance rituals observed by the bereaved.[3] One viewer, V. N. Serov, a teacher from Moscow, wrote to recommend that the minute's silence be a permanent feature and that a memorial with an eternal flame be erected in Moscow.[4]

The success of the minute's silence, the accompanying television program, and the centrality of eternal flames at many memorials around the Soviet Union suggest that the dominant tone of World War II commemorations in this period, for all their insistent articulation of the narrative of victory, in fact focused on grief, and with the desire for peace as a dimension of that grief more than had been the case previously. This tone, along with the ongoing sense that veterans could be an unruly group, is part of the success of the 1971 film *Belorussian Station* (*Belorusskii vokzal*, dir. Andrei Smirnov), which tells the story of four veterans who gather at the funeral for a fifth. Following various adventures, which include breaking the law, they end up singing their battalion song in the flat of their unit's nurse. The song, "We Need One Victory" ("Nam nuzhna odna pobeda"), by Bulat Okudzhava, strikes a balance between the tragic and the triumphant, as his biographer put it.[5] This tragic note, however, was what enabled the film to escape censorship, since its depiction of the militia was deemed subversive. It was saved only because Brezhnev cried while watching it.[6]

While there were no 9 May military parades in the Brezhnev period apart from the one in 1965, his rule saw an expansion of the military, as well as the projection of military power, which became the glue holding society together, according to some accounts of the period.[7] Correspondingly, there were still enormous military parades, but they occurred on 7 November; thus, the symbolic framework for militarism remained the Soviet communist festivities, whereas 9 May was not used in this manner. The Victory cult clearly was at this point not yet the dominant, hegemonic memory it has sometimes been claimed to be.

Nevertheless, war memory performed an important function, and a key dimension of this period was an intensifying attempt both to return to the sense that the war conferred greatness upon the nation and to turn away from the emphasis on Stalin's mistakes and the reverses of the early years of the war, as was characteristic of the narrative in the Khrushchev period. Thus, the 1937–1938 purges of the military were passed over in the 1974 *History of the Second World War*.[8] Yet there could be no return to the total silence and control of the Stalin era. The 1960s had seen the publication of many war memoirs, often written by those from the lower military ranks, and this tendency continued, albeit also with more memoirs by higher-ranking officers, including the most important of all, those of Marshal Zhukov, which eventually came out in 1969.[9] Nevertheless, the flow of information was more strictly controlled than under Khrushchev, with a stronger prejudice against the use of new material or publication of new facts, which, if they were to be released, had to be corrected so as to agree with earlier published accounts.

While these restrictions were part of the Brezhnev retrenchment, it was true, however, that the format of memoirs was inherently restrictive and tended to narrow vision, potentially leading to a loss of a sense of the bigger picture, as well as the overall narrative and significance of the war.[10] This has been referred to as a "privatization" of war memory in the 1960s.[11] Such a danger threatened to undermine the legitimizing symbolic force of the war by fragmenting and atomizing memory of it. Film's special power to convey meaning-conferring narratives and symbols meant that the Brezhnev administration paid particular attention to enlisting it in the task of articulating its view of the war and overcoming fragmentation of war memory through renewed emphasis on epic, monumental forms, with their collectivist slant.

RETURN TO THE "FICTIONAL DOCUMENTARY" AND EPIC FORM

The films of the late 1950s and 1960s had brought the war theme to the fore, making it more central to Soviet cinema than it had been in the late Stalin era and gaining substantial international acclaim.[12] The likes of *The Cranes Are Flying* (*Letiat zhuravli*, dir. Mikhail Kalatozov, 1957), *Ballad of a Soldier* (*Ballada o soldate*, dir. Grigorii Chukhrai, 1959), *Fate of Man* (*Sud′ba cheloveka*, dir. Sergei Bondarchuk, 1959), and *Ivan's Childhood* (*Ivanovo detstvo*, dir. Andrei Tarkovskii, 1962) all presented in-depth studies of the effects of war on individuals and their moral and psychological world. However, such films were not concerned with depicting the overall narrative of the war, which was in any case difficult to encapsulate in the space of the feature-film format. At times, the films also sought to reevaluate and doubt previous representations of the war experience and might even be said to focus primarily on its negative sides, such as the price paid for victory.

It was in this context that, in 1965, the Ministries of the Armed Forces and of Finances, along with a representative of the Cinematography Committee, commissioned director Iurii Ozerov to make the ambitious, gargantuan five-part feature film cycle *Liberation* (*Osvobozhdenie*). This was a project beyond the scope of the film industry alone, hence the support of other ministries for the project. *Liberation* was intended to remind the Soviet people of the epochal importance of the war and the Soviet Union's central and decisive role in it.[13] The Victory Banner was a crucial part of the fourth and fifth films, providing a suitably uplifting payoff for the extended narrative.

Key to this message was a particular approach to form: making an enormous, "epic" film cycle suggested an analogy between greatness of scale and great significance, by exceeding contemporary films by all measures of size and scope, and by employing the latest technologies, which here meant color and widescreen format.[14] Justifying this shift to the epic form, *Liberation* director Iurii Ozerov, a veteran, was critical of 1950s and 1960s films that, he suggested, represented the war in a small-scale manner just as a backdrop to a standard studio-style (*kamernyi*) romantic plot:

> Films about the war made in the 1950s and 60s . . . shared one defining characteristic: the majority of them were devoted to the first years of the war, the difficulties of defensive battles in which a lot of blood was shed. In them, as a rule, we saw the actions of a single artillery detachment, or a platoon or the crew of a single bomber. The thoughts and feelings of these few people were meant to convey the condition of all those who fought for the Motherland. My own memories of the war resisted such images. I felt from my own experience that our memories are meant to store good things. People are cleverly designed, and we're lucky like that. What I wanted to see on screen was the inexorable might of Soviet troops attacking, the joy of liberated towns and

> villages, the thrill of the triumphant advance through the countries of liberated Europe. . . .
>
> This is how *Liberation* was born.[15]

Ozerov was unapologetic about his orientation toward military strategy and the chief of staff: "From the trench or dugout of a Battalion, you can't see the whole front. We wanted to make a film that would show millions of spectators how it was done, how the war was won."[16]

Key here is a sense that the films of the post-Stalin 1950s and 1960s did not sufficiently emphasize the fact that the Soviets had won the war or dwell on the uplifting effect of victory. The recourse to an epic, monumental form was connected to the emphasis on the narrative of victory, and this entailed a reversion to the kind of Soviet war film typified by *The Fall of Berlin* or Igor′ Savchenko's *The Third Blow* (*Tret′i udar*, 1948), on which Ozerov had made his debut in cinema, something many critics comment upon. The narrative sweep is also comparable: *The Fall of Berlin* avoids depicting the defeats and reverses of the first part of the war by having Alesha, the main protagonist, lose consciousness. *Liberation* simply begins at Kursk, enabling the film to focus solely on Soviet victories.

When asked why his film starts in 1943, Ozerov said that there had already been many films about the beginning of the war: "There was, it seems to me, a tendency toward that, which was not quite right."[17] He expanded on the point in a 1971 article:

> At times in these films the scale of the representation of military reality was reduced disproportionately and what was left off the screen was the true heroism, the patriotic rallying of the whole people, without which our victory would have been impossible.
>
> Of course, the contemporary spectator must know about the many tragic trials people had to undergo in those terrible years. But you can't limit the story of the war to that, and you can't fail to show the genuine historical meaning of the events of the war, their true scale, and the majestic character of our heroic people, a people of victors.[18]

The reversion and resemblance to Stalin-era depictions did not stop there, however. In stressing the monumental scale and momentous significance of the war victory, the film also depicted Stalin in a fiction film for the first time since his death. The combination of the epic and the image of Stalin are also echoed in the way in which the final film of the cycle uses the Victory Banner imagery to cement its emphasis on victory. This high-profile film's emphasis on Stalin-era tropes confirms the claims that there was a "neo-Stalinist" tendency in the Soviet elite around Brezhnev.[19] This tendency was already evident in the mention of Stalin in the 1965 Victory Day speech by Brezhnev himself.

Nevertheless, as Iurii Khaniutin argues, the excesses of *The Fall of Berlin* led to a twenty-year gap in which Soviet film avoided attempts to create a broad canvas depicting the major battles of the war in military terms.[20] This approach was also somewhat one-sided in that a sense of the bigger military and historical importance of the conflict was a part of the war story that also needed to be told: there was a place for the historical film of the war that made history, rather than psychology or drama, central. Indeed, it could be argued that by the end of the 1960s, approaching the war through the prism of individual psychology was itself becoming a tired cliché, paving the way for a new, epic style.[21] However, although *Liberation* responds to this gap, and in so doing returns to an emphasis on combat and strategy, it attempts to avoid repeating the shortcomings of *The Fall of Berlin*.[22] One way it attempts to do this is by combining the features of previous Soviet cinema—the monumental and individualized—syncretically. As Denise Youngblood argues, Ozerov made here a film that showed how thaw-era tendencies had penetrated Soviet culture "even in a vehicle that rejected its key values." Thus, the characters are individualized and humanized: the rivalry between Zhukov and Konev is shown, and there is an erotic element in the romance scenes that end tragically, as the lovers are not reunited.[23]

Yet, while Ozerov's film can be understood primarily as a response to trends in Soviet remembrance of the war, it was also partly provoked by the changing Soviet media and by international trends, which also struck a contrast with the narrower focus of recent Soviet films. As Ozerov put it, "While we were getting carried away with psychological microstudies, our Western colleagues were using their works to 'correct' the history of the war."[24] One particular example he is referring to is the US film *The Longest Day* (1962).[25] At the time of its release, it was the most expensive war film ever made and was one of a number of US films articulating a simplistically patriotic vision of World War II, echoing the strident confidence of the United States in the early 1960s.[26]

There is a perceived need in *Liberation* to explain to the world how significant the Soviet Union's contribution to victory was. The idea of scale is also important in competing with American representations.[27] While it should be noted that all of these films focused on scale in part so as to compete with the rise of television, *Liberation*'s sense of scale was also a form of aesthetic escalation—an attempt to create a different kind of even more gargantuan scale than that seen in the US films, which had themselves created a sense of the monumental, but on the basis of material from a single day or hour and from an episode of the war that, in the Soviet view of things, was not the key one in terms of its ultimate outcome.

Certainly, the spectacular effects of *Liberation* were achieved largely through the use of an enormous quantity of military hardware, rather than illusionistic ingenuity.[28] Indeed, Ozerov saw his role as a movie director as being very similar to that of a general. On the set, the same language of "command points" and "battle" was used, and he argued that the same kinds of skills were required.[29]

Ozerov and his team take this relation beyond the metaphoric, stressing the direct role of the military in the film. Thus, Kun, who was Ozerov's assistant, asserts that "the army high command, in making military hardware available to the filmmakers, treated the filming as military exercises."[30]

In the context of Hollywood cinema, Guy Westwell has written of the "mutual exploitation" of war movies and the military-industrial complex, with the loan of military hardware and personnel effectively reducing costs and assuring a positive representation of the military. He stresses that what we are seeing on the screen in a war film is "the actual apparatus of war: real airplanes, real warships, real uniforms, even real soldiers who act as extras and advisors" and have the power to shape scripts and can withdraw support if the depiction is unflattering. Ultimately, Westwell argues, there is an indexical relationship between war, movies about war, and the cultural imagination of war.[31] There is certainly an overlap between the way in which *Liberation* was filmed and the role of military consultants, whose ostensible responsibility was historical accuracy. Ozerov stressed this link:

> I would like to draw attention to the extraordinary help of the army, who set aside for us not only the required quantity of troops and hardware but also appointed as the main consultant of the film general S. M. Shtemenko. Besides him, we were greatly aided in the first films of the cycle by guidance from our three unofficial advisors: Marshal G. K. Zhukov, Marshal I. S. Konev, and Marshal K. S. Moskalenko. They all take an enthusiastic part in the film, even watching rushes, for which we are extraordinarily grateful to them.[32]

However, while the films enjoyed strong support from the top, including from the military, even here there was a fear of letting too much information out. The KGB's control of military history, evident in Ozerov's *Liberation*, is mentioned in correspondence between Iurii Andropov, head of the KGB and the Central Committee, in February and March 1971, in which he expressed anxiety as to the way in which military consultants were being used for military films. He suspected that they were being chosen as a way of getting them to reveal certain information to which the filmmakers would not otherwise have access. As a result, the Central Committee decided that military consultants could be chosen only from a pool approved by higher-ups.[33] This tactic was similar to the approach to archives in this period: there were attempts to control historical representations and wider public memory of the war by limiting access to information.

Nevertheless, the film was impressive in its painstaking attention to documentary detail, and collaboration with the military enhanced the film's authenticity. Ozerov's team, most of whom were, like him, veterans of the war, had an extraordinary degree of access to an enormous range of materials in the Soviet military archives: to maps, orders, and reports. They also drew extensively on historical and memoir accounts and on personal conversations with the consultants mentioned above: General Shtemenko, Marshals Konev and Moskalenko, and the advice of the GDR Military-Historical Institute and the military historian Job von Witzleben (who was the nephew of an executed conspirator from the 1944 attempt to assassinate Hitler).[34] The filmmakers even interviewed those present at the Tehran conference as to how the building interiors had looked.[35]

In addition to making extensive use of sources and hardware, the film also presented itself as documentarylike in its style, drawing extensively on documentaries, even incorporating some sequences of newsreel footage (stretched and tinted to fit the widescreen color format) and using voice-over and intertitles in the manner of documentaries.[36] To this end it also included fifty-one historical figures, each of whom had to be cast, in part at least, according to their resemblance to the actual individuals.[37]

The most important of these, other than Stalin, was Marshal Zhukov, whose memoirs, read in manuscript form with his permission, were also an important source that Ozerov was able to use.[38] The depiction of Zhukov is one of the successes of the film, as well as one of the ways in which it clearly improves on *The Fall of Berlin*.[39]

However, the relationship between the historical and fictional elements was problematic for *Liberation*, and it is probably indicative of its excessive concern about visual authenticity that the casting of the historical figures was made a greater priority than that of the fictionalized "compound" characters who represent the lower-ranking soldiers and officers.[40] The problem was to make characters psychologically distinct and seem like individuals in the way that the historical characters did, "to ensure that the epic sweep of events would not eclipse the individual heroes."[41]

However, the film did not really succeed in creating believable characters who were also a "type." Thus, while the historical authenticity and importance of the film were highlighted by a review by Evgenii Boltin, a top Soviet military historian who had been responsible for writing the *History of the Great Patriotic War*, even among the enormously positive reviews for this film there are some comments that explain why it did not do so well, especially internationally: the lack of character development, due to the focus on history, chronology, and events.[42] As Iurii Khaniutin put it, "the hero is the army, strategy, the talent of commanders, military might, the military machine, grandiose and invincible in its movement, the professional ability, duty and talent of soldiers and officers. Individual stories in the film resemble traditional cinematic filler."[43]

In privileging the look and feel of documentary and authenticity over fiction, *Liberation* revisits footage of the battle of Berlin and the storming of the Reichstag, which is the focus of the last film: *The Final Storm*. The subject and its treatment serve as a concentrated restatement of the film's emphasis on the overall narrative of the war culminating in an uplifting sense of the victory and an implicitly authoritarian subtext.

REPEATING THE END

In 1967 a controversial documentary about the battle of Moscow early in the war, *If Your Home Is Dear to You* (*Esli dorog tebe tvoi dom*, dir. Vasilii Ordynskii) came out and enjoyed enormous success. In a review of it for *Iskusstvo kino*, Roman Karmen asked what was new and distinct about this film, since its images had already been used, and he answers his own question, saying that it is primarily the analytical nature of the film.[44] With Ozerov's *Liberation*, while there are some new images, they are attached to familiar ones and serve to repeat the established narrative of Soviet victory: the repetition is part of the ritualization of meaning. There is no analysis; the quasi-documentary qualities of the film invite belief and narrative investment rather than distance and analysis. The resemblance between *The Fall of Berlin* and *Liberation* is commented upon by many critics, but the two films are particularly close in their depiction of the storming of the Reichstag and raising of the Victory Banner, as Youngblood has pointed out.[45] However, a closer analysis reveals a certain contrast between the two films.

The final two films of the five-film cycle follow a single narrative sweep, covering the whole of the battle for Berlin. The fifth film, entitled *The Final Storm*, starts with the title appearing above images of street fighting in Berlin, over which the silhouetted form of the Reichstag looms on the horizon, through the veil of dust and smoke. This scene echoes the 1945 *Berlin* documentary footage, in which the artillery assault on the building is taking place while the distant contours of the Reichstag are visible. There follows a scene in which Major General Shatilov, commander of the 150th Rifle Division, comes to the unit with the Victory Banner as the troops prepare to attack the Reichstag. He has a conversation with a fictional character, Lieutenant Colonel (Podpolkovnik) Orlov and is shown to Captain Neustroev's unit; they are ready to launch an assault on the Reichstag. Shatilov and Orlov refer to it as the last stronghold (*oreshek*) of the Germans.

The published script is a great deal more pompous and momentous than the finished film: "'There it is, the banner that we must raise on that cupola. Take it from me, Orlov, that you have been chosen for a historic task—to storm the Reichstag,' said Shatilov, stepping back from the observation point. 'This is not simply an attack, Orlov, it is much more, it is everything! Do you understand?'"[46]

Shatilov later addresses the soldiers about to storm the building as "lucky," because they will have the chance to be the first to raise the Victory Banner. However, in the final film, instead of this speech we see an episode with the taking of photographic portraits for party membership cards. Political officer Berest is the one organizing the photography and party membership applications. This implicitly evokes the widespread (and even more widely represented) practice whereby soldiers wanted to go into a battle as communists: it was a kind of volunteering for leadership and willingness to submit yourself to greater danger, since communists were expected to lead by example in an attack. This is interrupted by the entrance of divisional commander Shatilov with fictional character Orlov, who calls for the regimental commander. Here we see a visually—rather than textually—moving moment when Colonel Zinchenko (a historical figure, commander of the 756th Rifle Regiment of the 150th Division) bestows the banner upon Egorov and Kantariia. The symbolic power of the banner is conveyed by his gesture of kissing it and by the way the camera zooms in so that the red banner, with the hammer and sickle in the center of the shot, occupies the whole of the frame at the end of the sequence as he tells them to raise it on the cupola of the Reichstag.

This representation, even in its earlier script variant, marks quite a contrast with what we see in *The Fall of Berlin*, where Egorov and Kantariia, along with the fictional Ivanov, are told that they have been chosen for the great honor of raising the Victory Banner over Berlin, fulfilling Stalin's order. They kneel and kiss it, and Zinchenko kisses each of them before battle, and we have a stronger sense that this is a sacred moment. The banner itself in *The Fall of Berlin* is also different from that in *Liberation*: it already bears the name of the unit that raised it, as does the actual banner preserved in the Central Museum of the Armed Forces, in Moscow. This suggests a greater attention to detail: evidently, the banner would not have borne the name and number of the unit that raised it before being raised, since this was something added after the fact by that unit to ensure that they alone received the credit for raising it. The approach taken in *The Fall of Berlin* is all about intensifying the effect of the symbolism, even at the expense of documentary authenticity, whereas *Liberation* pays greater attention to the latter, which is perhaps not surprising after the greater emphasis on the documentary in the post-Stalin period.

Ozerov's film shows the sequence of the assault on the Reichstag in a way that visually resembles that in *The Fall of Berlin*, to a degree: the lateral movement of the assault is emphasized in both films through a tracking shot. Both films also show soldiers falling in the assault, but this is treated in a slightly different way: in *The Fall of Berlin* Alesha's primary companions both die in the assault, Kostia on the steps of the Reichstag, passing his blood-stained handkerchief to Iusup to be raised on the building, while Iusup is also killed at the last moment, on the roof of the Reichstag. In Ozerov's film, as the tank man, Dorozhkin, is shot, his dying eyes see, in a point-of-view shot, Egorov and Kantariia climbing onto the roof to raise the flag from the cupola. We then see the moment of raising from the more distant perspective of the high command, in a shot that shows the whole Reichstag building, occupying the whole frame. The "trench" and "high command" perspectives are combined neatly here.

The main contrast in the two films' treatment of this episode, however, is the way in which *Liberation* cuts between the storming of the Reichstag sequence and other plot lines, such as Hitler's and then Goebbels's last moments, the broadcast by the antifascist German pastor, and the surrender negotiations with the Soviet high command. It does not, however, cut back to Stalin, nor does Stalin fly to Berlin in the famously superlative scene from Chiaureli's film. When the soldiers take the ground floor of the Reichstag, they radio through to General Kuznetsov, commander of the Third Strike Army, who tells them to get the banner up quickly. In turn he calls Zhukov, who calls Stalin. Likewise, when the German general Krebs attempts to negotiate a cease-fire and asks to talk to Moscow when the commanders of the First Belorussian Front tell him that they will accept nothing short of unconditional surrender, he is told that Moscow will say the same. Stalin's presence is implicit here but palpable all the same. *Liberation* rehabilitates the association of Stalin with victory but without the hyperbole of the original cult.

Moreover, in a further indication of *Liberation*'s greater historical accuracy, the raising of the flag and the news of the Berlin garrison's

4.2. Dorozhkin's last moments, as his eyes follow the Victory Banner's raising, in Iurii Ozerov's five-part film *Liberation*.

4.3. The Victory Banner, seen through Dorozhkin's dying eyes, in the film *Liberation*.

surrender on 2 May are not elided as they are in *The Fall of Berlin*. However, the scene of victory celebrated on the steps of Reichstag on 2 May echoes *The Fall of Berlin*, which in turn references Krivonogov's painting: the lateral tracking shot also quotes the moment of the assault on the Reichstag from that film. But the contrasting post-Stalin elements are no less significant, as the scene is tinged with loss: we see several soldiers, and the character Zoia, mourning fallen comrades, all of which contrasts with the more simplistically triumphant tone of *The Fall of Berlin*. It ends by cutting, in split screen, between the celebrations on the steps of the Reichstag to a montage of victory celebrations and the greeting of victorious troops by crowds throughout Europe. It then cuts to images of the 24 June 1945 Victory Parade and ecstatic welcoming home of Red Army soldiers at Belorussian Station, before a sequence detailing the figures of wartime dead for each nation of Europe, ending with the figure of

20 million Soviet dead. The final image is a shot of the Tomb of the Unknown Soldier by the Kremlin Wall in Moscow.

The combination of these symbols—the Victory Banner, figures for the dead, and the eternal flame from the Tomb of the Unknown Soldier—was easily decoded by the critics:

> The fierce tension of the battle inside the Reichstag is conveyed precisely and convincingly. . . . It was still dark when Egorov and Kantariia got to the base of the Reichstag cupola. Everything was glimmering in the sky and everything glimmering on the ground below. In the sky, long-distance artillery shells were exploding, and the shrapnel hit the roof. Below, the batteries of guns, tanks, and rockets were all firing. Breathless, they climbed up the cupola and lay motionless for a long time, their strength completely spent. Then Egorov and Kantariia started fixing the banner. The red banner was unfurled, it fluttered in the spring breeze. . . . Then the soldiers near the Reichstag fired into the air with every type of weapon and were all shouting, smiling, embracing, and everywhere a single word resounded: "Victory! Victory!" All around, the great, happy day of our victory raged, seethed, laughed, and cried out. Meanwhile, against the background of the eternal flame by the Kremlin Wall, figures appear, reminding us of the lives lost in the world due to fascism. Painfully, we read: "Soviet People 20,000,000." This intertitle is a requiem to the fallen, to those who gave their lives for the freedom of our Motherland, to those who liberated the world from the brown plague. This intertitle is a warning to those who would want to start another world war.[47]

For all its commitment to a rhetoric of authenticity, this symbolism is achieved at the expense of simplifying some of the script's commitments to historical detail and impoverishing its already feeble attempts to add depth to the characters. There is, for example, one Victory Banner on the Reichstag, on its cupola, and not many, as was the case in reality and even in the script.[48] By the final film, Egorov and Kantariia have lost the number of lines of dialogue they had and are shown in a much more peripheral way, whereas they had been the focus previously. The same is true of the historical figure of political instructor Berest, although he retains a couple of lines, but his very mention is noteworthy (see chapter 3).

There had been attempts to compensate for these shortcomings in other ways, as, between the script and the finished film, it was possible to add a greater sense of authenticity through the use of real locations:

> Work on the film *Liberation* began in 1966. Soon after this we filmed the first shots of the last part: "The Battle for Berlin." The remains of the ruins were still standing back then, and the Berlin mayoralty allowed us to film using them as a background to battles for the fording of the Spree, the storming of

> the metro, and the capture of the Reichstag. In cinema, this is what is called filming "a disappearing location." There is not a single other film about the last war where filming on that scale took place in Berlin itself. They filmed *The Fall of Berlin* by Chiaureli, for example, elsewhere or in the studio.[49]

These real locations were going to be demolished, and that is why they could be used as a set. Even by the time the film was released, those parts of Berlin had become unrecognizable.[50] These efforts to use the locations to enhance authenticity were lauded by the critics, and even battle participants said they resembled documentary footage.[51] According to one reviewer, "The storming of the Reichstag is filmed so as to create the illusion of the absolute authenticity of what is happening."[52]

Although Stalin himself is not present at the end of the film, the repetition of themes and motifs from *The Fall of Berlin* serves to reassert a vision of the war that echoes that articulated in the Stalin era. It is a reworking, especially in the Victory Banner scene, of imagery evoking the magical, glorious, charismatic power of the Soviet victory. This emphasis on the Victory Banner is the natural culmination of the plot that contains only Soviet victories, or what one account calls "the victorious stage of the Second World War."[53]

However, while *Liberation* avoids *The Fall of Berlin*'s tendency to spell everything out, verbalizing the symbolic importance of the moment, its nuances of joining the Communist Party before battle and the sacral resonances of the flag would be lost on international audiences. Thus, while *Liberation* was shown in 114 countries and supposedly attracted the colossal figure of 300 million viewers, claims that it exerted a tremendous effect around the world are unconvincing.[54]

In part, the enormous scale and thoughts about foreign reception were encouraged by the 1968 four-part epic adaptation of *War and Peace*. This film, described as a "film epic," was also critically acclaimed and won the Soviet Union considerable international prestige, including an Oscar. *Liberation* was intended as the *War and Peace* of the Great Patriotic War.[55] Iurii Ozerov himself clearly thought that his film would, like *War and Peace*, achieve international acclaim:

> Why not make use of both new technology and new ways of filming? Surely you would agree that all of this will help us to reach a large number of screens around the world and make an impact on them, which is much needed now in particular. Just to be clear: I don't mean the benefits of "import-export," although that is also important, but primarily that every Soviet film that is widely shown on screens around the world is another argument in the debate between ideologies that is heard by all. That is why I think that with

> each year we will increasingly film large-scale, multiseries films, devoted to burning issues, the big topics. Would you not agree that the worldwide success of *War and Peace* is an argument in favor of my point of view?[56]

However, the prioritization of ideology over commercial imperatives implicit in this statement was always likely to hamper the film's reception in the West, where the latter dominate. As Sumenov and Sul′kin point out, *The Longest Day* and other US war films were not shown on Soviet screens, in part for political reasons, and correspondingly *Liberation* was not widely shown in the West and was still less widely acclaimed. Whether intended this way or not, its ultimate primary audience was Soviet spectators and people in other socialist countries, despite the filmmakers' intentions.

Youngblood comments on the film's popularity, saying that despite the first two of the five films doing well at the box office, in large part due to very strong official promotion of the film that involved the party encouraging people to attend, neither part was ranked the best film of the year, and interest dropped sharply for the final two parts, shown in 1971.[57] While *Liberation* was not a box-office smash, it garnered a different kind of acclaim: in 1972 a number of the filmmakers (Ozerov, Bondarev, Kurganov, Slabnevich, Miagkov), but notably none of the actors, received the Lenin Prize.

Lauded in official culture, the attempt to reinvent the monumental epic form with *Liberation* set the mold for a series of 1970s Soviet epic films that followed it, most notably *The Soldiers of Freedom* (*Soldaty svobody*, dir. Iurii Ozerov, 1977), which, for the first time, featured episodes of the war contributions of Leonid Brezhnev, played by an actor. This film was even less successful than *Liberation*: Brezhnev was incapable of inspiring charismatic devotion. The Victory Banner scenes in *Liberation* were weakened by the sheer narrative scale of the form: for one thing, by the time that even domestic Soviet spectators had reached the final point of the raising of the flag, they were fewer in number, but the film's length also undermined the emotional power of the ending. The way in which the episode was presented, with less attention to the individual characters and failure to exploit its dramatic potential, was characteristic of the problems inherent in the monumental form. Ozerov claimed that gigantic-scale films were highly contemporary, a response to a new media landscape. As with *The Longest Day*, this is an attempt to compete with television.[58] But the audience's declining interest in the film cycle was an inherent weakness of the cinematic epic form, because it was difficult to sustain interest over an eight-hour span. The result was that *Liberation* was "more tiresome than bad."[59] The same kinds of things were said of *The Longest Day*: "so monumental that it discouraged emotion . . . [although it] cries out to be liked, it can only be respected . . . there is no plot."[60] *Liberation*'s attempt to reinvent the Stalinist epic form for cinema in a new media age was unsuccessful, as were its attempts to reach international audiences. The epic form and the symbol of the Victory Banner had to be reimagined for the rising, increasingly hegemonic form of television.

THE RISE OF TELEVISION AND *THE GREAT PATRIOTIC/UNKNOWN WAR*

While the reach of Soviet television had expanded steadily in the 1950s and 1960s, by 1970 it was available to half the country, with about 35 million television sets, one for every two families. This figure had risen to 55 million by 1975.[61] While the spectacular visuals and authentic feel of *Liberation* had limited success with audiences, experiments in even more spectacular cinematic forms continued, with the novel multiple-screen system, Mosfil′m's Sovpolikadr, patented in the late 1960s. Films such as *Our March* (*Nash marsh*, dir. Aleksandr Shein, A. Svetlov, 1970), *Internationale* (*Internatsional*, dir. A. Svetlov, Aleksandr Shein, 1971), *March on, Land of Mine* (*Shagai strana*, dir. Aleksandr Shein, G. Brenner, 1981) were all compilation documentaries on officially sanctioned anniversary themes (e.g., the centenaries of Lenin's birth and the Paris Commune), but their conservative subject matter was more than compensated for by their innovative approach to form, so that each of these films uses footage of the raising of the Victory Banner, but in novel ways. *Our March* is indicative: three screens, arranged horizontally, show two streams of newsreel footage, and in the third screen there is a red military flag (not depicted in black and white) bearing Lenin's portrait and the words "For Our Soviet Homeland." The effect is to lend the images greater dynamism, and intensity, since while one screen shows the infantry assault on the Reichstag, the other already shows the Germans surrendering. A twenty-minute film is thus able to pack in an account of the whole century, without this feeling insubstantial. On the other hand, the presence of a red flag adds the color red and insists on victory in the war being a communist-, Soviet-, and Lenin-inspired feat. The effects can be visually overwhelming, as it is hard to take in all of the information, and they point forward to the immersive and horizontal montage techniques of the digital age. However, these films were not destined to reach a wide audience and tended to be screened at festivals (where they were acclaimed) or at exhibitions or art galleries.[62]

A more influential approach to conveying the epic war narrative would be to reinvent it for television. As Christine Evans has argued, the

4.4. *Our March*, directed by Aleksandr Shein and Aleksandr Svetlov, 1970.

more direct, intimate, and informal medium of television was better able to overcome the tension between political message and entertainment than could cinema, because it was "ideally positioned to address the political and ideological challenges of the late Soviet state."[63] Rather than competing with it, film would achieve greater success by adapting to the new medium.

One way in which film adjusted to the possibilities and proclivities of television was through the development of the memoir form in documentary, which on the face of it might be said to represent a complete contrast with Ozerov's monumentalism. One such highly successful adaptation was by Sergei Smirnov, who had worked with Roman Karmen on the first treatment of 1965's *The Great Patriotic* (see chapter 3) and fronted the long-running television series *Tales of Heroism* and later, *Tales of Heroes* (*Rasskazy o geroiakh*, from 1968). In these shows, Smirnov would tell the story of a given person, often on the basis of a letter he had received, parts of which he would read aloud, even stumbling over parts that were hard to make out, before then meeting and interviewing the person whose story was the focus of the program. The interview would itself invite further participation, as Smirnov would address some of those named in the program, inviting them in turn to get in contact. As the titles imply, the focus here throughout is on heroes, and the implication is that this is the key story to tell about the war. Fates that are less than heroic—those of victims, of traitors, of the simply unheroic and unremarkable—would by implication be of no or of less interest. Yet, at the same time, millions saw themselves in those interviewed, and this made the heroic ordinary and accessible.

It was this dimension that made Smirnov's programs so popular, so much so that there was a television documentary made about him, *Sergei Sergeevich Smirnov*, which aired on Soviet television in July 1965. The idea was to invert the premise of his shows: he talks about heroes, but this program would tell viewers about him. What emerges here is the enormous popularity of the show: the woman who delivers Smirnov's mail says that he receives two hundred to three hundred letters a day, and she has to bring them to his door personally because there are too many to fit into his mailbox. Moreover, at the central telegraph office we see that he receives a further two thousand messages a day from people who don't write to his address.[64] These figures were no exaggeration, as the television archives show: in April 1965 more than twelve thousand letters were received about the coverage of the twentieth anniversary of Victory, and ten thousand of them were addressed to Smirnov.[65]

At one point in this program, Smirnov refers to television as a kind of "information bureau" (*spravochnyi biuro*): a kind of Soviet version of directory inquiries, where one would find out someone's address and telephone number. The numbers of letters received by Soviet Central Television had doubled in 1965 compared to the previous year.[66] In addition to the enthusiastic response of viewers to the coverage of the Victory commemorations, Smirnov was a large part of the reason why. He spoke to a need in the audience and understood the inherently interactive potential of the form. The critic Nikolai Nikolaievich Klado commented on Smirnov's popularity:

> For example, I was in the town of Efremov. In the evening, in the hotel everyone gathers around the television. When Sergei Sergeevich appeared on the screen, a small boy sitting nearby me exclaimed, "It's Uncle Television!" For many Smirnov really is the embodiment of television; his talents have become everyone's friend. But what is it that attracts us in Smirnov's characters? In *Katiusha*, for instance, Katia Mikhailova is a simple Russian girl.
>
> KLADO: You see . . . what attracts spectators and readers in the film *Katiusha* and in Smirnov's stories is the fact that his subjects are ordinary people. So, everyone understands that he could have become one of these heroic characters. This plants in people a sense of their own worth and belief in their own powers. But, most importantly, Smirnov wonderfully embodies in himself the power and possibilities of television.[67]

This tendency of television to offer war memoirs was echoed in documentary film too. This was in part due to the growing capacity of film to record interviews with lightweight portable recording apparatus, but it was also due to the success of films such as *If Your Home Is Dear to You* in revealing the enormous possibilities of the interview. The scenario for that film was written by Konstantin Simonov, and the film featured a revealing interview with Marshal Zhukov about the catastrophically precarious situation of the battle of Moscow.[68] This candid analysis by a figure of unimpeachable authority was a large part of the reason this film ran into enormous difficulties with censors, who were generally unhappy with its focus on the military reverses of 1941 and its attribution of blame for them on the Great Terror, the crimes of Stalin, and his commitment to the Nazi-Soviet pact.

Simonov, who had himself been extending the memoir genre in literature, was particularly energetic in pursuing this genre in film, with later works such as *A Soldier Was Walking* (*Shel soldat*, dir. Marina Babak, 1975) and his television series *Soldiers' Memoirs* (*Soldatskie memuary*, dir. Marina Babak, 1976). This approach was combined with an emphasis on the individual, the concrete, and the many hardships endured by soldiers at war. The effect of this focus also fragmented a sense of the whole of the war, its epic sweep, and overall significance. Indeed, the commentary to *A Soldier Was Walking* explicitly states its lack of interest in the narrative of the war or its strategic and historical dimensions: "The history of the war is already well known. . . . We remember how it started, where it ended. Everyone knows that . . . it is not the strategy of battles, not the history of the war that interests the authors of this film, but the image of the hero of the war." It also had the effect of moving wartime documentary and newsreel footage from its previously privileged position as the key visual representation and record of the war to a status as more of a tool for interpretation and reflection. While *A Soldier Was Walking* used newsreel footage, it stressed the unrepresentative nature of it and made the interviews with veterans central. This was even more so the case with *Soldiers' Memoirs*. In addition to possessing the authority of the witness, the interviews with veterans had the advantage of the direct, apparently spontaneous and unmediated appeal of the live voice, something that television was so suited to conveying. However, the interview and testimony were potentially fragmentary and had to be treated with caution by historians and those using film to convey historical narratives. As Annette Wieviorka has argued, "how can a coherent historical discourse be constructed if it is constantly countered by another truth, the truth of individual memory?"[69] While general understandings of the war, as well as notions such as victory and heroism, had served as social frameworks through which individual testimony could be organized, new narrative forms were required to synthesize these elements for the television format. The question that confronted Soviet filmmakers was how to convey the authoritative and overarching narrative of victory through the new medium of television. This entailed adapting and repackaging the Victory Banner imagery.

These challenges were negotiated in a fascinating way in one of Soviet television's most significant contributions to public memory of the war:

the 1978 twenty-part serial *The Unknown War*, a joint Russian and US project made for initial distribution in the United States, a development that was the product of détente. Indeed, some of the initial discussions in 1976 refer to the Soiuz-Apollo joint space project, a symbolic high point of US-Soviet cooperation.[70]

As an initial treatment makes clear, for the US side the attraction of the series was to satisfy viewers' appetite for historical compilation series, but from a different point of view:

> Well-produced war documentaries have received excellent acceptance by United States commercial television broadcasters. Most of the World War II programs that have appeared on American television, including *Victory at Sea*, *The World at War* . . . have been produced by American and British companies and have accented involvement by four of the five major powers involved in this great war. The United States of America, Great Britain, Germany, and Japan.
>
> The dramatic involvement of the Soviet Union, the fifth major power, has never been presented to the American television viewer.
>
> . . .
>
> Never before had man seen war on such a scale. It changed the face of Europe and determined the fate of the world.[71]

Most of all, though, the attraction appears to have been financial: the films were to be made in the Soviet Union at the Soviets' expense, albeit on US color film stock (three thousand meters of Kodak negative and ninety thousand meters of Intermediate [i.e. positive]).[72] Evidently, this arrangement would be cheaper than having the whole project made and edited by Americans at US facilities. However, the price for this was Soviet control over the message. Thus, after receiving the initial approach from the US company Air Time International, Filip Ermash, the minister of cinema, was told by Sergei Dobrynin, Soviet ambassador to the United States in January 1977, that the proposal could be accepted only if a Soviet author wrote the screenplay.[73] The following month the Soviets consulted Roman Karmen on the feasibility of the project. Karmen, who had dreamed of the possibilities of making a much longer film or series of films about the war when making *The Great Patriotic* in 1965, was now given the opportunity to realize these aspirations and was thrilled by the possibilities:

> Soviet documentary makers should do what they can to fulfill this task. To show to millions of American TV viewers what our people achieved in the years of World War Two, to reflect events and phenomena about which the Americans have no idea[;] this particularly relates to the current generation of Americans.

> Our dead, our losses, the heroism of our people, the great organizing role of the Communist Party, galvanizing our people for great deeds, the superiority of Soviet military science, the mighty power of our socialist system—all this must be reflected in the series of films.
>
> We must, while formally fulfilling the thematic plan proposed by "Air-Time," fill these films to the brim with our content. This is an opportunity for us to land a serious ideological blow at the American viewers' brains, doing this, in essence, with the Americans' own hands. A rare opportunity! . . . It is hard to overestimate the significance of millions of Americans seeing these films on the eve of the 60th anniversary of the Soviet state.[74]

Elsewhere, Karmen wrote, "If it all ends positively it will be an unprecedented salvo, it will be an enormous Soviet ideological victory, it is hard to overstate the power of this enterprise."[75]

Karmen sets out his vision for how work on the film should be organized—with him as overall director, supervising the directors of the individual films. Very soon this means that he has to decide on the film's form, and he faces difficulties finding an approach that is acceptable to the US public but that at the same time ensures that the Soviets retain control. In reusing wartime footage, it was clear that the narrative text would have to be rewritten and adapted to the present both in stylistic and ideological terms so that the voice-over would be in accord with the latest published Soviet history of the war:

> There is another challenge. All the old films reflecting the events of the Great Patriotic War and its major battles today require reexamination from the perspective of contemporary historical thought. The multivolume work *The History of the Great Patriotic War*, which is coming out now, should become the key basis for creating Soviet films anew. A profound reevaluation of a number of events, phenomena, and stages of the war will be needed.
>
> This all makes it unavoidable that every film be based on a new scenario, to have a new voice-over, and consequently a new approach to editing.[76]

When the Americans began asking for color footage, the Soviet team started to consider the possibilities of the interview form: such footage would look contemporary, feel direct and be in color, and could at the same time confirm the dominant message:

> By the way, the Americans are suggesting that the basis of this series of films should be color. What are we to make of this? All of our wartime newsreel is black-and-white, apart from the color film of the 1945 Victory Parade. So they are talking about shooting some extra scenes, which will obviously be the recollections of those who took part in the war: commanders and war he-

> roes. Here we can support the Americans fully, since this will strengthen the material's propaganda value. There could be color interviews with legendary war heroes such as Mares′ev, Kozhedub, Pokryshkin, both with heroes of Stalingrad such as General Chuikov, Podimtsev, Batov, [and] Shumilov as well as with Kantariia, who raised the Victory Banner over the Reichstag.[77]

Thus, initially, talking heads feature prominently in early drafts of the script: there are interviews with Zhukov, survivors of the blockade, Soviet air aces, and key figures in the battle of Stalingrad—Chuikov, Rodimtsev, and Sergeant Pavlov.[78] However, only a tiny fragment of the interview with Zhukov remained in the final version, in the battle of Moscow episode, taken from *If Your House Is Dear to You*, but it does not include Zhukov's most pessimistic and bleak assessments of the situation or his statement that he was not in the least certain of holding the German advance from 6 to 13 October. Presumably this is in part because that view was so controversial. There are also still a number of other talking heads, including the survivors of the blockade, Marshal Chuikov, US special envoy Averell Harriman, and, in the final episode, Leonid Brezhnev himself. His is the longest and, needless to say, the least interesting of the interviews, most of which are very short.

A key reason for reducing the number of talking heads was concern over how to control the information in interviews; these concerns surfaced over a proposed trip to Poland that was to depict the liberation of Poland and the 1944 Warsaw Uprising. The studio's request to film Poles, on location, in regard to sensitive issues was turned down by the Ministry of Cinema.[79]

Instead of interviews and extensive location filming, the demands of the television aesthetic were solved by the decision to have an American presenter, filmed at various locations, introduce the films. This brought in color and looked contemporary. Moreover, it had the benefit of allowing the Soviets to manage and script the message. First, however, the team had to find an appropriate actor. Names considered included Frank Sinatra, Paul Newman, John Wayne, and Kirk Douglas. The Soviets rejected Yul Brynner as a candidate for the voice-over before Burt Lancaster was agreed on.[80] However, both Air Time International and Lancaster were worried that they might end up being used for Soviet propaganda. They were reassured by their Soviet partners that there would be a US voice-over consultant who would see the final cut and who would be paid by the American side.[81] The contract stressed that the US consultant's purpose would be "assisting Soviet authors with the presentation of the program material as related to the specific character of American TV audience viewing demands at the stage of work when the rough version of the program screen image and the version of the program narration texts are completed."[82] But the message was to be a Soviet one that the Americans would only have the right to adapt: "The American side will have the right to show the series only in the version agreed by both sides."[83] But for all their ultimately propagandist intentions, the Soviets understood the need to make concessions in tone:

> III. When finalizing the texts for the series, pay particular attention to the way the material is delivered, bearing in mind that the text will be read from the perspective of an American speaker and the normal tone of a text for Soviet audiences could be judged overt propaganda in the USA.
>
> IV. Taking into account that American viewers are not well informed, increase the quantity of factual material in the texts.[84]

The Soviets also reluctantly accepted former *New York Times* Moscow correspondent Harrison Salisbury being brought in at the end to work on making the text more appealing to the US audience, even though they had originally wanted Albert Maltz, who had adapted the 1942 film *The Defeat of the Germans near Moscow* (*Razgrom nemetskikh voisk pod Moskvoi*) for US screens, leading to its being awarded an Oscar.[85] But this process of adaptation was not without its crises, such as when the Soviets got annoyed by the way in which the series presented itself as being made by Americans. Tereishvili, head of the Soviet organization overseeing relations with foreign filmmakers, sent an angry Telex to Fred Weiner of Air Time International, in imperfect English:

> The problem which worries me, and I think that you violate the obligations of the Contract, is the problem of publicity in the press media on the creators of the programme. I considered the text of the press-release and I think that it is not proper to say about Roman Karmen by-the-way. The programme is being actually done by Karmen and the other Soviet directors, and it does not seem serious when you name Isaac Kleinerman to be the principal person out of other creaters of the programme, who is, as Contract says, the consultant . . . it causes justified offence of the people wholeheartedly giving themselves up to the programme, i.e. Roman Karmen and other Soviet directors.[86]

Karmen also wrote a letter to Weiner complaining that the material "doesn't mention a single word about the fact that the serial is being made by the Soviet documentary filmmakers" and that he has not been thanked for "supplying qualified personnel."[87] He, in turn, is reassured by Weiner, who explains to Karmen that this is all part of a strategy to place the film on American television: "I must see to it that most Americans will view '[T]he Unknown War,'" adding, "Please trust my judgment in promotion and publicity. You are the artist, I am the salesman."[88]

The resulting series was an extraordinarily pro-Soviet one, albeit articulated through the mouth of an American. This is particularly noteworthy in *Unknown War*'s treatment of the Holocaust and the Victory Banner. The following discussion focuses on the English-language version of the script. However, the series was later dubbed by Vasilii Lanovoi for Russian release under the title *The Great Patriotic* (*Velikaia otechestvennaia*), denoting a repetition of titles as well as images from the earlier film, and the English- and Russian-language versions differed in sometimes subtle and important ways (which I will comment on below).

TREATMENT OF THE VICTORY BANNER

A brief comparison with *The World at War* (Thames Television, produced by Jeremy Isaacs, 1973–1974) illustrates how distinct the Soviet emphasis on the Victory Banner was. In the British series the imagery of the storming of the Reichstag was absent, with the last moments of the Nazis instead being devoted to events in Hitler's bunker. Whereas *Liberation*, or before it *The Fall of Berlin*, and numerous Soviet documentary films about the war depict the last days of Hitler just as the Western documentaries do, those Western accounts tend to ignore the story of the Victory Banner. Against this background, *The Unknown War* stands out all the more, because it makes the Victory Banner unusually prominent by not only using the famous filmic and photographic material but also filming Burt Lancaster in the Hall of Victory for the eighteenth episode of the series, entitled "The Battle of Berlin."

Lancaster spent fifteen days filming. He and the crew traveled around the Soviet Union to a certain number of significant and symbolic destinations: Moscow's line of defense (the farthest point of the German advance) and Tomb of the Unknown Soldier, as well as monuments in Leningrad, Volgograd, Kiev, Brest, Minsk, Novorossiisk, and Murmansk.[89] The decision to start the eighteenth episode in the Hall of Victory of Moscow's Central Museum of the Soviet Army was one that had been made at an early stage in the scripting for the film, in summer 1977:

1. The American presenter in the Museum of the Armed Forces of the USSR talks about the names left by the victors, Russian soldiers, on the Reichstag building in Berlin.
2. The commentator by the historical Victory Banner, raised in May 1945 over the defeated Nazi capital.[90]

There was indecision, however, as to how to combine this scene with the Victory Banner with other representations of it. A later version started the episode with the footage of the storming of the Reichstag:

> This episode begins with the historical footage of the raising of the Victory Banner above the Reichstag in Berlin. Later in the film this episode will be repeated. For the moment, it is just a short fragment. Then we can show this genuine banner in the Museum of the Soviet Army. It is in a place of honor. The American presenter stands by this banner. He looks at it intently, and then, turning to the camera, says:
>
> —This is the actual banner that was raised by Soviet soldiers in May 1945 over the cupola of the Reichstag in the center of Berlin. Now it has been put here in the Museum of the Soviet Armed Forces. This is a relic for the Russians, a memory of the final decisive battle of the Second World War.[91]

While the emphasis on the authentic and sacred quality of the Victory Banner remains in the final film, the 1945 footage is moved to the center of the film, placed chronologically in the narrative of the battle. Here the association of the Reichstag with the turning point in the Nazis' rise to power is made central, and the building is said to be burning once again, as it had when the Nazis seized power. This neat narrative, with the Reichstag forming a center point, realizes the aspirations of Raizman's original film and also echoes Karmen's 1965 documentary.

The images of the infantry assault are repeated, and as the flag is raised, the film cuts to crowds of soldiers celebrating. We then see images of the Berlin garrison's surrender, on 2 May. The symbol is made to stand for the moment of victory, even if, as we have seen, the fighting went on in the Reichstag and Berlin for days, and thus there could be no immediate celebrations. The sequence is therefore an imagined response that is no more historically accurate or "documentary" than what we found in *The Fall of Berlin*. In some ways it is less accurate than *Liberation*.

The episode ends with Red Army soldiers writing on the walls of the Reichstag, but the final sequence is of the camera slowly scanning Khaldei's photograph of the Victory Banner. Here we see the three representations working together: newsreel, still photograph, and live footage, but it is significant that it is the still photograph that is chosen for the conclusion of the program. This appears to confirm that still photography's freezing of a single moment possesses greater power to underline its importance as a historical turning point than does the moving image.

While this is not the final film in the series, since it is followed by episodes about the Soviet Union's brief war with Japan and a reflection on the cost of war and the remembrance of it in the final film, the Victory Banner and Berlin imagery still function to end the narrative of the war in Europe, which had been one of existential importance for the Soviets. Lancaster describes Berlin as the "last decisive battle" and "last major battle" of World War II and the culmination of Soviet efforts to avenge the attack on their homeland. The Victory Banner imagery serves here once again to complete a narrative that began with the invasion of the Soviet Union and the defense of Moscow. It does so at the expense of a certain tendency toward repetition, criticized by US producer Isaac Kleinerman in December 1977.[92] However, this is part of the Soviets' need to maintain the structural coherence and, with it, ideological coherence of the war narrative over the course of the twenty episodes.

DIFFICULTIES OVER THE PLACE OF THE HOLOCAUST

While the imagery of the Victory Banner over the Reichstag is a key element helping to maintain the coherence of the war narrative in *The Unknown War* series, the fate of Soviet and European Jews is something that the filmmakers find difficult to place in this narrative, since their fate is more connected with their ethnicity and less with their identity as Soviet citizens. At this point, the approach to ethnicity from the very beginning of the project, whereby in the US commentary the word "Russian" had been used to refer to all Soviet citizens, became particularly problematic. It was the descriptor used during the war by the British and Americans, and it made sense up to a point, downplaying the ideological character of the Soviet regime, but it compounded the Soviets' reticence over representation of the Holocaust, in turn creating tensions with the American partners.

A key episode that highlighted these tensions was the thirteenth, "The Liberation of Ukraine." Initially it was to begin with a sequence of Burt Lancaster, filmed at Babyi Iar, speaking to the US audience at the most important site of the Holocaust in the Soviet Union. In the final version of the film, the footage shot at Babyi Iar had been moved to the start of the second half of the nearly one-hour episode. This enabled a greater concentration on the heroism and feat of arms to push the narrative of victimhood to one side.

While the Babyi Iar footage was retained, subsequent treatments discarded a sequence about the Nazi crimes committed in Kharkiv and in Crimea, at Kerch, where there was even a mention of the Nazis' use of mobile "gas wagons" for asphyxiation killings and an assertion that the Chilean dictator Augusto Pinochet was harboring the perpetrators of such crimes. However, even after having decided to retain the sequence filmed at Babyi Iar, the Soviet writers agonized over what Lancaster should say there. Initially, the text he is to speak uses the time-worn Soviet formula for referring to the ethnicity of Nazi victims, said to be

"Soviet people"—"Jews, Russians, and Ukrainians"—although Russians are mentioned first in some script variants.[93] The marginality of Jews in this central site of Jewish memory in the Soviet Union was increased further, as the text referred to Soviets as Russians: "since these tragic events occurred on the Russian land 35 years have passed, a new generation of Russians has grown up."[94] Even the initial attempts to use Babyi Iar as a symbol for all of the various mass graves containing the bodies of Soviet Jews refer to graves like this as being all over "Russia" or "occupied Russia." The liberating soldiers were also repeatedly referred to as Russian.[95]

Following a prescreening in January 1978, however, the American side requested a number of corrections that concerned the way in which the ethnic character of the Nazis' victims was described and that objected to the marginalization of the Jews. The Americans' concerns first addressed the "Liberation of Ukraine" episode: "To tone down the rhetoric of the line about Russian and Ukrainian soldiers or to explain it in the text. To add figures about the battle of Korsun′-Shevchenko. To heighten the dramatic tone of the text explaining about Babyi Iar, citing the figures about the Jews killed and those saved by the Red Army, or evacuated from Poland, the Western regions of Ukraine, Belarus and the Baltic Republics."[96]

These corrections were all accepted by the Soviet side, and new text was proposed that made Jews more prominent while still retaining an emphasis on Russians: "*The Liberation of Kiev.* The first great Russian city to be reclaimed from the Germans. Russian troops swept in as the central city was blasting to the skies under Nazi demolition bombs. They found thousands of Jews and Russians had been exterminated and unearthed the great pit of Baby Yar where thousands of Jews had met their death."[97]

The completed film starts with Lancaster on location on the banks of the Dniepr, representing the military dimension of the conflict—the challenge of crossing the Dniepr. After twenty minutes, following a commercial break, Lancaster presents the story of the liberation of Kiev. Speaking at Babyi Iar, he refers to the victims murdered there as "Russians, Ukrainians, Jews. Mostly Jews." He also mentions Shostakovich's Thirteenth Symphony and quotes Evtushenko's poem "Babyi Iar," written "for the Jewish dead," which serves as the libretto for Shostakovich's work. The later Russian commentary, however, tellingly does not include the phrase "mostly Jews." While this passage refers to and quotes Evtushenko's poem, it does not quote or mention its Jewish dimension or Shostakovich's symphony.

The US consultant made analogous criticisms and suggested corrections to the sixteenth episode, "The Liberation of Poland." While a compromise had been found over Ukraine, when it came to Poland the differences in how Nazi atrocities and the Warsaw Uprising would be described required a substantial rewriting: "VI. Acknowledging that the nature of disagreements over the 'Liberation of Poland' episode is of a fundamental character, the respective sides have agreed, using certain proposals by the American side (attached to the protocol), for Soviet authors in Moscow to write a new version of the text, and to discuss it during the American delegation's trip at the end of March."[98]

After original plans for a trip to Poland were shelved, Lancaster instead was recorded in the studio for the Poland episode, saying to camera that he is recording narration for the *The Unknown War*. The studio recording was not only cheaper and less emotionally powerful, but it also downplayed the importance of specific places and moments. An early attempt at depicting the liberation of Poland had a similarly vague effect, by intention, in that all of the atrocities committed by the Nazis in Poland were bundled together in a sequence during which Lancaster was seated at a table looking at photographs of Nazi atrocities: "In the course of all these occupations, the Nazis were unable to suppress Polish resistance entirely. In the autumn of 1944 it became clear that the complete liberation of Poland from the Nazi yoke was close. The film begins with footage of the Soviet troops' mass offensive."[99]

Instead, images of Soviet troops and the joyful moment of liberation were to dominate, as they do throughout the film's narrative. In talking about concentration camps, the finished film refers to the repression of Poles, "a proud Slavic race" regarded by the Nazis as subhuman, and it refers to a list of fates, including the gas chambers. It then shifts to examining Poland's Jews as "a special case," telling the story of the Warsaw ghetto, including the 1943 uprising, and the deportation to camps. Later, when showing the images of Majdanek, there is a mixing up of images as we see famous images from Auschwitz, including bales of human hair and twins showing their tattooed ID numbers.

The anxieties over how to control the narrative about Poland are brought to the fore in the way in which the treatment deals with the 1944 Warsaw Uprising, which the Red Army famously failed to support. One script variant from 1977 touches upon the uprising briefly before the script moves on to Majdanek. The script says, "There are various interpretations of the history of these tragic days," but this is crossed out in favor of a tribute to the insurgents' courage, and then there is a shift to the liberation of Majdanek.[100] The final film simply asserts that the Soviets were exhausted and unable to cross the Vistula and pays tribute to the courage of the Poles who took part in the rising.

With regard to the even thornier issue of the massacre of Polish military officers at Katyn, the final film refers to the Soviet invasion of Poland in 1939 as "crossing the border and entering its Eastern provinces in 1939." It later reports the Nazi allegations about Katyn and says that the "London Poles thought that this might be true" but then endorses the Soviet version, albeit in a fairly muted way. Howard Rosenberg, in a review for the *Los Angeles Times*, quoted Kleinerman on the disagreements:

> "Originally, they (the Soviets) didn't want anything about [Katyn] in the documentary, but we insisted it be in," said Kleinerman, a veteran documentarian who was film editor for "Victory at Sea" and producer of "The Twentieth Century" on CBS.
>
> Although the Soviet Union traditionally has regarded history as an arm of propaganda and instrument to affect social attitudes, "The Unknown War" includes nothing that can be construed as propaganda, the Americans insist. Air Time had creative control, says [Air Time International's Fred] Weiner, and discussed everything with the Soviets only as a courtesy.
>
> "In about every case, we had our way," adds Kleinerman. "At times they were unhappy, but began to understand we were trying to make a damn good documentary."[101]

As we have seen, the Soviets ultimately thought that they would be able to get their message across and that certain compromises were acceptable toward this end. Permitting the United States to present themselves as getting their way was an acceptable price to pay. Looking at the final films, it is hard to escape the conclusion that the series overwhelmingly succeeds in getting across the Soviet narrative of the war. Even where there were compromises, these were toned down in the version released to Soviet audiences.

Thus, while the Soviets do permit a depiction of the Holocaust that is more frank about the extent of Jewish victimhood in the war than they would normally allow, we still see an account of the war that makes sense of the suffering and, after a twenty-episode epic sweep and despite the intimate feel of television, still returns and confirms the grandiose overarching narrative of the war as heroic, meaningful, and redemptive rather than dissipating and breaking into fragmentary individual stories.

A reluctance to narrate the story of the Holocaust systematically, with exact figures, dates, and precision over what image comes from where, as well as a differentiation of the groups of the dead, is something that we already saw with regard to Roman Karmen's 1965 film, *The Great Patriotic*. In *The Unknown War*, seen as Roman Karmen's legacy because he did not live until the premiere and saw the somber final part as particularly important, the same tendency dominates. In the final episode of the series, "A Soldier of the Unknown War," images of the Tomb of the Unknown Soldier in Moscow and mourners laying wreaths on 9

May are followed by a series of images of memorials to the Soviet war dead throughout the countries they liberated. These are underlined and made more poignant by showing the numbers of those who died in the various campaigns and battles. There then follow images of the Nuremberg tribunal, and frames from the films shown there of the camps, including Auschwitz, Majdanek, Buchenwald, Mauthausen, Dachau, and Ravensbruck. These are grouped into a montage so that the specific story in each geographical location is underplayed in favor of a generalized and indistinct sense of grief and suffering. This is a slightly different approach than what we see in other Soviet documentaries on this theme, but the effect, curiously, is rather similar—to create a universalized image of the dead, in which ethnic specificity and the distinct fate of Soviet Jewry are subsumed in an overall, Soviet story of meaningful sacrifice and redemption in victory.

There are many images from the Nazis' slaughter of the Jews, including the Einsatzgruppen killings, but while the figure of 6 million Jews does appear in the US version, accompanying the famous image of the young Sinti girl being loaded on a train at the Westerbork camp in the Netherlands, the same image is used but the figure of 6 million is absent from the Russian version. Finally, after platitudes about peace from Leonid Brezhnev, the film returns to Moscow's Tomb of the Unknown Soldier and footage of apparently carefree contemporary Soviet citizens, whose images are used to emphasize the meaningful sacrifice of Soviet soldiers as vindication and thus the narrative coherence of this film, the whole series, and of the war as such.

The Victory Banner image plays an important role in the narrative, framing the whole episode devoted to the battle of Berlin, but the need to reach out to US audiences meant that here it does not play quite the same kind of central narrative role it plays in many other war narratives: its communist and Soviet associations are perhaps too much for Americans to take. The Tomb of the Unknown Soldier and Brezhnev himself had become more prominent. Indeed, two years prior to the completion of *The Unknown War*, in 1976, a biographical film about Brezhnev called *Tale of a Communist* (*Povest′ o kommuniste*, dir. Igor′ Bessarabov, Aleksandr Kochetkov) was released. In the culminating moment of the general secretary receiving his Marshal of the Soviet Union epaulettes on 9 May 1976, the film showed the Victory Banner footage as if its hoisting at the Reichstag had been his personal achievement. When his 1978 ghostwritten war memoir *Minor Land* (*Malaia zemlia*) came out, expanding on the experience of taking part in the 24 June 1945 Victory Day parade, it contained this passage: "So my dream of reaching victory was also realized: this was the dream of millions of Soviet soldiers, who not only fought to the death, defending their land, but also honorably carried the Victory Banner through the hard roads of war and raised it in Berlin over the Reichstag."[102]

The Victory Banner, and the war cult more broadly, was now being made to serve the Brezhnev cult, just as it had the Stalin cult. Brezhnev's absurd new cult was now being more widely employed than the Victory Banner in this effort to produce a charismatic aura, with unfortunate consequences for both.

RECEPTION OF *THE UNKNOWN WAR*

Like *Liberation*, *The Unknown War* was an attempt to convey the Soviet interpretation of World War II to a wider international audience and to use the Soviets' sacrifice and victory in that war to garner sympathy and thus bolster its power in the Cold War. After the film was finished in a little over a year, it received a premiere in September 1978 at Washington DC's Kennedy Center, attended by civil servants, senators, congressional representatives, university presidents, scholars and directors of US historical associations, and leading journalists. In reviewing the film, author Erskine Caldwell commented that the Soviets had won the war because they believed in their system. The film also received screenings at colleges, and Harrison Salisbury wrote a special booklet to accompany the film.[103] The series then premiered simultaneously on television networks in New York, Los Angeles, Washington DC, and Chicago and was ultimately broadcast in numerous major American cities, reaching more than 30 million Americans in fall 1978 as they tuned in every Saturday evening.[104] This was less than the originally envisaged 50 channels reaching 150 million Americans but has not deterred some Soviet commentators from claiming that it had a great effect abroad, probably greater than any previous (Soviet) documentary film, which suggests an ignorance of the reception of wartime Soviet films in the United States. Nevertheless, it won a prize at the New York International Film Festival and at the Miami International Film Festival.[105]

However, while there were criticisms of its bias from the start, *The Unknown War* attracted more vocal protests following the Soviet invasion of Afghanistan in December 1979.[106] That led to its removal from American screens and to the Soviet Union's increasing international ostracization.[107] In pro-Soviet East Germany, however, it received the top prize, the Golden Dove, at the Leipzig Festival of Documentary and Animated Films, in 1980, and was also shown on national television.[108] At the festival, a minute's silence was observed in honor of the recently deceased Karmen.

At the very beginning of work on *The Unknown War*, in February 1977, Roman Karmen had predicted that the series would also be interesting for Soviet viewers, "of course in a somewhat different and shorter version than what is being done for America."[109] The series was not adapted other than being dubbed into Russian, however, with certain changes to the text as we saw above, but it was shown first of all in cinemas, starting with a Red Army day (23 February 1979) premiere of the first two episodes at the Rossiia cinema in central Moscow (where *The Great Patriotic* had been shown in 1965).[110] There then followed a series of ten screenings of two episodes each scheduled over a couple of weeks in forty-two of the country's most prestigious movie theaters, which were packed. After starting in Moscow, the film made its way through the capitals of Union republics and Hero cities, following the established hierarchy of war commemoration. In many places it was the most widely viewed film: in Leningrad it was watched by three times as many people as had gone to see *An Office Romance* (*Sluzhebnyi roman*, 1977), by the hugely popular comic director El′dar Riazanov, which admittedly had been running for a year.[111]

One of the dimensions of the series that greatly appealed to the Soviet public was the immediacy and directness of the experience of watching the whole series. The Soviet media had not seen anything like *The Unknown War*: all the compromises made to ensure that the film worked for American audiences in style and content meant that the series felt fresh to Soviet viewers, leading at least one critic to claim that there was no precedent for the series in world cinema.[112] In fact, it followed the established format of multipart television historical documentary series that had been popular in the United States for twenty years, but through its use of a celebrity narrator (dubbed into Russian) in choice locations such as the Hall of Victory, the series creates a sense of immediacy and directness that compensates for the scant use of interviews and overcomes the increasing remoteness of wartime documentary footage.

There is a sense, however, in which *The Unknown War* represented a new genre—the "documentary epic"—distinct from other television series about the war, due to its more insistent narrative cohesion. It overcomes fragmentation through the same means as *The World at War* and others, through repeated credits and music, the repetition of iconic images, the preview of the next episode at the end of the preceding one, and the use of the same presenter throughout. However, *The Unknown War* goes further than *The World at War* in its more insistent narrative thread, minimizing the use of the interview, and focusing overwhelmingly on the Soviet side in the conflict. Yet it was the way in which the film was shown and consumed in the Soviet Union that compounded its aspirations to epic status: by being screened theatrically and then on television on consecutive evenings in a short space of time, it created a festival-like intensity, a sense of the unmissable described by Christine Evans as characteristic of Soviet television.[113] In some sense this is akin to the modern day "binge-watching" of box-sets. Watching in this way at the same time encouraged audiences to perceive the war in monumental and epic terms, with unifying narrative sweep.

The Unknown War succeeded through the medium of documentary at what *Liberation* had attempted to do in features: conveying the epic scale and significance of the war for the Soviets. Indeed, despite being conceived as a filmic response to television, *Liberation* too was ultimately shown on the small screen, where it was a much greater success, prompting one commentator to argue that it revealed a hidden "TV aesthetic" when shown on television.[114] Its enormous length made *Liberation* better suited to the programming possibilities of Soviet television, especially during festivals and public holidays such as 9 May, which created extended periods of viewing that were a defining characteristic.[115]

In both cases, the Victory Banner imagery served to underpin the significance of the 9 May festivities. However, the banner itself was very seldom used in the period from 1965 to 1985. While mentions of and visual references to the Victory Banner continued to be frequent in newspaper coverage of Victory Day in this period, access to events involving the Victory Banner, unlike the practice of laying wreaths or flowers on graves, which everyone could do, was strictly limited: thus, a select company of thousands gathered around it in the Central Museum of the Soviet Army on 9 May 1969, where it was accorded a guard of honor.[116] The Victory Banner was similarly accompanied by a guard of honor the following year, for the larger-scale twenty-fifth anniversary of the end of the war. For that anniversary there was a large meeting and concert given to an invited audience in the Kremlin Palace of Soviets, at which the Victory Banner's entrance, accompanied by Egorov, Kantariia, and Samsonov, was thunderously applauded and people rose to accompany its being taken from the venue to the accompaniment of a march. They remained standing for the national anthem and minute of silence, suggesting these connected symbolic actions were treated similarly.[117]

There was a similar meeting in 1975, and there were likewise mentions of the Victory Banner over the course of Victory Days during the 1970s. Moreover, according to a guide for organizing such events, local ceremonies were also supposed to incorporate banners that would themselves be honored by being ceremonially carried into a meeting while attendees stood as a sign of respect, and the entrance of this banner would also be accompanied by the sounds of an appropriate march.[118]

While not a part of 9 May parades in this period, the Victory Banner was used to lead the 7 November (October Revolution) military parades in 1975 and 1977. The short articles explaining the unusual format of the parade in the military newspaper *Krasnaia zvezda* are almost identical word for word, with the exception that the 1975 article refers to the thirtieth anniversary of victory.[119] This in itself was indicative of a widespread fear of saying anything new, a facet of the logic of authoritarian repetition and the ritualization of discourse.

It is hard to be sure why there was no 9 May parade in 1975: as we saw with the final part of *The Unknown War*, the Soviet state was bolstering its symbolic legitimacy through the leader cult of Brezhnev, especially in association with an inflated account of his war record designed to bolster his symbolic power as his physical body grew weak.[120] Thus, it may be that the Brezhnev cult required fewer uses of the Victory Banner since the "charisma" of Brezhnev was thought enough in and of itself and there was thus less need for the Victory Banner as a charismatic object.

The lack of a parade in 1975 may have been related to the contexts of the Helsinki security conference, détente, and the Soviet Union's championing of peace, which would have been contradicted by an extra military parade that included the latest missiles; having the Victory Banner at the annual 7 November parade was less of a confrontational and aggressive gesture, because that parade was a permanent fixture. It may also be speculated that Brezhnev's declining health was a factor: he was finding it so hard to ascend the mausoleum steps that Poland's leader, General Wojciech Jaruzelski, quipped that this was the major show of strength (and not the missiles) on these occasions. In 1979 Brezhnev reduced the size of the 7 November parade from four hours to ninety minutes, because he found it hard to remain on his feet so long. Introducing a further parade would tax his ailing constitution unnecessarily.[121]

By contrast, while the physical rituals of parades were inconsistently observed in this period, 9 May film and television schedules were dominated by ritualistic screenings, with *The Unknown War* still being shown episode by episode in 1985, culminating in the twentieth episode being shown on 9 May itself. There were a number of attempts to repeat this pattern, notably with a partially dramatized seventeen-episode documentary series, *The Strategy of Victory* (*Strategiia Pobedy*, dir. Viktor Rabinovich, Stanislav Belianinov, Viktor Kriukov, Igor′ Beliaev, Samarii Zelikin, 1984). Although this series used some of the ubiquitous footage of the Victory Banner, including in its credits, it was oriented toward documents and memoirs, especially of the high command, which were read out by actors in studios. This meant that the series was less emotionally effective and visually arresting than *The Unknown War*.[122] Even though they made extensive use of Victory Banner footage and imagery, the same tended to be true of the many documentary productions aired in the Victory Day holiday period. These offerings had titles such as *Then in 1945* (*Togda v 45-m*, dir. Iurii Zanin, 1985) and *Legendary People* (*Liudi-legendy*, dir. I. Gutman, 1985), the first part of which, "Standard Bearers of Victory" ("Znamenostsy pobedy"), was devoted to Egorov and Kantariia.

But these productions, including that of *The Unknown War*, did not function equally effectively for viewers across the different generations. When *The Great Patriotic* was shown in 1965, there was a sense articulated in the film's voice-over that this was the audience's own experience, that most of the audience knew the participants. With *The Unknown War* there still were those who were said to have recognized themselves or loved ones, but the picture was more varied. As one critic put it, "the epic is oriented to the memory of the older generation, the conscience of the middle one, and the consciousness of those just entering life."[123] Part of the task now was to convey the wartime experience to a generation that had no direct experience of the war and who might not have understood its importance. Thus, Marshal of the Soviet Union Vasilii Chuikov, twice decorated with the Hero of the Soviet Union medal, praised the series: "A major event not only in cinematography, but in the whole country's public life, was the showing on cinema and on television screens of the multipart documentary film *The Great Patriotic*. This film, unprecedented in the breadth of its design, was truly aimed at the whole people. The unforgettable documentary footage, gleaned in the grit of battle, is for the veterans, who watch their youth with curiosity, and for those born after 1945, and to our grandchildren."[124]

However, while these images may have been in part addressed to younger people, they did not always have the desired effect, as one viewer of *The Unknown War* discovered in 1982:

> I remember I watched the third episode of the film (*The Great Patriotic*) on 19th May. There were also schoolchildren watching, as a group. I won't say the number of the school—it's too embarrassing. During the screening, the adults repeatedly asked the schoolchildren to keep the noise down—to no avail.
>
> I understand: not everyone remembers the grief of war. Not everyone had their mother blown up by a shell, as I have. Yes, I understand, not everyone has. But we are talking about something elementary: a sentimental education.
>
> I feel guilty too, because there's so much that we, the parents, have not succeeded in explaining to the children and have somehow decided that if we feel this, then they must also feel it too.[125]

This disconnect apparently felt by schoolchildren whom teachers had forced to watch the film echoes the sentiments expressed by journalist Dmitrii Radyshevskii to Nina Tumarkin: when, as a teenager in 1975, he won the right to be photographed next to the Victory Banner, he had wondered, "Why did our teachers think we would have any desire to look at Soviet banners, when every day we saw them everywhere?"[126] In his eyes, it was neither unique nor sacred; that was how he remembered it in the 1990s. Whether (and if so to whom) he expressed those sentiments in 1975 is not recorded.

The depiction of Brezhnev with his little granddaughter in the final episode of *The Unknown War*, looking decidedly infirm as he slurred his speech, illustrated the theme of bringing together the younger and the older generations, uniting society, and doing so in particular around memory of the war. This is related to a sense that those who fought in the war possessed a unique authority that could not be questioned; like the Victory Banner, as well as the medals, their experience was something beyond common rational scrutiny.

Although it has been argued that what has been called the Soviet "cult" of the war reached its peak with the fortieth-anniversary commemorations in 1985, it might also be argued that memory of the war was already a less influential and declining force.[127] Even in the Politburo, wartime veterans now faced being replaced by a generation who had not experienced the war directly except perhaps as children, and from this very demographic came the new general secretary: Mikhail Gorbachev.

The Politburo had been dominated by older people under Brezhnev, and there was very little renewal of its membership under his leadership, largely due to the key Brezhnev orientation toward "stability of cadres."[128] This stability meant greater employment security for party officials. The conservative tendencies of this "gerontocracy" were compounded by the collective leadership principle, which strove for consensus, ensuring that Politburo members signed off on all speeches.[129] In practice, this mitigated against bold and innovative turns of speech and led to the repetition of the ritualistic formulas observed by Yurchak. The verbal pattern and visual image of the Victory Banner illustrated this authoritarian repetition, such as that at the 9 May parading of the Victory Banner, recorded and shown live on television.

But the 1985 parade, like the Soviet leadership, was also subject to change: Mikhail Egorov was now dead and Kantariia not well enough to march, so their absence alone marked a contrast with 1965. However, the departures from precedent, as before, were not addressed in the commentaries and coverage; officials were anxious to dispel any danger of a perceived break in continuity: "The sounds of the orchestra rework the beat of drums. They merge with the storm of applause: the Victory Banner floats over the square. The very same banner . . . penetrating thick clouds of smoke and soot, it was raised on 30 April at 21:50 above the conquered Reichstag. The modest red banner that history was preparing to make the Victory Banner."[130]

To assure this sense of continuity, Kantariia was used to manufacture a false memory of the banner from the 1945 parade (at which the Victory Banner was not present):

> The Victory Banner flutters by the gray Kremlin walls. One man is particularly anxious as he fixes it with his gaze. His name is known to everyone: M. V. Kantariia.
>
> Protecting the banner more than themselves, Mikhail Egorov and Meliton Kantariia stormed the hardest and most important tall building of the war. There they are on the cupola of the Reichstag. The May breeze unfurled the flag, and its red calico shone out above Berlin. The enemy opened fire, fiercely. You can say of the Victory Banner, as if of a soldier: it has seven bullet wounds.
>
> "I remember the rejoicing with which the Victory Banner was met on the parade," recalls Meliton Varlaamovich. It was triumphantly transported along Red Square in a car, above the seats of which there was an enormous globe. The flagpole protruding from the circle had the word "Berlin" written on it—the victorious point of the war.
>
> The thousand-piece orchestra for military music sounded triumphantly. Another Red Square parade has been completed. This was a special one: it was dominated by the Victory Banner marked by war. Swearing an oath of allegiance to this banner, and the cause of today, we dream of other victories together on the field of peaceful battle. For life, for the future. For a world in which there will be no more wars, in which there will be no wars or weapons.[131]

This third but not final military Victory Parade of the Soviet era occurred under the leadership of Mikhail Gorbachev, general secretary since March 1985. While Gorbachev "did little during his first year in office to mark himself out as unusual," the first Victory Day military parade since 1965 suggested a continuity that was illusory.[132] Gorbachev had in fact already begun to maneuver his own team into place, behind the scenes, and the decision to hold a military parade on 9 May 1985 appears to have been made during the brief administration of Konstantin Chernenko. In an echo of his mentor Leonid Brezhnev's bold, extemporized move of 1965, once again the parade was a signal of conservative credentials but also an attempt, in the absence of a new leader cult or charismatic symbol, to project stability and credibility after the prestige and authority of the Soviet system had been undermined by the death of two general secretaries in a matter of years. However, this did not work: in the face of the declining authority of the Soviet system, Chernenko "finished the job, finally stripping the general secretaryship of its last remnants of charisma."[133]

Despite the 9 May parade bearing all the hallmarks of Chernenko, it may also have been motived by the greater tensions of the 1980s chapter in the Cold War, when the introduction of new US mobile rockets on European sites (in response to already deployed Soviet ones) and the threat of the US "Star Wars" missile defense system were destabilizing the international status quo. It is a poignant paradox that this parade occurred on Gorbachev's watch, because Gorbachev was to take on the Soviet military, instituting a new "defensive doctrine," significant military expenditure cuts, and an enormous reduction in personnel. While he presided over the May 1985 display of missiles, he spoke in January 1986 of his hopes for a nuclear-free world by the year 2000.[134] This was anticipated by earlier moves to stress political rather than military solutions to conflict, the downgrading of the military's presence on the Politburo, and declarations in his 8 May 1985 speech that the contemporary world could not be compared to the polarizations of the 1930s and thus there was no pressing need to invest in defense.[135] Yet this speech has been seen as a tactical appeal to conservatives or as part of a tendency to present old ideological slogans and formulas but with a few revisionist elements inserted.[136] The revisionism was nonetheless real, and his 1987 decision to withdraw Soviet troops from Afghanistan, implemented in 1989, may be seen as a bold departure from Soviet policy norms and one that underlined the waning power and prestige of the military in Soviet society, ultimately contributing to the Soviet Union's collapse.[137]

In cinema, too, away from the ritualized television schedules, the 1985 anniversary was also marked by a high point in the demythologizing and critiquing of the war narrative, as the ritualistic atmosphere of unanimity began to fracture, most notably in Elem Klimov's *Come and See* (*Idi i smotri*, 1985), which presented a child's perception of the war as a relentless and morally corrupting force. This made cinematic depictions of the Great Patriotic War problematic and initiated a steep decline in the World War II film genre for the next twenty years.[138] For the Victory cult, reverence for the Victory Banner, and the war narrative all to be revived, it would take societal collapse and the rise of a new Russian patriotic consciousness in the 2000s.

5

ICONOCLASM, RESANCTIFICATION, AND THE POST-SOVIET VICTORY CULT

While it might have appeared that the Soviet "cult" of the war was reaching a peak with the ritualized repetitions of the 1985 fortieth-anniversary commemorations, in fact memory of the war was about to be transformed.[1] The glasnost era led to heightened attention to society and history as part of a frank reassessment of the Soviet Union's mistakes, past and present. This meant a more prominent role for history, with the news media publishing detailed, properly documented accounts of events. The interview with the professional historian became one of the glasnost-era press's most popular genres.[2] Russian Marxist philosopher Valentin Tolstykh stresses this period as an "awakening of historical consciousness in society, of its desire to free real socialism from various kinds of illusions, inventions, and timeless formulas."[3]

A particularly popular theme consisted in revelations that "refuted or at least shed a different light on the accounts promoted in official texts and rituals."[4] This tendency has been somewhat hyperbolically characterized by Richard Stites as "iconoclasm, demythologizing, and open irreverence. The ridicule of sacred icons."[5] However, even when there was not ridicule, there was a striving to reassess and desacralize. This attitude meant that the war, surrounded for so long by an impenetrable holy aura, emerged once again, even more ambitiously and openly than in the Khrushchev era, as an object for both sober historical inquiry and more sensationalist exposé.

As with the post-Stalin period, there was also a refocusing on the start of the war, with a round-table discussion of prominent Soviet military historians published in *Izvestiia* on 8 May 1990. It detailed the ways in which the country was poorly prepared for war purely in terms of logistics and training and how Stalin was personally responsible for the mistakes at the start of the war.[6] However, at this, the peak of glasnost, the subjects for reassessment now went beyond the 1960s focus on the Soviet Union's inadequate preparation for the start of the war in 1941 and included even more telling revelations about the 1940 Katyn massacre of Polish officers by the NKVD, the Nazi-Soviet pact, penal battalions, Soviet collaborators, and revelations as to the falsified nature of Soviet leaders' war records.[7]

One of the key changes was that the dominant framing paradigm was not heroism anymore but suffering. This new paradigm inverted the previous hierarchy: whereas previously both were present, heroism, a key part of which was the Victory Banner imagery, had overshadowed and disciplined representations of suffering.[8] Now a sense of the war's suffering dominated, unchecked. Typical of this is a story published in *Izvestiia*, in the run-up to Victory Day, about a soldier who lost his memory and spent years in a mental hospital only to regain it very recently and find his family.[9] This is not so much glorious, not so much a reflection of the overarching narrative of the significance of victory but one of suffering, endured randomly, by an individual and his family. This shift reflected the struggle between rival interpretations of the war that had surfaced from 1986, with the release and publication of many sources that had previously been censored, and demands for full respect to be accorded to Soviets who had been prisoners of war.[10]

This period also saw the demythologizing and critiquing of the whole idea of the Victory Banner. Some of the inaccurate claims about the storming of the Reichstag had of course already been contested and corrected earlier, in the 1960s or later, as the findings of the 1960 and 1961 conferences began to leak out. In 1975 (the year Egorov died in a car accident), he published a memoir in which he conceded that he and Kantariia's flag had been erected after many others, but this claim was not endorsed by the official *History of the Second World War*, the ninth volume of which, published in 1979, described the storming of the Reichstag.[11] While this publication was silent about the time the Victory Banner was raised, the claim that it was raised at 14:25 was corrected in a third edition of Zhukov's memoirs in 1978. Other memoirs, such as Colonel Fedor Zinchenko's, published in 1983, while taking care not to show disrespect or directly impugn the authority of Zhukov, say that 14:25 is the incorrect time and that the flag was raised in the evening.[12] This sense of vagueness and fear of contradicting the stories of those in command was quickly overcome in the glasnost period in a new wave of publications. One of the first of these was an article by Vladimir Seoev, a historian involved in the ongoing project to rewrite the multivolume *History of the Great Patriotic War*, in the Ukrainian newspaper *Rabochaia gazeta* on

1 May 1989. More prominent and influential, though, was an interview published in *Pravda* on 30 April 1990 with Seoev and historian Georgii Kumanev. Headlined "The Banner Bearers of Victory" ("Znamenonostsy Pobedy"), it explained how the incorrect time of 14:25 had come about (a premature claim made by divisional commander Shatilov) and the process by which it became widespread and accepted. As conscientious professionals, Seoev and Kumanev produce a rounded historical account that compared memoir accounts with documents and gave a detailed account of the mythmaking, the falsification, and the suppression of truth that had occurred since the 1960–1961 conferences.[13] They also refer to Bobrov, a member of the group storming the Reichstag, who had been jailed after the war and was thus not mentioned in the 1960s-era *History of the Great Patriotic War.*

Kumanev received joyful congratulatory letters from Sergeant Mikhail Minin and V. D. Shatalin, former commander of the 380th Rifle Regiment, whose accounts had now been vindicated. On the other hand, General Shatilov, shown to be responsible not only for the incorrect premature claim that the flag had been raised at 14:25 but also for continuing to perpetuate that distortion, wrote to Minister of Defense Dmitrii Iazov demanding the formation of a special commission to look at this question.[14]

The *Pravda* piece also mentioned the fact that the banner was not part of the June 1945 parade. This startling revelation was one that Neustroev himself expanded upon in a publication that came out around the same time: "In the decades following the war there have been many different fantasized legends written about the storming of the Reichstag[;] they are what we call in Russian, lies. There were also attempts to make me fall into line with numerous authoritative figures. 'What you say contradicts this person and that person. You have to rewrite it, to find a compromise,' I was repeatedly advised by comrades responsible."[15]

Kumanev subsequently expanded his analysis in a book published in 2000. Drawing on archival documents and eyewitness accounts, he claims to set the record straight as to who raised the Victory Banner and when. His conclusions are very much in line with the picture that emerged at the 1960 and 1961 conferences but was not fully published at the time. In brief: the first onto the roof of the building were Captain Makov (756th Rifle Regiment, 150th Rifle Division, Seventy-Ninth Rifle Corps, Third Strike Army) and his group (Aleksei Bobrov, Gizii Zagitov, Aleksandr Lisimenko, and Mikhail Minin), who put a flag on an equestrian statue of Germania (also known as the Goddess of Victory) at 22:40. This was a flag given to them by the command of the Seventy-Ninth Rifle Corps.[16] Egorov and Kantariia were in the second wave, accompanied by

Aleksei Berest and a group under Il′ia S′ianov, which put up the official flag no. 5 of the 150th Rifle Division on the same statue later that night, at 3:00 a.m., and it was then moved on 2 May to the cupola. This was the flag intended to become, and which later was officially dubbed, the Victory Banner. In the aftermath of the battle, Makov's group was recommended for the Hero of the Soviet Union award but received instead a lesser medal, the Order of the Red Banner, possibly because they cited the actual time of 22:40, which conflicted with the premature order of 14:25 that had become official. Egorov and Kantariia were also awarded Orders of the Red Banner in 1945 but made Heroes of the Soviet Union in May 1946.[17] Kumanev's reasoned account was repeated in the press but somehow had little effect.[18] It has been followed by others, often with a more popularizing orientation, such as the 2006 book by Nikolai Iamskoi, which confirms Kumanev's account of the first flag being raised by Makov's group but goes beyond the documentation to imagine dialogue and naïvely treats the photographs and newsreel of the raising of the banner as evidence.[19] More recently, the Central Museum of the Armed Forces has produced its own account, written by Arkadii Dement′ev, building on Kumanev and referencing numerous new archival documents from the difficult-to-access Ministry of Defense archive.[20]

Just as the actual account of events was critiqued, this period also saw films and articles demythologizing and critiquing the 1945 images. Taking advantage of looser travel restrictions, Soviet film historian Sergei Drobashenko attended an August 1985 conference at the Institut für Wissenschaft und Film (IWF) in Göttingen on the subject of film depictions of history. There he gave a presentation on the subject of the Soviet film record of the raising of the Victory Banner over the Reichstag that did not question the assumption that the footage records the actual moment the flag was raised.[21] His account was flatly rejected by US historian Richard Raack, who referred to the film as a restaging of a myth, rephrasing philosopher George Santayana's maxim: "those who deny the past will constantly repeat it: repeat it in history so that the historical myths sustaining the apparatus of the system can go critically untested; repeat it in behavior so that the designs of yesterday will prefigure those of today and tomorrow."[22] Challenging Soviet propaganda myths, in this scholar's view, was a precondition for reforming the system that had produced them.

Raack also referred to the multiplicity of photographs of the Victory Banner, stating that they do not in fact record the actual raising of this flag. This was of course true, and Khaldei's famous photograph of the Victory Banner would soon be exposed as staged. In 1991, German artist and art historian Ernst Volland was among the first to track Khaldei down in Moscow, and he exhibited and published the multiple takes of the Victory Banner scene in Germany.[23] In the run-up to the 1995 fiftieth anniversary of the end of the war, journalists from around the world began to take an interest in his work, and Belgian filmmaker Marc-Henri Wajnberg made a documentary entitled *Evgenii Khaldei: A Photographer under Stalin* in 1997 in which the photograph representing the Victory Banner over the Reichstag features prominently alongside Khaldei's account of making it. Here Khaldei claims to have taken the shot on 2 May, using a flag made for him and that he brought himself from Moscow. While he does not say that the battle was already over and that his was not the first flag to be raised, he does say that he got the soldiers to try putting up the flag in a variety of compositions. Clearly this was not the first flag to be raised, since it is hard to imagine soldiers risking their lives to pose while under fire. Moreover, this was when it became public knowledge that, when Khaldei returned to Moscow late on 2 May, Palgunov, chief editor at TASS, drew his attention to the fact that the soldier holding up the flag was wearing two watches, a sign of looting. Khaldei was told to scratch out the watch from one of the photographs, and he did so, thus enabling it to be published. Implicitly in Wajnberg's film, and more explicitly subsequently, this became a story of staging and falsification illustrating the deceitful and morally bankrupt nature of the Soviet regime.[24] However, this reorientation toward the historical and critical view of the war did not necessarily translate into changes in public memory and the rituals by which memory of the war was commemorated on Victory Day.

THE EVOLUTION OF VICTORY DAY COMMEMORATIONS

While the 9 May military parade became a contested practice at the end of the Soviet era, the institution of Victory Day, with its ritualistic television programming for the days leading up to the holiday as well as the day itself, continued to be observed to the end of the Soviet Union in 1991 and has continued in the post-Soviet period. The 1990 commemorations are particularly interesting, displaying as they do a totally different approach to the war than that which dominated during the previous twenty-five years.[25]

In the late 1980s, the Soviet public were allowed to vote on whether a monument inspired by the Victory Banner would be the appropriate symbol with which to commemorate the war at the new Victory Park war memorial complex. They rejected this project.[26] While the precise reasons are a matter of speculation, it seems likely that the popular rejection was a product of the skepticism felt toward the official cult of

ИЗВЕСТИЯ

№ 129 • 8 мая 1990 года • 3

ПРЯМАЯ СВЯЗЬ

Передают корреспонденты «Известий»

ЛИТВА ОБЪЯВЛЯЕТ САНКЦИИ

ДПР—ПАРТИЯ БЕЗ АППАРАТА

КИРОВЦЫ БРОСАЮТ ПЕРЧАТКУ

ВЕРНУТЬ ИМЯ ГОРОДУ

ВОЙНА. НАРОД. ПОБЕДА

1945-1990

5.1. Victory Banner logo, from *Izvestiia*, 8 May 1990.

World War II by the Soviet population at this time, fueled in turn by a widespread mood of iconoclasm.

Yet despite the increasing skepticism and numerous revelations, much of the iconography remained unchanged: Khaldei's photograph was used as a logo for *Izvestiia*'s coverage of Victory Day in 1990. The contradictory combination of radically discontinuous verbal content with the established symbolism was also a feature of Gorbachev's speech at the traditional ceremonial meeting on the eve of Victory Day. According to tradition, the meeting was preceded by the usual fanfare and parade of the Victory Banner, but his emphasis was groundbreaking, focusing on the price of victory through the new, higher figure of 27 million Soviet war dead, the catastrophic losses of the first year of the war due in great part to Stalin's repression of 40,000 officers and misreading of the intelligence warning of the impending German attack, and the ruinous situation in the villages after the war, where there were 1.1 million disabled veterans, whose needs are a greater priority than monuments to the dead, he argued. To support this argument, Gorbachev audaciously turned the Victory Banner symbol into one of loss that should no longer be used to deflect questions as to the price of victory: "What was the cause of the unimaginable scale of the death and destruction we suffered? Why was the path to the raising of the Victory Banner over the Reichstag so hard for our army? Again and again, we address these and other key questions because our mind and conscience are not satisfied by the previous incomplete and sometimes inaccurate responses."[27]

Nevertheless, despite this emphasis on losses, Gorbachev rejected the notion that the war was won by blood alone, arguing instead that the war was won because it became "truly the people's war," as those who "condemned Stalin as a tyrant" and those who admired him as savior joined together regardless of their ethnic and political differences. Gorbachev's interpretation was contradictory, as he also stressed the role of the party as key to victory but at the same time condemned totalitarianism, claiming that the reasons for the fact that the winners (i.e., the Soviets) are now poorer than the losers of the war (i.e., the West Germans) is due to the authoritarian system stifling the sense of freedom, dignity, and respect for the individual that soldiers began to develop during the war:

> Having spent time at the front line, advancing across Europe, many people for the first time began to realize or at the very least suspect that our country was not so advanced as they had been taught. Having returned from the war, they did not feel themselves to be "little screws" and did not want to be "little screws." But this feeling of dignity and freedom was first given an outlet only after the 20th party congress. The main aim of Perestroika is to restore respect for the personality, the self-worth of humanity, to liberate people's creative potential.[28]

While condemning Stalinism for reducing the Soviet people who had defeated Hitler to "little screws," Gorbachev in the next breath asserted that the war was in fact one between humanism and inhumanity, democracy and fascism, which effectively makes the Soviet Union under Stalin democratic, undermining, or at least contradicting, his own critique of

Stalinism. Compounding this confusion, Gorbachev's emphasis on the wartime alliance, described as one of "democratic forces," is one he sees as a paradigm for cooperation in the future, vindicating his emphasis on "common human interests and values": "The war showed the capacity of democratic forces around the Earth to unite before a common mortal danger. This outcome is highly relevant for us, who are living in this historically groundbreaking time of great responsibility."[29]

Instead of the habitual use of Victory Day to emphasize Soviet credit for victory so as to bolster a sense of exceptionalism and a display of strength to project martial prowess, Gorbachev ended his speech with details of his proposed reforms of the military and reflections on the future given the demise of what the Yalta and Potsdam conferences had created, and he wondered how to ensure that a united Germany would be peaceful. These are not ritualistic formulas but apparently sincere ruminations, deviating from the previous script.

A greater focus on the wider picture of the war, encompassing Western efforts, the sense that the victory was one for democracies more widely, and greater attention to the social history elements instead of exclusively heroic Soviet military feats were all common features of the wider media coverage.[30] Nevertheless, the military parade on Red Square took place in what was essentially the same *form* as it had five years earlier, in 1985. The television commentary and newspaper coverage claimed that the change as to the individual who officially ordered the parade to take place, from the minister of defense to the president of the Soviet Union, possessed a deeper symbolism: "our Fatherland is not demonstrating military might, but a striving toward peace."[31] The dominant tone was a critical attitude toward the militaristic implication of such parades.

As with the 1985 parade, the Victory Banner in 1990 was no longer being borne by one of those originally associated with its raising on the Reichstag (Egorov, Kantariia, Neustroev, or Samsonov), presumably because they were no longer alive or were in poor health. Instead, the television commentary described the flag bearer, Vasilii Zdunov, as being a participant in the storming of the Reichstag, and he was further associated with the banner because he was one of the group who accompanied it in transit from Berlin to Moscow on 23 June 1945. The Victory Banner symbol was, however, somewhat overshadowed in this parade because it was preceded by footage of a facsimile scale model of the statue, from Treptower Park cemetery in Berlin, of a soldier-liberator carrying a sword in one hand and cradling a young child in the other.

One debate prior to the 1990 commemoration day was over whether the expense of a military parade could be justified in times of economic hardship. The project to build a grandiose Victory Park museum and memorial complex at the Hill of Prostrations (Poklonnaia gora) in Moscow had been frozen in 1987 in part for the same reasons.[32] Nikolai Kalinin, commander of the Moscow military *okrug* (district), argued that it must be justified: "'Is it just a question of money?' he said. 'There are things that you cannot measure in rubles. The parade is a symbol of our immortal glory, the continuation of the glorious traditions of our people, an injection of belief in our own success. Including in the success of Perestroika. Do you think things were easier in June 1945?'"[33]

The attempt to inflect the meaning of the parade so as to express ideas quite different from those of the continuity and vitality of the communist system that it had originally been conceived to convey meant that the unlikely figure of Minister of Defense Dmitrii Iazov (later to play an important part in the August 1991 coup against Gorbachev) in his 9 May speech on Red Square stressed the importance of democracy, something he would attempt to destroy the following year.

The 1990 parade reflected this uncertainty. Nina Tumarkin, an eyewitness, describes it as brief, small in scale, and lacking in the "swagger" of previous years as a result of the state of the crisis facing the country, as well as the widely held perception that the Soviet Union's social system and ideology were not, after all, superior to those of the West.[34] The true irony of the situation was, however, that Gorbachev, in his short six-year reign, presided over two Red Square Victory Parades, whereas Stalin and Brezhnev, who had both effectively invented the format, each held only one during their longer reigns.

Nevertheless, the Victory Banner, as well as the other traditional trappings of the parade, were still featured in 1990 and thereafter. Thus it was that, seeking to break with the symbolism of the Soviet Union and emphasize a new democratic identity, under the Russian Federation's first president, Boris Yeltsin, officials called for a very low-key marking of Victory Day on 9 May 1992, with no parade and an emphasis in the media on a victory being achieved despite, rather than because of, Stalin and the communist system. In part, this was due to the Communist Party of the Russian Soviet Federal Socialist Republic having been banned in 1991. However, having re-formed as the Communist Party of the Russian Federation (CPRF) in February 1993, Yeltsin's communist opponents were unwilling to reconcile themselves to this more historically nuanced and less triumphalist vision of war commemoration, and they successfully harnessed and articulated a wider perception that the commemoration of Victory was being belittled by the current government. In turn, this was linked to a wider societal sense of loss of the Soviet Union, the state for which the veterans had fought.[35] Following violence at Moscow May Day demonstrations in 1993, the city's mayor, Iurii Luzhkov, attempted to ban the Communist Party of the Russian Federation and other left-wing groups from gathering and marching to Red Square on 9 May.[36] The communists marched to Red Square anyway. They also took part in the gathering of veterans at the as yet uncompleted Victory Park memorial complex at the Hill of Prostrations, where the president spoke at the ceremony for the opening of the museum building.[37] The *Pravda* report described one pro–Communist Party veteran raising a red flag and asserting that it, not the Russian tricolor, was the flag under which they had fought and that had been raised over the Reichstag.

Following the October 1993 siege and shelling of the Russian parliament, the CPRF consciously renounced violence, and the December 1993 Duma elections signaled the CPRF's rise (or return) to national political influence.[38] From this point onward, the Communist Party and other left-wing parties began to use peaceful 9 May gatherings and marches to invoke the Soviet-era myth of Victory and to agitate so that the fiftieth anniversary of the end of the war would be commemorated properly, in their view.[39] While they also commemorated 7 November and 1 May, this was the one element of the Soviet symbolic calendar that still resonated with wide swaths of the Russian population. Indeed, it was the only one of those days that remained a public holiday. The disappearance of parades and festivities for the communist festivals left a certain gap that only 9 May could fill.

This campaign brought results, because, in order not to let the fiftieth anniversary events fall into communist hands along with the emotive symbolism of victory, Yeltsin was forced to officially sponsor large-scale Victory Day events in 1995 and to permit the red flag of the Victory Banner to coexist in a parade with the new tricolor of the Russian state.[40] However, the hesitancy over this compromise was evident in the way the 1995 parade occurred in two distinct parts: a historical portion and a contemporary one. In the historical part, veterans assembled on Red Square, where, at the traditional time of 10:00 a.m., they were inspected by generals in limousines and the Victory Banner was paraded according to the model established in 1965. However, while troops wearing World War II–era uniforms and bearing period submachine guns marched in the parade, the display of contemporary military hardware and the air force fly-by took place later that day, at one o'clock in the afternoon at Victory Park, where the new memorial complex was being opened. Western leaders had been invited to that parade too but preferred not to be part of a military parade involving tanks, presumably because they deemed it too Soviet and reminiscent of the Cold War.[41] One element that linked both parades, though, was the Victory Banner, which was carried aloft at both events.

At the historic Red Square parade, for all the continuity evident, there was a noticeable attempt to articulate a new vision of memory of the war and to break with the Soviet parades: an enormous image of a Soviet soldier and an American one was displayed on the State Historical Museum facing Red Square. Among other political leaders in attendance, US president Bill Clinton and British prime minister John Major were prominent, standing in a group of VIP invitees next to the mausoleum. Combined with the shift in imagery, their presence was not mere empty symbolism, as Yeltsin also mentioned in his speech the importance of Britain's and the United States' wartime roles and noted that the Cold War was a terrible thing. Yeltsin also built on Gorbachev's change in emphasis regarding the war, which permitted memory of the Holocaust to emerge in the mainstream of Russian historical memory to a greater extent than previously: he publicly admitted some of the Soviet Union's contorted and paranoid acts of repression, such as the arrest and murder of Raoul Wallenberg, the Swedish diplomat who had saved Jews in Budapest during the Holocaust.[42] Now Yeltsin went further than his predecessor and used his Red Square speech to refer to the Nazi plan to destroy Russians and other peoples, mentioning Auschwitz and Majdanek, which he described as death camps. This came quite close, but did not quite succeed, in integrating the Soviet tradition of memory of the war conceived as victory with memory of the Holocaust as it had come to be understood in the West.

Together these changes symbolized the most extensive examples of the attempted Yeltsin-era break with the narrative of the victory as exclusively Soviet and with the overtly militaristic message. Despite these changes, the fact that the parade had even taken place was effectively a recognition that Yeltsin's Democrats had not succeeded in creating their own distinct and resonant rituals and symbols. The fact that there was no winner in Yeltsin's 1996 search for a new national idea for Russia suggested that the Russian past, as opposed to the Soviet past, possessed no emotive symbols of civic patriotism or nationalism.[43] This ambivalence was also evident in that there was no voice-over commentary for television coverage of the parade, as there had been in the Soviet era. The role of the voice-over had been to verbally underline the importance and backstory of the various elements of ritual and emphasize a sense of continuity, but in 1995 Russia's rulers were not sure themselves as to the meaning of the various rituals and symbols and did not want to emphasize a continuity, especially of historical elements such as the Victory Banner, that was in many ways an unwelcome burden. Nor were they sure how to articulate discontinuity and what a new commentary would be. Consequently, they were forced to reconcile themselves to and resurrect the rituals of commemoration invented in the Stalin and Brezhnev periods.[44] Thus, as with Soviet leaders, Yeltsin and his entourage still surveyed the parade from the traditional viewing platform at Lenin's mausoleum, despite having anathematized his political legacy, banned the Communist Party, and dismantled the state he created. Beginning in 1997 they would fix this anomaly and no longer watch the parade from Lenin's mausoleum.

The uncertainty as to how to rethink the parade evident in 1995 was addressed directly in some of the journalistic commentary. As *Izvestiia* journalist Stanislav Kondrashov put it, the emphasis upon the established rituals of war commemoration was due to a desire not to "rub salt on the wounds of the living at the same time as laying flowers on the countless graves of the fallen[,] since the country that these heroes defended no longer exists. Yet if anything is visible in the new country, then it is the pain and suffering of birth, even if its leaders, since they of course possess power, will declare their rights to the Great Victory."[45]

Kondrashov sees the symbolism of reconciliation with the West as a key departure but suggests that it will not be emphasized too much for fear of offending the veterans whose sacrifice secured victory for democracy throughout the world more widely. The problem, he argues, is the very cult of Victory itself, and the Victory Banner in particular, as a distraction from the country's real problems and an incitement to militarism: "However, over the course of half a century, wrapping itself in Victory Banners, the ruling system has paid less attention to the solution of wider national problems and more to the overarching task of preparing for a new war and new victory, throwing a pile of money, effort, talent, and brains at the creation and eternal perfection of the Cyclops-like military machine."[46]

Kondrashov sees the Chechnya conflict as a particularly topical and poignant illustration of the difficult heritage of victory. He writes that Stalin deported Chechens on the eve of the original 1945 victory (in fact it was in 1944), and Yeltsin and Minister of Defense Pavel Grachev had just annihilated Groznyi on the eve of this victory. The two events are linked, he argues, by the fact that the original victory strengthened the grip of the totalitarian party system and the elites' hold on power created by that totalitarian system. The same elite have still not relinquished that grip, Kondrashov claims, despite the apparent "metamorphoses of victory."[47]

Some liberal commentators, from within and outside Russia, thought the Victory cult was on the way out, perceiving that the younger generation would think of it as an irrelevant "abstraction."[48] Indeed, Sergei Urusliak's 1998 film *Composition for Victory Day* (*Sochinenie k Dniu Pobedy*), about the adventures of three veterans reunited, is narrated by a child speaking from a future about the legendary time, the present of 1998, when Victory Day was still commemorated on Red Square.

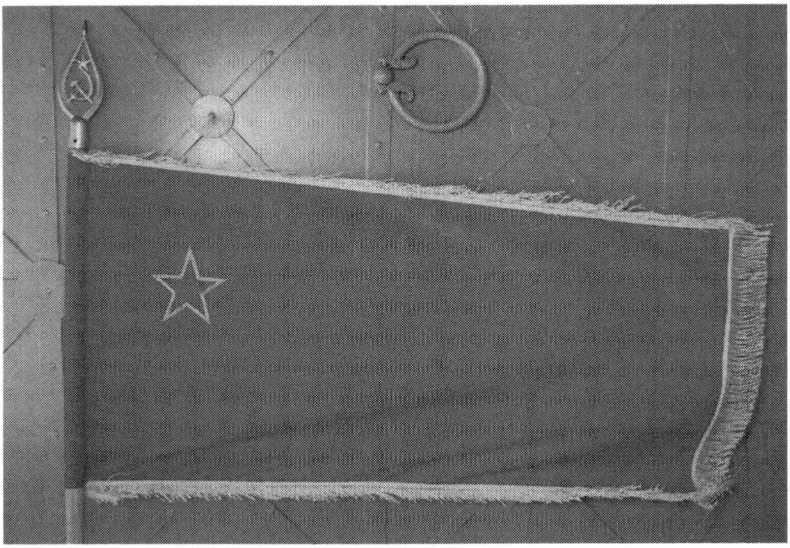

5.2. The "Symbol of the Victory Banner," a version having only a five-pointed yellow star but no hammer and sickle, from the late 1990s.

However, this scenario smacked of wishful thinking (even if, in Urusliak's case, tinged with nostalgia). Instead, rather than being a once in twenty years affair, the Victory Parade was again held on Red Square in 1999 and has been held every year since. Moreover, the forces that the CPRF had mobilized to push for Victory Day commemorations were not solely the elderly, and even they were not going away soon. There was also a wider sense of the loss of national purpose and belonging, quite apart from the social problems of poverty and law and order. The CPRF was able to speak to all of these concerns and had become the largest party in the 1995 parliamentary (State Duma) elections, a position it maintained throughout Yeltsin's rule, until 2003.

This political threat was why Yeltsin, despite mentioning the Victory Banner in his Red Square speech and permitting it to be used in the 9 May parades, was still anxious to control and restrict the circulation of Soviet-era imagery, including that of the Victory Banner. For this reason, he introduced a law in 1996 that permitted facsimile copies of the Victory Banner to be used as a state symbol but only for official state ceremonies on Victory Day and Defender of the Fatherland Day (23 February). In all other cases, organizers of local parades and so on were to use not exact copies but the "Symbol of the Victory Banner," which was a red flag with a five-pointed yellow star on it but no hammer and sickle.[49] However, while being restricted in use outside of state ceremonies, the

Victory Banner and its role in the Victory Parade now expanded: from 1996 onward, the annual parade began not with an inspection of troops by the minister of defense but with the ceremonial parading of the Victory Banner. It also continued to be used as part of the main parade. With this according of a more prominent role to the Victory Banner, expanded television commentary was introduced, including ritualistic verbal formulas that do not correspond even to official late Soviet-era published histories of the Victory Banner and storming of the Reichstag; the voice-over repeated the incorrect time it was raised as 14:25 and claimed it was the first flag raised. They were perhaps quoting previous television depictions of parades rather than historical scholarship. While making the Victory Banner more prominent, television commentary for the 1996 and 1997 live broadcasts stressed that the banner was a state symbol, presumably in case anyone mistook it for the symbol of the Communist Party. This need to make use of but at the same time regulate the use of so powerful a symbol was a further indication of the Yeltsin government's ineffective attempts to break with the communist heritage and its failure to find a symbol with comparable resonance. The communists (i.e.., the CPRF) ridiculed this symbol of the Victory Banner as a cross between the Chinese and Vietnamese flags and as a contemptible sign of the government's embarrassment before the symbol of Russia's greatest historical achievement, something that should elicit only pride.[50]

VICTORY PARADES IN THE PUTIN ERA

The Victory cult and the ritual of holding Victory Day parades underwent another shift with Vladimir Putin's rise to power in 1999. Even before he was inaugurated as president on 7 May 2000, Vladimir Putin's public speeches invoked the memory of World War II, and he associated himself with Russia's victory.[51] Such remembrance of the war has since become a central part of the Putin project to restore national pride and project Russian power globally. The association of the war with Stalin, and thus with authoritarianism, has not concerned Putin's administration, since democracy, while nominally observed, has not been a central aspiration for the Putin project and has certainly always been trumped by the need for a strong state.[52] Thus, since 2000, and even more so since 2005, the parade has been a feature of Russia's most important national holiday and day of commemoration.

Two days after Putin's inauguration on 7 May 2000, the 9 May parade was held on Red Square. With Yeltsin and Gorbachev in attendance, Putin did not break significantly with the norms of parades held under his two immediate predecessors: the parade included veterans but no tanks or other military vehicles; the television voice-over narration claimed that this was because tanks could not go through the narrow Iverskie Gates, which had been recently restored. In fact, when military parades were later reintroduced, they simply no longer passed through these gates.

Putin's message in 2000 was also close to that of the previous decade. He talked of Russia "raising high the banner of democracy and freedom" and spoke to the importance of the parade, helping the people to build a strong, prosperous country, free and "democratic." Putin's speech also referred to the need to remember everything, stressing the losses as well as the victories. The press echoed this tone, as *Izvestiia* published a series of articles about the war, including about POWs and the lack of individual graves, including graves for dead Germans.[53] Nevertheless, all this was ultimately subject to the narrative of victory and heroism central to Victory Day. One note that was indicative of the deeper, more troubling context of the second Chechen war, initiated by the new Putin administration, was the way the commentators, in mentioning the various non-Russian ethnicities participating, stressed the presence of Chechens, who also participated in the 1945 parade. Coming immediately after the recapture of Groznyi and imposition of direct Russian rule over Chechnya, the parade was intended to symbolically enact and display the integration of Chechnya into the Russian state.

For the 2000 observance of Victory Day, the Victory Banner was paraded on Red Square, accompanied by new, incorrect claims in the television commentary that its initial raising had informed the world of the victory over Nazism and, even more erroneously, that it had been part of the 1945 parade. While the Victory Banner was not part of the 1945 parade, as all journalistic, filmic, and photographic records of the parade confirm, the claim is indicative of a need for an unbroken tradition into which the Victory Banner, and other elements of the parade, could fit. This has been described by Stephen Hutchings and Natalia Rulyova as a tendency in the Victory Day parades in the Putin era—"a commemoration of commemoration itself."[54] The focus is on this parade's relation to previous rituals of commemoration in the Soviet past, even if the commentary also refers to prerevolutionary traditions of parades. The original event being commemorated is thus not the war itself but the 24 June 1945 Victory Parade and Stalinism, and the parade is a performative compensation for the contradiction between the fact that "Russia must stand in for the Soviet Union, but at the same time assert its difference from it."[55] The quotation of past parades evokes the Soviet past and at the same time distances it. This is a new dimension to the ritualized repetition of war memory evident in the Victory Banner imagery. Now the image of heroism and glory more generally and that of the Victory Banner in particular are repeated so as to block out not just inconvenient aspects of Soviet history but also the unpleasant memory of the collapse of the Soviet Union and greater complexities of the world it revealed.

The music used at Victory Parades is, needless to say, also highly quotational: all parades since 1945 have used pieces from Glinka's *A Life for the Tsar*, with its not exactly democratic subtext, following the inspection of the troops. Since 1975, the parades have also featured the popular song "Victory Day," composed that year by David Tukhmanov. However, the collapse of the Soviet Union led to changes in the Soviet national anthem, Aleksandrov's 1943 "hymn," which had itself been rewritten following the death of Stalin to remove references to him. Thus, although between 1995 and 2000 a new Russian national anthem, a piece of music that never succeeded in inspiring and becoming a national symbol, was featured at the parades, in the 2001 parade the national anthem played was a reworked version of the Soviet one, recently restored by Putin. This further return to a more implicitly Soviet symbolism was also echoed in Putin's 9 May speech, which no longer stressed democracy and made mention instead of sovereignty and independence.

One theme evident in these early parades of the Putin presidency was military reform, which echoed a Gorbachev-era priority. Thus, in 2000 the voice-over narrative on television referred to structural reforms of the military, and in 2001 the generals are said to be responsible for deciding whether or not Russia's army can become professional. This contrasted with the fact that for the first time the person commanding the parade, the minister of defense, was a civilian, Sergei Ivanov, and he was wearing civilian clothes. Changing the military, along with its place in society and attitudes to it, was central to the Gorbachev and Yeltsin reform projects, involving reducing defense budgets and changing military doctrine, hence the attempt to rethink the military parades as well.

By contrast, the renewed centrality of the military in post-Soviet Russia was symbolized on 9 May 2005, when for the first time since the Soviet era, Red Square saw a full military parade with ballistic missiles, tanks, and other military vehicles. This set the pattern and became the norm, with the Victory Banner retaining the central place it had acquired during the Yeltsin era. One refinement was added: until 2005 the Victory Banner had been brought alone to start the parade; from 2006 onward, however, it was accompanied by the state flag of the Russian Federation. This made it clear in visual terms what previously the commentary had spelled out: for 9 May at least, the Victory Banner was a symbol of the Russian state. The reintroduction of parades with military hardware on Red Square every year suggested continuity with the Soviet-era military establishment.[56] Indeed, the practice of unveiling new military hardware, such as a new missile or tank, may ultimately be seen as a way of justifying their expense by reference to the Great Patriotic War.

From the perspective of 2020, if we look at the 2000 and 2005 parades we may be struck by the extent to which there is still a sense of the coming together of Russia and the West. Putin's speeches at both of those events refer to cooperation during World War II between different political systems in order to fight fascism. Indeed, in 2005 George W. Bush was present, seated alongside Putin, and the openly articulated lesson of the war was that all must work together to fight the universal scourge of terrorism.

Similarly, earlier in 2005, on Holocaust Memorial Day (27 January) Putin gave a speech marking the sixtieth anniversary of the liberation of Auschwitz, and in it he made an analogy between terrorism and the crimes of the Nazis. As well as making it clear that the Nazis specifically targeted Jews, Putin referred to the Holocaust as "the greatest crime against humanity."[57] Nevertheless, this message is also combined with an emphasis on the heroism of the Red Army in liberating Auschwitz and other camps, as well as on the sacrifice made by the Soviet people, who "did the most of all to fight Nazism, to vanquish Nazism, to save the Jewish people."[58] There is a similar emphasis on Soviet heroism, explicitly including long-ignored or underplayed Jewish heroism, at the speech Putin made on the seventieth anniversary of the liberation of Auschwitz, this time not at Auschwitz itself but at Moscow's newly opened Jewish Museum and Tolerance Center.[59] Memory of the Holocaust was now permitted, but only within the framework of the war as a Great Patriotic one, a paradigm that went against the tragic understanding of the Holocaust dominant in the West.[60]

For all the shortcomings and the short-term instrumentalizing dimension of these speeches, they are more substantial than the speeches given at the 9 May parade, which are less analytical and far more self-congratulatory. There is a virtual absence of ideology, especially the ideologies of communism and Nazism, which are not discussed or analyzed.[61] As Hutchings and Rulyova argue, while the ideology is evacuated from the words, it is ubiquitous in the images, the flags in particular, and, one might add, especially on the Victory Banner. While the writing on the flag serves to make it a symbol of the war victory, thus serving the agenda of Russian state and national pride, it still remains the red flag symbolic of communism, with roots in socialist movements since at least the French Revolution of 1848 (see introduction). This makes it still a potential site of conflict, even if largely dormant at present, as the CPRF is largely in agreement with the Putin administration's patriotic agenda. Most importantly, the CPRF and Putin share a largely positive view of Stalin, and this is an implicit subtext of the whole 9 May parade, the prototype for which was ordered by Stalin. The increased frequency of these Victory Parades since the end of the Soviet era (there were only four in the 1945–1991 portion of the Soviet period, but the 2020 parade was the twenty-sixth in the post-Soviet era from 1992 to the present) may thus be seen as indicative of a more positive attitude toward the Stalin era of Soviet history than was permissible even under Brezhnev.

Hutchings and Rulyova have suggested that the 2005 Victory Day commemorations came at a particularly propitious moment for Putin for a number of domestic and international political reasons: the war on terror brought him closer to the West, and his government had just achieved effective control over the media, by which the authors primarily mean television. Their study illustrates how the resources of television in particular were mobilized in a coordinated and effective manner in tandem with Victory Day organizers to create a "media event" highlighting the collective memory of the war so as to present society in an ideal, harmonious way, constructing the sense of stable identity that is key to any "imagined community" of nationalism.[62] This was a particularly precarious undertaking, given the tension between the fact that it was the Soviet Union and not Russia that won the war. Consequently, Victory Day coverage celebrates the Soviet Union, but only within limits, asserting a continuous, stable identity through performance and recitation but still marking a distance to it through the presence of the Russian tricolor and the framing of the Soviet flag as the Victory Banner. Hutchings and Rulyova's analysis of the 2005 Victory Day could be easily extended to any subsequent parade.

The scale of direct participation, apart from the television audience, is itself impressive: in addition to the Red Square parade, there are smaller gatherings of various kinds across the capital and regions. In 2005 more than 9 million people had directly taken part in the celebrations by 9:00 p.m. Moscow time, with more than half of those attending events in Moscow. With each year the numbers of troops parading on Red Square have also increased: seven thousand in 2005, fourteen thousand in 2010, and eighty thousand (plus two thousand pieces of military hardware) in 2015.[63]

Even for those at home, it was hard not to become involved, as Russian television committed itself to the commemoration without restraint: every single program on Channel One on 9 May 2005 centered on Victory Day, and such programming dominated in the days leading up to it too.[64] Moreover, the way in which the coverage of the parade itself was filmed and presented also created a sense of participation and involvement, with what has been described as an "emphasis on the sensuous voyeurism of modern media technology."[65] While the sensuousness is undeniable, the purpose seems to be to convey a vicarious feeling of being part of the parade. Curiously, this possibility was anticipated in a review of the television coverage of the first 9 May parade, in 1965, which imagined the possibilities of showing the parade in such a way as to enhance the viewing experience for the viewer at home, even making their sense of the spectacle more complete and direct than that of those present on Red Square:

> We often say that, thanks to television, millions can be present on Red Square. But this is not so. The camera enables us to see not only what someone standing on Red Square can see but also what they cannot see. Television is a multitude of eyes and points of view. It permits you to watch what is happening with a bird's eye view or from beneath a tank track. Gone is the time when the happy holder of a pass for the Red Square parade would tell people at home how it was. Now, he asks those who stayed at home following the parade on television "how it was."[66]

Columnists Sergei Muratov and Georgii Fere argue that while the television viewer gets a better view, the person present at the parade is a participant. They get a "sense of personal common presence." But the television view creates a new event in and of itself: "an event on a TV screen is simultaneously the image of the event"; the ceremony is not so much the actual one that occurred but its televisual representation.[67]

Those frustrated at the very limited techniques employed in 1965 would no doubt have been overjoyed to watch the 2005 and subsequent years' coverage of the parades, which made widespread use of innovative camera angles through aerial and spider-cam shots, with cameras mounted on all kinds of moving objects. The 2019 coverage even showed the inner workings of the Kremlin clock, thus giving close-ups and panoramic sweeps unavailable to the unenhanced human eye. As Hutchings and Rulyova put it, this approach "establish[es] the broadcaster's viewpoint as that of a privileged, all-seeing observer aligned with the impersonal state to which it gives its voice."[68] They also see this as possessing a kind of erotic, voyeuristic attraction, as well as a way of pulling together the fragments of varying angles and varying kinds of images of victory.

However, one element of the 1965 parade that was still tediously repeated in the post-Soviet parades was that use of narrative voice-overs in the broadcast coverage. These were and remained ritualistically inane, which Muratov and Fere describe, using a play on words between the Russian term for a long shot (*obshchii plan*) and a commonplace (*obshchee slovo*), as linked to the unimaginative filmic language: "on screen wide angles and commonplaces dominate":

> With every year the technology of the coverage improves. The number of cameras grows. Their points of view become more unusual. Unfortunately, the only thing that does not change is the verbal accompaniment. There is an abundance of superfluous phrases: "Look how they advance in close formation . . ." These are the fixed expressions that we heard last year or the year before. These are words, the aim of which is to fill a pause: ballast words do not raise up but weigh down the televisual representation.
>
> The broadcast of an event is not an art solely of the cameramen but also, to a lesser extent, of the commentators and directors.[69]

This mismatch is striking, because precisely the same could be said of recent television coverage: innovation on the level of the visual is not matched by changes to the highly anodyne voice-over, often repeating information that historical studies have long since widely and unambiguously debunked, because they were scared to change too much, lest the sense of nostalgia be spoiled and the sense of unity and tradition, the ritualistic atmosphere, be broken. It can be argued that different constituencies see different things in the Victory Day parade.[70] However, in this disparity between verbal and visual, the repetitive, ritualistic orientation of the voice-over undermines the aspiration to keep the Victory Day ritual relevant for the present generation. While the dizzying visuals are in part intended to do this, there is a real and palpable fear that the young will become disconnected from these rituals, as the 1970s and 1980s generation did.

However, the Victory cult is not solely dependent on the parades: the desire for relevance through a sense of immersion and directness has been realized through other forms and technologies. We see an attempt to reach out to a new generation, to wrap the most hidebound, ritualistic content in the most cutting-edge technology in the hope that it will become more palatable. This same tendency to recycle ever older wine in new bottles can of course be found in the cinema and other genres on television, as well as in military reenactments and in the sphere of gaming. These forms all interact and compete for immediacy of impact in a phenomenon of "convergence" characteristic of new media.[71]

THE VICTORY BANNER IN VIDEO GAMES

Since 2003, the iconic imagery of the Victory Banner has been widely used in the medium of the video game *Call of Duty*. While there have been many new versions of this game spanning different kinds of warfare, the

Victory Banner figures in 2003's *Call of Duty 1* and in its enormously successful fifth sequel, *Call of Duty: The World at War* (Activision-Blizzard, 2008), which sold eleven million copies.[72] Although the game is from the United States, it is widely played in Russia and as such has influenced the Russian-media environment as much as any Russian production has. Both the original 2003 and the 2008 variants of *Call of Duty* include noninteractive "cut scenes" of the original Soviet footage of Berlin in 1945, suggesting a historical authenticity that anchors the CGI action of the game, such as the assault on the Reichstag, through the point-of-view perspective of a Soviet combatant, "allow[ing] players to experience the movie-like intensity."[73] Indeed, reviews consistently compare the experience of playing the game with that of watching or even being in films.[74] The games could even be said to go further: many of the scenes fill in the gaps in the iconic imagery, showing the fight inside the Reichstag itself and the first-person point of view of the soldier hoisting the Victory Banner.

Thus, while the trailer and introduction for *Call of Duty 1* include black-and-white footage of the Reichstag and Red Army men advancing toward it with a red flag, the game culminates in the storming of the Reichstag with the gamer advancing across the open ground in front of the Reichstag building in a direct echo of Raizman's 1945 newsreel footage. The character adopted by the player in the Russian sequences is the fictional Sergeant Alexei Voronin of the 150th Rifle Division of the Third Strike Army, one of the divisions that took the building.

When the character puts up the flag, the game is over, triggering another montage of black-and-white footage of the raising of the flag over the Reichstag, accompanied by a Red Army man's voice-over reading a letter to his mother referring to the raising of the flag. It ends, however, by tempering this pro-Russian image and sentiment through commentary on images of the Americans and Soviets meeting and shaking hands at the Elbe River, in Germany.

The primary aim in using the original footage is evidently to suggest historical authenticity, as well as to confer monumental and epic connotations: the dramatic quality of some of the original footage, such as that of the assault on the building, is restaged in the game, adding to the central purpose of producing an interactive version of famous film footage.

The subtitle of the 2008 *Call of Duty* release, *The World at War*, evokes the Thames Television series of the 1970s, and the player moves beyond Europe to play first Private Miller, an American who is an infantryman in the Pacific, and then a Red Army man, Private Dmitrii Petrenko, who fights at Stalingrad before ultimately taking part in the battle of Berlin and the storming of the Reichstag. Despite being wounded in the act, he is the one who puts up the Victory Banner.

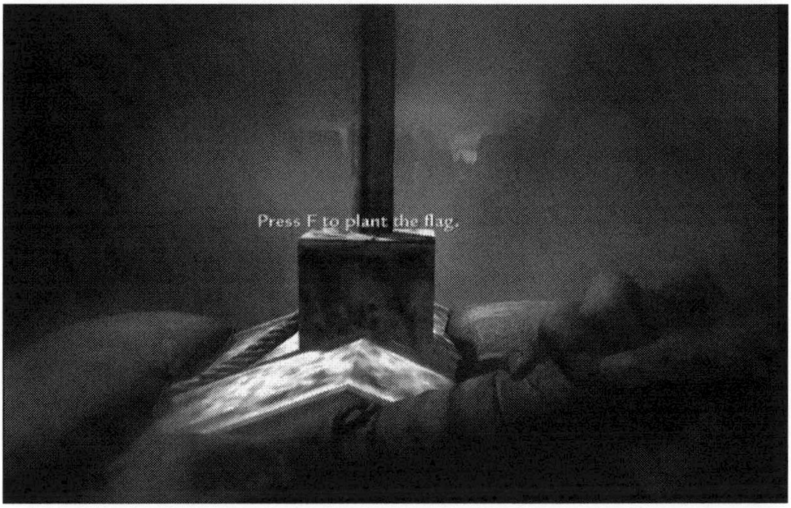

5.3. Raising the Victory Banner in the first-person shooter video game *Call of Duty 4: The World at War.*

5.4. The Victory Banner raised, in *Call of Duty 4: The World at War.*

The game overall, and individual episodes, are introduced through brief montages of black-and-white newsreel footage. With the storming of the Reichstag episode, we see a number of images of the final assault on the building, including that of rockets with "for the Reichstag" written on them in Cyrillic (the Russian reads both "po reikhstagu" and "v reikhstag"), which were used in Raizman's film, as well as other images from that footage, but we do not see the actual footage of the assault or that of the hoisting of the Victory Banner. Effectively, the game imagery, itself more detailed and movielike than its precursor, is now restaging and taking the place of the iconic photographic images far more fully than in *Call of Duty 1*. This process of cannibalizing previous visual media is termed "remediation" in studies of new media and is part of its neverending pursuit of immediacy.[75]

The most profound difference between the two versions of the game, however, is the greater complexity, the greater difficulty, and greater time investment required by the player of the raising of the Victory Banner episode, entitled "Downfall," which begins as the character enters the Reichstag. Whereas in the first *Call of Duty* the storming of the Reichstag, including the flag-raising episode, was brief, maybe taking five or ten minutes, for *The World at War* release it is two protracted episodes that are likely on a first play to consume several hours of the player's time. This greater difficulty is very important in gaming, with the player wanting to be consumed or immersed and to find the game addictive: with the first release of *Call of Duty*, many users complained that the game took "only" eight hours to play.[76] Jesper Juul has described this trade-off between the need to win and the no less important demand from the players that it not be too easy: "failure adds content" is a central tenet of the structure of games.[77]

The need to overcome the game's difficulty, wherein the character is likely to be killed many times as the player acquires skill in completing the various missions, adds not just "content" but a sense of the task's importance as the hours mount up. Taking ten or twenty hours to complete the game is an investment of time, making this the gaming equivalent of the epic, such as with the five-film *Liberation* or the twenty-part television series *Unknown War*: one definition of that form is simply that a piece is long or wide in scope.[78] The sheer temporal magnitude, however, is coupled with a sense of the personal experience, as the epic trajectory culminates with raising the Victory Banner. But this is slightly different every time, illustrating the new media's tendency toward variability and the production not of exact copies but variants that reflect personal participation.[79]

While the length of the game contributes to a sense of immersion as the player becomes engrossed in the task, at the same time, by collapsing a sense of distance and the analytical, immersion also increases the tendency to take representation for granted. Hans Belting, following a tradition in so-called media ecology pioneered and popularized by Marshall McLuhan, argues that new media are very effective at concealing a quoted image's presence, with the effect that we do not notice the process of the medium itself and "are captured by the image."[80] Immersion similarly colors the video game medium's consumption of history and its representations: players do not think of the images as a version, as a mediated representation, and instead perceive them as part of their own experience.[81] This can be seen very clearly with Russian gamers' reviews of *Call of Duty: The World at War*, which is rated the third most interesting of 2008, despite flaws as a game. The positive reception was in part due to the Soviet sequences being appreciated, simply because the player identifies with the characters:

> *Call of Duty: World at War* can be divided into two parts: the boring and the one about the Russians. Therefore, it should be played in the following way: grit your teeth and switch on the usual first-person shooter game autopilot, and run through the tedious Pacific campaign, until you get to the first level at Stalingrad when your jaw will drop. Because what's there is: Sergeant Reznov with a submachine gun (dead ringer for Lenin), attacks under German machine fire, Red Army Ushankas, "For the Motherland!," and the raising of the flag over the Reichstag.[82]

This view is quite common for Russian players of the game, with some saying that placing the flag on the Reichstag makes them feel proud, while others even claim to like playing it every 9 May.[83] Even more so than with a popular historical novel or a historical film, with a video game such as *Call of Duty*, which uses historical images, the player is encouraged to take the dramatic simplification, and not the array of conflicting sources, as the authentic historical context. This further compounds the ritualized repetition of meaning.

The video games thus become a further way of perpetuating and popularizing misconceptions, such as the suggestion that the Reichstag was a symbol of Nazism, when it was in fact never used by the Nazis as a parliament and therefore never had a Nazi eagle in its debating chamber. Distracted through immersion, the player finds it hard to contest such errors. Moreover, whereas the economic, ideological, and diplomatic dimensions of modern war are key, first-person shooter games possess an inherent bias for combat—and weapons—as the decisive factor, what has been termed "combat gnosticism."[84]

In US-produced games such as *Call of Duty*, the Soviet epic narrative, which endows events with a certain historical meaning, is quoted without being seriously endorsed.[85] However, a vague sense of the historically momentous remains. Despite the player's need to fail and be engrossed before winning, victory itself is important in games, and the Victory Banner imagery, deliberately staged to connote victory, is a rather effective way of identifying the moment a player wins. The fact that winning here is attached to a difficult combat objective presents an emotionally satisfactory payoff. Ultimately there is a narrative here, and it is conveyed in part through the Victory Banner, mobilizing its rich associations for a privileged moment of historical closure to complete the game, despite the antinarrative tendency of games. While it recasts the footage of the Victory Banner as an interactive, palpable experience, at the same time the game "reasserts a linear, singular, and teleological conception of history," because the narrative is predetermined and the meanings narrowly limited.[86] For all the interactivity, the narrative is always set and the player cannot change the course of historical events.

Doubts persist as to the extent to which gamers take in the historical implications of the imagery they consume. All the same, it is clear is that games offer a new kind of approach to history in which the gamer feels directly part of it, and millions of young people connect and engage with them. To reach young people, television and cinema producers, as well as Russian society more widely, had to begin responding to the video game aesthetic.

FILM AND TELEVISION'S RESPONSES TO THE RISE OF WAR GAMES

The visual and narrative influence of video games has resulted in a number of reworkings of the Victory Banner imagery on Russian television. These include the miniseries *The Fog 2* (*Tuman 2*, dir. Ivan Shukhovetskii, 2012) and *The Final Fight* (*Poslednii boi*, dir. Ivan Shukhovetskii, 2013), as well as the eighteen-part documentary *The Great War* (*Velikaia voina*, dir. Anna Grazhdan, 2010–2012).[87]

In attempting to make war films that visually resemble and compositionally echo video games, Russian television also strove to alter the films' political messages to suit its immediate domestic agenda. Thus, for all of *Call of Duty*'s mobilization of the Victory Banner imagery's momentous associations, its commingling with references to the US contribution to victory dilutes its exclusive focus on Soviet and Russian glory. This transnational orientation in the video game is also part of a commercial strategy to make its appeal as wide as possible. Just as Russian gamers were often dismissive of the US dimension of the historical games, for Russian television the audience and message remain primarily national.

An early indication of this patriotic inflection of video game imagery in Russian war films is *We Are from the Future* (*My iz budushchego*, dir. Andrei Maliukov, 2008), a film in which the main characters, who are presented as insensitive to the true meaning of the war as they search for military artifacts to sell for money, are literally transported into the past and forced to experience the war firsthand. They return to the present chastened, as well as respectful of memory of the war. Here the narrative traditions of cinema are dispensed with, and the first-person experience and immersion of gaming transform the means of representing the war. Indeed, the immersion is literal, as the characters swim from the present to the past. In place of a frame narrative or flashback, *We Are from the Future* offers its characters a literal experiencing of the war. It is reminiscent of the US science fiction comedy *Back to the Future* (dir. Robert Zemeckis, 1985) but differs in its mystical motivation of time travel and patriotic purpose.

The flashback and the frame narrative have been widely used in Soviet cinema to stress the personal connection to the war, especially since the beginning of the thaw era. As Alissa Timoshkina, drawing on Youngblood and Tumarkin, has argued, the films of the Brezhnev period changed this slightly, making particularly broad use of flashbacks and frame narratives to stress the connection of the younger generation to memory of the war.[88] This technique has been deployed in the television series *The Last Fight* (*Poslednii boi*, 2013), in which disrespect for memory of the war has gone so far as to make a young man rob a veteran (played by legendary actor Iurii Nazarov) and steal his medals. While retrieving his stolen property, the pensioner recounts his wartime experiences in flashback to the police officers in charge of the investigation. The pensioner's experiences include his hoisting of a red flag over a Berlin building that was not the Reichstag and, in so doing, overcoming a personal fear of heights. Having told his story and made the decision not to press charges, the pensioner then meets the young man and they are reconciled. This more traditional way of narrating the story of youth's redemption through remembering the war is curiously also more considered than in *We Are from the Future*, as it is critical of the manufactured nature of the iconic image of the Victory Banner, showing not only the staging of images but, at the same time, the personal appropriation of the Victory Banner by the main character.

With *We Are from the Future*, however, the importance of the past is experienced directly, and this same, novel formula of time travel, along with the look and feel of a video game through the widespread use of CGI, has since been repeated in a sequel to *We Are from the Future*, as well as in the 2010 made-for-television films *Fog* and its (for us) more relevant 2012 sequel, *Fog 2*, in which the main characters are transported to the war period while celebrating Victory Day and nearly kill Meliton Kantariia—one of those (incorrectly) credited with raising the Victory Banner over the Reichstag. In a conscious echo of *Back to the Future*, where the main character nearly prevents himself from being born (by

5.5. Still image of the Victory Banner being brought to the Reichstag, from the television series *The Great War*, 2010–2012.

obstructing his parents' courtship), the characters are concerned that if their actions lead to the death of Kantariia, then the Victory Banner will not be raised over the Reichstag and the Soviets will not win World War II. This is a strange reversal of causality, where the image representing victory is taken to be the cause of victory itself, and an even stranger take on *Back to the Future*'s oedipal plot. But it also suggests that correct historical knowledge of the war enables the characters to survive, and it is contrasted with their experiences in the present, where the war is trivialized in a Victory Day thematic nightclub evening during which the DJ and bar staff wear Red Army uniforms but erotic dancers sport swastika armbands.

The urgent desire to get through to a younger generation has also influenced the approach of *The Great War* documentary series, which used much more CGI animation, creating a video game feel to some of the sequences alongside reenacted scenes. It began with eight episodes, commissioned by Channel One for Victory Day 2010, with the final program ending with the Victory Banner imagery. An additional ten episodes appeared in 2012.[89] The whole thus broadly echoes the twenty-part *Unknown War* in the construction of its eighteen parts with an overwhelmingly Soviet focus. In this eighteen-part format, the seventeenth part (the eighth and final episode of the original) shows the battle of Berlin and devotes a great deal of space to the battle for the Reichstag and the raising of the Victory Banner. While it uses some of the documentary footage, both the still and moving images, *The Great War* integrates those images with reconstructions and CGI images of battle, pausing to identify prominent participants, especially generals, with photographs and typewritten documents from manila folders. The film's focus on the elements and characteristics of military hardware is also particularly noteworthy, since this both echoes the tendency of first-person shooter video games, where gamers can select the appropriate weapons, and the subtext of Victory Day parades, with their hailing of new weaponry. The makers claimed that the combination of CGI, digital animation, and dramatic reenactment enabled them to create a sense of scale that was hard to achieve in other historical documentaries.[90] Certainly, despite the small number of reconstructors involved, the sense of scale is reminiscent of films like *Liberation*, and the immediacy and echoing of a first-person perspective serves to personalize the images, stressing the raising of the flag as an uplifting, exhilarating moment and as a source of pride, which appears to have been well received.[91] The documentary does nothing to dispel the myth about Egorov and Kantariia or establish the identities of those who actually put up the first banner. Instead, the scene depicted here is of the first and only flag being raised as part of the storming of the building. This contrasts with the more analytical tone of many recent Russian television documentary treatments of the subject, as we shall see.

Jaimie Baron has argued that the flip side to widespread belief in the authenticity and power of what she calls "meta-archival" documents, something close to the notion of "iconic images," is a desire to question and undermine those claims.[92] This more critical attitude, in which the justification for compilation films is all about getting people to look at familiar shots in a new way or drawing attention to broader meanings of familiar material, is not evident in *The Great War*'s treatment of the Victory Banner. By contrast, other recent television documentaries on the Victory Banner have revised canonical accounts of the actual raising of the banner; Igor′ Kholodkov's *Parade of the Century: The Victory Banner* (*Parad veka: Znamia Pobedy*, 2009) challenges the accepted account of Egorov and Kantariia putting up the first Victory Banner over the Reichstag and stresses the staged and falsified nature of the Victory Banner imagery, as does *The Victory Banner* (*Znamia Pobedy*, dir. Aleksandr Kas′ianov, 2015). Both of these accounts, which are broadly accurate and reliant on the published historical work as to the raising of the Victory Banner, draw attention to the myths and misconceptions that have plagued the whole episode.

Despite these more critical perspectives, the more immersive and popular forms have reverted to ritualized repetition of the old Victory Banner myth. This is compounded by the tendency, evident in the video game and its appropriations in film, to collapse the distance of history and mediations separating the Victory Banner artifact from the present by ignoring the historical controversies as to who put it up and when and treating it as an unambiguous historical fact. This is part of a wider striving for an immediate and immersive relationship with history that has manifested itself in further uses of the Victory Banner in which it has freed itself from the confines of the museum and ritual uses on Victory Day and become part of a far wider range of activities, including World War II reenactment in Russia and the post-Soviet space.

REENACTMENTS AND DEMONSTRATIONS BEYOND THE MUSEUM

The Victory Banner has been a feature of the Central Museum of the Armed Forces (previously Central Museum of the Soviet Army) since being consigned there prior to the 24 June 1945 Victory Parade. Following the removal of a bust to Stalin and the 1965 creation of new museum premises with a room devoted to the Victory Banner, the storming of Berlin, and the Moscow Victory Parade of 24 June 1945, the presence of the Victory Banner in the Central Museum of the Armed Forces has remained remarkably similar, even if the name of the museum has changed. The manner of display has changed several times since 1945, most recently in 2011, with one constant being that the banner itself has been raised ever higher, just as it has become more elevated in status. The flag on display in a glass case has been a facsimile, however, since 1965, with the actual flag now kept in a sealed capsule in the basement so as to arrest its decay.[93]

There were plans to move it to the new museum of the Great Patriotic War in the Victory Park and house it in a new Hall of Glory, and a dedicated memorial to it was also to be constructed.[94] When completed in 1995, however, the complex was without the Victory Banner itself or the monumental sculpture dedicated to it. Instead, the Victory Banner, or the official identical copy, left the museum for official Victory Day ceremonies, such as the 8 May Kremlin commemoration or Victory Day itself, when it was paraded on Red Square. The Victory Banner also became a focus for rituals performed by visitors to the museum: from its first arrival in what was then called the Central Museum of the Red Army, in 1945, it was common for members of the Pioneers, the official Soviet youth organization, to make their promise by it.[95] In the wake of the 1956 decision to permit the forming of a Union-wide veterans' organization, Victory Day became a focus for their activity and veterans began to gather together in Moscow in the period between 15 April and 10 May.[96] The Central Museum of the Armed Forces' Victory Hall in this period would frequently be packed, as thousands of people, especially participants in the storming of the Reichstag, came to pay their respects to the dead and to reminisce.[97] Their choice to visit the Victory Hall, dominated by the Victory Banner, was symbolic. Emboldened by discovery of their power to organize, veterans strove to seize greater control over the narrative of the war in general and of the Victory Banner in particular as a symbol of it. The flag itself began to leave the premises of the museum and become part of their gatherings. A 1962 guidebook describes this phenomenon: "Participants in the Battle of Berlin often come to the Museum, to the Victory Banner. On numerous occasions, heroes of the Soviet Union Egorov, Kantariia, Neustroev, S′ianov, and other veterans of the Great Patriotic War have spoken in the Museum about their memories of the raising of the Victory Banner. On occasion the Victory Banner, accompanied by a guard of honor, has been ceremonially displayed at meetings devoted to notable events in the history of the Soviet Army."[98]

As we saw earlier (chapter 3), the use of the flag in commemorative political meetings was part of growing grassroots pressure from veterans in the post-Stalin period for whom the war was central. The decision to declare Victory Day a public holiday and to stage the enormous 1965 parade was not solely a myth imposed from above but also the state's assertion of control over an independent impulse to intensify commemoration of the war.[99] As Boris Dubin has argued, the state mobilized every possible institutional means, from parades, medals, monuments, film, literature, and so forth, to ensure that it retained "the monopoly as keeper of memory and constructor of history," as part of a "symbolic politics."[100]

In the post-Soviet period, in 2007, the CPRF proposed a bill in the Duma to replace the whole notion of the "Symbol of the Victory Banner" (adopted under Yeltsin) with exact replicas of the original flag, bearing both the hammer and sickle and the name of the unit. Ceding to Communist Party pressure and at the same time stealing their thunder, President Putin enacted a law on 7 May 2007 that overturned the 1996 Yeltsin-era statute and abolished the notion of the "Symbol of the Victory Banner."[101] Thus, facsimile copies of the Victory Banner could now be used by any organization or anyone honoring the memory of the war.[102]

The 2007 change in the law fueled a rise in the use of facsimiles of the Victory Banner, which has been paralleled by the growing popularity of military reenactment, termed "reconstruction" (*rekonstruktsiia*) in Russia since the 1990s. As Jenny Thompson has noted, for reenactors, genuine or replica artifacts play a key role in authenticating the bearer's right to own or control history.[103] In addition to replica uniforms and weapons, copies of the Victory Banner, as an artifact, have become used in public reenactments of the storming of the Reichstag, thus confirming its potency as a symbol authenticating the dominant Russian account of the Great Patriotic War as a glorious victory.

The fact that the movement began following the collapse of the Soviet Union, in the early 1990s, when official military parades on Red Square had ceased, meant that "reconstruction," by virtue of employing banned communist symbols, immediately possessed a more intense political charge than was the case in places like the United States, where the politics, if present, are implicit and not central.[104] Moreover, American reenactors rarely stage particular events, being more oriented toward re-creating and reliving the experience of the common soldier. In the Russian and Ukrainian context, the restaging of particular events such as the liberation of specific towns and cities or the storming of the Reichstag are more popular scenarios. One significant expression of this political dimension in the growth of military reenactment, and practices close to it, is the use of objects of veneration normally housed in museums, or at least replicas of them, as with as the Victory Banner. Moreover, the crossover between practices of reenactment and politics is evident most acutely in the events surrounding the tensions and armed conflict in eastern Ukraine. It is probably no coincidence that Igor′ Strelkov (aka Igor′ Girkin), the one-time prominent insurgent leader in eastern Ukraine, had long been an ardent military reenactor. Indeed, former *Guardian* Russia correspondent Shaun Walker interviewed a prominent Donetsk separatist, Aleksandr Khodakovskii, who recalled that storming the Reichstag and raising the Victory Banner was his favorite childhood game.[105]

The use of these exact copies has gone well beyond military reconstruction, becoming a part of numerous demonstrations; the Victory Banner thus has escaped from its fixed position in the Central Museum of the Armed Forces to appear on the streets, brandished and revered by crowds of demonstrators in parades around Russia and Ukraine. Ukrainian nationalists, however, revile and desecrate the banner whenever possible.

Thus, following the Victory Banner's 2007 reinstatement as an officially sanctioned symbol of Russian and Soviet victory in the war, the flag also became a symbol of pro-Russian identity in Ukraine. Following the 2010 election of Viktor Ianukovich, from Ukraine's Party of the Regions, as president, the Ukrainian government began to actively promote the banner: in April 2011, in the run-up to Victory Day, Ianukovich's government passed a law requiring Ukrainian national and regional governments to fly facsimiles of the Victory Banner on 9 May and to use it in remembrance ceremonies.[106] The symbol had not formerly played an important role in post-Soviet Ukraine, and this was a highly provocative

5.6. This Russian tank in Simferopol, during Russia's annexation of Crimea in 2014, bears a Victory Banner. From Crimeanews.com.

5.7. This image from a YouTube video shows Ukrainians burning a Victory Banner to protest Russian influence in Ukraine.

and divisive move, one that flew in the face of local authorities in the Ukrainian-speaking west of the country, which banned use of the red flag in all its guises.[107] In Russian-speaking cities such as Kharkiv and Odessa, however, Ianukovich's new law was enthusiastically obeyed on Victory Day 2011 with the parading of a copy of the Victory Banner, in imitation of the Moscow parade, albeit alongside the Ukrainian flag. This was preceded by dancing and a parade by reenactors in World War II–period uniforms. In Kyiv itself, there was a parade featuring people in facsimile uniforms and with period weapons.

As had been the case in Russia beginning in the mid-1990s, the Communist Party of Ukraine (KPU), especially in Russian-speaking regions, attempted to seize the initiative, and the party organized its own demonstrations featuring an enormous replica of the Victory Banner.[108] In a trajectory that again echoes Russia in the 1990s, such events were also organized by Ianukovich's Party of the Regions, the main vehicle of the Russian-speaking population, and in 2012 its Odessan chapter staged a reconstruction of the storming of the Reichstag before a festive crowd gathered under bright sunshine on the beach, where a copy of the Victory Banner was carried into battle and raised to signify the Soviet triumph.[109] The following year, on 22 June 2013, a reconstruction of the wartime battle for Kyiv was followed by the hoisting of a copy of the Victory Banner by Party of the Regions–dominated local authorities. In each case, the events were photographed and filmed for subsequent dissemination on the internet and had the effect of attracting the support of many of those who had previously backed the communists.

Predictably, in the Ukrainian-speaking west of the country there was a hostile reaction to the revival of this Soviet-era symbol. On 9 May 2011 in L′viv, copies of the Victory Banner were publicly defiled; a motor cavalcade repeatedly drove over them, before they were burned to the sound of the chant, "Sickle and hammer—death and famine."[110] Following Ianukovich's 2014 toppling from power, pro-Russian demonstrators and forces in Ukraine, Crimea, and Donbas used copies of the Victory Banner as a symbol of their movement. Since 2015, however, such displays have been banned, along with all Communist Party and Soviet symbolism, throughout Ukraine, including Odessa.[111]

Following the public demonstrations on Kyiv's Maidan Square and Crimea's annexation by (or accession to) the Russian Federation, in 2014, the Victory Banner has in parallel become an even more important and widely disseminated symbol in Russia, especially with the Russian state-sponsored anti-Maidan movement. Among the most significant uses of it was in March 2015, when a giant two-hundred-square-meter copy of the Victory Banner began a twenty-five-thousand-kilometer journey, starting in Sevastopol, in Crimea, through ninety towns and cities, ending up in Novorossiisk on Victory Day. It was transported as part of a supposedly long-running "international" project, a motor race entitled Our Great Victory. A report from the Kuban regional site on the Rossiia news channel explained the symbolism: "In the three years that the project 'Our Great Victory' has been running, thousands of hands of people from various ethnicities, generations, and social groups have already touched it. The ritual symbolized the unity of the peoples who fought the German-Fascist invaders in the years of the Great Patriotic War for the freedom of our multiethnic Motherland."[112]

The emphasis here on the international dimension of war memory is significant. The Victory Banner is not just a symbol with resonance in the Russian Federation, as we have seen with regard to Ukraine; rather, it symbolizes precisely the international or imperial claims of Russian nationalism, as well as Russia's efforts to exert influence beyond its borders, especially in the former countries of the Soviet Union (the race also passed through Belarus and Kazakhstan) and also, but not exclusively, among Russian-speaking populations. At the same time, this campaign was a way of underlining that Crimea is part of Russia, as is implied by the fact that the flag began its journey in Sevastopol, on the anniversary of Russia's reincorporation of Crimea, and was evidently intended to link that event with victory in the Great Patriotic War and the symbolism of the 9 May Victory Day parade. A version of this race, or procession, occurred for the fourth time in 2018, and the Victory Banner was ever present as bikers rode to Berlin, stopping at symbolic sites on the way, including Auschwitz. It seems, from this context, that the events in Crimea have had the effect of making the Victory Banner imagery even more prominent, especially in demonstrations.

This international culture of Russian war commemoration is analyzed in Ukraine director Sergei Loznitsa's 2018 documentary film *Victory Day* (*Den′ Pobedy*), which is an observational film about the crowds observing Victory Day 2017 at the Treptower Park memorial complex and cemetery in Berlin. Loznitsa's approach may be seen as fundamentally opposed to the tendency of iconic images to color and organize interpretations. While the film is set in the shadow of the famous statue of the soldier-liberator, he does not show us this familiar and emotive image that is calculated to condition a familiar response. Similarly, the chronicle of commemorations presents a richly varied picture of speeches, singing, and dancing, the laying of flowers, drinking, and much waving of flags, the Victory Banner in particular. Among the crowds we see the Night Wolves motorcycle club, who pose with facsimiles of the Victory Banner as if they had personally placed it on the Reichstag cupola.

5.8. This image from a YouTube video shows the Storm of Berlin—with contemporary Reichstag cupola, from the April 2017 reconstruction of the "Storming of Berlin" in Moscow's Patriot Park.

There are also many period uniforms: in one instance, a mother tries to make her little boy wear one and he cries. All of this is accompanied by an incessant cacophony of digital clicks and bleeps, as everything is recorded.

Intercut and contrasted with these images of celebration, self-satisfaction, and triumphalism are those of wartime death and destruction from the bas-reliefs on the original 1949 memorial. The observational style and focus on the practices of commemoration make *Victory Day* something of a companion to Loznitsa's 2016 film, *Austerlitz*, about tourists visiting concentration camp sites. Rather than judging the subjects of his films, Loznitsa invites his audience to reflect on the correct way of remembering. Indeed, there is something comforting about the chaos and spontaneity of these Berlin bacchanalia when compared to the strict and meticulous choreography of the Moscow 9 May parade. Nevertheless, Loznitsa seems to comment overtly at the end of the film as we hear the nondiegetic music of Bulat Okudzhava's "Pick up your greatcoat and go home" ("Beri shinel′, poshli domoi," 1975). The inference is clear: it is time to forget the war and think about something else.

Back in Russia, however, critical distance is rare, and there have been an increasing number of impressive reenactments of the storming of the Reichstag. The one held in Groznyi in 2015 was more spectacular than most, and it concluded with the raising of the Victory Banner over a specially constructed cupola. The evident subtext here was the display of Chechen loyalty to the Russian state.

A further notable attempt to convey the importance of the victory in palpable terms accessible to a wide public, including the young, was in Moscow's Patriot Park in 2017. On 23 February 2017 (i.e., on Defender of the Fatherland Day, previously Red Army Day), Russia's minister of defense, Sergei Shoigu, announced that a replica of the Reichstag would be built in Moscow's Patriot Park.[113] The idea was that it could be used for exercises by the Youth Army (Iunarmiia) organization. Founded in 2016, this was a kind of post-Soviet Russian scout or Young Communists group open to children between eleven and eighteen years of age, but with a clear "military-patriotic" orientation.[114] As Shoigu put it, "We are building a Reichstag. Not a complete version, but so that our Youth Army people can storm not just anything but a concrete place."[115]

Thus, Patriot Park became the setting on 23 April 2017 for a reconstruction of the storming of Berlin, culminating in the battle for the Reichstag. Organized by Moscow's Synergy University at enormous cost, it involved more than a thousand reconstructors from more than eight countries, dozens of period military vehicles, and an air display.[116] Vadim Lobov, executive director of Synergy University, which claims to combine "contemporary educational technologies" with age-old academic traditions, was attempting to use new methods to serve a traditional educational goal of conveying a sense of pride in Russia's history.[117] The goal was an effect something like that of cinema, with Lobov saying that it was the biggest reconstruction outside of cinema: "It will be the largest-scale [*samoe masshtabnoe*] historical re-creation of the events of the Great Patriotic war, organized not on a film set, not for a director and film producers, but for spectators who will watch what is happening from stands."[118]

To convey the importance of the war and victory narrative, the representation had to be on a grand scale, to possess the same quality of *masshtabnost′* sought after by epic representations of the war from the Stalin era onward. What was different here is the idea to achieve that through complete immersion, giving people an emotional and direct sense of the greatness of the events and making that somatic experience reinforce the message:

> The meaning of such events lies in the total immersion in a historical atmosphere. On the one hand, we construct contemporary visuals: from the site of the event and videos on social media to images on multimedia screens. On each communication channel, people can become acquainted with the main stages of the historical development of the events we are talking about. On the other hand, visitors to this "open-air history lesson" get the chance to feel the drama and importance of those events for the history of our country

> in an intensely emotional way. Thus, the spectacle that they will see, in its format and quality of performance, corresponds to professional drama productions and is accompanied by spectacular elements: stunts performed by stuntmen, aerial battles, and military hardware in action.[119]

The underlying purpose is educational: "Victory Day is the most important holiday and is of course the main reason to feel pride in contemporary Russia's history." According to Lobov, to fulfill that pedagogic task, the effectiveness of the reconstruction depended not only on its immersive power and the realistic special effects but also on the historical accuracy of what is depicted, guaranteed by a scenario authorized by the most authoritative Russian historians. This is needed, he argues, because contemporary students find it hard to read. This is supposed to take the place of that.[120] However, for all these claims of accuracy, the model of the Reichstag that was stormed was a copy of the contemporary building—a beacon of German democracy and transparency—and not the building as it was during the war. Given the emphasis on authentic detail, this was quite probably deliberate, and if it was inadvertent, it is still suggestive of an anti-Western and antidemocratic subtext to these events.

VICTORY BANNER AS COMMUNIST SYMBOL

Ultimately, what distinguishes the Victory Banner from the Soviet flag is its association with the end of the war and, visually, the fact that it bears the name (in Cyrillic lettering) of the unit that raised it. This insists on its Russianness, its unique resonance in a Russian-speaking space, and its association with Soviet martial glory and military feats of arms. The rituals through which the flag is displayed further cement this sense that this is not an internationalist but a specifically Russian symbol. Indeed, when Russian athletes and fans were not permitted to use the Russian tricolor flag at the 2018 Winter Olympics in PyeongChang in South Korea, as punishment for a state-sponsored doping program, the Victory Banner was used as an alternative to the national flag. Russian Olympian Svetlana Gladysheva, former head of Russian skiing and snowboarding, wrapped herself in the Victory Banner and refused to remove it.[121] With its use in the anti-Maidan activities in Ukraine, it has become a nationalist symbol, the very opposite of a symbol of international revolution and of socialism. However, despite its uses and associations, the Victory Banner is still in essence a red flag and still evokes other—communist and socialist—connotations.

One illustration of this residual communist charge came during the 2018 presidential elections, in which the CPRF candidate, Pavel Grudinin,

5.9. Retired Olympic skier Svetlana Gladysheva wearing a Victory Banner while attending the 2018 Winter Olympics in South Korea. Image from ok.ru.

was the principal challenger to Vladimir Putin and eventual, albeit distant, runner-up (liberal anticorruption campaigner Aleksei Navalnyi was not permitted to campaign for office). At the height of the run-up to the election, in February 2018, a strange version of the Victory Banner with no hammer and sickle or five-pointed star was being used in observance of the seventy-fifth anniversary of victory at the battle of Stalingrad. The regional authorities claimed, implausibly, that these symbols had washed off in a dry-cleaning process (but the rest of the writing remained intact).[122] What seems more likely is that the communist symbolism was deemed problematic in the context of the presidential elections, since the classic banner displays the hammer, sickle, and star that are symbols of the Communist Party. CPRF State Duma deputy Denis Parfenov expressed his outrage at this disrespect for "the sacred relics of the Fatherland" and linked this to attacks on Russia from all quarters:

> I regard as categorically unacceptable all expressions of disrespectful attitudes to the sacred relics of our Fatherland. The present time is characterized by increased international tensions, an attack of forces hostile to Russia on all fronts (informational, economic, diplomatic, and others), by constant attempts to promote Nazi criminals and inflame anti-Soviet and Russophobic hysteria in the post-Soviet space. Such actions directly threaten the national and state interests of the Russian Federation, enabling it to be weakened. In such a situation, the removal of state symbols of the USSR from the Victory Banner can be interpreted as ideological sabotage and an attempt to revise the role of the Soviet Union in the Second World war.[123]

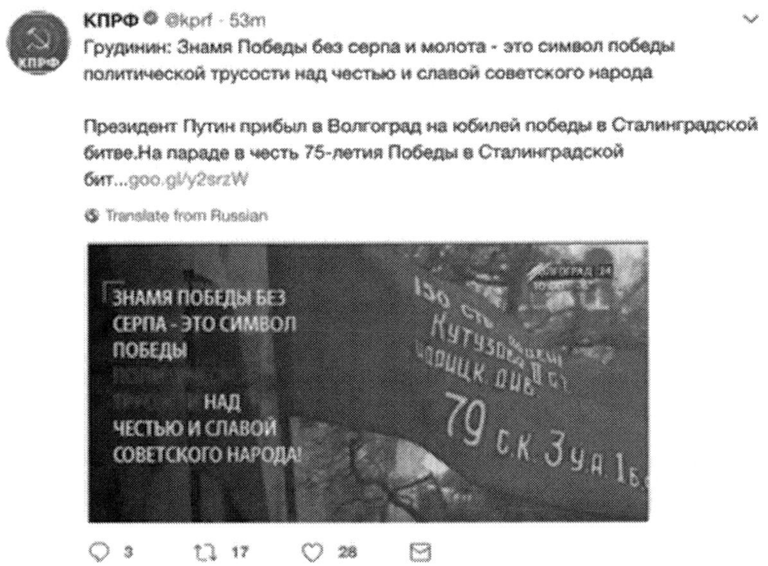

5.10. This tweet from the Communist Party of the Russian Federation in 2018 indicates presidential candidate Pavel Grudinin's condemnation of a doctored Victory Banner.

Expanding on the same line, Grudinin condemned this as "a symbol of political cowardice toward the honor and glory of the Soviet people." The communists were incensed and wanted to make more of this suppression of the symbols associated with their movement; they called for a debate on this in the Volgograd regional Duma and for those responsible for this crime to be prosecuted.[124] What they did not do here is to stress the importance of the red flag, with its internationalist pretensions, as the precursor of this symbol. In this respect, it symbolizes the problem faced by the communists: the Soviet-era symbolism, and the Victory Banner in particular, confer great power on the Russian communists, who are in a sense the custodians of that memory more than anyone else. However, this also makes it harder for them to move on from, for example, the nationalist and imperialist dimensions of the Soviet legacy. Parallel to the growing power of the symbol was the way in which the CPRF reframed itself, through the influence of Gennadii Ziuganov, so that the whole post-1993 communist project was presented as a reconciliation with religion and tradition, while the state possessed quasi-religious qualities transcending those of the individual. The communists' attempts to articulate a vision of social justice are still bound up

5.11. Troops raise a Soviet-era red flag over Raqqa, Syria, in this image from *Morning Star.*

with their reliance for legitimacy on a historical symbol tainted with the repressive and authoritarian legacy of the Soviet Union.[125]

However, while it is especially potent in Russia, the Victory Banner symbolism, especially in references to Khaldei's photograph, still possesses considerable resonance beyond Russia and the former Soviet Union—almost exclusively among left-wing, socialist, and communist groups. Thus, the small group of volunteers from the leftist International Freedom Battalion, fighting with the Syrian Kurds against the so-called Islamic State group, staged a raising of the red flag over a prominent building in Raqqa in 2018, symbolically celebrating their own socialist contribution to victory over the Islamic State and equating that organization to Nazism.[126] It is still used by antifascist groups, and, as a symbol of the socialist cause, it has even been appropriated by socialist currents within the green movement. These reuses and recyclings, especially of Khaldei's photograph, attest to the enduring power of the Victory Banner to symbolize a moment of triumph for the Soviet state and socialism and for the defeat of Nazism. Detached from the Russian context, without the name of the 150th Rifle Division of the First Belorussian Front's Third Strike Army on it or any other ritualized discourse, its authoritarian associations are likewise less significant.

OTHER COMMEMORATIVE PRACTICES

While the Victory Banner is a key symbol of the Russian war cult, one that crosses many media and crystallizes wider themes in memory of the war, it is of course not the only symbol of the war, nor is the 9 May parade the sole commemorative activity for the war. Moreover, while the

5.12. Poster using the Victory Banner as an antifascist symbol to advertise a discussion accompanying a reading of East German author Willi Bredel's account of a Nazi concentration camp. From DKP, https://dkp-luebeckostholstein.blogspot.com/p/vor-ort-aktiv.html.

Victory Banner is a symbol that for most of its existence has been closely controlled by the state, it is important to remember that it possesses a palpable power as an artifact that has genuine resonance for people and thus does not depend solely on state sponsorship. Indeed, previous studies of the war cult have been criticized for paying too much attention to the state's role in commemoration in the post-Soviet sphere or for drawing too sharp a distinction between the public cult of the war, seen as inauthentic, and what happens on a private level, seen as authentic.[127] As an object that can be experienced directly, or indirectly via a replica, it has been part of grassroots insurgencies for commemoration of the war in the 1960s, the 1990s, and in the twenty-first century. Its power is

5.13. Poster advertising the radical bookshop Jepps Books employing the iconic imagery of the Victory Banner on the Reichstag. Courtesy of Jim Jepps.

such that by attending a parade where a copy of the banner is carried, by personally bearing it or waving it, someone overcomes the distance that characterizes history as represented by remote museums and feels its direct presence. It is in this sense that we can understand the influence of and analogy to reenactments, to living history. Thus, through its use in meetings and alternative practices, including as an internet meme, the Victory Banner illustrates the ways in which remembrance of the war is sustained in Russia today through an interaction between private initiative and state intervention.[128]

This combination of private and public facets is true not only of the minute of silence, the visits to the eternal flame, and the laying of flowers at tombs of the Unknown Soldier and other graves but also of the ritual of watching the Victory Day parade on television; all of these practices were formalized by the state and given an impetus at or immediately

5.14. A Victory Day crowd wearing St. George ribbons carries Victory Banner facsimiles while participating in an Immortal Regiment procession, 2019.

after the 1965 commemorations. Two entirely post-Soviet commemorative practices are of note: the wearing of St. George ribbons (*georgievskie lentochki*) and the Immortal Regiment (Bessmertnyi polk) processions on 9 May. Unlike the Victory Banner, both of these practices avoid communist imagery. The former came into existence in 2005 as an initiative by RIA Novosti Press Agency and Moscow University students. It is a black ribbon with orange stripes on it, representing a prerevolutionary medal awarded for bravery; Stalin reinstated it after 1943. These are given out to be tied on clothing, usually the lapel, in the run-up to Victory Day every year, and they quickly became ubiquitous.[129] As Serguei Oushakine has pointed out, the ribbons invoke a heroic image of Russia's past and are attractive for their literal solidity, their "tactile and visual specificity." This tangible, incontrovertible physicality may again be compared with the Victory Banner.[130]

The same immediacy is characteristic of the Immortal Regiment, or the practice of marching through a town center holding a large portrait of a relative who took part in World War II. This started as a local initiative in Tomsk in 2012 but was soon taken up to become a state-sponsored and politically manipulated affair, quite different from the quiet, contemplative focus envisaged by its originators.[131] Nevertheless, it shares with the St. George ribbon a more personal, affective connection with official historical memory and is an activity in which individuals directly participate.

Like the use of the Victory Banner in parades, reenactments, and demonstrations, these practices may be contrasted to the epistemological uncertainty about the war that emerged in the late Soviet and early post-Soviet years, when eyewitnesses, including those who had raised the Victory Banner over the Reichstag, came forward to contest accepted accounts of all manner of official versions of history and when the photographic record of events such as the raising of the Victory Banner was subjected to criticism and critique.[132] Unlike those state-created images, photographs, and films, these forms of remembrance are interactive and personal. They are not subject to critique and historical revision, since their connection to the historical events of the war is primarily vague and emotional rather than being subject to rational scrutiny and sober reassessment. This is the opposite of historical critique, which has been marginalized by these tendencies.

THE BACKLASH AGAINST HISTORY

Mikhail Gorbachev, in permitting revelations as to the mistakes (and worse) committed by the communists, hoped that the widespread and unfettered publication of historical analysis of difficult moments in Soviet history would lead to a new historical consciousness and the overcoming of attitudes based on myth. It seemed at the time that the demythologizing tendency, accompanying a democratizing and opening of society, was a process that was unstoppable, as Tumarkin's book poignantly suggests and even assumes. Ultimately, however, this process was reversed, especially under Putin, as historical revelations as to mistakes made and crimes committed by the Soviet Union were seen as damaging to the post-Soviet Russian state. In parallel with the shift to a ritualized ahistorical discourse about the war, the state has attempted to regulate historical works through its 3 May 2014 law banning the rehabilitation of Nazism, for which prosecutions are rising, and through the reimposing of control over archives to limit the flow of such materials, which are the documents on which the articles were based.[133] As Leonid Maksimenkov put it, while individuals can decide to watch the television coverage of the parades and observe the minute's silence, the state serves as a monopolist on the archival records of the war, thus controlling the source as well as the validity of historical accounts.[134] The same law also punished showing disrespect to symbols of Russian martial glory, including the Victory Banner.[135] Mythologized symbols were to receive the protection of the law but historical research would not.

A particular factor preventing a frank reassessment of the war's many less uplifting dimensions is the attitude at the Russian Ministry of

Defense archive. One researcher has even described it as "conducting an undeclared, but none the less effective war against military history, paralyzing research with the blunt instrument of restrictions."[136] The stated rationale for keeping files secret—stopping falsifiers and those intending to blacken the name of Russian soldiers—makes no sense: those intent on doing so have no need for factual substantiation of their claims. The archive has been "infected with the virus of unmotivated secrecy."[137] This tendency, while it does not affect all Russian archives by any means, hinders research on a number of important aspects of the war.

Memoirs and easily dismissed popular historical works without a solid source base in the archives tend to dominate over genuine works of history. There has also been a trend toward rehabilitation of Stalin, described as an "effective manager" in a history textbook issued in 2007, as well as a more uncritical attitude to World War II.[138] However, this trend is contradictory, with echoes of but not a return to the Soviet era. This is evident from the whole tone of the twelve-volume *History of the Great Patriotic War*, a 2015 publication with a title that contrasted even with that of its Brezhnev-era analogue, the *History of the Second World War*, and suggests suspicion toward the Western Allies' participation in the war, thus evoking Soviet attitudes.[139] However, it was not a total reversion, and, unlike the earlier Soviet publication, the 2015 history now contained the account of the Victory Banner first articulated by Kumanev—that Makov's group had been the first to raise a red banner atop the Reichstag roof and that Egorov and Kantariia only put up an official flag later.[140] It also acknowledged that the flag was not used in the 24 June 1945 Victory Parade.[141]

Moreover, there have been attempts in these publications to approach the topic of the Holocaust in a far franker way than was the case in the Soviet era. Thus, volume 10 of this later work, in a section about "informational and ideological work," Nazi atrocities against the Jews (but not the word *Holocaust*) are mentioned in passing, in the context of appeals to the Jews of America and the United Kingdom.[142]

However, the 2015 work contains an emphasis on Nazi atrocities against Jews outside the Soviet Union, and when discussing atrocities within the Union the tendency is to universalize the fate of all those attacked, treating the violence as inflicted evenly against the whole Soviet population. Thus, the Holocaust is more present, but in the enormous twelve-volume work it occupies a peripheral place. The same is true more broadly for representations of the Holocaust in contemporary Russian museums, history books, films, and major commemorations: they are present, not suppressed, but always marginal and subordinated to the discourse of Russian heroism.[143] Thus, the narrative of the Holocaust is subordinated to the patriotic, to the Soviet focus, the one that ends with victory and with the symbolically potent scene of the raising of the Victory Banner. Moreover, the Victory Day parade ritual practices, like the historical discourse of victory itself, may be seen as "cumulative rather than subtractive"; by contrast with historical debate, the new discourse of the Holocaust is added without revising the overall framework.[144] The vernacular way of naming the end of the conflict "Victory," with a capital *V*, underlines the positive result, the outcome of a complex narrative conferring meaning. "Victory" helps people to remember what is important and to forget what is not, dismissing it as an irrelevance or temporary blip. The notion of "Victory" is one reinforced through an interlocking and overlapping system of symbols across many media.

This pattern illustrates how it is that Russian society maintains an ennobling and glorious narrative of the war. Russians are able to exorcise and counterbalance facts about the war that threaten its uplifting tenor, most notably the enormous toll of death and suffering that is inextricably associated with it, including the Holocaust. From this perspective, constructing memory of the war through the prism of victory, and the Victory Banner, serves not just to vindicate the sacrifice and price paid as meaningful but also to distract from elements of the war that cannot be assimilated into this paradigm, that do not fit notions of meaningful sacrifice. It repairs, smooths over, and fetishizes the traumas, the wounds, and scars of war to create a pleasing, edifying narrative.

CONCLUSION

My task in this book has been to show how imagery featuring the Victory Banner has been a central part of the shifting constructions of Russian war memory over the years since World War II. In showing how use of this imagery has evolved in the context of changes in politics and the media, it is not my intention to belittle the significance of the Soviet Union's defeat of Nazi Germany. On the contrary, this is a subject I would not want to research and write about if I did not think it was important, for Russians as well as humanity in general.

Instead, my intention has been to illustrate in detail the process by which history and memory of the war have been contested; they have not been a fixed constant, conveyed through an agreed-upon, objective account but have been shaped from the very start and adapted to fulfill political need. I cannot claim to have touched upon every single iteration of the Victory Banner imagery, and there are certainly many iterations of it in literary works and art, especially book illustrations, that I have passed over due to my primary focus on the moving image. My focus on the Victory Banner, a consciously created symbol used to sum up the meaning of the war, one that straddles the "soft memory" of films and the "hard memory" of the museum artifact, has enabled an in-depth and multifaceted picture to emerge, illustrating that war memory in Russia is not singular or monolithic. I hope to have shown that the cluster of images and the artifact itself are like an "iconic image" but that, unlike Hariman and Lucaites's account of iconic images in the United States, the Victory Banner imagery is more plural, spreading over a wide range of media, and it is primarily a site of contestation in unstable periods when Soviet or Russian war memory is being reassessed. Overwhelmingly, its often ritualized repetition tends to restrain and control memory of the war, underlining an authoritarian version of it, hence my suggestion of the notion of "authoritarian repetition" as an alternative to or variant of Hariman and Lucaites's notion of the iconic image.

Thus it is that the Victory Banner and depictions of it were created to bolster the Stalin cult by associating victory in the war with his own personal achievements and the Soviet state. It was not always effective in doing this, as the 1945 Victory Parade showed. Following the war, the Victory Banner was subsumed in more direct articulations of the Stalin cult, as was memory of the war more widely. Cinema was at this point a key mode articulating the cult; there were no histories and few memoirs with which it had to negotiate. In the post-Stalin period, the movement to free Soviet communism from the influence of Stalin meant that the Victory Banner was reassessed; attempts were made to establish the historical truth about who raised it and how. Treatments of it in film, notably the 1965 documentary *The Great Patriotic*, and the growing genres of historical writing and memoir literature in this period played out tensions between denouncing and demythologizing Stalin, between the empowering of eyewitnesses, historians, artists, and others to reassess the war, as well as the need to control this process by emphasizing the role of the Communist Party. The Victory Banner was a contested symbol, a site over which these conflicts between history and myth played out, but fear of undermining the force of this symbol meant that these debates were not made public.

When Brezhnev took power in October 1964, he immediately commissioned activities across many media and cultural spheres aimed at using the twentieth anniversary of victory in the war as a rallying point, one serving to unify and reinvigorate the country. In the initial absence of a new personality cult, memory of the war served to inject a charismatic aura and legitimacy into Communist Party rule. The Victory Banner played a special role here, as it was made central to the Kremlin memorial meeting on 8 May and the Red Square parade held on 9 May 1965, as well as being given an honored place in the relocated Central Museum of the Soviet Army. In addition to the actual artifact, film and television played a pivotal role not just in disseminating this image but also in emphasizing its place in the narrative of the war, endowing it with layers of myth and meaning, establishing a sacred aura around it to be approached only through ritualistic formulas and through monumental, epic forms suggesting collective power and the irrelevance of the single, individual perspective uncorroborated by higher powers.

While the pattern had been set by the 1965 commemorations, the Soviet media made repeated efforts to ensure that the Victory Banner imagery was repeated and reimagined but not reassessed for new trends in media and new audiences. Thus, it was featured in various documentaries, such as the made-for-television *The Unknown War* and the blockbuster epic film *Liberation*, in each case serving to impart a sense that the war was sacred and heroic and to control and ritualize the way people talked about it. These attempts to remake the story of the war across various media, in an attempt to reach across generations, were not ultimately successful. Moreover, it was at times subsumed within the unlikely cult of Brezhnev's personality, itself framed in terms of his wartime contribution, and this had the paradoxical effect of both sidelining it and contaminating it. Thus, by the mid-1980s the war cult and aura of the Victory Banner had come to seem marginal relative to the more pressing task of reassessing the whole Soviet project under Gorbachev. At worst, the Victory Banner was a distraction from that political exigency. While, paradoxically, there were more Red Square Victory Day military parades held under Gorbachev than any other Soviet leader, the climate of openness over which he presided led to revelations and reconsideration of the actual story of the Victory Banner, as its staged, constructed, and fabricated nature became the subject matter of historical studies, memoirs, and television documentaries.

Yet, under Yeltsin, post-Soviet Russia's democrats failed either to appropriate the memory of the war for their own political project or to create other charismatic symbols legitimizing their rule. Their communist opponents were able to use 9 May and Victory Banner symbolism as a focus for mobilizing and galvanizing their hostility to the liberal economic policies and pro-Western orientation of Yeltsin's team. Yeltsin had to permit a 9 May parade in 1995 but still tried to control the use of the Victory Banner and copies of it. One of Vladimir Putin's great successes has been his use of history to imbue contemporary Russians with a sense of pride in their nation, and reviving the cult of the Great Patriotic War has been central to that. This has meant annual 9 May parades becoming ever larger in scale and increasingly militarized, with ever more modern and destructive military technologies on display. The Victory Banner has been a central feature in these parades and has also become a more widely used symbol, appearing in many films and television programs, as well as in demonstrations across both Russia and Ukraine, in the events preceding Crimea's 2014 accession to (or annexation by) the Russian Federation, and in the context of the Donetsk separatist movement in eastern Ukraine.

While there have been countercurrents in critical works of history and documentary films, the cultivation of large-scale commemoration and rituals, including the use of the Victory Banner, has been paralleled by legal restrictions on historical inquiry into the Great Patriotic War, a tendency to close down or circumscribe archival access, and a wider shift away from conscientious rational scrutiny of history in favor of ritualized repetition of an emotive, unifying, and heroic vision. Moreover, while there is no minimizing of the enormous wartime losses sustained by the Russians and Soviets, there is a reluctance to break the larger figure of an estimated 27 million dead into the various categories, including Jews, and little appetite to approach loss through notions of mourning or trauma detached from an overall sense of victory as heroic and ultimately redemptive. The fact of ultimate victory for the Russian nation is what makes this historical experience meaningful and a source of pride, and attempts to question that are considered to be ultimately inadmissible, antipatriotic, heretical, treasonous. Moreover, in the eyes of the Russian public, victory tends to overshadow and minimize the violence of the Stalinist repressions and the Gulag, as well as crimes committed by a Moscow-centered Soviet regime against the other ethnicities of the Soviet Union or countries that it occupied.

However, more recently, the enormous disparity in wealth in Russian society has fed an as yet marginal current of discontent, leading to tensions again between the communist opposition, which sees the 9 May parade and victory as communist, and Putin's governing United Russia Party and the Russian state more broadly, which attempt to regulate and control representations of the war as a source of unity. If the communists develop as an oppositional force, it is possible that such differences may increasingly come to the fore over the Victory Banner, since it is a symbol of national pride revered not only by communists with a residual claim to the social justice agenda but also by nationalists with an unashamedly capitalist vision of Russia's development. The Victory Banner may be seen as illustrating the predicament of Russian communists, since it dissolves the internationalist aspirations of socialist ideas inherent in the red flag but also buttresses a nationalist or imperial vision of Russian greatness, through the Soviet state emblem and the inscription identifying the unit that raised the Victory Banner.

On one level, it seems that all these layers of meaning and commemorative practices are cumulative rather than subtractive.[1] While there is potentially a stark choice between the sharply contrasting visions of Russian society implicit in these two visions, neither is excluded by the Victory Banner symbol, and victory in the war can be seen, depending on your perspective, as the triumph of the communist worldview and system or of the Soviet and especially the Russian people. The Victory Banner can support these interpretations and more, including a sense of victory as the achievement of a multiethnic state, since its raising has over the years been credited to a Georgian, or to a Ukrainian, or to other non-Russian ethnicities, depending on the account. However, its uplifting, triumphant nature is not easily compatible with the narrative of the Holocaust as understood in the West, which we do not conventionally see as an uplifting or redemptive ending.

But it is the very ritualized nature of commemoration of the war that makes it difficult to change and revise, a paradox, since it creates a visual idiom that is endlessly replicated across myriad media, including the latest immersive digital technologies, but still serves to validate an ultimately authoritarian tradition. It is part of a pattern that has been described somewhat provocatively as an obsessive-compulsive reenactment: pursuit of the illusory goal of a stable national identity.[2] Acknowledging this pathologization of Russian war memory may be seen as insulting. Yet, rather than get outraged on Russia's behalf, we might attempt to apply this approach more widely and then briefly consider whether such a focus on the repetition of images and a discourse less as a site of contest and more as a tool of authoritarian disciplining of historical inquiry and criticism has wider relevance for societies other than Russia. Could it be that Hariman and Lucaites's account of contested iconic images is one flattering to the self-image of American democracy and that a glance in the distorted mirror of the potentially authoritarian repetition of an image or cluster of imagery is a salutary one, even for a democratic society, as a warning of what might come to pass, of how a central image can organize and discipline, or even manipulate, narratives? Nevertheless, the suggestion that Russia's war memory is pathological, or "obsessive-compulsive," is part of the central memory studies metaphor of a society remembering collectively as if it were a single individual. This view would certainly help to explain why memories of the war that might seem excessively verbose, digressional, irrelevant, and even self-indulgent are valorized as important, even holy. The tendency toward quotation, or remediation, inherent in digital culture suggests that this trend may intensify.

In Russia, it would take another eruption of historical scholarship into the mainstream, as happened under Khrushchev and even more so under Gorbachev, and probably social change as well, for there to be any chance of revising this ritualized, repetitious logic, with its ultimately authoritarian undertow. In the meantime, the world outside evolves, sometimes in ways that make the contrast with Russia's view of events all the more striking: the Reichstag's evolution into a symbol of a democratic Germany contrasts with its primary association, for Russians, with the end of the war, the victory over the Nazis.

There may, however, be a shift in attitudes toward the Victory Banner and the war: in 2018 there were some signs of a new tendency, such as the declining numbers of those wearing St. George ribbons in Moscow after that symbol increasingly became associated with aggressive Russian nationalism in the Donetsk region. It may be that attitudes toward the war, as well as the ways in which the Victory Banner symbolism is used, may have changed between the writing of this book and the reading of it, as has been the case with other charismatic cults. But, apart from the fact that the Victory Banner's construction as a cult is not dependent on a single individual, thus making its complete collapse unlikely, any challenge or revision of it would prove my point: the Victory cult, seen from early 2020, seems eternal and appears to teach one thing, but this is a construction, and this book has been an attempt to peel away the veneer of timelessness, of ritual, of the sacred, of epic, of the monumental to show the mechanics of how the Victory cult was constructed. Memory of the war, the ways it is commemorated, and the meaning attributed to it are actually still in flux and, beneath the surface unanimity, remain so. They can be changed to reflect changes in society and social attitudes. Russian memory of the war may yet take a liberal turn and undergo a shift in which critical historical reappraisal based on painstaking use of archival sources comes to dominate. Russian society may come to see the defeat of Nazi tyranny as a victory for democracy. Equally, the communist ideological legacy that may be seen as a part of victory may come to the fore, if leftist forces become a more significant challenge to the ruling Putin administration than Western-facing liberals. Whatever happens, if there are lasting changes, they will entail a reappraisal of the ritualized symbolic legacy of war memory, including the Victory Banner. Any new formation will have to create its own symbols, memories, and rituals or risk reverting to the old ones.

NOTES

INTRODUCTION

The Victory Banner shall be referred to throughout the body of the text in capital letters, likewise Victory Parade and the Reichstag. In Russian, "victory banner," "victory parade," and "reichstag" are inconsistently capitalized, depending on when the text was written and the attitudes of the author. I have preserved these inconsistencies in transliterated titles in the endnotes and bibliography but standardized them according to English-language norms in translations and elsewhere.

1. David Moos, "Utopian Construction? The Work of Frank Thiel," in *Frank Thiel: A Berlin Decade, 1995–2005*, ed. Robert Hobbs and David Moos (Madrid: Hatje Cantz, 2006), 9.

2. Earl F. Ziemke, *The Battle for Berlin: End of the Third Reich*, vol. 6 of *Purnell's History of the Second World War* (London: Macdonald, 1968), 110.

3. Ziemke, *Battle for Berlin*, 121.

4. Murray Edelman, *Constructing the Political Spectacle* (Chicago: University of Chicago Press, 1988), 8.

5. Murray Edelman, *The Symbolic Uses of Politics* (Urbana: University of Illinois Press, 1964), 6.

6. Astrid Erll, "Cultural Memory Studies: An Introduction," in *A Companion to Cultural Memory Studies*, ed. Astrid Erll, Ansgar Nünning, and in collaboration with Sara B. Young (Berlin: De Gruyter, 2010).

7. Alexander Etkind, "Hard and Soft in Cultural Memory: Political Mourning in Russia and Germany," *Grey Room*, no. 16 (2004): 36–59.

8. Astrid Erll, *Memory in Culture*, trans. Sara B. Young (Basingstoke: Palgrave Macmillan, 2011), 141.

9. Robert Hariman and John Louis Lucaites, *No Caption Needed: Iconic Photographs, Public Culture, and Liberal Democracy* (Chicago: University of Chicago Press, 2007).

10. Hariman and Lucaites, *No Caption Needed*, 1.

11. Hariman and Lucaites, *No Caption Needed*, 2.

12. Boris Uspensky, *The Semiotics of the Russian Icon*, ed. Stephen Rudy (Lisse, Netherlands: Peter de Ridder Press, 1976), 8.

13. Nina Tumarkin, *The Living and the Dead: The Rise and Fall of the Cult of World War II in Russia* (New York: Basic Books, 1994), 137.

14. Tumarkin, *Living and the Dead*, 226.

15. Eric Hobsbawm, "Introduction: Inventing Traditions," in *The Invention of Tradition*, ed. Eric Hobsbawm and Terence Ranger (1983; Cambridge: Cambridge University Press, 2002), 1.

16. Aleida Assmann, "Transformations between History and Memory," *Social Research* 75, no. 1 (2008): 66.

17. Assmann, "Transformations between History and Memory," 67.

18. Danièle Hervieu-Léger, *Religion as a Chain of Memory*, trans. Simon Lee (Cambridge: Polity Press, 2000), 83.

19. Pierre Nora, "Entre mémoire et histoire: La problématique des lieux," in *Les lieux de mémoire*, ed. Pierre Nora (Paris: Gallimard Quarto, 1997), 29.

20. Emile Durkheim, *The Elementary Forms of Religious Life*, trans. and intro. Karen E. Fields (New York: Free Press, 1995), 37.

21. Alexei Yurchak, *Everything Was Forever, Until It Was No More: The Last Soviet Generation* (Princeton, NJ: Princeton University Press, 2006), 26, 59–60.

22. Nikolai Iamskoi, *Kto bral Reikhstag. Geroi po umolchaniiu* (Moscow: Olma Press, 2006); Georgii Kumanev, *Podvig i podlog. Stranitsy Velikoi Otechestvennoi voiny 1941–1945 gg* (Moscow: Russkoe slovo, 2000).

23. Susan Sontag, *Regarding the Pain of Others* (London: Penguin, 2003), 49, 50.

24. Shaun Walker, "Russian War Film Set to Open amid Controversy over Accuracy of Events," *The Guardian*, 23 November 2016, https://www.theguardian.com/film/2016/nov/23/russian-war-film-set-to-open-against-controversy-over-accuracy-of-events.

25. Vladimir Medinskii, *Voina. Mify SSSR; 1939–1945*, 2nd ed. (Moscow: OLMA Media Grupp, 2014), 240–42, 657.

26. Medinskii, *Voina*, 565.

27. Catherine Merridale, *Night of Stone: Death and Memory in Twentieth-Century Russia* (New York: Viking, 2001), 226, 240.

28. Hayden White, *Metahistory: The Historical Imagination in Nineteenth-Century Europe* (Baltimore: Johns Hopkins University Press, 1973), 5.

29. Nina Tumarkin, "The Great Patriotic War as Myth and Memory," *European Review* 11, no. 4 (2002): 598.

30. Joshua Hirsch, *Afterimage: Film, Trauma, and the Holocaust* (Philadelphia: Temple University Press, 2004).

31. Jean-Paul Sartre, "Discussion on the Criticism of *Ivan's Childhood*," *L'Unità*, 9 October 1962; published in French in Jean-Paul Sartre, *Situations VII* (Paris: Gallimard, 1965).

32. Anna Krylova, "'Healers of Wounded Souls': The Crisis of Private Life in Soviet Literature, 1944–1946," *Journal of Modern History* 73, no. 2 (2001): 307–31.

33. Catherine Merridale, *Ivan's War: The Red Army 1939–1945* (London: Faber and Faber, 2005).

34. Anonymous, *A Woman in Berlin*, trans. James Stern (London: Secker & Warburg, 1955); Norman M. Naimark, *The Russians in Germany: A History of the Soviet Zone of Occupation, 1945–1949* (Cambridge, MA: Belknap Press of Harvard University Press, 1995); Mark Solonin, *Zavetnaia pravda o Velikoi Otechestvennoi. Net blaga na voine!* (Moscow: Iauza-katalog, 2014), respectively.

35. Michael Rothberg, *Multidirectional Memory: Remembering the Holocaust in the Age of Decolonization* (Stanford, CA: Stanford University Press, 2009), 12–14.

36. Alexander Etkind, *Warped Mourning: Stories of the Undead in the Land of the Unburied* (Stanford, CA: Stanford University Press, 2013), 208.

37. E. A[rfon]. Rees, "Leader Cults: Varieties, Preconditions and Functions," in *The Leader Cult in Communist Dictatorships: Stalin and the Eastern Bloc*, ed. Balázs Apor et al. (Basingstoke: Palgrave Macmillan, 2004), 6–7.

38. Rees, "Leader Cults," 7, 12.

39. Yurchak, *Everything Was Forever*, 19, 21.

40. Bishnupriya Ghosh, *Global Icons: Apertures to the Popular* (Durham, NC: Duke University Press, 2011).

41. Maurice Dommanget, *Histoire du drapeau rouge des origines à la guerre de 1939* (Paris: Librairie de l'Étoile, 1967), passim, 72, 157, 229, 271.

42. Geoffrey A. Hosking, *Russia: People and Empire, 1552–1917* (Cambridge, MA: Harvard University Press, 1997).

CHAPTER 1. THE RAISING OF THE VICTORY BANNER

1. It should be noted that a number of accounts, including Zhukov's memoirs, cite the earlier time of 14:25, but that has been definitively disproved and was probably the consequence of an unconfirmed report from advanced units. See Georgii Zhukov, *Vospominaniia i razmyshleniia* (Moscow: Izdatel′stvo agentstvo pechati novosti, 1972), as well as below in this chapter and chapter 5.

2. V. N. Saprykov, *Dvazhdy pobednoe* (Moscow: Moskovskie uchebniki—SiDipress, 2008), 29.

3. P[etr] N[ikolevich] Pospelov, E[vgenii] A[rsenevich] Boltin, and V. P. Moskovskii, *Istoriia Velikoi Otechestvennoi voiny Sovetskogo Soiuza 1941–1945* (Moscow: Voennoe izdatel′stvo ministerstva oborony SSSR, 1963), 5:284.

4. Dmitrii Lozin, *Znamia Pobedy—gosudarstvennaia relikviia Rossii. Voenno-istoricheskie ocherki* (Moscow: Zhizn′, 2014), 51–68.

5. Antony Beevor, *Berlin 1945: The Downfall* (London: Penguin, 2003), xxxiv.

6. Alexandra Richie, *Faust's Metropolis: A History of Berlin* (London: HarperCollins, 1999), 553; Zhukov, *Vospominaniia i razmyshleniia*, 594–95.

7. Richie, *Faust's Metropolis*, 555.

8. Joseph Stalin, "Doklad na torzhestvennom zasedanii Moskovskogo Soveta deputatov trudiashikhsia s partiinymi i obshchestvennymi organizatsiiami goroda Moskvy 6 noiabria 1944 goda," 1944, in *Sochineniia*, vol. 15, part 2 (Moscow: Izdatel′stvo ITRK, 2009), 818.

9. Richie, *Faust's Metropolis*, 595; Erich Kuby, *The Russians and Berlin, 1945*, trans. Arnold J. Pomerans (London: Heinemann, 1965), 66. Ian Kershaw's account of Germany in the last year of the war sees the Reich Chancellery, "the epicentre of Nazi rule," as the Soviets' primary objective. Kershaw, *The End: Germany 1944–45* (London: Penguin, 2011), 339. This was definitely not the case.

10. Zhukov, *Vospominaniia i razmyshleniia*, 622.

11. Tony Le Tissier, *Race for the Reichstag: The 1945 Battle for Berlin* (London: Frank Cass, 1999), 32; John Erickson, *The Road to Berlin*, vol. 2 of *Stalin's War with Germany* (London: Weidenfeld and Nicolson, 1983), 599.

12. Richie, *Faust's Metropolis*, 596.

13. Maksim Svoichakov, *Oni brali reikhstag* (Moscow: Voennoe izdatel′stvo 1973), 73.

14. Saprykov, *Dvazhdy pobednoe*, 11.

15. "Stenogrammy dokladov i vystuplenii v nauchnoi konferentsii po izucheniiu Berlinskoi operatsii voisk 1 Belarusskogo Fronta," Babelsberg, 9–12 April 1946, TsAMO RF, 233/2356/804, sheets 528–35.

16. Le Tissier, *Race for the Reichstag*, 3.

17. Fedor Zinchenko, *Geroi shturma reikhstaga* (Moscow: Voennoe izdatel′stvo, 1983), 87.

18. Arkadii Dement′ev, *Znamia Pobedy. Glavnaia relikviia Velikoi Otechestvennoi voiny v svete istoricheskikh issledovanii* (Moscow: Granitsa, 2015), 6.

19. V. Briskin, "Vodruzim znamia pobedy nad Berlinom," *Za chest′ rodiny*, 24 April 1945, 3.

20. Samuil Marshak and Kukryniksy, "Poverzhennyi Berlin," *Pravda*, 1 May 1945, 4.

21. Stalin, "Doklad na torzhestvennom zasedanii Moskovskogo Soveta deputatov trudiashikhsia," 818.

22. David Shneer, *Through Soviet Jewish Eyes: Photography, War and the Holocaust* (New Brunswick, NJ: Rutgers University Press, 2011), 226.

23. I. Zolin, "Vozdruzhivshie znamia pobedy nad Berlinom," *Pravda*, 8 May 1945, 2.

24. Quoted in Shneer, *Through Soviet Jewish Eyes*, 136.

25. Kuby, *Russians and Berlin, 1945*, 66.

26. Vassily Subbotin, "How Wars End," in *How Wars End: Eye-Witness Accounts of the Fall of Berlin*, ed. Vladimir Sevruk (Honolulu, HI: University Press of the Pacific, 2005), 282.

27. Victor Barbat, "Bannières et drapeaux, sur quelques manières de les les ver et de les représenter: L'exemple du Reichstag, mai 1945," *1895*, no. 74 (2014): 92.

28. Orlando Figes and Boris Kolonitskii, *Interpreting the Russian Revolution: The Language and Symbols of 1917* (New Haven, CT: Yale University Press, 1999); Graeme Gill, *Symbols and Legitimacy in Soviet Politics* (Cambridge: Cambridge University Press, 2011).

29. James von Geldern, *Bolshevik Festivals, 1917–1920* (Berkeley: University of California Press, 1993), 199–200.

30. Leon Trotsky, *The History of the Russian Revolution, Volume 3: The Triumph of the Soviets*, proofed and reset by Pablo Stern, converted to eBook format by Kollektiv Yakov Perelman in 2013 and posted at the Marxists Internet Archive, accessed 2 May 2018, https://www.marxists.org/archive/trotsky/1930/hrr/ch44.htm.

31. Quotation from von Geldern, *Bolshevik Festivals*, 201.

32. Robert A. Rosenstone, *History on Film/Film on History*, 2nd ed. (Harlow: Pearson 2012), 75.

33. Mikhail Romm, *Izbrannye proizvedeniia*, vol. 2, *O sebe, o liudiakh, o fil′makh*, ed. Natal′ia Kuz′mina (Moscow: Iskusstvo, 1981), 180.

34. Zinchenko, *Geroi shturma reikhstaga*, 123.

35. Khmel′nitskii to Saakov, "Correspondence with Film Group of Belarussian Front 02.01.45–14.04.45," RGALI, 2487/1/1004, 5/1, sheet 134.

36. Military historian Tony Le Tissier also discusses the puzzling decision to make the Reichstag into a military objective, saying that, as the nucleus of Nazi power, it came to acquire symbolism as a counterpart to the Kremlin. Le Tissier, *Race for the Reichstag*, 3.

37. Zhukov, *Vospominaniia i razmyshleniia*, 662; Sergei Shtemenko, *The Soviet General Staff at War, 1941–1945*, trans. Robert Daglish (Moscow: Progress, 1970), 388.

38. Jan Plamper, *The Stalin Cult: A Study in the Alchemy of Power* (New Haven, CT: Yale University Press, 2012), 57, 68–69.

39. Evgenii Dolmatovskii, "Nad Berlinom reet znamia nashei pobedy," *Krasnaia armiia* (newspaper of First Belorussian Front), 3 May 1945, 3; Oleg Knorring, "Berlinskii reportazh," in *Poslednii shturm*, ed. Konstantin Telegin (Moscow: Izdatel′stvo politicheskoi literatury, 1965), 234.

40. Stepan Neustroev, *Put′ k reikhstagu* (Moscow: Voennoe izdatel′stvo Ministerstva Oborony Soiuza SSR, 1961). Kumanev, drawing on documents

from the Ministry of Defense Archive, claims it was put up at 22:40 and discusses how the incorrect claim that a banner had been raised at 14:25 ended up in Zhukov's memoirs. Kumanev, *Podvig i podlog*, 330–33.

41. Beevor, *Berlin 1945*, 336.

42. Richie gets Khaldei's staging mixed up with the issue as to when a photograph was first raised, and is dependent upon a 1997 obituary for Khaldei.

43. Ernst Volland, *Das Banner des Sieges* (Berlin: Berlin Story Verlag, 2008), 44; Aleksandr Abramov and Varvara Kochetova, *Znamia pobedy nad Berlinom* (Nizhnii Novgorod: Ekstra N, 2007), 5; Barbat, "Bannières et drapeaux," 94; L. Vysokostrovskii and P. Troianovskii, "Nad reikhstagom vodruzheno znamia nashei pobedy," *Krasnaia zvezda*, 1 May 1945, 2.

44. Roman Karmen, "Berlin: Nad zdaniem reikhstaga reet znamia pobedy," *Krasnaia zvezda*, 1 May 1945, 4. Moreover, the flag over the cupola was apparently photographed from the air the following day by Timofei Mel′nik, but this image was not found until 1965. See Abramov and Kochetova, *Znamia pobedy nad Berlinom*, 5.

45. Sergei Gerasimov to Karmen and Galadzhev, 5 May 1945, in Correspondence with Filmgroup of First Belorussian Front, 16 April 1945–16 June 1945, RGALI 2487/1/1005, 6/1, sheet 94.

46. Mark Grosset, *Khaldei: Un photoreporteur en Union Soviétique* (Paris: Éditions du Chêne, 2004), 129.

47. Alice Nakhimovsky and Alexander Nakhimovsky, *Witness to History: The Photography of Yevgeny Khaldei* (New York: Aperture, 1997), 10.

48. Nakhimovsky and Nakhimovsky, *Witness to History*, 10. The Nakhimovskys sidestep the generally accepted notion that Khaldei's photo was taken the following day. He denied staging it, but the fact that it was put up on 2 May means that it was not the first flag to be raised.

49. Volland, *Das Banner des Sieges*, 11.

50. Grosset, *Khaldei*, 129.

51. Aleksandr Rodchenko, "The Paths of Contemporary Photography," in *Experiments for the Future: Diaries, Essays, Letters, and Other Writings*, ed. Alexander N. Lavrentiev (New York: Museum of Modern Art, 2005), 207–21; Andrei Tolstoi, "Khudozhnik na fronte," in *Evgenii Khaldei: Znamia pobedy*, ed. A. V. Maksimova (St. Petersburg: Rosfoto, 2015), 5.

52. Julia Hell and Andreas Schönle, "Introduction," in *Ruins of Modernity*, ed. Julia Hell and Andreas Schönle (Durham, NC: Duke University Press, 2010), 1–16.

53. Grosset, *Khaldei*, 129.

54. Quoted in Valerii Fomin, ed., *Kino na voine. Dokumenty i svidetel′stva* (Moscow: Materik, 2005), 770.

55. Quoted in Fomin, *Kino na voine*, 776.

56. Fomin, *Kino na voine*, 776.

57. Fomin, *Kino na voine*, 775.

58. Fomin, *Kino na voine*, 771.

59. Sergei Gerasimov, telegram to Galadzhev, head of Politupravlenie First Belorussian Front, Correspondence with Film Group of First Belorussian Front, 2 February–14 April 1945, RGALI 2487/1/1004, 5/1, sheet 123.

60. Popov to Film Group of Second Belorussian Group, 16 March 1945, in Correspondence with Film Group of Second Belorussian Front, 1 January–25 June 1945, RGALI, 2487/1/1006, 7/2, 1945, sheet 68.

61. Vladimir Mikhailov, *Frontovoi kinoreportazh* (Moscow: Nauchno-issledovatel′nyi institut teorii i istorii kino, 1977), 140. Not everyone appreciated how important this was—the film group under Raizman's command had to turn down requests for the camera operators filming the battle of Berlin to be diverted to other tasks, saying they were needed to film the battle.

62. The official flag of the Third Strike Army's Military Council first seems to have been put on an equestrian statue sometimes referred to as the Goddess of Victory but is in fact an allegory of Germania. The official flag was later moved to the cupola. This statue was later removed from the Reichstag.

63. Mark Zak, *Iulii Raizman. Mastera kinoiskusstva* (Moscow: Iskusstvo, 1962), 151.

64. Iulii Raizman, *Vchera i segodnia* (Moscow: Biuro propogandy sovetskogo kinoiskusstva, 1969), 39.

65. L. Saakov to Troianovskii, 14 March 1945, RGALI 2487/1/1006, 7/2, sheet 30.

66. Viktor Shtatland, telegram to Saakov, 31 March 1945, RGALI, 2487/1/1004, 5/1, sheet 188.

67. Viktor Shtatland, telegram to Saakov, 7 May 1945, RGALI, 2487/1/1004, 5/1, sheet 135.

68. Popov to Kuznetsov, 25 May 1945, RGALI, 2487/1/1004, 5/1, sheet 136.

69. Mikhailov, *Frontovoi kinoreportazh*, 145; Raizman, *Vchera i segodnia*, 46. In fact, the final film has eighteen hundred meters, but some of this is archival footage not taken for this film. However, the Krasnogorsk archives hold only 11,992.40 meters of outtakes from the Berlin film.

70. Sergei Gerasimov to Karmen and Galadzhev, 5 May 1945, RGALI 2487/1/1005, 6/1, sheet 94. Victor Barbat has doubted the attribution of this image to Karmen, finding no further mention of it, but this telegram is clear, and the scandal would explain the subsequent silence.

71. Ivan Panov, "Nad reichstagom znamia," in *Ikh oruzhie—kinokamera*, ed. Valentin Zeltov and Aleksei Lebedev (Moscow: Iskusstvo, 1970), 280; Semen Shkol′nikov, "Tiazhkii put′ kinokhronikera," *Iskusstvo kino*, no. 6 (2008), accessed 22 May 2018 at http://kinoart.ru/ru/archive/2008/06/n6-article14.

72. Vladimir Berman, "Znamia nad reikhstagom. O tekh, kto snimal istoricheskie kadry," *Lekhaim*, May 2005, accessed 1 May 2005, http://lechaim.ru/ARHIV/157/berman.htm.

73. Raizman, *Vchera i segodnia*, 39.

74. Gerasimov to Saakov, 3 May 1945, Correspondence with Film Group of First Belorussian Front, vol. 2, 16 April–16 June 1945, RGALI, 2487/1/1005, 6/1, sheet 88.

75. Iulii Raizman, "Berlin," in *Ikh oruzhue—kinokamera*, ed. V. I. Zheltov and A. A. Lebedev (Moscow: Iskusstvo, 1970), 287.

76. Barbat, "Bannières et drapeaux," 84.

77. Viktor Shtatland and Iulii Raizman, telegram to Saakov, 11 May 1945, RGALI 2487/1/1005, 6/1, sheet 114. The fact that Raizman demands medium shots and long shots is interesting: it suggests that the defective footage may have contained some close-ups. It also suggests that there were not any good shots in which the Reichstag itself was visible: the actual storming sequence would thus seem to be part of the footage that was staged later.

78. The demand for smoke is part of the genre of such images, as we saw with the March 1945 request for footage for Lukov's film, but it is also possibly indicative of the need to cover up the fact of the staging—as with Khaldei's famous still photograph. Volland, *Das Banner des Sieges*, 22.

79. Panov and Dul′tsev, 7 June 1945, Information about Film Material Arriving from Fronts of Great Patriotic War, January 2–June 7, 1945, RGALI 2487/1/1001, 26/23, sheet 46.

80. Raizman and Khmel′nitskii to Kuznetsov and Volk, 19 June 1945, RGALI 2487/1/1005, 6/1, sheet 192.

81. Iulii Raizman and Nikolai Shpikovskii, "'Berlin' Plan for Documentary Film, Berlin-Moscow May 1945," RGALI 2487/1/141, sheet 42.

82. RGALI 2487/1/141, sheet 52.

83. John Barber, "The Image of Stalin in Soviet Propaganda and Public Opinion during World War Two," in *World War 2 and the Soviet People: Selected Papers from the Fourth World Congress for Soviet and East European Studies, Harrogate, 1990*, ed. John Garrard and Carol Garrard (Basingstoke: Macmillan, 1993), 42–43.

84. Iulii Raizman and Khmel′nitskii to Kuznetsov, 19 June 1945, RGALI 2487/1/1005, 6/1, sheet 192.

85. Plamper, *Stalin Cult*, 68–69.

86. Malte Rolf, *Soviet Mass Festivals, 1917–1991*, trans. Cynthia Klohr (Pittsburgh, PA: University of Pittsburgh Press, 2013), 182.

87. Iurii Khaniutin, "'Kogda pushki streliaiut . . . ,'" *Iskusstvo kino*, no. 5 (1965): 23.

88. Edelman, *Symbolic Uses of Politics*, 16; von Geldern, *Bolshevik Festivals*, 145.

89. Richard S. Wortman, *Myth and Ceremony in Russian Monarchy: From Peter the Great to the Abdication of Nicholas II*, abridged one-volume ed. (Princeton, NJ: Princeton University Press, 2006), 113.

90. Wortman, *Myth and Ceremony in Russian Monarchy*, 146.

91. "Spravka i zamechaniia po paradu voisk Moskovskogo garnizona 1 maia 1945," Directorate of the Commandant of Moscow 1 May 1945 Parade, vol. 2, TsAMO RF, 514044/4, sheets 78, 344.

92. "Spravka i zamechaniia po paradu voisk Moskovskogo garnizona 1 maia 1945," Directorate of the Commandant of Moscow 1 May 1945 Parade, vol. 1, TsAMO RF, 514044/3, sheet 148.

93. TsAMO RF, 514044/3, sheet 151.

94. Mikhail Chertok, *Muzykanty Parada Pobedy* (Moscow: Kanon+, 2015), 8.

95. TsAMO RF, 514044/3, sheet 200 verso; Vadim Mal′tsev, *Po stranitsam voennogo dnevnika. Ot nachala voiny do parada pobedy*, 2nd rev. ed. (Moscow: Avanglion-print, 2013), 210.

96. Dmitrii Karavaev, "Newsreels of Soviet Military Parades as Component of Victory: Some Ineffective Examples" (paper presented at "The Iconic and the Archival: Images and Russian Memory of World War Two" workshop, Queen Mary University of London, 25 May 2017).

97. Victory Parade, Directorate of the Military Commandant of Moscow, TsAMO RF 701786/1, sheets 114–24 verso.

98. Mal′tsev, *Po stranitsam voennogo dnevnika*, 210.

99. TsAMO RF 701786/1, sheets 345–50.

100. Victory Parade, Directorate of the Military Commandant of Moscow, TsAMO RF 701786/2, sheet 55.

101. "Torzhestvo pobedy," *Pravda*, 24 June 1945, 1.

102. Rolf, *Soviet Mass Festivals*, 33.

103. I. F. Bobylev, *Vsadniki s Krasnoi Ploshchadi. Svidetel′stva ochevidtsa* (Moscow: Izdatel′skii tsentr "Fedorov," 2000), 73.

104. Bobylev claims that this music was used in the 1 May 1945 parade, but more reliable histories and documentary sources contradict this claim. Bobylev, *Vsadniki s Krasnoi Ploshchadi*, 73.

105. Chertok, *Muzykanty Parada Pobedy*, 12.

106. Chertok, *Muzykanty Parada Pobedy*, 13.

107. B. Asaf′ev, "*Ivan Susanin*. Spektakl′ v Bol′shom teatre," *Pravda*, 25 May 1945, 3.

108. Asaf′ev, "*Ivan Susanin*," 3.

109. Chertok, *Muzykanty Parada Pobedy*, 13.

110. Chertok, *Muzykanty Parada Pobedy*, 13, 443.

111. Chertok, *Muzykanty Parada Pobedy*, 13.

112. Bobylev, *Vsadniki s Krasnoi Ploshchadi*, 83.

113. Zhukov, *Vospominaniia i razmyshleniia*, 662.

114. Elena Rzhevskaia, *Berlin, mai 1945. Zapiski voennogo perevodchika* (Moscow: TERRA-Knizhnyi klub, 2005), 276–77; Mal′tsev, *Po stranitsam voennogo dnevnika*, 195.

115. Bobylev, *Vsadniki s Krasnoi Ploshchadi*, 81; Shtemenko, *Soviet General Staff at War*, 382.

116. Shtemenko, *Soviet General Staff at War*, 383.

117. Shtemenko, *Soviet General Staff at War*, 388.

118. In the Russian military, a regiment (*polk*) might have a thousand soldiers. It comprises two or more battalions (*battal′ony*) of two hundred or more, comprising two or more companies (*roty*) of one hundred or more troops. "Troop Organization," Wikipedia, accessed 7 June 2018, https://ru.wikipedia.org/wiki/Структура_вооружённых_сил.

119. Shtemenko, *Soviet General Staff at War*, 390.

120. "Znamia pobedy," *Izvestiia*, 23 June 1945, 3. It should be noted that in the Soviet press there were photos of another banner, also termed the Victory Banner, which was taken from the Reichstag to be transported to Moscow earlier on 20 May. Unlike the official Victory Banner, it had a large hammer and sickle in the center. This was ceremonially removed in what might be seen as a further rehearsal for the Victory Parade.

121. Stepan Neustroev, "O reikhstage na sklone let," *Oktiabr′* 5 (1990): 144.

122. Valentin Varennikov, *Parad Pobedy* (Moscow: Vagrius, 2005); V. V. Zainkin, ed., *Nashi prazdniki. (Sovetskie obshchegosudarstvennye, trudovye, voinskie, molodezhnye i semeino-bytovye prazdniki, obriady, ritualy)* (Moscow: Politizdat, 1977); E. A. Drozdovskii et al., *Tverichi na Parade Pobedy* (Tver′: Litera-M, 2000); Shtemenko, *Soviet General Staff at War*, 390; Chertok, *Muzykanty Parada Pobedy.*

123. Aleksei Surkov, "Gordost′ naroda," *Pravda*, 25 June 1945, 4; B. Borisov, "Parad Pobedy: Novyi dokumental′nyi kinofil′m," *Krasnaia zvezda*, 18 July 1945, 3.

124. Fedor Zinchenko, "Nash polk ovladel reikhstagom," *Trud*, 24 June 1945, 3.

125. "Istoricheskii parad armii-pobeditel′nitsy," *Pravda*, 25 June 1945, 1.

126. Catherine Merridale, *Red Fortress: The Secret Heart of Russia's History* (London: Penguin, 2013), 2, 277.

127. Rolf, *Soviet Mass Festivals*, 41.

128. Michel Pastoreau, *Une histoire symbolique du Moyen Âge occidental* (Paris: Seuil, 2004), 291.

129. Richard C. Raack, *Stalin's Drive to the West, 1938–1945: The Origins of the Cold War* (Stanford, CA: Stanford University Press, 1995), 111.

130. *Tsentral′nyi Muzei Krasnoi Armii. Kratkii putevoditel′ po zalam ekspozitsii. V pomoshch′ posetiteliu* (Moscow: Izdanie Tsentral′nogo Muzeia Krasnoi Armii, 1946), 1–2.

131. *Tsentral′nyi Muzei Krasnoi Armii*, 3–4.

132. Elena Zubkova, *Russia after the War: Hopes, Illusions, and Disappointments, 1945–1957*, trans. Hugh Ragsdale (Armonk, NY: M. E. Sharpe, 1998), 15.

133. Robert Service, *Stalin: A Biography* (London: Pan, 2010), 482.

134. Oleg V. Khlevniuk, *Stalin: New Biography of a Dictator*, trans. Nora Seligman Favorov (New Haven, CT: Yale University Press, 2015), 263.

135. Ivan Bol′shakov et al., "Vsesoiuznoe soveshchanie rabotnikov khuedozhestvennoi kinematografii po obsuzhdeniiu resheniia Tsk Vkp(B) o kinofil′me 'Bol′shaia zhizn′ (2 Seriia), 14–15 Oktiabria 1946 Goda," in *Zhivye golosa kino. Govoriat vydaiushchiesia mastera otechestvennogo kinoiskusstva (30-e–40-e gody). Iz neopublikovannogo*, ed. L. A. Parfenov (Moscow: Belyi bereg, 1999), 308–84.

CHAPTER 2. VICTORY AND THE POSTWAR STALIN CULT

1. V. F. Zima, *Golod v SSSR 1946–47 godov. Proiskhozhdenie i posledstviia* (Moscow: Institut rossiiskoi istorii RAN, 1996), 12–13.

2. Yoram Gorlizki and Oleg Khlevniuk, *Cold Peace: Stalin and the Soviet Ruling Circle, 1945–1953* (Oxford: Oxford University Press, 2004), 124.

3. Karen Petrone, *Life Has Become More Joyous, Comrades: Celebrations in the Time of Stalin* (Bloomington: Indiana University Press, 2000), 16.

4. "Slavnymi trudovymi podvigami oznamenuem 1 maia i Den′ Pobedy!," *Pravda*, 15 April 1946, 1.

5. "Prizyvy TsK VVP(B) k 1 maia 1946 goda," *Pravda*, 24 April 1946, 1.

6. "Pervomaiskie prizyvy bol′shevistskoi partii," *Pravda*, 25 April 1946, 1.

7. "Pervomaiskie prizyvy bol′shevistskoi partii," 1.

8. Iosif V. Stalin, "Prikaz Ministra Vooruzhennykh Sil Soiuza SSR," *Pravda*, 1 May 1946, 1.

9. "Nadezhnaia opora interesov Sovetskogo Soiuza," *Pravda*, 3 May 1946, 1.

10. "Nakanune dnia pobedy," *Pravda*, 8 May 1946, 1.

11. "Vsia strana torzhestvenno i radostno prazdnovala pervuiu godovshchisnu nashei velikoi pobedy. Moskva prazdnichnaia," *Pravda*, 10 May 1946, 1.

12. "Parad soiuznykh voisk v Berline," *Pravda*, 10 May 1946, 4.

13. "Vsia strana torzhestvenno i radostno prazdnovala pervuiu godovshchisnu nashei velikoi pobedy," 1.

14. Jeffrey Brooks, *Thank You, Comrade Stalin! Soviet Public Culture from Revolution to Cold War* (Princeton, NJ: Princeton University Press, 2000), 201.

15. "Nadezhnaia opora interesov Sovetskogo Soiuza," 1.

16. Quoted in Brooks, *Thank You, Comrade Stalin!*, 201.

17. "Prazdnik Pobedy," *Pravda*, 9 May 1946, 1.

18. M. Andzhaparidze and V. Tsirgiladze, "Kak sozdavalsia fil′m 'Padenie Berlina,'" *Iskusstvo kino*, no. 4 (1950): 22–26.

19. Tumarkin writes that Victory Day was no longer a holiday in 1947 (*Living and the Dead*, 104), a claim repeated by most English-language histories,

such as Service, *Stalin*, 543. In fact, the holiday was only abolished at the end of that year.

20. "Ukaz ot 23 dekabria 1947 goda. Ob ob′iavlenii 1 ianvaria nerabochim dnem," in *Sbornik zakonov SSSR i ukazov Prezidiuma Verkhovnogo Soveta SSSR, 1938 g.—iiul′ 1956 g.*, ed. Iu. I. Mandel′shtam (Moscow: Gosudarstvennoe izdatel′stvo iuridicheskoi literatury, 1956), 376.

21. Mark Edele, *Soviet Veterans of the Second World War: A Popular Movement in an Authoritarian Society, 1941–1991* (Oxford: Oxford University Press, 2008), 154–59.

22. Tumarkin, *Living and the Dead*, 99.

23. Tumarkin, *Living and the Dead*, 110.

24. E. Gerasimov, ed., *Shturm Berlina. Vospominaniia, pis′ma, dnevniki uchastnikov boev za Berlin* (Moscow: Voennoe izdatel′stvo ministerstva vooruzhennykh sil SSSR, 1948).

25. Gerasimov, *Shturm Berlina*, 12, 402.

26. Konstantin Simonov, *Glazami cheloveka moego pokoleniia* (Moscow: Agenstvo pechati Novosti, 1988), 291.

27. Sergei Kudryashov, "Remembering and Researching the War: The Soviet and Russian Experience," in *Experience and Memory: The Second World War in Europe*, ed. Jörg Echternkamp and Stefan Martens (New York: Berghahn Books, 2010), 99–100; Alexander Statiev, "'La Garde meurt mais ne se rend pas!': Once Again on the 28 Panfilov Heroes," *Kritika: Explorations in Russian and Eurasian History* 13, no. 4 (2012): 769–98.

28. Aleksandr Vasilevskii, *Delo vsei zhizni*, 2nd ed. (Moscow: Politizdat, 1975), 5–6; Tumarkin, *Living and the Dead*, 104.

29. Jeremy Black, *Rethinking World War Two: The Conflict and Its Legacy* (London: Bloomsbury Academic, 2015), 102. Soviet generals began to publish in earnest in the 1960s, though Eremenko and Chuykov were allowed to publish first (1958 and 1959, respectively), because they had fought alongside Khrushchev and so could serve to legitimize the emergent post-Stalin association of Khrushchev and the war. Kudryashov, "Remembering and Researching the War," 113n43. Also see chapter 3.

30. Kudryashov, "Remembering and Researching the War," 113, 98, respectively.

31. V. M. Kulish, "Sovetskaia istoriografiia Velikoi Otechestvennoi voiny," in *Sovetskaia istoriografiia*, ed. Iu. N. Afanas′ev (Moscow: Rossiiskii gosudarstvennyi gumanitarnyi universitet, 1996), 274.

32. Service, *Stalin*, 451.

33. Iosif Stalin, *O Velikoi Otechestvennoi Voine Sovetskogo Soiuza*, 5th ed. (Moscow: Gospolitizdat, 1948), 16–17.

34. G. F. Aleksandrov et al., eds., *Joseph Stalin: A Short Biography*, 2nd rev. ed. (Moscow: Foreign Languages Publishing House, 1949), 182, 184–85.

35. Kudryashov, "Remembering and Researching the War," 113, 98; Kulish, "Sovetskaia istoriografiia Velikoi Otechestvennoi voiny," 279.

36. Viacheslav Molotov, *Stalin and Stalin's Leadership* (Moscow: Foreign Languages Publishing House, 1950), 11.

37. K. E. Voroshilov, *Stalin i vooruzhennye sily SSSR* (Moscow: Gosudarstvennoe izdatel′stvo politicheskoi literatury, 1951), 99.

38. Kulish, "Sovetskaia istoriografiia Velikoi Otechestvennoi voiny," 276.

39. Kulish, "Sovetskaia istoriografiia Velikoi Otechestvennoi voiny," 277.

40. Iosif V. Stalin, "Prikaz narodnogo komissara oborony SSSR," *Pravda*, 23 February 1946, 1.

41. *Berlinskaia operatsiia 1945 goda* (Moscow: Voennoe izdatel′stvo soiuza SSSR, 1950), 2.

42. *Berlinskaia operatsiia 1945 goda*, 555.

43. Ronald Smelser and Edward J. Davies II, *The Myth of the Eastern Front: The Nazi-Soviet War in American Popular Culture* (Cambridge: Cambridge University Press, 2008), 64–80.

44. Smelser and Davies, *Myth of the Eastern Front*, 90–114.

45. As Alec Nove's classic study of the Soviet economy showed, after an initial period of demobilization following the war, by 1949 the Cold War was sucking labor from the economy. The armed forces more than doubled in size between 1948 and 1955, with much of the increase having occurred, Nove surmises, by 1952, since military budgets rose year on year in this period, from under a fifth of total expenditure in 1950 to nearly a quarter in 1952. Alec Nove, *An Economic History of the U.S.S.R.* (Harmondsworth: Penguin, 1969), 319.

46. Kulish, "Sovetskaia istoriografiia Velikoi Otechestvennoi voiny," 282.

47. Seweryn Bialer, ed., *Stalin and His Generals: Soviet Military Memoirs of World War II* (Boulder, CO: Westview Press, 1984), 17.

48. Yurchak, *Everything Was Forever.*

49. "O vsesoiuznoi khudozhestvennoi vystavke," *Iskusstvo*, no. 1 (1947): 6.

50. "O vsesoiuznoi khudozhestvennoi vystavke," 9.

51. "O vsesoiuznoi khudozhestvennoi vystavke," 10.

52. Tumarkin, *Living and the Dead*, 100.

53. Plamper, *Stalin Cult*, 93.

54. Khristofor Ushenin, *Petr Aleksandrovich Krivonogov* (Moscow: Sovetskii khudozhnik, 1956), 22.

55. Petr Krivonogov, "Den′ pobedy. Iz dnevnika voennogo khudozhnika," *Sovetskoe Iskusstvo*, no. 37 (1951): 1.

56. Quoted in Ushenin, *Petr Aleksandrovich Krivonogov*, 24.

57. Ushenin, *Petr Aleksandrovich Krivonogov*, 22.

58. Tumarkin, *Living and the Dead*, 102; Plamper, *Stalin Cult*, 75–78.

59. Richard Taylor, *Film Propaganda: Soviet Russia and Nazi Germany*, 2nd ed. (London: I. B. Tauris, 1998), 100.

60. Andzhaparidze and Tsirgiladze, "Kak sozdavalsia fil´m," 22–26.

61. Petr Pavlenko, "'Padenie Berlina' ('Vo imia budushchego'). Kinopovest´ variant," 1947–1949, RGALI 2199/1/32, sheet 40.

62. Andzhaparidze and Tsirgiladze, "Kak sozdavalsia fil´m," 23.

63. Quoted in Taylor, *Film Propaganda*, 121–22.

64. I. Manevich, *Mikhail Chiaureli* (Moscow: Goskinoizdat, 1953), 119. On "artistic" documentary cinema, see N. Kolin, "V Pomoshch´ Nachinaiн ushchemu stsenaristu," in *Konkurs na kinotsenarii* (Moscow: Goskinoizdat, 1938), 11–25.

65. Petr Pavlenko, *Kinotsenarii* (Moscow: Goskinoizdat, 1952), 5.

66. Denise J. Youngblood, *Russian War Films: On the Cinema Front, 1914–2005* (Lawrence: University Press of Kansas, 2007), 97.

67. Mikhail Chiaureli, "Ob Izobrazitel´noi forme kinofil´ma," in *Voprosy masterstva v sovetskom kinoiskusstve. Sbornik statei*, ed. B. Kravchenko (Moscow: Goskinoizdat, 1952), 72–73.

68. N. Shcherbina, *Padenie Berlina (Ocherk o kinofil´me)* (Moscow: Goskinoizdat, 1950), 27.

69. "Perepiska s kinostudiei 'Mosfil´m' i storonnimi organizatsiiami o kinofil´me 'Padenie Berlina.' O priobretenii materialov, veshchei inostrannykh i otechestvennykh, vooruzheniia, tekhniki, otpravki imushchestva i akterov za granitsu. Ob oplate akteram. Smeta i proizvodstvo fil´ma i dr." (1948–1949), RGALI, 2456/2/74, sheet 42.

70. "Perepiska s kinostudiei 'Mosfil´m,'" RGALI, 2456/2/74, sheet 42.

71. RGALI, 2456/2/74, sheet 213.

72. Andzhaparidze and Tsirgiladze, "Kak sozdavalsia fil´m," 23.

73. Andzhaparidze and Tsirgiladze, "Kak sozdavalsia fil´m," 24.

74. Taylor, *Film Propaganda*, 119.

75. Chiaureli, "Ob Izobrazitel´noi forme kinofil´ma," 47.

76. "Stenogramma zasedaniia sektsii po obsuzhdeniiu fil´ma 'Padenie Berline'" (1950), RGALI, 2923/1/285, sheet 65.

77. Manevich, *Mikhail Chiaureli*, 119.

78. Manevich, *Mikhail Chiaureli*, 120.

79. Andzhaparidze and Tsirgiladze, "Kak sozdavalsia fil´m," 23.

80. V. Kolodiazhnaia, *Boris Andreev* (Moscow: Goskinoizdat, 1951), 27.

81. RGALI, 2923/1/285, sheet 9.

82. "Otchety i informatsii direktorov kinoteatrov, otzyvy zritelei i reklame nyi material o rabote s kinofil´mom 'Padenie Berlina'" (1949–1950), RGALI, 2473/1/487, sheet 4.

83. "Otchety i informatsii direktorov kinoteatrov, otzyvy zritelei i reklame nyi material o rabote s kinofil´mom 'Padenie Berlina'" (1949–1950), RGALI, 2473/1/487, sheet 24.

84. L. Pogozheva, "Padenie Berlina," *Iskusstvo kino*, no. 4 (1950): 12.

85. Pogozheva, "Padenie Berlina," 12.

86. Paul Innes, *Epic* (London: Routledge, 2013), 3, 19–20.

87. "Stenogramma zasedaniia sektsii po obsuzhdeniiu fil′ma 'Padenie Berlina'" (1950), RGALI, 2923/1/285, sheet 39.

88. David Brandenberger, *National Bolshevism: Stalinist Mass Culture and the Formation of Modern Russian National Identity, 1931–1956* (Cambridge, MA: Harvard University Press, 2002), 192.

89. Petr Pavlenko, *Kinostsenarii* (Moscow: Goskinoizdat, 1952), 5.

90. "Stenogramma zasedaniia sektsii po obsuzhdeniiu fil′ma 'Padenie Berline'" (1950), RGALI, 2923/1/285, sheet 12; Shcherbina, *Padenie Berlina*, 27.

91. Andzhaparidze and Tsirgiladze, "Kak sozdavalsia fil′m," 23.

92. Brooks, *Thank You, Comrade Stalin!*, 195.

93. "Stenogramma zasedaniia sektsii po obsuzhdeniiu fil′ma 'Padenie Berlina'" (1950), RGALI, 2923/1/285, sheet 66.

94. "Stenogramma zasedaniia tvorcheskoi sektsii o vstreche s tvorcheskimi rabotnikami fil′ma 'Padenie Berlina' 28.10.48," RGALI, 2453/2/108, sheet 14.

95. "Materialy po rezhisserskomu sstenariiu 'Padenie Berlina,'" RGALI, 2453/2/108, sheet 19 verso.

96. Chiaureli, "Ob Izobrazitel′noi forme kinofil′ma," 59.

97. Chiaureli, "Ob Izobrazitel′noi forme kinofil′ma," 75.

98. The film released as *Grunia Kornakova* is also known by its working title, *The Nightingale*.

99. RGALI 2923/1/285, sheet 78.

100. Kolodiazhnaia, *Boris Andreev*, 31.

101. Shcherbina, *Padenie Berlina*, 22.

102. Taylor, *Film Propaganda*, 120.

103. Petr Pavlenko and Mikheil Chiaureli, "'Padenie Berlina': Kinopovest′; Variant" (1949), RGALI, 2199/1/35, sheet 97.

104. RGALI, 2199/1/32, sheet 91.

105. RGALI, 2199/1/32, sheet 92.

106. RGALI, 2199/1/32, sheets 102–3.

107. Petr Pavlenko and Mikheil Chiaureli, "'Padenie Berlina'" ('Vo imia budushchego'): Kinopovest′ variant IV" (1948), RGALI, 2199/1/33, sheet 102.

108. Mikheil Chiaureli and Petr Pavlenko, "'Padenie Berlina'. Rezhisserskii stsenarii" (1948), RGALI, 2453/2/106, sheet 28.

109. RGALI, 2199/1/32, sheet 93.

110. RGALI, 2456/2/74, sheet 8.

111. RGALI, 2453/2/108, sheet 5 verso.

112. RGALI, 2199/1/32, sheet 6.

113. RGALI, 2199/1/32, sheet 18.

114. Taylor, *Film Propaganda*, 119.

115. Brooks, *Thank You, Comrade Stalin!*, 205.

116. Simonov, *Glazami cheloveka moego pokoleniia*, 175; RGALI, 2199/1/35, sheet 1.

117. Rolf, *Soviet Mass Festivals*, 181–82.

118. Boris Groys, *The Total Art of Stalinism: Avant-Garde, Aesthetic Dictatorship, and Beyond*, trans. Charles Rougle (Princeton, NJ: Princeton University Press, 1992), 113.

119. Mikheil Chiaureli, "Rezhisserskii stsenarii M. E. Chiaureli 'Padenie Berlina' (Seraiia 2)" (1948), RGALI, 2456/1/2078, sheet 98.

120. Taylor, *Film Propaganda*, 121.

121. Chiaureli, "Ob Izobrazitel′noi forme kinofil′ma," 75.

122. RGALI, 2923/1/285, sheets 77–78.

123. RGALI, 2199/1/32, sheet 30.

124. RGALI, 2923/1/285, sheet 28.

125. RGALI, 2923/1/285, sheet 15.

126. RGALI, 2199/1/33, sheet 70.

127. Shcherbina, *Padenie Berlina*, 10.

128. RGALI, 2199/1/32, sheet 106.

129. RGALI, 2199/1/32, sheet 17.

130. RGALI, 2199/1/32, sheet 108.

131. RGALI, 2199/1/32, sheet 104.

132. Taylor, *Film Propaganda*, 121–22.

133. Youngblood, *Russian War Films*, 83.

134. Tumarkin, *Living and the Dead*, 104.

135. Taylor, *Film Propaganda*, 108.

136. Tony Shaw and Denise J. Youngblood, *Cinematic Cold War: The American and Soviet Struggle for Hearts and Minds* (Lawrence: University Press of Kansas, 2010), 42.

137. Bialer, *Stalin and His Generals*, 17; Youngblood, *Russian War Films*.

138. Timothy Dunmore, *Soviet Politics, 1945–1953* (London: Macmillan, 1984), 153.

CHAPTER 3. THE DEATH OF STALIN AND THE BIRTH OF THE VICTORY CULT

1. Plamper, *Stalin Cult*, 68–69.

2. Edele, *Soviet Veterans*, 7.

3. Graeme Gill, *Symbols and Legitimacy in Soviet Politics* (Cambridge: Cambridge University Press, 2011), 164.

4. Victoria E. Bonnell, "The Leader's Two Bodies: A Study in the Iconography of the Vozhd′," *Russian History/Histoire russe* 23, no. 1–4 (1996): 122.

5. Bonnell, "Leader's Two Bodies," 130.

6. Robert C. Tucker, *The Soviet Political Mind: Studies in Stalinism and Post-Stalin Change* (London: Pall Mall Press, 1963), 53.

7. Joshua Rubenstein, *The Last Days of Stalin* (New Haven, CT: Yale University Press, 2016), 96.

8. The subversive humor mocking the Stalin cult and wishing for his death is explored with subtlety in Jonathan Waterlow, *It's Only a Joke, Comrade: Humour, Trust and Everyday Life under Stalin* (Oxford: n.p., 2018), 57–64.

9. Mikhail Chiaureli, "Bessmertie," *Sovetskoe iskusstvo*, 14 March 1953, 2.

10. Chiaureli, "Ob Izobrazitel′noi forme kinofil′ma," 43–78.

11. Chiaureli, "Ob Izobrazitel′noi forme kinofil′ma," 59.

12. V. Stepanov and A. Sazonov, "Dokladnaia zapiska otdela khudozhestvenn noi literatury i iskusstva Tsk KPSS M. A. Suslovu o kinos" emkakh pokhoron I. V. Stalina," 19 May 1953, in *Kul′tura i vlast′ ot Stalina do Gorbacheva. Kremlevskii kinoteatr 1928–1953. Dokumenty*, ed. K. M. Anderson and L. V. Maksimenkov (Moscow: ROSSPEN, 2005); Rashit Iangirov, "Proshchanie s mertvym telom. Ob odnom siuzhete Rossiiskogo ekrannogo ofitsioza i ego podtekstakh," *Otechestvennye zapiski* 35, no. 2 (2007), http://www.strana-oz.ru/2007/2/proshchanie-s-mertvym-telom.

13. Jeremy Hicks, *Dziga Vertov: Defining Documentary Film* (London: I. B. Tauris, 2007), 40.

14. Rubenstein, *Last Days of Stalin*, 98.

15. Aleksei Surkov, "Velikoe Proshchanie/Diktorskii tekst dokumental′nogo kinofil′ma O Proshchanii s Velikim Vozhdem Trudiashikhsia Iosif Vissarionovich Stalinym. Perepiska i diktorskii tekst fil′ma. Proshchanie s Vozhdem," 5–20 March 1953, RGALI, 2487/1/605, sheet 7.

16. RGALI, 2487/1/605, sheet 40.

17. RGALI, 2487/1/605, sheet 61.

18. RGALI, 2487/1/605, sheet 86.

19. Iangirov, "Proshchanie s mertvym telom"; RGALI, 2487/1/605, sheet 113.

20. Quoted in Aleksandr Pyzhikov, *Opyt modernizatsii sovetskogo obshchestva v 1953–1964 godakh. Obshchestvenno-politicheskii aspekt* (Moscow: Gamma, 1998), 114–15.

21. Sergei Loznitsa, *State Funeral* (*Gosudarstvennye pokhorony*, 2019). See also the excellent review of the film: Birgit Beumers, "Sergei Loznitsa, 'State Funeral (2019),'" *Kinokultura*, no. 67 (2020), accessed 9 January 2020, http://www.kinokultura.com/2020/67r-statefuneral.shtml.

22. RGALI, 2487/1/605, sheet 62.

23. RGALI, 2487/1/605, sheet 97.

24. RGALI, 2487/1/605, sheet 62.

25. Rubenstein, *Last Days of Stalin*, 99.

26. Tucker, *Soviet Political Mind*, 54.

27. Chiaureli, "Bessmertie," 2.

28. S. Kuznetsov, "('Padenie Berlina'), Direktor Mosfil′ma S. Kuznetsov—B. N. Vasil′evskomu, nachal′niku otdela po kontroliu za Kinorepetuarom," 20 November 1953, Gosfil′mofond, *Padenie Berlin*, delo 1652, n.p.

29. Pyzhikov, *Opyt modernizatsii sovetskogo obshchestva*, 27.

30. Pyzhikov, *Opyt modernizatsii sovetskogo obshchestva*, 27.

31. Pyzhikov, *Opyt modernizatsii sovetskogo obshchestva*, 28.

32. Matthew Gallagher, "Trends in Soviet Historiography of the Second World War," in *Contemporary History in the Soviet Mirror*, ed. John Keep and Liliana Brisby (New York: Frederick A. Praeger, 1964), 223–24.

33. Boris Tel′pukhovskii, ed., *Ocherki istorii Velikoi Otechestvennoi Voiny 1941–1945* (Moscow: Akademiia nauk SSSR, Institut istorii, 1955), 472–73.

34. One suggestion to the contrary comes from Edele, *Soviet Veterans*, 10.

35. Joachim Hösler, "Chto znachit 'Prorabotka proshlogo?' Ob istoriografii Velikoi Otechestvennoi Voiny v SSSR i Rossii," in *Pamiat′ o voine 60 let spustia. Rossiia, Germaniia, Evropa* (Moscow: Novoe literaturnoe obozrenie, 2005).

36. Polly Jones, *Myth, Memory, Trauma: Rethinking the Stalinist Past in the Soviet Union, 1953–70* (New Haven, CT: Yale University Press, 2013), 224; Roger Markwick, *Rewriting History in Soviet Russia: The Politics of Revisionist History, 1956–74* (New York: Palgrave, 2001), 209–19.

37. Leonid Maksimenkov, "Arkhivno-istoricheskoe obespechenie nyneshnek go i buduiushchikh iubileev," in *Pobeda-70: Rekonstruktsiia iubileia*, ed. Gennadii Bordiugov (Moscow: AIRO-XXI, 2015), 386.

38. Iurii Aksiutin, *Khrushchevskaia "ottepel′" i obshchestvennye nastroeniia v SSSR v 1953–1964 gg.* (Moscow: ROSSPEN, 2010), 565; Thomas C. Wolfe, *Governing Soviet Journalism: The Press and Soviet Journalism after Stalin* (Bloomington: Indiana University Press, 2005), 106–7.

39. Pyzhikov, *Opyt modernizatsii sovetskogo obshchestva*, 238.

40. Pyzhikov, *Opyt modernizatsii sovetskogo obshchestva*, 240.

41. Pyzhikov, *Opyt modernizatsii sovetskogo obshchestva*, 259.

42. Jones, *Myth, Memory, Trauma*, 189.

43. Pyzhikov, *Opyt modernizatsii sovetskogo obshchestva*, 77–78.

44. Sergei Kapterev, *Post-Stalinist Cinema and the Russian Intelligentsia, 1953–1960: Strategies of Self-Representation, De-Stalinization and the National Cultural Tradition* (Saarbrücken, Germany: VDM Verlag Dr Müller, 2005), 47–48 and passim.

45. Pyzhikov, *Opyt modernizatsii sovetskogo obshchestva*, 69–72.

46. Pyzhikov, *Opyt modernizatsii sovetskogo obshchestva*, 83.

47. P. N. Pospelov, "Perepiska s otdelami Tsk KPSS, Prezidiuma Verkhovnogo Soveta Sovetskogo Soiuza i Ministerstvami SSSR" (March 1959–December 1961, RGASPI, 71/22/1, sheet 1.

48. Pyzhikov, *Opyt modernizatsii sovetskogo obshchestva*, 76.

49. "Stenogramma zasedaniia redaktsionnoi komissii po V tomu Istorii Velikoi Otechestvennoi Voiny ot 30 noiabria 1961 goda," RGASPI, 77/22/44, sheet 4.

50. Marina Balina, "Prose after Stalin," in *The Cambridge Companion to Twentieth-Century Russian Literature*, ed. Evgeny Dobrenko and Marina Balina (Cambridge: Cambridge University Press, 2011), 153; Smelser and Davies, *Myth of the Eastern Front*, 90–114.

51. Kudryashov, "Remembering and Researching the War," 113, 104–5.

52. Denis Kozlov, "The Historical Turn in Late Soviet Culture: Retrospectivism, Factography, Doubt, 1953–91," *Kritika* n.s. 2, no. 3 (2001): 581.

53. Maksimenkov, "Arkhivno-istoricheskoe obespechenie nyneshnego i buduiushchikh iubileev," 381.

54. Kumanev, *Podvig i podlog*, 326.

55. "Stenogramma soveshchaniia, posviashchennogo obsuzhdeniiu rukopisi piatogo toma 'Istoriia Velikoi Otechestvennoi Voiny Sovetskogo Soiuza 1941–1945gg,'" (1960), RGASPI, 71/22/99, sheet 7.

56. Evgenii Boltin and Petr Pospelov, "Perepiska s otdelami TsK KPS, Prezid-iuma Verkhovnogo Soveta i Ministerstvami SSSR" (January 1962–December 1962), RGASPI, 77/22/2, sheets 213–15.

57. "Stenogramma soveshchaniia otdela istorii Velikoi Otechestvennoi Voiny na temu 'Shturm Reikhstaga'" (1961), RGASPI, 71/22/102, sheets 3–4.

58. RGASPI, 71/22/102, sheets 113–14.

59. "Stenogramma soveshchaniia otdela istorii Velikoi Otechestvennoi Voiny na temu 'Shturm Reikhstaga' (prodolzhenie)" (1961), RGASPI, 71/22/103, sheet 7.

60. "Stenogramma soveshchaniia, posviashchennogo obsuzhdeniiu rukopisi piatogo toma 'Istoriia Velikoi Otechestvennoi Voiny Sovetskogo Soiuza 1941–1945gg'" (1960), RGASPI 71/22/99, sheet 21.

61. RGASPI, 77/22/44, sheet 17.

62. RGASPI, 71/22/103, sheet 83.

63. RGASPI, 71/22/102, sheets 12–13.

64. *Berlinskaia operatsiia 1945 goda* (Moscow: Voennoe izdatel´stvo soiuza SSSR, 1950).

65. RGASPI, 71/22/102, sheets 6–7.

66. "Stenogramma vstrechi s geroiami Sovetskogo Soiuza, uchastnikami shturma Berlina" (1960), RGASPI, 77/22/98, sheet 3.

67. RGASPI, 77/22/44, sheets 9–11.

68. RGASPI, 71/22/102, sheet 9.

69. RGASPI, 71/22/102, sheet 11.

70. Konstantin Samsonov, *Shturm Reikhstaga* (Moscow: DOSAAF, 1955).

71. RGASPI, 71/22/102, sheet 129.

72. RGASPI, 71/22/102, sheets 9–10.

73. RGASPI, 71/22/102, sheet 50.

74. RGASPI, 77/22/98, sheet 66.

75. RGASPI, 77/22/98, sheets 31–32.

76. RGASPI, 77/22/98, sheet 57.

77. RGASPI, 71/22/103, sheets 28–31.

78. RGASPI, 71/22/103, sheet 126.

79. RGASPI, 71/22/103, sheet 45.

80. RGASPI, 71/22/102, sheet 32–33.

81. RGASPI, 71/22/102, sheets 94–95.

82. RGASPI, 71/22/102, sheet 33.

83. Stephen Hutchings and Natalia Rulyova, "Commemorating the Past/Performing the Present: Television Coverage of the Second World War Victory Celebrations and the (De)Construction of Russian Nationhood," in *The Post-Soviet Russian Media: Conflicting Signals*, ed. Birgit Beumers, Stephen Hutchings, and Natalia Rulyova (London: Routledge, 2009), 142.

84. RGASPI, 71/22/103, sheet 87.

85. RGASPI, 71/22/102, sheet 61.

86. RGASPI, 71/22/102, sheet 96.

87. RGASPI, 71/22/103, sheet 56.

88. RGASPI, 77/22/98, sheet 74.

89. RGASPI, 71/22/103, sheet 92.

90. Pospelov et al., *Istoriia Velikoi Otechestvennoi Voiny*, 5:285.

91. Edele, *Soviet Veterans*, 7.

92. As Rubenstein notes, fictional scenes from *Eugene Onegin* and *War and Peace*, as well as the show trials of Bukharin in 1938 and of Gary Powers in 1960, had all taken place in the Columned Hall of the House of the Unions.

93. B. Dobrodeev and K. Slavin, "Oni vodruzili Znamia Pobedy. Literaturnyi stsenarii" (1960), RGALI, 2487/1/504, sheet 29.

94. RGALI, 2487/1/504, sheet 32–33.

95. RGALI, 2487/1/504, sheet 31.

96. Pyzhikov, *Opyt modernizatsii sovetskogo obshchestva*, 259.

97. *Geroicheskaia oborona Brestskoi kreposti. Po dokumentam i relikviiam Tsentral′nogo muzeia Sovetskoi Armii* (Voennoe izdatel′stvo Ministerstva oborony SSSR, 1955), 10.

98. Sergei Smirnov, *Sobranie sochinenii* (Moscow: Molodaia gvardiia, 1973), 1:13.

99. "Delo fil′ma 'Velikaia Otechestvennaia,'" vol. 1 (1964), RGALI, 2487/2/681, sheet 10.

100. "Delo fil′ma 'Velikaia Otechestvennaia,'" vol. 2 (1964–1965), RGALI, 2487/2/682, sheet 187; G. Senchakova, "Put′ k pobede," *Sovetskii ekran*, no. 9 (1965): 4–5.

101. RGALI, 2487/2/682, sheet 6.

102. RGALI, 2487/2/682, sheet 93.

103. "Delo fil′ma 'Velikaia Otechestvennaia,'" vol. 3 (1965), RGALI, 2487/2/683, sheet 27.

104. RGALI, 2487/2/681, sheet 30.

105. RGALI, 2487/2/681, sheet 42.

106. RGALI, 2487/2/682, sheets 103–4 (original emphases).

107. RGALI, 2487/2/683, sheets 38–39.

108. RGALI, 2487/2/683, sheet 51.

109. RGALI, 2487/2/683, sheet 17.

110. RGALI, 2487/2/682, sheet 111.

111. RGALI, 2487/2/681, sheet 88.

112. RGALI, 2487/2/682, sheet 2.

113. RGALI, 2487/2/682, sheets 9–10.

114. RGALI, 2487/2/682, sheet 116.

115. RGALI, 2487/2/683, sheet 53.

116. RGALI, 2487/2/683, sheet 57.

117. RGALI, 2487/2/683, sheet 241.

118. On the US context, see Hariman and Lucaites, *No Caption Needed.*

119. RGALI, 2487/2/683, sheets 251–52.

120. Yurchak, *Everything Was Forever.*

121. "Delo fil′ma 'Velikaia Otechestvennaia'" (1965), RGALI, 2487/2/684, sheet 57.

122. "Teksty televizionnykh peredach za ianvar′–mai 1965 g.," GARF, 6903/26/578, sheet 584.

123. Konstantin Slavin, "Velikaia voina i nashe vremia," *Sovetskii ekran*, no. 13 (1965): 12.

124. RGALI, 2487/2/681, sheets 13, 146.

125. Boris Medvedev, "Eto bylo pri nas . . . ," *Iskusstvo kino*, no. 8 (1965): 22.

126. RGALI, 2487/2/682, sheet 152.

127. RGALI, 2487/2/681, sheet 122.

128. RGALI, 2487/2/681, sheets 69–71.

129. RGALI, 2487/2/683, sheets 247, 249.

130. Roi Medvedev, *Lichnost′ i epokha. Politicheskii portret L. I. Brezhneva; Kn. 1* (Moscow: Novosti, 1991), 13. While in recent years Brezhnev's reputation has risen and a number of publications have appeared, such as a biography in the prestigious Life of Remarkable People series (Zhizn′ zamechatel′nykh liudei), for many years he remained an embarrassing and almost forgotten figure. See Leonid Mlechin, *Brezhnev* (Moscow: Molodaia gvardiia, 2011).

131. As an anonymous letter from a thirty-six-year old worker to *Pravda* pointed out, if the party thought that personality cults were bad practice, then why did they continue to elevate a cult around Lenin? Oleg Leibovich, *Reforma*

i modernizatsiia v 1953–1964 gg. (Perm′: Izd. Permskogo universiteta, 1993), 129.

132. Wolfe, *Governing Soviet Journalism*, 38; R. Medvedev, *Lichnost′ i epokha*, 161.

133. Pyzhikov, *Opyt modernizatsii sovetskogo obshchestva*, 293.

134. Aleksandr Maisurian, *Drugoi Brezhnev* (Moscow: Vagrius, 2004), 162–63.

135. Maisurian highlights the contrast between the somewhat clandestine dismantling of the Stalin cult and the revolutionaries' own triumphant destruction of statues, churches, and opening of graves; in 1961, Stalin's remains were removed from the mausoleum at night, with Red Square closed off with chains. Statues of Stalin were also removed at night, in strict secrecy. See Maisurian, *Drugoi Brezhnev*, 112–13.

136. R. Medvedev, *Lichnost′ i epokha*, 168–69.

137. Leonid Brezhnev, "Velikaia Pobeda sovetskogo naroda: Doklad tov. L. I. Brezhneva na torzhestvennom sobranii v kremlevskom dvortse s″ezdov, posviashchennom 20-letiu Pobedy sovetskogo naroda v Velikoi Otechestvennoi Voine, 8 Maia 1965," *Literaturnaia gazeta*, 9 May 1965, 1, 2, 7, 8.

138. R. Medvedev, *Lichnost′ i epokha*, 166.

139. Maksimenkov, "Arkhivno-istoricheskoe obespechenie nyneshnego i buduiushchikh iubileev," 385.

140. "Zasedaniia Prezidiuma TsK KPSS ot 1 aprelia 1965, 'O prazdnovanii 20-letiia pobedy sovetskogo naroda v Velikoi Otechestvennoi Voine Sovetskogo Soiuza za 1941–1945gg.' Protokol No. 197" (1965), RGANI, 3/16/659, sheet 129.

141. "Zasedaniia Prezidiuma KPSS ot 15 aprelia 1965g. XXII sozvyz. Protokol No. 199" (1965), RGANI, 3/18/337, sheet 8.

142. On the new museum, see RGANI, 3/16/659, sheets 136–37.

143. RGANI, 3/16/659, sheets 136–37.

144. B. Sudarov, "Labirinty zhizni Nikolaia Mesiatseva," accessed 1 June 2018, http://tvmuseum.ru/catalog.asp?ob_no=10852 (no longer available).

145. "Teksty televizionnykh peredach za aprel′–iiun′1965g.," GARF, 6903/26/575, sheet 146.

146. "Teksty televizionnykh peredach za mai 1965 g.," GARF, 6903/26/561, sheet 353.

147. GARF, 6903/26/ 561, sheets 355–56.

148. GARF, 6903/26/561, sheet 356.

149. "Obzory pisem telezitelei za fevral′ 1965 g.," GARF, 6903/10/65, sheet 6.

150. Sudarov, "Labirinty zhizni Nikolai Mesiatseva," accessed 1 June 2018, http://tvmuseum.ru/catalog.asp?ob_no=10852 (no longer available).

151. Vladimir Stepaniuk, Korrespondent GRI TsT (DIP 1-go kanala) s 1961–2004, "Vekhi istorii glavnoi redaktsii informatsii TsT," accessed 1 June 2018, http://tvmuseum.ru/catalog.asp?ob_no=11699 (no longer available).

152. RGANI, 3/16/659, 136–37.

153. "Zasedaniia Prezidiuma KPSS ot 15 aprelia 1965g. XXII sozvyz: Protokol No. 199" (1965), RGANI, 3/18/337.

154. "Pis′ma, telegrammy, vypiski protokolov zasedaniia biuro TsK KPSS po RSFSR" (25 January 1965), RGANI, 5/34/126.

155. Wolfe, *Governing Soviet Journalism*, 38.

156. "Stenogramma soveshchanii sekretarei i zaveduiushchikh otdelami propagandy i agitatsii obkomov i kraikomov KPSS po voprosam raboty sistemy politicheskogo prosveshcheniia, sostoiavshikhsia pri otdele v marte, mae i iiune 1965 g.," RGANI, 5/34/118, sheet 61.

157. RGANI, 5/34/118, sheet 61.

158. Edele, *Soviet Veterans*, 9.

159. Edele, *Soviet Veterans*, 9; "Proekty postanovlenii TsK KPSS (Ideologicheskii otdel), 20 ianvaria 1965 g.," RGANI, 5/55/142, sheet 33. Eleonory Gilburd charts the reception of Erich Maria Remarque's novels in the Soviet Union in the post-Stalin period, where they enjoyed enormous popularity until a backlash against them began in 1959 for their pacifism and apolitical stance. See Eleonory Gilburd, *To See Paris and Die: The Soviet Lives of Western Culture* (Cambridge, MA: Belknap Press of Harvard University Press, 2018), 130–44.

160. Edele, *Soviet Veterans*, 10.

161. Boris Dubin, "Pamiat′, voina, pamiat′ o voine. Konstruirovanie proshlogo v sotsial′noi praktike poslednikh desiatiletii," *Otechestvennye zapiski* 4, no. 43 (2008), http://www.intelros.ru/intelros/reiting/reyting_09/material_sofiy/5023-boris-dubin-pamyat-vojna-pamyat-o-vojne-konstruirovanie-proshlogo-v-socialnoj-praktike-poslednix-desyatiletij.html.

162. Edele, *Soviet Veterans*, 9.

163. Barbat, "Bannières et drapeaux," 70–95.

164. RGASPI, 71/22/102, sheet 111.

165. Maksimenkov, "Arkhivno-istoricheskoe obespechenie nyneshnego i buduiushchikh iubileev," 381.

166. Kudryashov, "Remembering and Researching the War," 113, 104–5.

167. Maisurian, *Drugoi Brezhnev*, 112–13.

168. Rolf, *Soviet Mass Festivals*, 41; Hobsbawm, "Introduction," 4.

CHAPTER 4. THE VICTORY CULT IN THE AGE OF TELEVISION

1. Leonid Brezhnev, Nikolai Podgornyi, and Aleksei Kosygin, "Pervomu sekretariu Tsentral′nogo Komiteta Kommunisticheskoi Partii Chekhoslovakii tovarishchu Aleksandru Dubcheku," *Izvestiia*, 10 May 1968, 1.

2. Val Gol′tsev, "Neugasimyi ogon′ vechnoi slavy," *Izvestiia*, 8 May 1967, 1, 2.

3. "Itogovaia spravka o rezul′tatakh anketnogo oprosa telezritelei o peredachakh, posviashchennykh prazdnovaniiu 20-letiia so dnia Pobedy[,] 1965," GARF, 6903/3/278, sheet 8.

4. GARF, 6903/3/278, sheet 9.

5. Dmitrii Bykov, *Bulat Okudzhava* (Moscow: Molodaia gvardiia, 2009), 604–5.

6. Susanne Schattenberg, *Velichie i tragediia cheloveka i strany*, trans. V. A. Brun-Tsekhovskii, (Moscow: Politicheskaia entsiklopediia, 2018), 113.

7. Mark O'Neil, "The Cold War on the Ground, 1945–1981," in *The Military History of the Soviet Union*, ed. Robin Higham and Frederick W. Kagan (New York: Palgrave, 2002), 232–33.

8. R. W. Davies, *Soviet History in the Gorbachev Revolution* (Basingstoke: Macmillan, 1989), 101.

9. Davies, *Soviet History in the Gorbachev Revolution*, 101.

10. Samuel Hynes, *The Soldier's Tale: Bearing Witness to Modern War* (New York: Penguin, 1998), 16.

11. Balina, "Prose after Stalin," 153.

12. See Josephine Woll, *Real Images: Soviet Cinema and the Thaw* (London: I. B. Tauris, 2000), 71–124; Youngblood, *Russian War Films*, 107–41.

13. Alexander Prokhorov and Elena Prokhorova, *Film and Television Genres of the Late Soviet Era* (New York: Bloomsbury, 2017), 43; G. Tsitriniak, "NapravY lenie glavnogo udara," *Iskusstvo kino*, no. 5 (1970): 9.

14. James Russell, *The Historical Epic and Contemporary Hollywood: "From Dances with Wolves" to "Gladiator"* (New York: Continuum, 2007), 10.

15. Iurii Ozerov, "Na NP," *Iskusstvo kino*, no. 5 (1975): 72.

16. Quoted in Tsitriniak, "Napravlenie glavnogo udara," 12.

17. Quoted in Tsitriniak, "Napravlenie glavnogo udara," 10.

18. Iurii Ozerov, "Vosslavit′ podvig naroda," *Iskusstvo kino*, no. 2 (1971): 2.

19. William J. Tompson, *Soviet Union under Brezhnev* (Harlow: Pearson, 2003), 27, 98. This notion of "re-Stalinization" is contested by Schattenberg, who sees any such emphasis as the result of Brezhnev's consensual style of politics. See Schattenberg, *Velichie i tragediia cheloveka i strany*, 397.

20. Iurii Khaniutin, "Vozvrashchennoe vremia," *Iskusstvo kino*, no. 7 (1977): 96.

21. Aleksandr Kamshalov, *Geroika podviga na ekrane. Voenno-patrioticheskaia tema v sovetskom kinematografe* (Moscow: Iskusstvo, 1986), 64.

22. Khaniutin, "Vozvrashchennoe vremia," 96.

23. Denise J. Youngblood, "'When Will the Real Day Come?' War Films and Soviet Post-war Culture," in *Histories of the Aftermath: The Legacies of the Second World War in Europe*, ed. Frank Biess and Robert G. Moeller (London: Berghahn Books, 2010), 132.

24. Ozerov, "Vosslavit′ podvig naroda," 2.

25. Tsitriniak, "Napravlenie glavnogo udara," 9.

26. Guy Westwell, *War Cinema: Hollywood on the Front Line* (London: Wallflower, 2006), 55.

27. Ozerov, "Vosslavit′ podvig naroda," 1.

28. S. Abramov and S. Kruzhkov, "Iurii Ozerov v rabote i razmyshleniiakh," *Iskusstvo kino*, no. 5 (1974): 96.

29. Abramov and Kruzhkov, "Iurii Ozerov v rabote i razmyshleniiakh," 97.

30. Quoted in Tsitriniak, "Napravlenie glavnogo udara," 8.

31. Westwell, *War Cinema*, 3.

32. Quoted in Tsitriniak, "Napravlenie glavnogo udara," 17.

33. N. G. Tomlinina et al., eds., *Apparat Tsk KPSS i kul′tura 1965–1972: Dokumenty* (Moscow: ROSSPEN, 2009), 1050–51.

34. Nikolai Sumenov and Oleg Sul′kin, *Iurii Ozerov* (Moscow: Iskusstvo, 1986), 133.

35. Sumenov and Sul′kin, *Iurii Ozerov*, 134.

36. Tsitriniak, "Napravlenie glavnogo udara," 13.

37. Sumenov and Sul′kin, *Iurii Ozerov*, 136.

38. Tsitriniak, "Napravlenie glavnogo udara," 12–13, 17.

39. Mikhail Ul′ianov, *Real′nost′ i mechta* (Moscow: Vagrius, 2007), 266–67.

40. S. Chertok, "Nikolai Olialin," in *Ekran 1971–72* (Moscow: Iskusstvo, 1972), 62.

41. S. Chertok, "Nikolai Olialin," 61–62.

42. Evgenii Boltin, "Epopeia osvobozhdeniia. Mysli voennogo istorika," *Iskusstvo kino*, no. 5 (1972): 41–54; "Bitva za Berlin," in *Ekran 1970–71* (Moscow: Iskusstvo, 1971).

43. Khaniutin statement in *Kino i vremia* (Moscow: Iskusstvo, 1977), 64, quoted in Sumenov and Sul′kin, *Iurii Ozerov*, 127.

44. Roman Karmen, "Surovaia pravda," *Iskusstvo kino*, no. 2 (1968): 39.

45. Youngblood, *Russian War Films*, 161.

46. Quoted in Iurii Bondarev, Oskar Kurganov, and Iurii Ozerov, "Bitva za Berlin. Osvobozhdenie fil′m 5," *Iskusstvo kino*, no. 5 (1970): 52, 53.

47. Sumenov and Sul′kin, *Iurii Ozerov*, 115.

48. Bondarev, Kurganov, and Ozerov, "Bitva za Berlin," 65.

49. "Bitva za Berlin," in *Ekran 1970–71*, 20.

50. Sumenov and Sul′kin, *Iurii Ozerov*, 138.

51. Sumenov and Sul′kin, *Iurii Ozerov*, 114.

52. Dal′ Orlov, "Zavershenie epopei," *Iskusstvo kino*, no. 2 (1972): 8.

53. Ozerov, "Vosslavit′ podvig naroda," 2.

54. N. Zaitsev, "Epos i lichnost′," in *Pamiat′ grozovykh let. Velikaia Otechestvennaia Voina v sovetskom kino 1970-kh godov*, ed. N. Zaitsev, L. Muraa tov, N. Vol′man, and V. Ivanova, (Leningrad: Iskusstvo, 1980), 63; Sumenov and Sul′kin, *Iurii Ozerov*, 95–97.

55. Youngblood, *Russian War Films*, 158.

56. Quoted in Tsitriniak, "Napravlenie glavnogo udara," 10.

57. Youngblood, *Russian War Films*, 158.

58. Tsitriniak, "Napravlenie glavnogo udara," 9–10.

59. Youngblood, *Russian War Films*, 161.

60. Bernard F. Dick, *The Star-Spangled Screen: The American World War II Film* (Lexington: University Press of Kentucky, 1985), 138.

61. Christine E. Evans, *Between Truth and Time: A History of Soviet Central Television* (New Haven, CT: Yale University Press, 2016), 256n14.

62. For more on this, see Maksim Kaz[i]uchitz, "'Sovpolikadr'. Poliekrannyi i polikadrovyi fil′m v istorii kinematografii 1960-kh–1980-kh," *Kinovedcheskie zapiski*, no. 104–105 (2013): 388–96. My thanks to Keti Chukhrov and William Brown for bringing these films to my attention with their excellent September 2019 retrospective at the Whitechapel Gallery: "V-A-C Live: Alexander Shein and Sovpolikadr," accessed 9 January 2020, https://www.whitechapelgallery.org/events/v-a-c-live-this-is-not-a-cinema-2/.

63. Evans, *Between Truth and Time*, 2.

64. "Teksty televizionnykh peredach za ianvar′–iiun′ 1965. Glavnaia redaktesiia literaturno-dramaticheskikh program. Otdel literatury i iskusstva," GARF, 6903/26/588, sheet 574.

65. "Obzory pisem telezritelei za aprel′–avgust, oktiabr′1965," GARF, 6903/10/66, sheet 2.

66. GARF 6903/10/66, sheet 1.

67. "Teksty televizionnykh peredach za ianvar′–mai 1965 g.," GARF 6903/26/578, sheet 581.

68. Konstantin Simonov, *Simonov i voina* (Moscow: Vremia, 2016), 478.

69. Annette Wieviorka, *The Era of the Witness*, trans. from French by Jared Stark (Ithaca, NY: Cornell University Press, 2006), 143–44.

70. "Neizvestnaia voina. Delo fil′ma, tom. 1," RGALI, 3160/1/730, sheet 8.

71. RGALI, 3160/1/730, sheet 56.

72. "Neizvestnaia voina. Vostochnyi front. Dogovor s kompaniei 'Air Time Incorporation' (SShA) na proizvodstvo zvukovogo fil′ma 'Neizvestnaia voina. Vostochnyi front, '" RGALI, 3160/1/155, sheet 1.

73. "Neizvestnaia voina," RGALI, 3160/2/3255, sheet 1.

74. Karmen—Ermash (chair Goskino), Kozyrev (director TsSDF), Tereishvili, 12 February 1977, RGALI, 3160/1/730, sheets 42–43, 49.

75. Karmen, writing to his son, from *Sovetskaia kul′tura*, 27 November 1981, quoted in Hynes, *Soldier's Tale*, 16.

76. RGALI, 3160/1/730, sheet 48.

77. RGALI, 3160/1/730, sheet 49.

78. RGALI, 3160/1/730, sheet 69.

79. "Neizvestnaia voina. Delo fil′ma, tom 2," RGALI, 3160/1/731, sheet 55.

80. RGALI, 3160/2/3255, sheet 73; "Neizvestnaia voina. Delo fil′ma, soglashveniia, protokoly, perepiska, t. 2," RGALI, 3160/2/3256, sheet 36.

81. RGALI, 3160/1/731, sheet 78; RGALI, 3160/1/155, sheet 5.

82. RGALI, 3160/1/155, sheet 15.

83. RGALI, 3160/1/730, sheet 8.

84. RGALI, 3160/2/3256, sheets 43–44.

85. "Neizvestnaia voina. Delo fil′ma. (Otchety, akty, spravki i dr). tom. 1," RGALI, 3160/2/3260, sheet 58.

86. Telex Tereishvili to Weiner, 26 October 1977, "Neizvestnaia voina. Delo fil′ma. (Otchety, akty, spravki i dr), tom. 1," RGALI, 3160/2/3260, sheet 115. Fred Weiner was the young vice president of Air Time who "had dreamed up the idea of the television series after a 1976 visit . . . that impressed him with his own ignorance of the sacrifice and heroism of the Russians in the war." Kevin Klose, "Fresh Footage from 'The Unknown War,'" *Washington Post*, December 22, 1977, https://www.washingtonpost.com/archive/lifestyle/1977/12/22/fresh-footage-from-the-unknown-war/10c28862-9dfc-4d3e-b6da-d76dd15add66/.

87. RGALI, 3160/2/3260, sheet 50.

88. RGALI, 3160/2/3260, sheets 54, 58.

89. RGALI, 3160/1/155, sheet 4.

90. RGALI, 3160/1/731, sheet 64.

91. RGALI, 3160/1/155, sheet 104.

92. RGALI, 3160/1/155, sheet 86.

93. R. L. Karmen, "'Velikaia otechestvennaia' = Neizvestnaia voina: Stsenarnyi plan, tekst dlia amerikanskogo diktora i plan s″emok televizionnogo dokumental′nogo fil′ma v 20 seriiakh [1977]," RGALI, 2989/1/65, sheet 27.

94. RGALI, 3160/1/155, sheet 101.

95. RGALI, 2989/1/65, sheets 39, 48.

96. RGALI, 3160/2/3256, sheets 44–45.

97. RGALI, 3160/1/730, sheet 61.

98. RGALI, 3160/2/3256, sheet 49.

99. RGALI, 2989/1/65, sheet 79.

100. RGALI, 3160/2/3255, sheet 17.

101. "'Unknown War' on Channel 9," *Los Angeles Times*, October 5, 1978, clipping in RGALI, 3160/2/3256, sheet 66.

102. Leonid Brezhnev, *Vospominaniia* (Moscow: Politicheskaia literature, 1982), 86.

103. Joshua Rubenstein, "World War Two—Soviet Style," in *New Challenges for Documentary*, ed. Alan Rosenthal (Berkeley: University of California Press, 1988), 469.

104. N. Vol′man, "Pamiat′ i dokument," in *Pamiat′ grozovykh let. Velikaia Otechestvennaia Voina v sovetskom kino 1970-kh godov*, ed. N. Zaitsev, L. Muratov, N. Vol′man, and V. Ivanova (Leningrad: Iskusstvo, 1980), 48.

105. Vol′man, "Pamiat′ i dokument," 48.

106. For a reaction to the film, see the May 1979 *Commentary* critique of *The Unknown War*'s silences and distortions, reprinted in Rubenstein, "World War Two—Soviet Style," 465–70.

107. Gerald D. Swick, "WW2 Documentary Unseen for 30 Years Returns on DVD," HistoryNet, accessed 2 June 2018, http://www.historynet.com/ww2-documentary-unseen-for-30-years-returns-on-dvd.htm.

108. Andrei Kochetov, "Magnitnye Polia Leiptsiga," *Sovetskii ekran*, no. 16 (1980): 16–17.

109. RGALI, 3160/1/730, sheet 49.

110. Vol′man, "Pamiat′ i dokument," 48.

111. "O sovetskom cheloveke, o sovetskom narode," *Iskusstvo kino*, no. 8 (1982): 97.

112. Kamshalov, *Geroika podviga na ekrane*, 163.

113. Evans, *Between Truth and Time*, 2, 24.

114. Sumenov and Sul′kin, *Iurii Ozerov*, 95.

115. Evans, *Between Truth and Time*, 13.

116. "Podvig Zhivet," *Izvestiia*, 10 May 1969, 1.

117. "Kremlevskii dvorets s″ezdov, 8 maia," *Izvestiia*, 9 May 1970, 1.

118. V. A. Rudnev, *Prazdniki, obriady, ritualy v trudovom kollektive* (Moscow: Profizdat, 1984), 10.

119. "V Prazdnichnom stroiu," *Krasnaia zvezda*, 5 November 1975, 1; "V paradnom stroiu," *Krasnaia zvezda*, 5 November 1977, 2.

120. Schattenberg, *Velichie i tragediia cheloveka i strany*, 550–51.

121. Schattenberg, *Velichie i tragediia cheloveka i strany*, 571–72.

122. Ivan Pavlovskii, "Iakzykom faktov i dokumentov," *Sovetskaia kul′tura*, 9 May 1985, 8.

123. Vol′man, "Pamiat′ i dokument," 50.

124. Vasilii Chuikov, "Podvig bessmerten," *Sovetskii ekran*, no. 9 (1980): 1.

125. "O sovetskom cheloveke, o sovetskom narode," 103.

126. Quoted in Tumarkin, *Living and the Dead*, 138.

127. The decline is even apparent in the title of Tumarkin's book: *The Rise and Fall of the Cult of World War II in Russia*.

128. Schattenberg, *Velichie i tragediia cheloveka i strany*, 281.

129. Schattenberg, *Velichie i tragediia cheloveka i strany*, 282–90, 572–76.

130. A. Beliko, L. Beranskii, V. Dzhalagoniia, O. Moskovskii, V. Oleinichenko, and N. Sevruk, "Krasnaia ploshchad′, 9 maia," *Vecherniaia Moskva*, 9 May 1985, 3, 4.

131. Beliko et al., "Krasnaia ploshchad′, 9 maia," 3, 4.

132. John Miller, *Mikhail Gorbachev and the End of Soviet Power* (Basingstoke: Macmillan and St. Martin's Press, 1993), 40.

133. Ilya Zemtsov, *Chernenko: The Last Bolshevik; The Soviet Union on the Eve of Perestroika* (New Brunswick, NJ: Transaction, 1989), 166.

134. William E. Odom, *The Collapse of the Soviet Military* (New Haven, CT: Yale University Press, 1998), 128.

135. John W. Parker, *Kremlin in Transition*, vol. 2, *Gorbachev, 1985 to 1989* (Boston: Unwin Hyman, 1991), 31.

136. Parker, *Kremlin in Transition*, 4; Odom, *Collapse of the Soviet Military*, 89.

137. Rafael Reuveny and Aseem Prakash, "The Afghanistan War and the Breakdown of the Soviet Union," *Review of International Studies*, no. 25 (1999): 693–708.

138. On the decline and subsequent return of the World War II film genre in Russia, see: Youngblood, *Russian War Films*, 218–30.

CHAPTER 5. ICONOCLASM, RESANCTIFICATION, AND THE POST-SOVIET VICTORY CULT

1. Nina Tumarkin refers to it as "the last hurrah." Tumarkin, *Living and the Dead*, 28.

2. Thomas C. Wolfe, "Past as Present, Myth, or History? Discourses of Time and the Great Fatherland War," in *The Politics of Memory in Postwar Europe*, ed. Richard Ned Lebow, Wulf Kansteiner, and Claudio Fogu (Durham, NC: Duke University Press, 2006), 271.

3. Valentin Tolstykh, *Khochu—mogu—dolzhen. Opyt obshchestvennoi avtobiografii lichnosti* (Moscow: Progress-traditsiia, 2015), 155.

4. Wolfe, "Past as Present, Myth, or History?," 271.

5. Richard Stites, *Russian Popular Culture: Entertainment and Society since 1900* (New York: Cambridge University Press, 1992), 178.

6. V. Litovkin, "Voina, narod, Pobeda," *Izvestiia*, 8 May 1990, 3.

7. Wolfe, "Past as Present, Myth, or History?"; Pavel Polian, *Istoriomor, ili trepanatsiia pamiati* (Moscow: AST, 2016), 163–69.

8. See Polian, *Istoriomor*, 121.

9. M. Shimanskii, "Vernulsia chtoby uiti. 40 let shel soldat domoi s voiny," *Izvestiia*, 7 May 1990, 4.

10. Davies, *Soviet History in the Gorbachev Revolution*, 111.

11. Mikhail Egorov, *Znamia Pobedy. Boi pervyi. Boi poslednii* (Moscow: Molodaia gvardiia, 1975), quoted in Lozin, *Znamia Pobedy—gosudarstvennaia relikviia Rossii*, 172.

12. Zinchenko, *Geroi shturma Reikhstaga*, 150.

13. Georgii Kumanev and Vladimir Seoev, interviewed in "Znamenostsy Pobedy," *Pravda*, 30 April 1990, 1–2.

14. Lozin, *Znamia Pobedy—gosudarstvennaia relikviia Rossii*, 174.

15. Neustroev, "O Reikhstage na sklone let," 130.

16. Kumanev here quotes an archival source: TsAMO, 3-darnoi armii/4306/528, sheet 45.

17. Kumanev, *Podvig i podlog*, 332–33.

18. "Egorov i Kantariia byli ne pervymi," *Argumenty i fakty*, 7 May 2003, http://www.aif.ru/archive/1628792.

19. Iamskoi, *Kto bral Reikhstag*.

20. Dement′ev, *Znamia Pobedy*.

21. K. R. M. Short, preface to *Hitler's Fall: The Newsreel Witness*, ed. K. R. M. Short and Stephan Dolezel (London: Croom Helm, 1988), xii; Sergei Drobashenko, "Soviet Film Chronicles and the Fall of Nazi Germany," in *Hitler's Fall: The Newsreel Witness*, ed. K. R. M. Short and Stephan Dolezel (London: Croom Helm, 1988), 50–56.

22. Richard C. Raack, "The Red Army Beflags the Reichstag: Film as Historical Fantasy," in *Hitler's Fall: The Newsreel Witness*, edited by K. R. M. Short and Stephan Dolezel (London: Croom Helm, 1988), 64.

23. Ernst Volland and Heinz Krimmer, *Von Moskau nach Berlin: Bilder des russischen Fotografen Jewgeni Chaldej* (Berlin: Nicolaische Verlagsbuchhandlung, 1994).

24. See, for example, Michael Sontheimer, "The Art of Soviet Propaganda: Iconic Red Army Reichstag Photo Faked," *Spiegel Online*, 7 May 2008, http://www.spiegel.de/international/europe/the-art-of-soviet-propaganda-iconic-red-army-reichstag-photo-faked-a-551972.html.

25. Following a common misunderstanding, one author claims that there was a military parade on Victory Day every year in the Soviet period. See Nataliya Danilova, *The Politics of War Commemoration in the UK and Russia* (London: Palgrave-Macmillan, 2015), 188.

26. Tumarkin, *Living and the Dead*, 218–20.

27. Mikhail Gorbachev, "Uroki voiny i pobedy. Torzhestvennoe sobranie v Moskve, posviashchennoe 45-letiiu Pobedy sovetskogo naroda v Velikoi Otechestvennoi voine; Doklad M. S. Gorbacheva," *Izvestiia*, 9 May 1990, 1–2.

28. Gorbachev, "Uroki voiny i pobedy," 1–2. "Little screws" is a reference to Stalin's 24 June 1945 Victory Parade speech in the Kremlin, in which he referred to the people in this manner.

29. Gorbachev, "Uroki voiny i pobedy," 1–2. Note that some accounts see the 2005 acknowledgment of the Allies' contribution as groundbreaking. This is not so. See Danilova, *Politics of War Commemoration*, 194.

30. N. Burbyga, "Ia shel k El′be v riadakh soiuznicheskoi armii," *Izvestiia*, 9 May 1990, 6; P. Gutiontov, "Vstrecha prezidenta SSSR s veteranami voiny i truda," *Izvestiia*, 9 May 1990, 1; "Vstrecha s veteranami voiny, truda i vooruzhennykh sil SSSR," *Izvestiia*, 9 May 1990, 1.

31. N. Burbyga and V. Litovkin, "V odnom stroiu ottsy i synov′ia," *Izvestiia*, 10 May 1990, 3.

32. Nurit Schleifman, "Moscow's Victory Park: A Monumental Change," *History and Memory* 13, no. 2 (2001): 5–34.

33. Quoted in Burbyga and Litovkin, "V odnom stroiu ottsy i synov′ia," 3.

34. Tumarkin, *Living and the Dead*, 200.

35. "My slyshim vas, frontoviki," *Pravda*, 9 May 1992, 1.

36. Iurii Makhrin, "Prazdnik na Krasnoi ploshchadi," *Pravda*, 8 May 1993, 1.

37. Valentina Nikiforova, "Narodu vse ploshchadi maly," *Pravda*, 12 May 1993, 1; Benjamin Forest and Juliet Johnson, "Unraveling the Threads of History: Soviet-Era Monuments and Post-Soviet National Identity in Moscow," *Annals of the Association of American Geographers* 92, no. 3 (2004): 532.

38. Luke March, *The Communist Party in Post-Soviet Russia* (Manchester: Manchester University Press, 2002), 173, 75.

39. Valentina Nikiforova, "Dva lika prazdnika," *Pravda*, 11 May 1994, 1.

40. Kathleen E. Smith, *Mythmaking in the New Russia: Politics and Memory during the Yeltsin Era* (Ithaca, NY: Cornell University Press, 2002), 89.

41. Konstantin Eggert, "9 Maia zarubezhnye gosti prepochtut ne videt′ nashikh tankov," *Izvestiia*, 6 May 1995, 2.

42. "Kholokost: Istoriia geroizma, predatel′stva i ravnodushiia," *Messianskii komitet*, 2 December 2010, http://www.messcom.org.ua/2010/12/06/holocost-2/; "Raul′ Vallenberg byl kaznen po prikazu Stalina i Molotova, vyiasnilos′ iz tainykh dnevnikov KGB," Newsru.com, 8 August 2016, https://www.newsru.com/russia/08aug2016/wallenberg.html.

43. Wolfe, "Past as Present, Myth, or History?," 277.

44. Smith, *Mythmaking in the New Russia*, 85–91.

45. Stanislav Kondrashov, "Velikaia otechestvennaia ostanetsia v geneticheskoi pamiati naroda," *Izvestiia*, 6 May 1995, 1.

46. Kondrashov, "Velikaia otechestvennaia ostanetsia v geneticheskoi pamiati naroda," 3.

47. Kondrashov, "Velikaia otechestvennaia ostanetsia v genetichsekoi pamiati naroda," 3.

48. Leonid Kapeliushnii, "Voina na vsiu ostavshuiusia zhizn′," *Izvestiia*, 6 May 1995, 3. For an external observer with this perspective, see Tumarkin, *Living and the Dead*, passim.

49. "Ukaz Prezidenta Rossiiskoi Federatsii ot 15 aprelia 1996 'o Znameni Pobedy' N. 561" [Decree of the president of the Russian Federation 15 April 1996, "on the Victory Banner"], *Sbornik zakonov*, accessed 12 November 2015, http://sbornik-zakonov.ru/215419.html.

50. Stanislav Slivko, "Kommunisty vernuli Khabarovskomu kraiu Znamia Pobedy," Communist Party of the Russian Federation, accessed 28 July 2016, https://kprf.ru/party-live/regnews/127563.html.

51. Elizabeth A. Wood, "Performing Memory: Vladimir Putin and the Celebration of WWII in Russia," *Soviet and Post-Soviet Review* 38 (2011): 173.

52. Richard Sakwa, *Putin Redux: Power and Contradiction in Contemporary Russia* (London: Routledge, 2014), 12, 142–43; Shaun Walker, *The Long Hang-*

over: Putin's New Russia and the Ghosts of the Past (Oxford: Oxford University Press, 2018), 31.

53. Ella Maksimova and Aleksei Belianchev, "Plen," *Izvestiia*, 4 May 2000, 3.

54. Hutchings and Rulyova, "Commemorating the Past/Performing the Present," 149.

55. The 24 June 1945 parade is incorrectly referred to by Hutchings and Rulyova as the 9 May 1945 parade. They also refer to the Victory Banner as coming from the "national flag museum" rather than the Central Museum of the Armed Forces. Hutchings and Rulyova, "Commemorating the Past/Performing the Present," 138, 140, 148.

56. Zoltan D. Barany, *Democratic Breakdown and the Decline of the Russian Military* (Princeton, NJ: Princeton University Press, 2007); William E. Odom, "The Military and the State: Contemporary Russia in Historical Perspective," in *The Military History of the Soviet Union*, ed. Robin Higham and Frederick W. Kagan (New York: Palgrave, 2002), 303.

57. President Vladimir Putin, "Speech at the Forum 'Let My People Live!' Commemorating the Memory of the Victims of Auschwitz," delivered in Krakow, Poland, 27 January 2005, President of Russia, http://en.kremlin.ru/events/president/transcripts/22800.

58. Putin, "Speech at the Forum 'Let My People Live!'"

59. Vladimir Putin, "International Holocaust Remembrance Day," Jewish Museum and Tolerance Center, Moscow, 27 January 2015, President of Russia, http://en.kremlin.ru/events/president/transcripts/47529.

60. Stefan Rohdewald, "Post-Soviet Remembrance of the Holocaust and National Memories of the Second World War in Russia, Ukraine and Lithuania," *Forum for Modern Language Studies* 44, no. 2 (2008): 173–84.

61. Hutchings and Rulyova, "Commemorating the Past/Performing the Present," 146–47.

62. Hutchings and Rulyova, "Commemorating the Past/Performing the Present," 137–38.

63. Danilova, *Politics of War Commemoration*, 192; Vikas Shukla, "Russia's World War II Victory Day Parade: Who Is Coming and Who Isn't," *ValueWalk*, 7 May 2015, https://www.valuewalk.com/2015/05/russia-world-war-ii-victory-day-parade/.

64. Hutchings and Rulyova, "Commemorating the Past/Performing the Present," 139.

65. Hutchings and Rulyova, "Commemorating the Past/Performing the Present," 149.

66. Sergei Muratov and Georgii Fere, "Sovetskoi kul′tury" and "Ekrany Maia" columns, *Sovetskaia kul′tura*, 3 June 1965, from "Stat′i o tsentral′nom televidenii, opublikovannye v tsentral′noi i mestnoi presse (vyrezki iz gazet) t. 1," GARF, 6903/3/308, sheet 21.

67. GARF, 6903/3/308, sheet 21.

68. Hutchings and Rulyova, "Commemorating the Past/Performing the Present," 149.

69. GARF, 6903/3/308, sheet 21.

70. Danilova, *Politics of War Commemoration*, 194.

71. Jay David Bolter and Richard Grusin, *Remediation: Understanding New Media* (Cambridge, MA: MIT Press, 1999), 224.

72. "*Call of Duty*," Wikipedia, accessed 14 June 2013, https://en.wikipedia.org/wiki/Call_of_Duty.

73. "*Call of Duty*: Product Description," Amazon.com, accessed 15 July 2014, http://www.amazon.co.uk/Call-of-Duty-PC-CD/dp/B00009WBGS/ref=sr_1_3?ie=UTF8&qid=1394793358&sr=8-3&keywords=call+of+duty+1.

74. A Customer (pseudonym), "Could Have Been Great (Review of *Call of Duty*)," Amazon UK, accessed 2 June 2018, http://www.amazon.co.uk/review/RXCIN0N93D0WM/ref=cm_cr_pr_viewpnt—RXCIN0N93D0WM (no longer available).

75. Bolter and Grusin, *Remediation*, 9.

76. A Customer (pseudonym), "Could Have Been Great (Review of *Call of Duty*)."

77. Jesper Juul, "Fear of Failing? The Many Meanings of Difficulty in Video Games," in *The Video Game Theory Reader 2*, ed. Bernard Perron and Mark J. P. Wolf (London: Routledge, 2009), 237–52; Trent Cruz, "'It's Almost Too Intense': Nostalgia and Authenticity in *Call of Duty 2*," *Loading . . . 1*, no. 1 (2007); "*Call of Duty* (Video Game)—Soviet Campaign," Wikipedia, accessed 16 January 2020, http:/en.wikipedia.org/wiki/Call_of_Duty_(video_game)—Soviet_campaign.

78. Masaki Mori, *Epic Grandeur: Toward a Comparative Poetics of the Epic* (Albany:

State University of New York Press, 1997), 11.

79. Joanne Garde-Hansen, Andrew Hoskins, and Anna Reading, eds., *Save As . . . Digital Memories* (Basingstoke: Palgrave Macmillan, 2009), 15–16.

80. Hans Belting, *An Anthropology of Images: Picture, Medium, Body*, trans. Thomas Dunlap (Princeton, NJ: Princeton University Press, 2011), 16.

81. Bolter and Grusin, *Remediation*, 99

82. "Shuter goda," Igromania, 8 March 2009, https://www.igromania.ru/article/14582/SHuter_goda.html.

83. kramarenko19, "Otzyv: Igra dlia PC 'Call of Duty: World at War' (2008)—OTLICHNAIA IGRA," Otzovik, accessed 10 January 2020, https://otzovik.com/review_76414.html; Rastaman35 (24 April 2011), comments quoting Skayler (6 March 2011), "Call of Duty: World at War," Igromania, accessed 10 January 2020, https://www.igromania.ru/game/4389/Call_of_Duty_World_at_War.html.

84. James Campbell, "Combat Gnosticism: The Ideology of First World War Poetry Criticism," *New Literary History* 30, no. 1 (1999): 203.

85. Indeed, the episodes of *Call of Duty*'s action span a number of military campaigns and include not only US but also British (in the first release) and Soviet characters. These qualities differentiated it from the first-person shooter game that introduced the World War II setting to gaming, *Medal of Honor* (1999), which was devoted entirely to the American experience.

86. Jaimie Baron, *The Archive Effect: Found Footage and the Audiovisual Experience of History* (London: Routledge, 2014), 164.

87. *The Great War* was broadcast as *Soviet Storm: WW2 in the East* on the History Channel in in the United States in 2011 and in the United Kingdom in 2012.

88. Alissa Timoshkina, "Representations of the Holocaust in Soviet Cinema," PhD diss., King's College London, 2015, 154–55.

89. "Velikaia voina (dokumental′nyi tsikl)," Wikipedia, 3 June 2018, https://ru.wikipedia.org/wiki/Великая_война_(документальный_цикл).

90. "Vokrug TV," 3 June 2018, https://www.vokrug.tv/product/show/velikaya_voina/.

91. See reviews at Kinopoisk, 3 June 2018, https://www.kinopoisk.ru/film/velikaya-voyna-2010-503264/.

92. Baron, *Archive Effect*, 62.

93. "Tsentral′nyi Muzei Vooruzhennykh Sil: Ofitsial′nyi Sait; Zal 18, Zal Pobedy," Central Museum of the Armed Forces, accessed 10 November, 2015, http://cmaf.ru/ekspo/inside/129; "Dmitrii Medvedev otkryl Zal 'Znamia Pobedy' v Tsentral′mom Muzee Vooruzhennykh Sil," *Rossiiskaia gazeta*, 8 May 2011, https://rg.ru/2011/05/08/znamya-anons.html. Lozin says that even in the 1965 parade an exact copy was used, and the actual flag has never left the museum since its arrival. Lozin, *Znamia Pobedy—gosudarstvennaia relikviia Rossii*, 126.

94. Synthart (pseudonym), "Eshche o pamiatnike Pobedy na Poklonnoi Gore," accessed 11 November 2015, http://synthart.livejournal.com/217953.html.

95. A. Arsenin, *Tsentral′nyi muzei Sovetskoi Armii* (Moscow: Moskovskii rabochii, 1953), 94.

96. Edele, *Soviet Veterans*, 162.

97. Vasilii Shatilov, *V boiakh rozhdennoe znamia*, 2nd rev. and expanded ed. (Moscow: Sovetskaia Rossiia, 1988), 188.

98. Central Museum of the Soviet Army, *Relikvii boevoi slavy* (Moscow: Voennoe izdatel′stvo Ministerstva oborony SSSR, 1962), 151–52.

99. Tumarkin, *Living and the Dead*, 133; Amir Weiner, *Making Sense of War: The Second World War and the Fate of the Bolshevik Revolution* (Princeton, NJ: Princeton University Press, 2001), 365.

100. Dubin, "Pamiat′, voina, pamiat′ o voine," n.p.

101. "Federal′nyi zakon Rossiiskoi Federatsii ot 7 maia 2007g. N 68-F3 'O Znameni Pobedy" [Federal law of 7 May 2007 N 68-F3 "on the Victory Banner"], *Rossiiskaia gazeta*, 8 May 2007, http://www.rg.ru/2007/05/08/znamya.html.

102. Sergei Kruglov, "Istoriiu ne perepishesh′," *Voenno-promyshlennyi kur′er*, 9 May 2007, http://vpk-news.ru/articles/3637.

103. Jenny Thompson, *War Games: Inside the World of Twentieth-Century War Reenactors* (Washington, DC: Smithsonian Books, 2010), 135.

104. Thompson, *War Games*, 125–34.

105. Walker, *Long Hangover*, 206.

106. "Rada obiazala podnimat′ Krasnoe Znamia v Den′ Pobedy," *Zerkalo nedeli*, 21 April 2011, http://zn.ua/SOCIETY/rada_obyazala_podnimat_krasnoe_znamya_v_den_pobedy.html.

107. "Rada obiazala podnimat′ Krasnoe Znamia v Den′ Pobedy."

108. Vladimir Ul′ianov (pseudonym), "Aktsiia kommunistov 'Znamia Pobedy,'" YouTube video, accessed 3 June 2018, https://www.youtube.com/watch?v=N7cAAJKRj_o.

109. Elena Chernysheva, "Voennaia Rekonstruktsiia Vziatie Berlina," *Odessit.ua*, 2012, http://www.odessit.ua/photo/389-voennaya-rekonstrukciya-vzyatie-reyhstaga.html (accessed 3 June 2018; no longer available).

110. The video accounts depicting these events have been deleted from YouTube. For a more detailed description of them, see Jeremy Hicks, "A Holy Relic of War: The Soviet Victory Banner as Artefact," in *Remembering the Second World War*, ed. Patrick Finney (London: Routledge, 2017), 197–216.

111. "V Odesse zapretili Znamia Pobedy," *Lenta.ru*, 23 October 2015, http://lenta.ru/news/2015/10/23/flag/; Alex Luhn, "Ukraine Bans Soviet Symbols and Criminalises Sympathy for Communism," *The Guardian*, 21 May 2015, https://www.theguardian.com/world/2015/may/21/ukraine-bans-soviet-symbols-criminalises-sympathy-for-communism.

112. "B Novorosiisk privezut -200metrovoe Znamia Pobedy," Kuban TV, accessed 25 March 2015, http://kubantv.ru/pobeda/91809-gigantskoe-znamia-pobedy-provezut-po-gorodam-kubani/?utm_source=dlvr.it&utm_medium=twitter (no longer available).

113. Patriot Park is a military theme park in Kubinka, near Moscow. Shaun Walker, "Vladimir Putin Opens Russian 'Military Disneyland' Patriot Park," *The Guardian*, 16 June 2016, https://www.theguardian.com/world/2015/jun/16/vladimir-putin-opens-russian-military-disneyland-patriot-park.

114. Anastasiia Anushevskaia, "Chto takoe dvizhenie 'Iunarmiia' i zachem ono nuzhno?," *Argumenty i fakty*, 4 August 2016, http://www.aif.ru/dontknows/actual/chto_takoe_dvizhenie_yunarmiya_i_zachem_ono_nuzhno.

115. "Shoigu soobshchil o stroitel′stve v Podmoskov′e kopi Reichstaga dlia trenirovok," *Gazeta.ru*, 22 February 2017, https://www.gazeta.ru/army

/news/9717851.shtml; Shaun Walker, "Russia Builds Replica Reichstag So Children Can Recreate 1945 Victory," *The Guardian*, 22 February 2017, https://www.theguardian.com/world/2017/feb/22/russian-replica-to-give-children-chance-to-storm-the-reichstag.

116. Vadim Lobov, "Zachem nam nuzhen 'Shturm Berlina,'" *Izvestiia*, 14 April 2017, https://iz.ru/news/682742.

117. See "Ob universitete," Synergy University, accessed 3 June 2018, https://synergy.ru/about/.

118. Lobov, "Zachem nam nuzhen 'Shturm Berlina.'"

119. "Na Parade Pobedy v Groznom vziali Reichstag,'" YouTube video, accessed 11 June 2018, https://www.youtube.com/watch?v=iWxEHYUfLMA.

120. Lobov, "Zachem nam nuzhen 'Shturm Berlina.'"

121. Peter Bjorn, "'Etot flag byl v Berline! Eto flag moego naroda,' Svetlana Gladysheva otkazalas′ubrat′ Znamia Pobedy," *Sports.ru*, 22 February 2018, https://www.sports.ru/tribuna/blogs/mama4h/1593866.html.

122. Denis Parfenov, "Vytravlivanie gosudarstvennykh simvolov SSSR so Znameni Pobedy mozhet byt′ rastseneno kak ideologicheskaia diversiia," Communist Party of the Russian Federation, 6 February 2018, https://kprf.ru/dep/gosduma/activities/172751.html.

123. Parfenov, "Vytravlivanie gosudarstvennykh simvolov SSSR so Znameni Pobedy."

124. "Volgograd: Na zasedanii oblastnoi Dumy 'edinorossy' otkazalis′ podsderzhat′ predlozhenie deputata-kommunista M. A. Tarasova obsudit′ situatsiiu so Znamenem Pobedy, popavshim na parad 2 fevralia bez zvezdy, serpa i molota," Communist Party of the Russian Federation, 8 February 2018, https://kprf.ru/dep/reg/172845.html.

125. It has been argued that the misuse of political symbolism from the communist era tainted politics more widely in the postcommunist era. Sakwa, *Putin Redux*, 20.

126. Gary Oak, "A Red Flag over Raqqa: Gary Oak Presents a Photograph of International Freedom Battalion Members Recreating the Famous 1945 Photo Raising a Flag over the Reichstag," *Morning Star*, 3 January 2018, http://www.morningstaronline.co.uk/article/red-flag-over-raqqa (accessed 3 June 2018; no longer available).

127. Seth Bernstein, "Remembering War, Remaining Soviet: Digital Commemoration of World War II in Putin's Russia," *Memory Studies* 9, no. 4 (2016): 422–36; Tumarkin, *Living and the Dead*, passim. See criticism in Wolfe, "Past as Present, Myth, or History?," 266. Also see discussion in Dubin, "Pamiat′, voina, pamiat′ o voine," n.p.

128. Danilova, *Politics of War Commemoration*, 184, 199.

129. Danilova, *Politics of War Commemoration*, 199–205.

130. Serguei Oushakine, "Remembering in Public: On the Affective Management of History," *Ab Imperio*, no. 1 (2013): 291.

131. Peter Hobson, "How Russian Authorities Hijacked a WWII Remembrance Movement," *Moscow Times*, 6 May 2016, https://themoscowtimes.com/articles/how-russian-authorities-hijacked-a-wwii-remembrance-movement-52776.

132. Neustroev, "O Reikhstage na sklone let," 130–44.

133. Grigory Levchenko, "How Russia Prosecutes Its Own People for 'Falsifying History,'" trans. Peter Marshall, *Meduza*, 11 May 2018, https://meduza.io/en/feature/2018/05/11/how-russia-prosecutes-its-own-people-for-falsifying-history; "Doklad Mezhdunarodnoi Agory. Istoriia stanovitsia opasnoi naukoi," *Agora*, 11 May 2018, http://agora.legal/news/2018.05.10/Doklad-Mezhdunarodnoi-Agory-Istoriya-stanovitsya-opasnoi-naukoi/713.

134. Maksimenkov, "Arkhivno-istoricheskoe obespechenie nyneshnego i budushchikh iubileev," 382.

135. Polian, *Istoriomor*, 238.

136. Georgii Ramazashvili, "Est′ takaia professiia—istoriiu zashchishchat′: TsAMO RF v predverii 60-iia Pobedy," in *Pamiat′ o voine 60 let spustia. Rossiia, Germaniia, Evropa*, ed. Il′ia Kalinin and Mikhail Gabovich (Moscow: Novoe literaturnoe obozrenie, 2005), 297.

137. Ramazashvili, "Est′ takaia professiia—istoriiu zashchishchat′," 298.

138. Miguel Vázquez Liñán, "History as a Propaganda Tool in Putin's Russia," *Communist and Post-Communist Studies* 43, no. 2 (2010): 167–78.

139. A. A. Grechko et al., eds., *Istoriia vtoroi mirovoi voiny*, 12 vols. (Moscow: Voennoe izdatel'stvo Ministerstva oborony SSSR, 1973–1982).

140. The 1979 volume refers to Makov's group entering the Reichstag first, then to Egorov and Kantariia later putting up an official Victory Banner that symbolized all of those previously put up on the Reichstag, including that raised by Makov's group. Grechko et al., *Istoriia vtoroi mirovoi voiny*, 10:341.

141. V. P. Baranov et al., eds., *Velikaia otechestvennaia voina 1941–1945 godov*, 12 vols. (Moscow: Kuchkovo pole, 2015), 5:403.

142. Baranov et al., *Velikaia otechestvennaia voina 1941–1945 godov*, 10:424.

143. Rohdewald, "Post-Soviet Remembrance of the Holocaust," 173–84.

144. Hutchings and Rulyova, "Commemorating the Past/Performing the Present," 142.

CONCLUSION

1. Hutchings and Rulyova, *Commemorating the Past/Performing the Present*, 142.

2. Hutchings and Rulyova, *Commemorating the Past/Performing the Present*, 152.

BIBLIOGRAPHY

ARCHIVES CONSULTED

Bundesarchiv-Filmarchiv, Berlin
GARF, State Archive of the Russian Federation, Moscow
Gosfil′mofond, Russian State Film Archive, Moscow
RGAKFD, Russian State Archive for Film and Photo Documents, Krasnogorsk (Moscow region)
RGALI, Russian State Archive for Literature and Arts, Moscow
RGANI, Russian State Archive for Recent History, Moscow
RGASPI, Russian State Archive for Social and Political Research, Moscow
TsAMO RF, Central Archive of the Ministry of Defense of the Russian Federation, Podol′sk (Moscow region)

BOOKS AND ARTICLES

Abramov, Aleksandr, and Varvara Kochetova. *Znamia pobedy nad Berlinom.* Nizhnii Novgorod: Ekstra N, 2007.

Abramov, S., and S. Kruzhkov. "Iurii Ozerov v rabote i razmyshleniiakh." *Iskusstvo kino*, no. 5 (1974): 88–102.

Aksiutin, Iurii. *Khrushchevskaia "ottepel′" i obshchestvennye nastroeniia v SSSR v 1953–1964 gg.* Moscow: ROSSPEN, 2010.

Aleksandrov, G. F., et al., eds. *Joseph Stalin: A Short Biography.* 2nd rev. ed. Moscow: Foreign Languages Publishing House, 1949.

Anderson, K. M., and L. V. Maksimenkov, eds. *Kul′tura i vlast′ ot Stalina do Gorbacheva. Kremlevskii kinoteatr 1928–1953; Dokumenty.* Moscow: ROSSPEN, 2005.

Anonymous. *A Woman in Berlin.* Translated by James Stern. London: Secker & Warburg, 1955.

Anushevskaia, Anastasiia. "Chto takoe dvizhenie 'Iunarmiia' i zachem ono nuzhno?" *Argumenty i fakty*, 4 August 2016. http://www.aif.ru/dontknows/actual/chto_takoe_dvizhenie_yunarmiya_i_zachem_ono_nuzhno.

Andzhaparidze, M., and V. Tsirgiladze. "Kak sozdavalsia fil′m 'Padenie Berline.'" *Iskusstvo kino*, no. 4 (1950): 22–26.

Arsenin, A. *Tsentral′nyi muzei Sovetskoi Armii*. Moscow: Moskovskii rabochii, 1953.

Assmann, Aleida. "Transformations between History and Memory." *Social Research* 75, no. 1 (2008): 49–72.

Balina, Marina. "Prose after Stalin." In *The Cambridge Companion to Twentieth-Century Russian Literature*, edited by Evgeny Dobrenko and Marina Balina, 153–73. Cambridge: Cambridge University Press, 2011.

Baranov, V. P., et al., eds. *Velikaia otechestvennaia voina 1941–1945 godov*. 12 vols. Moscow: Kuchkovo pole, 2015.

Barany, Zoltan D. *Democratic Breakdown and the Decline of the Russian Military*. Princeton, NJ: Princeton University Press, 2007.

Barbat, Victor. "Bannières et drapeaux, sur quelques manières de les lever et de les représenter: L'exemple du Reichstag, mai 1945." *1895*, no. 74 (2014): 70–95.

Barber, John. "The Image of Stalin in Soviet Propaganda and Public Opinion during World War Two." In *World War 2 and the Soviet People: Selected Papers from the Fourth World Congress for Soviet and East European Studies, Harrogate, 1990*, edited by John Garrard and Carol Garrard, 38–49. Basingstoke: Macmillan, 1993.

Baron, Jaimie. *The Archive Effect: Found Footage and the Audiovisual Experience of History*. London: Routledge, 2014.

Beevor, Antony. *Berlin 1945: The Downfall*. London: Penguin, 2003.

Belting, Hans. *An Anthropology of Images: Picture, Medium, Body*. Translated by Thomas Dunlap. Princeton, NJ: Princeton University Press, 2011.

Berlinskaia operatsiia 1945 goda. Moscow: Voennoe izdatel′stvo soiuza SSSR, 1950.

Berman, Vladimir. "Znamia nad reikhstagom. O tekh, kto snimal istoricheskie kadry." *Lekhaim*, May 2005. http://lechaim.ru/ARHIV/157/berman.htm.

Bernstein, Seth. "Remembering War, Remaining Soviet: Digital Commemoration of World War II in Putin's Russia." *Memory Studies* 9, no. 4 (2016): 422–36.

Beumers, Birgit. "Sergei Loznitsa, 'State Funeral (2019).'" *Kinokultura*, no. 67 (2020). http://www.kinokultura.com/2020/67r-statefuneral.shtml.

Bialer, Seweryn, ed. *Stalin and His Generals: Soviet Military Memoirs of World War II*. Boulder, CO: Westview Press, 1984.

"Bitva za Berlin." In *Ekran 1970–71*, 20–22. Moscow: Iskusstvo, 1971.

Bjorn, Peter. "'Etot flag byl v Berline! Eto flag moego naroda,' Svetlana GladysS heva otkazalas′ubrat′ Znamia Pobedy." *Sports.ru*, 22 February 2018. https://www.sports.ru/tribuna/blogs/mama4h/1593866.html.

Black, Jeremy. *Rethinking World War Two: The Conflict and Its Legacy*. London: Bloomsbury Academic, 2015.

Bobylev, I. F. *Vsadniki s Krasnoi Ploshchadi. Svidetel′stva ochevidtsa*. Moscow: Izdatel′skii tsentr "Fedorov," 2000.

Bol′shakov, Ivan, et al. "Vsesoiuznoe soveshchanie rabotnikov khudozhestvene noi kinematografii po obsuzhdeniiu resheniia TsK VKP(b) O kinofil′me 'Bol′shaia Zhizn′ (2 Seriia), 14–15 oktiabria 1946 goda." In *Zhivye golosa kino. Govoriat vydaiushchiesia mastera otechestvennogo kinoiskusstva (30-e–40-e gody). Iz neopublikovannogo*, edited by L. A. Parfenov, 308–84. Moscow: Belyi bereg, 1999.

Bolter, Jay David, and Richard Grusin. *Remediation: Understanding New Media*. Cambridge, MA: MIT Press, 1999.

Boltin, Evgenii. "Epopeia osvobozhdeniia. Mysli voennogo istorika." *Iskusstvo kino*, no. 5 (1972): 41–54.

Bondarev, Iurii, Oskar Kurganov, and Iurii Ozerov. "Bitva za Berlin. Osvobozhdenie fil′m 5." *Iskusstvo kino*, no. 5 (1970): 20–66.

Bonnell, Victoria E. "The Leader's Two Bodies: A Study in the Iconography of the Vozhd′." *Russian History/Histoire russe* 23, no. 1–4 (1996): 113–40.

Brandenberger, David. *National Bolshevism: Stalinist Mass Culture and the Formation of Modern Russian National Identity, 1931–1956*. Cambridge, MA: Harvard University Press, 2002.

Brandenberger, David. "Stalin as Symbol: A Case Study of the Personality Cult and Its Construction." In *Stalin: A New History*, edited by Sarah Davies and James Harris, 249–70. Cambridge: Cambridge University Press, 2005.

Brezhnev, Leonid. *Vospominaniia*. Moscow: Politicheskaia literature, 1982.

Brooks, Jeffrey. *Thank You, Comrade Stalin! Soviet Public Culture from Revolution to Cold War*. Princeton, NJ: Princeton University Press, 2000.

Burgoyne, Robert. Introduction to *The Epic Film in World Culture*, edited by Robert Burgoyne, 1–16. New York: Routledge, 2011.

Bykov, Dmitrii. *Bulat Okudzhava*. Moscow: Molodaia gvardiia, 2009.

Campbell, James. "Combat Gnosticism: The Ideology of First World War Poetry Criticism." *New Literary History* 30, no. 1 (1999): 203–15.

Central Museum of the Soviet Army. *Relikvii boevoi slavy*. Moscow: Voennoe izdatel′stvo Ministerstva oborony SSSR, 1962.

Chernysheva, Elena. "Voennaia rekonstruktsiia vziatiia Berlina." *Odessit.ua*, 2012. Accessed 3 June 2018 (no longer available). http://www.odessit.ua/photo/389-voennaya-rekonstrukciya-vzyatie-reyhstaga.html.

Chertok, Mikhail. *Muzykanty Parada Pobedy*. Moscow: Kanon+, 2015.

Chertok, S. "Nikolai Olialin." In *Ekran 1971–72*, 60–62. Moscow: Iskusstvo, 1972.

Chiaureli, Mikhail. "Bessmertie." *Sovetskoe iskusstvo*, 14 March 1953, 2.

Chiaureli, Mikhail. "Ob Izobrazitel′noi forme kinofil′ma." In *Voprosy masterstva v sovetskom kinoiskusstve: Sbornik statei*. Edited by B. Kravchenko. Moscow: Goskinoizdat, 1952. 43–78.

Christie, Ian. "Canons and Careers: The Director in Soviet Cinema." In *Stalinism and Soviet Cinema*, edited by Richard Taylor and Derek Spring, 142–70. London: Routledge, 1993.

Chuikov, Vasilii. "Podvig bessmerten." *Sovetskii ekran*, no. 9 (1980): 1.

Cruz, Trent. "'It's Almost Too Intense': Nostalgia and Authenticity in *Call of Duty 2*." *Loading . . . 1*, no. 1 (2007).

Danilova, Nataliya. *The Politics of War Commemoration in the UK and Russia*. London: Palgrave-Macmillan, 2015.

Davies, R. W. *Soviet History in the Gorbachev Revolution*. Basingstoke: Macmillan, 1989.

Dement′ev, Arkadii. *Znamia Pobedy. Glavnaia relikviia Velikoi Otechestvennoi voiny v svete istoricheskikh issledovanii*. Moscow: Granitsa, 2015.

Dick, Bernard F. *The Star-Spangled Screen: The American World War II Film*. Lexington: University Press of Kentucky, 1985.

Dommanget, Maurice. *Histoire du drapeau rouge: Des origines à la guerre de 1939*. Paris: Librairie de l'Étoile, 1967.

Drobashenko, Sergei. "Soviet Film Chronicles and the Fall of Nazi Germany." In *Hitler's Fall: The Newsreel Witness*, edited by K. R. M. Short and Stephan Dolezel, 50–56. London: Croom Helm, 1988.

Drozdovskii, E. A., et al. *Tverichi na Parade Pobedy*. Tver′: Litera-M, 2000.

Dubin, Boris. "Pamiat′, voina, pamiat′ o voine. Konstruirovanie proshlogo v sotsial′noi praktike poslednikh desiatiletii." *Otechestvennye zapiski* 4, no. 43 (2008). http://www.intelros.ru/intelros/reiting/reyting_09/material_sofiy/5023-boris-dubin-pamyat-vojna-pamyat-o-vojne-konstruirovanie-proshlogo-v-socialnoj-praktike-poslednix-desyatiletij.html.

Dunmore, Timothy. *Soviet Politics, 1945–1953*. London: Macmillan, 1984.

Durkheim, Emile. *The Elementary Forms of Religious Life*. Translated and with an introduction by Karen E. Fields. New York: Free Press, 1995.

Edele, Mark. *Soviet Veterans of the Second World War: A Popular Movement in an Authoritarian Society, 1941–1991*. Oxford: Oxford University Press, 2008.

Edelman, Murray. *Constructing the Political Spectacle*. Chicago: University of Chicago Press, 1988.

Edelman, Murray. *The Symbolic Uses of Politics*. Urbana: University of Illinois Press, 1964.

"Egorov i Kantariia byli ne pervymi." *Argumenty i fakty*, 7 May 2003. http://www.aif.ru/archive/1628792.

Erickson, John. *The Road to Berlin*. Vol. 2 of *Stalin's War with Germany*. London: Weidenfeld and Nicolson, 1983.

Erll, Astrid. "Cultural Memory Studies: An Introduction." In *A Companion to Cultural Memory Studies*, edited by Astrid Erll, Ansgar Nünning, and in collaboration with Sara B. Young, 1–15. Berlin: De Gruyter, 2010.

Erll, Astrid. *Memory in Culture*. Translated by Sara B. Young. Basingstoke: Palgrave Macmillan, 2011.

Etkind, Alexander. "Hard and Soft in Cultural Memory: Political Mourning in Russia and Germany." *Grey Room*, no. 16 (2004): 36–59.

Etkind, Alexander. *Warped Mourning: Stories of the Undead in the Land of the Unburied*. Stanford, CA: Stanford University Press, 2013.

Evans, Christine E. *Between Truth and Time: A History of Soviet Central Television*. New Haven, CT: Yale University Press, 2016.

Figes, Orlando, and Boris Kolonitskii. *Interpreting the Russian Revolution: The Language and Symbols of 1917*. New Haven, CT: Yale University Press, 1999.

Fomin, Valerii, ed. *Kino na voine. Dokumenty i svidetel′stva*. Moscow: Materik, 2005.

Forest, Benjamin, and Juliet Johnson. "Unraveling the Threads of History: Soviet-Era Monuments and Post-Soviet National Identity in Moscow." *Annals of the Association of American Geographers* 92, no. 3 (2004): 524–47.

Gallagher, Matthew. "Trends in Soviet Historiography of the Second World War." In *Contemporary History in the Soviet Mirror*, edited by John Keep and Liliana Brisby. New York: Frederick A. Praeger, 1964.

Garde-Hansen, Joanne, Andrew Hoskins, and Anna Reading, eds. *Save As . . . Digital Memories*. Basingstoke: Palgrave Macmillan, 2009.

Gerasimov, E., ed. *Shturm Berlina. Vospominaniia, pis′ma, dnevniki uchastnikov boev za Berlin*. Moscow: Voennoe izdatel′stvo ministerstva vooruzhennykh sil SSSR, 1948.

Gerasimov, Sergei. "O professii kinorezhissera." In *Voprosy masterstva v sovetskom kinoiskusstve: Sbornik statei*, edited by B. Kravchenko, 7–42. Moe scow: Goskinoizdat, 1952.

Geroicheskaia oborona Brestskoi kreposti. Po dokumentam i relikviiam Tsentral′nogo muzeia Sovetskoi Armii. Moscow: Voennoe izdatel′stvo Ministerstva oborony SSSR, 1955.

Ghosh, Bishnupriya. *Global Icons: Apertures to the Popular*. Durham, NC: Duke University Press, 2011.

Gilburd, Eleonory. *To See Paris and Die: The Soviet Lives of Western Culture*. Cambridge, MA: Belknap Press of Harvard University Press, 2018.

Gill, Graeme. *Symbols and Legitimacy in Soviet Politics*. Cambridge: Cambridge University Press, 2011.

Gorlizki, Yoram, and Oleg Khlevniuk. *Cold Peace: Stalin and the Soviet Ruling Circle, 1945–1953*. Oxford: Oxford University Press, 2004.

Grechko, A. A., et al., eds. *Istoriia vtoroi mirovoi voiny.* 12 vols. Moscow: Voennoe izdatel'stvo Ministerstva Oborony SSSR, 1973–1982.

Grosset, Mark. *Khaldei: Un photoreporteur en Union Soviétique.* Paris: Éditions du Chêne, 2004.

Groys, Boris. *The Total Art of Stalinism: Avant-Garde, Aesthetic Dictatorship, and Beyond.* Translated by Charles Rougle. Princeton, NJ: Princeton University Press, 1992.

Hariman, Robert, and John Louis Lucaites. *No Caption Needed: Iconic Photographs, Public Culture, and Liberal Democracy.* Chicago: University of Chicago Press, 2007.

Hell, Julia, and Andreas Schönle. Introduction to *Ruins of Modernity*, edited by Julia Hell and Andreas Schönle, 1–16. Durham, NC: Duke University Press, 2010.

Hervieu-Léger, Danièle. *Religion as a Chain of Memory.* Translated by Simon Lee. Cambridge: Polity Press, 2000.

Hicks, Jeremy. *Dziga Vertov: Defining Documentary Film.* London: I. B. Tauris, 2007.

Hicks, Jeremy. "A Holy Relic of War: The Soviet Victory Banner as Artefact." In *Remembering the Second World War*, edited by Patrick Finney, 197–216. London: Routledge, 2017.

Hirsch, Joshua. *Afterimage: Film, Trauma, and the Holocaust.* Philadelphia: Temple University Press, 2004.

Hobsbawm, Eric. "Introduction: Inventing Traditions." In *The Invention of Tradition*, edited by Eric Hobsbawm and Terence Ranger, 1–14. 1983. Cambridge: Cambridge University Press, 2002.

Hösler, Joachim. "Chto znachit 'Prorabotka proshlogo?' Ob istoriografii Velikoi Otechestvennoi Voiny v SSSR i Rossii." In *Pamiat′ o voine 60 let spustia: Rossiia, Germaniia, Evropa.* Moscow: Novoe literaurnoe obozrenie, 2005.

Hosking, Geoffrey A. *Russia: People and Empire, 1552–1917.* Cambridge, MA: Harvard University Press, 1997.

Hutchings, Stephen, and Natalia Rulyova. "Commemorating the Past/Performing the Present: Television Coverage of the Second World War Victory Celebrations and the (De)Construction of Russian Nationhood." In *The Post-Soviet Russian Media: Conflicting Signals*, edited by Birgit Beumers, Stephen Hutchings, and Natalia Rulyova, 137–55. London: Routledge, 2009.

Hynes, Samuel. *The Soldier's Tale: Bearing Witness to Modern War.* New York: Penguin, 1998.

Iamskoi, Nikolai. *Kto bral Reikhstag. Geroi po umolchaniiu.* Moscow: Olma Press, 2006.

Iangirov, Rashit. "Proshchanie s mertvym telom. Ob odnom siuzhete rossiiskogo ekrannogo ofitsioza i ego Podtekstakh." *Otechestvennye zapiski* 35, no. 2 (2007). http://www.strana-oz.ru/2007/2/proshchanie-s-mertvym-telom.

Innes, Paul. *Epic*. London: Routledge, 2013.

Iurenev, Rostislav. "Rosomakha." In *Boris Andreev: Vospominaniia, stat'i, vystupleniia, aforizmy*, edited by B. B. Andreev, 73–82. Moscow: Iskusstvo, 1991.

Jones, Polly. *Myth, Memory, Trauma: Rethinking the Stalinist Past in the Soviet Union, 1953–70*. New Haven, CT: Yale University Press, 2013.

Juul, Jesper. "Fear of Failing? The Many Meanings of Difficulty in Video Games." In *The Video Game Theory Reader 2*, edited by Bernard Perron and Mark J. P. Wolf, 237–52. London: Routledge, 2009.

Kamshalov, Aleksandr. *Geroika podviga na ekrane. Voenno-patrioticheskaia tema v sovetskom kinematografe*. Moscow: Iskusstvo, 1986.

Kapterev, Sergei. *Post-Stalinist Cinema and the Russian Intelligentsia, 1953–1960: Strategies of Self-Representation, De-Stalinization and the National Cultural Tradition*. Saarbrücken, Germany: Verlag Dr. Müller, 2005.

Karavaev, Dmitrii. "Newsreels of Soviet Military Parades as Component of Victory: Some Ineffective Examples." Paper presented at the workshop Iconic and the Archival: Images and Russian Memory of World War Two, Queen Mary University of London, 25 May 2017.

Karmen, Roman. "Surovaia Pravda." *Iskusstvo kino*, no. 2 (1968): 39.

Kaz[i]uchitz, Maksim. "'Sovpolikadr'. Poliekrannyi i polikadrovyi fil'm v istoѳrii kinematografii 1960-kh–1980-kh," *Kinovedcheskie zapiski*, no. 104–105 (2013): 388–96.

Kenez, Peter. *Cinema and Soviet Society from the Revolution to the Death of Stalin*. Rev. and updated ed. London: I. B. Tauris, 2008.

Kershaw, Ian. *The End: Germany 1944–45*. London: Penguin, 2011.

Khaniutin, Iurii. "'Kogda pushki streliaiut. . . . '" *Iskusstvo kino*, no. 5 (1965): 1–25.

Khaniutin, Iurii. "Vozvrashchennoe vremia." *Iskusstvo kino*, no. 7 (1977): 86–97.

Khlevniuk, Oleg V. *Stalin: New Biography of a Dictator*. Translated by Nora Seligman Favorov. New Haven, CT: Yale University Press, 2015.

Knorring, Oleg. "Berlinskii reportazh." In *Poslednii shturm*, edited by Konstantin Telegin. Moscow: Izdatel'stvo politicheskoi literatury, 1965.

Kochetov, Andrei. "Magnitnye polia Leiptsiga." *Sovetskii ekran*, no. 16 (1980): 16–17.

Kolin, N. "V Pomoshch' Nachinaiushchemu stsenaristu." In *Konkurs na kinotsenarii*, 11–25. Moscow: Goskinoizdat, 1938.

Kolodiazhnaia, V. *Boris Andreev*. Moscow: Goskinoizdat, 1951.

Kozlov, Denis. "The Historical Turn in Late Soviet Culture: Retrospectivism, Factography, Doubt, 1953–91." *Kritika*, n.s. 2, no. 3 (2001): 577–600.

Krivonogov, Petr. "Den' Pobedy. Iz dnevnika voennogo khudozhnika." *Sovetskoe iskusstvo*, no. 37 (1951): 1.

Kruglov, Sergei. "Istoriiu ne perepishesh′." *Voenno-promyshlennyi kur′er*, 9 May 2007. http://vpk-news.ru/articles/3637.

Krylova, Anna. "'Healers of Wounded Souls': The Crisis of Private Life in Soviet Literature, 1944–1946." *Journal of Modern History* 73, no. 2 (2001): 307–31.

Kuby, Erich. *The Russians and Berlin, 1945*. Translated by Arnold J. Pomerans. London: Heinemann, 1965.

Kudryashov, Sergei. "Remembering and Researching the War: The Soviet and Russian Experience." In *Experience and Memory: The Second World War in Europe*, edited by Jörg Echternkamp and Stefan Martens, 86–115. New York: Berghahn Books, 2010.

Kulish, V. M. "Sovetskaia istoriografiia Velikoi Otechestvennoi voiny." In *Sovetskaia Istoriografiia*, edited by Iu. N. Afanas′ev, 274–315. Moscow: Rossiiskii gosudarstvennyi gumanitarnyi universitet, 1996.

Kumanev, Georgii. *Podvig i podlog. Stranitsy Velikoi Otechestvennoi voiny 1941–1945 gg.* Moscow: Russkoe slovo, 2000.

Leibovich, Oleg. *Reforma i modernizatsiia v 1953–1964 gg.* Perm′: Izd. Permskogo universiteta, 1993.

Levchenko, Grigory. "How Russia Prosecutes Its Own People for 'Falsifying History.'" Translated by Peter Marshall. *Meduza*, 11 May 2018. https://meduza.io/en/feature/2018/05/11/how-russia-prosecutes-its-own-people-for-falsifying-history.

Le Tissier, Tony. *Race for the Reichstag: The 1945 Battle for Berlin*. London: Frank Cass, 1999.

Lozin, Dmitrii. *Znamia Pobedy—gosudarstvennaia relikviia Rossii. Voenno-istoricheskie ocherki*. Moscow: Zhizn′, 2014.

Maisurian, Aleksandr. *Drugoi Brezhnev*. Moscow: Vagrius, 2004.

Maksimenkov, Leonid. "Arkhivno-istoricheskoe obespechenie nyneshnego i budushchikh iubileev." In *Pobeda-70. Rekonstruktsiia iubileia*, edited by Gennadii Bordiugov, 381–448. Moscow: AIRO-XXI, 2015.

Mal′tsev, Vadim. *Po stranitsam voennogo dnevnika. Ot nachala voiny do Parada Pobedy*. 2nd rev. ed. Moscow: Avanglion-print, 2013.

Manevich, I. *Mikhail Chiaureli*. Moscow: Goskinoizdat, 1953.

March, Luke. *The Communist Party in Post-Soviet Russia*. Manchester: Manchester University Press, 2002.

Markwick, Roger. *Rewriting History in Soviet Russia: The Politics of Revisionist History, 1956–74*. New York: Palgrave, 2001.

Medinskii, Vladimir. *Voina. Mify SSSR. 1939–1945*. 2nd ed. Moscow: OLMA Media Grupp, 2014.

Medvedev, Boris. "Eto bylo pri nas. . . ." *Iskusstvo kino*, no. 8 (1965): 18–23.

Medvedev, Roi. *Lichnost′ i epokha. Politicheskii portret L. I. Brezhneva; Kn. 1*. Moscow: Novosti, 1991.

Merridale, Catherine. *Ivan's War: The Red Army 1939–1945*. London: Faber and Faber, 2005.

Merridale, Catherine. *Night of Stone: Death and Memory in Twentieth-Century Russia*. New York: Viking, 2001.

Merridale, Catherine. *Red Fortress: The Secret Heart of Russia's History*. London: Penguin, 2013.

Mikhailov, Vladimir. *Frontovoi kinoreportazh*. Moscow: Nauchno-issledovatel′nyi institut teorii i istorii kino, 1977.

Miller, John. *Mikhail Gorbachev and the End of Soviet Power*. Basingstoke: Macmillan and St. Martin's Press, 1993.

Mlechin, Leonid. *Brezhnev*. Moscow: Molodaia gvardiia, 2011.

Molotov, Viacheslav. *Stalin and Stalin's Leadership*. Moscow: Foreign Languages Publishing House, 1950.

Moos, David. "Utopian Construction? The Work of Frank Thiel." In *Frank Thiel: A Berlin Decade, 1995–2005*, edited by Robert Hobbs and David Moos. Madrid: Hatje Cantz, 2006.

Mori, Masaki. *Epic Grandeur: Toward a Comparative Poetics of the Epic*. Albany: State University of New York Press, 1997.

Muratov, L. "Fil′my v bor′be idei." In *Pamiat′ grozovykh let. Velikaia otechestvennaia voina v sovetskom kino 1970-kh godov*, edited by N. Zaitsev et al., 6–30. Leningrad: Iskusstvo, 1980.

Muratov, Sergei, and Georgii Fere. "Sovetskoi kul′tury" and "Ekrany maia" columns. *Sovetskaia kul′tura*, 3 June 1965.

Naimark, Norman M. *The Russians in Germany: A History of the Soviet Zone of Occupation, 1945–1949*. Cambridge, MA: Belknap Press of Harvard University Press, 1995.

Nakhimovsky, Alice, and Alexander Nakhimovsky. *Witness to History: The Photography of Yevgeny Khaldei*. New York: Aperture, 1997.

Neustroev, Stepan. *Put′ k reikhstagu*. Moscow: Voennoe izdatel′stvo Ministerstva Oborony Soiuza SSR, 1961.

Neustroev, Stepan. "O Reikhstage na sklone let." *Oktiabr′* 5 (1990): 130–44.

Nora, Pierre. "Entre mémoire et histoire: La problématique des lieux." In *Les lieux de* mémoire, edited by Pierre Nora, 23–43. Paris: Gallimard Quarto, 1997.

Nove, Alec. *An Economic History of the U.S.S.R.* Harmondsworth: Penguin, 1969.

Odom, William E. *The Collapse of the Soviet Military*. New Haven, CT: Yale University Press, 1998.

Odom, William E. "The Military and the State: Contemporary Russia in Historical Perspective." In *The Military History of the Soviet Union*, edited by Robin Higham and Frederick W. Kagan, 299–318. New York: Palgrave, 2002.

O'Neil, Mark. "The Cold War on the Ground, 1945–1981." In *The Military History of the Soviet Union*, edited by Robin Higham and Frederick W. Kagan, 221–36. New York: Palgrave, 2002.

Orlov, Dal′. "Zavershenie epopei." *Iskusstvo kino*, no. 2 (1972): 6–14.

"O sovetskom cheloveke, o sovetskom narode." *Iskusstvo kino*, no. 8 (1982): 94–105.

Oushakine, Serguei. "Remembering in Public: On the Affective Management of History." *Ab Imperio*, no. 1 (2013): 269–302.

"O vsesoiuznoi khudozhestvennoi vystavke." *Iskusstvo*, no. 1 (1947): 6–10.

Ozerov, Iurii. "Na NP." *Iskusstvo kino*, no. 5 (1975): 70–73.

Ozerov, Iurii. "Vosslavit′ podvig naroda." *Iskusstvo kino*, no. 2 (1971): 1–4.

Panov, Ivan. "Nad Reichstagom znamia." In *Ikh oruzhie—kinokamera*, edited by Valentin Zeltov and Aleksei Lebedev, 271–80. Moscow: Iskusstvo, 1970.

Parfenov, Denis. "Vytravlivanie gosudarstvennykh simvolov SSSR so Znameni Pobedy mozhet byt′ rastseneno kak ideologicheskaia diversiia." Communist Party of the Russian Federation, 6 February 2018. https://kprf.ru/dep/gosduma/activities/172751.html.

Parker, John W. *Kremlin in Transition*. Vol. 2, *Gorbachev, 1985 to 1989*. Boston: Unwin Hyman, 1991.

Pastoreau, Michel. *Une histoire symbolique du moyen* âge *occidental*. Paris: Seuil, 2004.

Pavlenko, Petr. *Kinostsenarii*. Moscow: Goskinoizdat, 1952.

Pavlovskii, Ivan. "Iazykom faktov i dokumentov." *Sovetskaia kul′tura*, 9 May 1985, 8.

Petrone, Karen. *Life Has Become More Joyous, Comrades: Celebrations in the Time of Stalin*. Bloomington: Indiana University Press, 2000.

Plamper, Jan. *The Stalin Cult: A Study in the Alchemy of Power*. New Haven, CT: Yale University Press, 2012.

Pogozheva, L. "Padenie Berlina." *Iskusstvo kino*, no. 4 (1950): 10–14.

Polian, Pavel. *Istoriomor, ili trepanatsiia pamiati*. Moscow: AST, 2016.

Pospelov, P[etr] N[ikolevich], E[vgenii] A[rsenevich] Boltin, and V. P. Moskovskii. *Istoriia Velikoi Otechestvennoi Voiny Sovetskogo Soiuza 1941–1945*. 6 vols. Moscow: Voennoe izdatel′stvo ministerstva oborony SSSR, 1963.

Prokhorova, Alexander, and Elena Prokhorov. *Film and Television Genres of the Late Soviet Era*. New York: Bloomsbury, 2017.

Pudovkin, Vsevolod. "Podlinnaia narodnost′." *Sovetskoe iskusstvo*, no. 4 (1950): 4.

Putin, Vladimir. "International Holocaust Remembrance Day." Jewish Museum and Tolerance Center, Moscow, 27 January 2015. http://en.kremlin.ru/events/president/transcripts/47529.

Putin, Vladimir. "Speech at the Forum 'Let My People Live!' Commemorating the Memory of the Victims of Auschwitz." 27 January 2005, Krakow, Poland. http://en.kremlin.ru/events/president/transcripts/22800.

Pyzhikov, Aleksandr. *Opyt modernizatsii sovetskogo obshchestva v 1953–1964 godakh. Obshchestvenno-politicheskii aspekt.* Moscow: Gamma, 1998.

Raack, Richard C. "The Red Army Beflags the Reichstag: Film as Historical Fantasy." In *Hitler's Fall: The Newsreel Witness*, edited by K. R. M. Short and Stephan Dolezel, 57–69. London: Croom Helm, 1988.

Raack, Richard C. *Stalin's Drive to the West, 1938–1945: The Origins of the Cold War.* Stanford, CA: Stanford University Press, 1995.

Raizman, Iulii. *"Berlin."* In *Ikh oruzhue—kinokamera*, edited by V. I. Zheltov and A. A. Lebedev, 282–88. Moscow: Iskusstvo, 1970.

Raizman, Iulii. *Vchera i segodnia.* Moscow: Biuro propagandy sovetskogo kinoiskusstva, 1969.

Ramazashvili, Georgii. "Est′ takaia professiia—istoriiu zashchishchat′: TsAr MO RF v predverii 60-iia Pobedy." In *Pamiat′ o voine 60 let spustia: Rossiia, Germaniia, Evropa*, edited by Il′ia Kalinin and Mikhail Gabovich, 293–313. Moscow: Novoe literaturnoe obozrenie, 2005.

Rees, E. A[rfon]. "Leader Cults: Varieties, Preconditions and Functions." In *The Leader Cult in Communist Dictatorships: Stalin and the Eastern Bloc*, edited by Balázs Apor et al., 3–28. Basingstoke: Palgrave Macmillan, 2004.

Reuveny, Rafael, and Aseem Prakash. "The Afghanistan War and the Breakdown of the Soviet Union." *Review of International Studies*, no. 25 (1999): 693–708.

Richie, Alexandra. *Faust's Metropolis: A History of Berlin.* London: HarperCollins, 1999.

Rodchenko, Aleksandr. "The Paths of Contemporary Photography." In *Experiments for the Future: Diaries, Essays, Letters, and Other Writings*, edited by Alexander N. Lavrentiev, 207–12. New York: Museum of Modern Art, 2005.

Rohdewald, Stefan. "Post-Soviet Remembrance of the Holocaust and National Memories of the Second World War in Russia, Ukraine and Lithuania." *Forum for Modern Language Studies* 44, no. 2 (2008): 173–84.

Rolf, Malte. *Soviet Mass Festivals, 1917–1991.* Translated by Cynthia Klohr. Pittsburgh, PA: University of Pittsburgh Press, 2013.

Romm, Mikhail. *Izbrannye proizvedeniia.* Edited by Natal′ia Kuz′mina. 3 vols. Moscow: Iskusstvo, 1980–1982.

Rosenstone, Robert A. *History on Film/Film on History.* 2nd ed. Harlow: Pearson, 2012.

Rothberg, Michael. *Multidirectional Memory: Remembering the Holocaust in the Age of Decolonization.* Stanford, CA: Stanford University Press, 2009.

Rubenstein, Joshua. *The Last Days of Stalin.* New Haven, CT: Yale University Press, 2016.

Rubenstein, Joshua. "World War Two—Soviet Style." In *New Challenges for Documentary*, edited by Alan Rosenthal, 465–70. Berkeley: University of California Press, 1988.

Rudnev, V. A. *Prazdniki, obriady, ritualy v trudovom kollektive.* Moscow: Profizdat, 1984.

Russell, James. *The Historical Epic and Contemporary Hollywood: From "Dances with Wolves" to "Gladiator."* New York: Continuum, 2007.

Rzhevskaia, Elena. *Berlin, mai 1945. Zapiski voennogo perevodchika*. Moscow: TERRA-Knizhnyi klub, 2005.

Sakwa, Richard. *Putin Redux: Power and Contradiction in Contemporary Russia*. London: Routledge, 2014.

Samsonov, Konstantin. *Shturm Reikhstaga*. Moscow: DOSAAF, 1955.

Saprykov, V. N. *Dvazhdy pobednoe*. Moscow: Moskovskie uchebniki—SiDipress, 2008.

Sartre, Jean-Paul. "Discussion on the Criticism of *Ivan's Childhood*." *L'Unità*, 9 October 1962. Published in French in Sartre's *Situations VII*. Paris: Gallimard 1965.

Schattenberg, Susanne. *Velichie i tragediia cheloveka i strany*. Translated by V. A. Brun-Tsekhovskii. Moscow: Politicheskaia entsiklopediia, 2018. Originally published as *Leonid Breschnew: Staatsmann und Schauspieler im Schatten Stalins; Eine Biographie*. Cologne: Böhlau, 2017.

Schleifman, Nurit. "Moscow's Victory Park: A Monumental Change." *History and Memory* 13, no. 2 (2001): 5–34.

Service, Robert. *Stalin: A Biography*. London: Pan, 2010.

Shatilov, Vasilii. *V boiakh rozhdennoe znamia*. 2nd rev. and expanded ed. Moscow: Sovetskaia Rossiia, 1988.

Shaw, Tony, and Denise J. Youngblood. *Cinematic Cold War: The American and Soviet Struggle for Hearts and Minds*. Lawrence: University Press of Kansas, 2010.

Shcherbina, N. *Padenie Berlina. (Ocherk o kinofil′me)*. Moscow: Goskinoizdat, 1950.

Shkol′nikov, Semen. "Tiazhkii put′ kinokhronikera." *Iskusstvo kino*, no. 6 (2008). Accessed 22 May 2018. http://kinoart.ru/ru/archive/2008/06/n6-article14.

Shneer, David. *Through Soviet Jewish Eyes: Photography, War and the Holocaust*. New Brunswick, NJ: Rutgers University Press, 2011.

Short, K. R. M. Preface to *Hitler's Fall: The Newsreel Witness*, edited by K. R. M. Short and Stephan Dolezel. London: Croom Helm, 1988.

Shtemenko, Sergei. *The Soviet General Staff at War, 1941–1945*. Translated by Robert Daglish. Moscow: Progress, 1970.

Shukla, Vikas. "Russia's World War II Victory Day Parade: Who Is Coming and Who Isn't." *ValueWalk*, 7 May 2015. https://www.valuewalk.com/2015/05/russia-world-war-ii-victory-day-parade/.

Simonov, Konstantin. *Glazami cheloveka moego pokoleniia*. Moscow: Agentstvo pechati Novosti, 1988.

Simonov, Konstantin. *Simonov i voina*. Moscow: Vremia, 2016.

Slavin, Konstantin. "Velikaia voina i nashe vremia." *Sovetskii ekran*, no. 13 (1965): 12.

Slivko, Stanislav. "Kommunisty vernuli Khabarovskomu kraiu Znamia Pobedy." Communist Party of the Russian Federation. Accessed 28 July 2016. https://kprf.ru/party-live/regnews/127563.html.

Smelser, Ronald, and Edward J. Davies II. *The Myth of the Eastern Front: The Nazi-Soviet War in American Popular Culture*. Cambridge: Cambridge University Press, 2008.

Smirnov, Sergei. *Sobranie sochinenii*. 3 vols. Moscow: Molodaia gvardiia, 1973.

Smith, Kathleen E. *Mythmaking in the New Russia: Politics and Memory during the Yeltsin Era*. Ithaca, NY: Cornell University Press, 2002.

Solonin, Mark. *Zavetnaia pravda o Velikoi Otechestvennoi. Net blaga na voine!* Moscow: Iauza-katalog, 2014.

Sontag, Susan. *Regarding the Pain of Others*. London: Penguin, 2003.

Sontheimer, Michael. "The Art of Soviet Propaganda: Iconic Red Army Reichstag Photo Faked." *Spiegel Online*, 7 May 2008. http://www.spiegel.de/international/europe/the-art-of-soviet-propaganda-iconic-red-army-reichstag-photo-faked-a-551972.html.

Stalin, Iosif. *O Velikoi Otechestvennoi Voine Sovetskogo Soiuza*. 5th ed. Moscow: Gospolitizdat, 1948.

Stalin, Joseph. "Doklad na torzhestvennom zasedanii Moskovskogo Soveta deputatov trudiashikhsia s partiinymi i obshchestvennymi organizatsiiami goroda Moskvy 6 noiabria 1944 goda." 1944. In *Sochineniia*, vol. 15, part 2. Moscow: Izdatel′stvo ITRK, 2009.

Statiev, Alexander. "'La Garde meurt mais ne se rend pas!': Once Again on the 28 Panfilov Heroes." *Kritika: Explorations in Russian and Eurasian History* 13, no. 4 (2012): 769–98.

Stepaniuk, Vladimir. "Vekhi istorii glavnoi redaktsii informatsii TsT." TV Museum. Accessed 1 June 2018 (no longer available). http://tvmuseum.ru/catalog.asp?ob_no=11699.

Stites, Richard. *Russian Popular Culture: Entertainment and Society since 1900*. New York: Cambridge University Press, 1992.

Subbotin, Vassily. "How Wars End." In *How Wars End: Eye-Witness Accounts of the Fall of Berlin*, edited by Vladimir Sevruk, 127–58. Honolulu: University Press of the Pacific, 2005.

Sudarov, B. "Labirinty zhizni Nikolaia Mesiatseva." TV Museum. Accessed 1 June 2018 (no longer available). http://tvmuseum.ru/catalog.asp?ob_no=10852.

Sumenov, Nikolai, and Oleg Sul′kin. *Iurii Ozerov*. Moscow: Iskusstvo, 1986.

Svoichakov, Maksim. *Oni brali reikhstag*. Moscow: Voennoe izdatel′stvo, 1973.

Swick, Gerald D. "WW2 Documentary Unseen for 30 Years Returns on DVD." HistoryNet. Accessed 2 June 2018. http://www.historynet.com/ww2-documentary-unseen-for-30-years-returns-on-dvd.htm.

Synthart (pseudonym). "Eshche o pamiatnike Pobedy na Poklonnoi Gore." Accessed 11 November 2015. http://synthart.livejournal.com/217953.html

Taylor, Richard. *Film Propaganda: Soviet Russia and Nazi Germany*. 2nd ed. London: I. B. Tauris, 1998.

Tel′pukhovskii, Boris, ed. *Ocherki istorii Velikoi Otechestvennoi Voiny 1941–1945*. Moscow: Akademiia nauk SSSR, Institut istorii, 1955.

Thompson, Jenny. *War Games: Inside the World of Twentieth-Century War Reenactors*. Washington, DC: Smithsonian Books, 2010.

Timoshkina, Alissa. "Representations of the Holocaust in Soviet Cinema." PhD diss., King's College London, 2015.

Tolstoi, Andrei. "Khudozhnik na fronte." In *Evgenii Khaldei: Znamia pobedy*, edited by A. V. Maksimova, 4–7. St. Petersburg: Rosfoto, 2015.

Tolstykh, Valentin. *Khochu—mogu—dolzhen. Opyt obshchestvennoi avtobiografii lichnosti*. Moscow: Progress-traditsiia, 2015.

Tomlinina, N. G., et al., eds. *Apparat Tsk KPSS i Kul′tura 1965–1972: Dokumenty*. Moscow: ROSSPEN, 2009.

Tompson, William. *The Soviet Union under Brezhnev*. Harlow: Pearson, 2003.

Trotsky, Leon. *The History of the Russian Revolution, Volume 3: The Triumph of the Soviets*. Proofed and reset by Pablo Stern, converted to eBook format by Kollektiv Yakov Perelman in 2013. Accessed 22 May 2018. https://www.marxists.org/archive/trotsky/1930/hrr/ch44.htm.

Tsentral′nyi Muzei Krasnoi Armii. Kratkii putevoditel′ po zalam ekspozitsii. V pmoshch′ posetiteliu. Moscow: Izdanie Tsentral′nogo Muzeia Krasnoi Armii, 1946.

Tsitriniak, Grigorii. "Napravlenie glavnogo udara." *Iskusstvo kino*, no. 5 (1970): 7–19.

Tucker, Robert C. *The Soviet Political Mind: Studies in Stalinism and Post-Stalin Change*. London: Pall Mall Press, 1963.

Tumarkin, Nina. "The Great Patriotic War as Myth and Memory." *European Review* 11, no. 4 (2002): 595–611.

Tumarkin, Nina. *The Living and the Dead: The Rise and Fall of the Cult of World War II in Russia*. New York: Basic Books, 1994.

"Ukaz ot 23 dekabria 1947 goda: Ob ob′iavlenii 1 ianvaria nerabochim dnem." In *Sbornik zakonov SSSR i ukazov Prezidiuma Verkhovnogo Soveta SSSR, 1938 g.—iiul′ 1956 g.* Edited by Iu. I. Mandel′shtam. Moscow: Gosudarstvennoe izdatel′stvo iuridicheskoi literatury, 1956.

Ul′ianov, Mikhail. *Real′nost′ i mechta*. Moscow: Vagrius, 2007.

Ul′ianov, Vladimir (pseudonym). "Aktsiia kommunistov 'Znamia Pobedy.'" YouTube video, 12 May 2011. https://www.youtube.com/watch?v=N7cAAJKRj_o.

Ushenin, Khristofor. *Petr Aleksandrovich Krivonogov*. Moscow: Sovetskii khudozhnik, 1956.

Uspensky, Boris. *The Semiotics of the Russian Icon*. Edited by Stephen Rudy. Lisse, Netherlands: Peter de Ridder Press, 1976.

Varennikov, Valentin. *Parad Pobedy*. Moscow: Vagrius, 2005.

Vasilevskii, Aleksandr. *Delo vsei zhizni*. 2nd ed. Moscow: Politizdat, 1975.

Vázquez Liñán, Miguel. "History as a Propaganda Tool in Putin's Russia." *Communist and Post-Communist Studies* 43, no. 2 (2010): 167–78.

Volland, Ernst. *Das Banner des Sieges*. Berlin: Berlin Story Verlag, 2008.

Volland, Ernst, and Heinz Krimmer. *Von Moskau nach Berlin: Bilder des russischen Fotografen Jewgeni Chaldej*. Berlin: Nicolaische Verlagsbuchhandlung, 1994.

Vol′man, N. "Pamiat′ i dokument." In *Pamiat′ grozovykh let. Velikaia Otechestvennaia Voina v sovetskom kino 1970-kh godov*, edited by N. Zaitsev, L. Muratov, N. Vol′man and V. Ivanova, 31–52. Leningrad: Iskusstvo, 1980.

von Geldern, James. *Bolshevik Festivals, 1917–1920*. Berkeley: University of California Press, 1993.

Voroshilov, K. E. *Stalin i vooruzhennye sily SSSR*. Moscow: Gosudarstvennoe izdatel′stvo politicheskoi literatury, 1951.

Walker, Shaun. *The Long Hangover: Putin's New Russia and the Ghosts of the Past*. Oxford: Oxford University Press, 2018.

Waterlow, Jonathan. *It's Only a Joke, Comrade: Humour, Trust and Everyday Life under Stalin*. Oxford: n.p., 2018.

Westwell, Guy. *War Cinema: Hollywood on the Front Line*. London: Wallflower, 2006.

Weiner, Amir. *Making Sense of War: The Second World War and the Fate of the Bolshevik Revolution*. Princeton, NJ: Princeton University Press, 2001.

White, Hayden. *Metahistory: The Historical Imagination in Nineteenth-Century Europe*. Baltimore: Johns Hopkins University Press, 1973.

Wieviorka, Annette. *The Era of the Witness*. Translated from French by Jared Stark. Ithaca, NY: Cornell University Press, 2006. Originally published as *L'ère du témoin*, 1998.

Wolfe, Thomas C. *Governing Soviet Journalism: The Press and Soviet Journalism after Stalin*. Bloomington: Indiana University Press, 2005.

Wolfe, Thomas C. "Past as Present, Myth, or History? Discourses of Time and the Great Fatherland War." In *The Politics of Memory in Postwar Europe*, edited by Richard Ned Lebow, Wulf Kansteiner, and Claudio Fogu, 249–83. Durham, NC: Duke University Press, 2006.

Woll, Josephine. *Real Images: Soviet Cinema and the Thaw*. London: I. B. Tauris, 2000.

Wood, Elizabeth A. "Performing Memory: Vladimir Putin and the Celebration of WWII in Russia." *Soviet and Post-Soviet Review* 38 (2011): 172–200.

Woodward, Rachel, and K. Neil Jenkins. *Bringing War to Book: Writing and Producing the Military Memoir*. London: Palgrave Macmillan, 2018.

Wortman, Richard S. *Myth and Ceremony in Russian Monarchy: From Peter the Great to the Abdication of Nicholas II*. Abridged one-volume ed. Princeton, NJ: Princeton University Press, 2006.

Youngblood, Denise J. *Russian War Films: On the Cinema Front, 1914–2005*. Lawrence: University Press of Kansas, 2007.

Youngblood, Denise J. "'When Will the Real Day Come?' War Films and Soviet Post-war Culture." In *Histories of the Aftermath: The Legacies of the Second World War in Europe*, edited by Frank Biess and Robert G. Moeller, 123–38. London: Berghahn Books, 2010.

Yurchak, Alexei. *Everything Was Forever, Until It Was No More: The Last Soviet Generation*. Princeton, NJ: Princeton University Press, 2006.

Zainkin, V. V., ed. *Nashi prazdniki (Sovetskie obshchegosudarstvennye, trudovye, voinskie, molodezhnye i semeino-bytovye prazdniki, obriady, ritualy)*. Moscow: Politizdat, 1977.

Zaitsev, N. "Epos i lichnost′." In *Pamiat′ grozovykh let. Velikaia Otechestvennaia Voina v sovetskom kino 1970-kh godov*, edited by N. Zaitsev, L. Muratov, N. Vol′man, and V. Ivanova. Leningrad: Iskusstvo, 1980.

Zak, Mark. *Iulii Raizman. Mastera kinoiskusstva*. Moscow: Iskusstvo, 1962.

Zemtsov, Ilya. *Chernenko: The Last Bolshevik; The Soviet Union on the Eve of Perestroika*. New Brunswick, NJ: Transaction, 1989.

Zhukov, Georgii. *Vospominaniia i razmyshleniia*. Moscow: Izdatel′stvo agentstvo pechati Novosti, 1972.

Ziemke, Earl F. *The Battle for Berlin: End of the Third Reich*. Vol. 6 of *Purnell's History of the Second World War*. London: Macdonald, 1968.

Zima, V. F. *Golod v SSSR 1946–47 godov. Proiskhozhdenie i posledstviia*. Moscow: Institut rossiiskoi istorii RAN, 1996.

Zinchenko, Fedor. *Geroi shturma reikhstaga*. Moscow: Voennoe izdatel′stvo, 1983.

Zubkova, Elena. *Russia after the War: Hopes, Illusions, and Disappointments, 1945–1957*. Translated by Hugh Ragsdale. Armonk, NY: M. E. Sharpe, 1998.

INDEX

actors, 68, 146, 153, 165; Boris Andreev, 70–71; Mikheil Gelovani, 80, 81; Burt Lancaster, 153, 155, 157, 158; Iurii Nazarov, 195; reenactors, 198–206

Air Time International Company, 151, 152, 153, 160

archives, 15–17, 101, 165, 172, 213; Germany's Bundesarchiv-Filmarchiv, 95; Gosfil′mofond (Russian state film archive), 95, 112; Krasnogorsk archives, 229n69; Russian Ministry of Defense, 106, 173, 213–14

Auschwitz. *See under* concentration camps

authoritarian repetition, notion of, 60, 120, 130, 165, 167, 216, 220

Baltic Republics, 5, 158

Belorus, 97, 103, 143, 158, 203

Berest, Aleksei, 106, 112, 144, 173

Beriia, Lavrentii, 95, 96

Berlin, 21, 103, 118, 120, 121; battle for, 20, 21–22, 34, 97, 114–15, 229n61; Brandenburg Gate, 21, 25, 39, 64; original footage of battle for, 140, 141, 156, 190. *See also Fall of Berlin, The*

Bobylev, Ivan, 45, 231n104

Boltin, Evgenii, 102, 103, 104, 106, 107

Brest Fortress, 16, 113, 121, 155

Brezhnev, Leonid, 117, 123–24, 128, 146, 161, 214; administration of, 134, 246n19; biography of, 243n130; cult of, 131, 165, 218; and Khrushchev, 111; and media, 133, 153, 217; speeches by, 98–99, 125, 137; and Stalin, 129, 130, 136–37

Brooks, Jeffrey, 53, 73

Bubrik, S. D., 118, 119

Bulganin, 55, 82, 87, 94, 97

camera operators, 34–35, 36, 37, 38, 39, 91; Kosmatov, 75, 83

censorship, 31, 65, 93, 133, 149–50, 171

Central Committee of the Party, the, 31, 93, 94–96, 105, 138–39; Presidium of the, 98, 99–100

Central Museum of the Armed Forces, 8, 27–28, 123, 125–26, 156, 173, 198–99; brochure for, 105; Petr Krivonogov painting titled *Victory* (*Pobeda*, 1948) at, 61–64; Victory Banner at, 7, 87, 142, 254n55, 256n93

Central Museum of the Red Army, 17, 28, 46, 48–49, 53, 198

Central Museum of the Soviet Army, 106, 109, 131, 155, 164, 217

Central Studio of Documentary Film (TsSDF), 32, 37
CGI (computer-generated imagery), 190, 195, 196, 197
Chechnya conflict, 181, 184, 204
Chiaureli, Mikheil, 68, 79–80, 81, 90, 91, 94–95; use of color in film by, 74–75, 77, 83; *The Vow* (*Kliatva*) by, 54, 66, 67, 80, 81. *See also Fall of Berlin, The*
Chuikov, Vasilii, 153, 166
Churchill, Winston, 21, 56, 57, 58
cinema, 70, 73, 138, 145, 163, 195; and documentary, 60, 66, 120; and epic form, 146, 147; Ministry of, 68, 80, 119, 120, 151, 153; Soviet, 31, 50, 75, 134, 137, 195; Soviet Council of Ministers' State Committee for, 126, 135; and Stalin cult, 54, 89–96, 115, 217; and television, 131, 148, 169, 189, 194; war and, 86, 98, 99, 130
cinemas and theaters, 122, 126, 131; Rossiia cinema, Pushkin Square, Moscow, 121, 163
cinematography, 31–41, 68, 119, 120, 130, 135, 166
Cold War, 86, 162, 169, 179, 180, 235n45
color film, 47, 68, 91, 135, 139, 151–53; Chiaureli and, 69, 73–75, 77, 83, 91
commemorations, 183, 187; documentary film, 47; in 1965, 217; in 1985, 167, 170; in 1990, 174, 177–78; in 1993, 179
commemorative practices, 126, 129, 209–13; coins and special medals, 128; ritualized nature of, 124, 220
Communist Party: of the Russian Federation (CPRF), 178, 179, 182, 183, 186–87, 199, 206–7, 208; of the Russian Soviet Federal Socialist Republic (banned in 1991), 89, 178; of the Soviet Union (CPSU), 98, 100; of Ukraine (KPU), 202
compilation, 122, 151; documentaries, 113, 147; films, 3, 15, 120, 197
concentration camps, 159, 161, 204; Auschwitz, 159, 161, 180, 186, 203; Majdanek, 159, 161, 180; Willi Bredel's account, 210
Crimea. *See under* Ukraine
cult of personality, 98, 99, 107, 115, 218

Danilov, 111, 112
Davydov, Captain, 53, 97, 111
Defender of the Fatherland Day (23 February), 182, 195
digital technologies, 147, 197, 204, 220
documentaries, 33–34, 90, 96, 107, 126, 149, 155, 166; compilation, 113, 147; "epic," 163, 217–18; fictional, 66–67, 81, 134–40; film, 18, 126, 139; newsreel, 15, 110; on television, 122
documentary filmmakers, 43, 93, 118, 151, 154. *See also* Raizman, Iulii
documentary footage, 145, 166, 196
Dolmatovskii, Evgenii, 28, 56
Donbass region, 50, 70, 202
Donetsk region, 35, 218, 220
Donskoi, Mark, 72, 84
Dubin, Boris, 128, 199
Duma, the, 179, 182, 208
Dzhugashvili, Iakov, 65, 84

Edele, Mark, 128, 129
Egorov, Mikhail, 10, 28, 46, 108, 109, 124, 125; absent from Moscow, 71, 106; dead, 167; in film, 75, 78–80, 111, 144; given awards, 53, 71, 173; with Konstantin Samsonov, 75,

164; with Meliton Kantariia, 20, 97, 104–6, 172–73, 129, 141, 197; memoir of, 171
Eisenhower, Dwight, 21, 56
Eisenstein, Sergei, 26, 68–69, 74
epic, 18, 66, 77, 86, 90, 99, 137, 190; adaptation of *War and Peace*, 145; and "fictional documentary," 65–72, 134–40, 163; form, 134–36, 146–47, 192, 217; narrative, 67, 71, 147–48, 193, 205; sweep of war, 72, 139, 150, 160, 164; tone, 67, 81
Etkind, Alexander, 6, 13–14
Evans, Christine, 147–48, 164

Fall of Berlin, The (*Padenie Berlina*, dir. Mikheil Chiaureli, 1949), 33, 58, 84, 137, 142, 144–45, 81–88; Chiaureli and, 54, 63, 65–66, 69, 73, 95; and disciplining memory, 77–81; epic grandeur of, 71–72; as "fictional documentary" and epic, 65–72; and *Liberation*, 140, 145, 156; still photography from, 74, 76, 85; and the victory banner in, 72–77, 141
fascism, 3, 5, 40, 52, 117, 176, 186; combat with, 114, 186; German, 72, 118; Hitler and, 115, 116; Soviets and, 103, 115–16, 144
film, 16, 50, 107, 112, 131, 138–39, 147, 229n69; festivals, 126, 162; flashbacks in, 91, 112, 120–21, 195; Institut für Wissenschaft und Film (IWF) in Göttingen, 173; scholars, 26, 42, 173; script variants, 84–86; studios, 39, 40, 80, 116, 118, 122; and war, 35, 134–35, 217
filmmakers, 15, 70, 90, 138–39, 146, 154, 157; Soviet 66, 33, 150; and *The Fall of Berlin*, 68, 69; and *The Great Patriotic*, 116, 117, 119
films: *Austerlitz* (dir. Loznitsa, 2016), 204; *Back to the Future*, 195–96; *A Ballad of a Soldier* (*Ballada o soldate*, dir. Grigorii Chukhrai, 1959), 135; *Battleship Potemkin* (*Brononosets Potemkin*, dir. Sergei Eisenstein, 1926), 26, 68–69; *Belorussian Station* (*Belorusskii vokzal*, dir. Andrei Smirnov, 1971), 133; *Come and See* (*Idi i smotri*, dir. Elem Klimov, 1985), 169; *Composition for Victory Day* (*Sochinenie k Dniu Pobedy*, dir. Sergei Urusliak, 1998), 181–82; *The Cranes Are Flying* (*Letiat zhuravli*, dir. Mikhail Kalatozov, 1957), 135; *The Death of Stalin* (dir. Iannucci, Armando, 2017), 90; *The Defeat of the Germans near Moscow* (*Razgrom nemetskikh voisk pod Moskvoi*, 1942), 154; *Evgenii Khaldei: A Photographer under Stalin* (dir. Marc-Henri Wajnberg, 1997), 174; *Fate of Man* (*Sud′ba cheloveka*, dir. Sergei Bondarchuk, 1959), 135; *The Final Storm* (see *Liberation*); *Fog* and *Fog 2* (made-for-television), 195; *The Great Farewell* (*Velikoe proshchanie*), 90, 91, 94–95; *The Great Glow* (*Velikoe zarevo*, dir. Mikheil Chiaureli 1938), 80; *A Great Life: Part 2* (*Bol′shaia zhizn′*, dir. Leonid Lukov, 1945), 50; *The Great Patriotic* (*Velikaia otechestvennaia*, dir. Roman Karmen, 1965), 112–14, 121–23, 148, 151, 160, 163, 166, 217; *Grunia Kornakova/aka* (The nightingale) (*Solovei-solovushka*, dir. Nikolai Ekk, 1936), 75; *If Your Home Is Dear to You* (*Esli dorog tebe tvoi*

dom, dir. Vasilii Ordynskii, 1967), 140, 149, 153; *In Defense of Peace*, 117; *Internationale* (*Internatsional*, dir. A. Svetlov, Aleksandr Shein, 1971), 147; *It Happened in the Donbas* (*Eto bylo v Donbasse*, dir. Leonid Lukov), 35; *Ivan's Childhood* (*Ivanovo detstvo*, dir. Andrei Tarkovskii, 1962), 12, 135; *July Rain* (*Iiul'skii dozhd'*, dir. Khutsiev, Marlen, 1966), 110; *Katiusha* (dir. Viktor Lisakovich, 1964), 113; *Lenin in October* (*Lenin v oktiabre*, dir. Mikhail Romm), 27, 69; *Liberation* (*Osvobozhdenie*, dir. Iurii Ozerov, 1970–1971), 18, 135–38, 140, 142–43, 145–46, 164, 192, 217; *The Longest Day* (1962), 137, 146, 147; *March On, Land of Mine* (*Shagai strana*, dir. Aleksandr Shein, G. Brenner, 1981), 147; *October* (*Oktiabr'*, dir. Sergei Eisenstein, 1927), 26, 69; *An Office Romance* (*Sluzhebnyi roman*, dir. El'dar Riazanov, 1977), 163; *Our March* (dir. Aleksandr Shein, Aleksandr Svetlov, 1970), 147, 148; *A Relic of Military Glory* (*Relikviia boevoi slavy*), 126; *The Soldiers of Freedom* (*Soldaty svobody*, dir. Iurii Ozerov, 1977), 146; *A Soldier Was Walking* (*Shel soldat*, dir. Marina Babak, 1975), 150; *The Storming of the Winter Palace* (dir. Nikolai Evreinov), 26–27; *Story of a Great Feat* (*Povest' o velikom podvige*), 126; *Tale of a Communist* (*Povest' o kommuniste*, dir. Igor' Bessarabov, Aleksandr Kochetkov), 161; *Tarzan*, 122; *They Raised the Victory Banner* (*Oni vodruzili Znamia Pobedy*, dir. L. Danilov, 1960), 110–12; *The Third Blow* (*Tret'i udar*, dir. Igor' Savchenko, 1948), 136; *Three Songs of Lenin* (*Tri pesni o Lenine*, dir. Dziga Vertov, 1934), 94; *20th Anniversary of the Great Feat* (*20-letie velikogo podviga*, dir. Irina Setkina, Elena Vermisheva, 1965), 123; *Victory Day* (*Den' Pobedy*, dir. Sergei Loznitsa, 2018), 203; *Victory Parade* (*Parad pobedy*, dir. Vasilii Beliaev, Irina Venzher, Iakov Posel'skii, 1945), 47; *The Vow* (*Kliatva*, dir. Mikheil Chiaureli), 54, 66, 67, 80, 81; *We Are from the Future* (*My iz budushchego*, dir. Andrei Maliukov, 2008), 194–95; *World at War*, 163

Firsov, General-Lieutenant, 106, 108, 109

First Belorussian Front, 22, 35, 47, 142

First Ukrainian Front, 22–23

foreign dignitaries: George W. Bush, 186; Bill Clinton, 180; Averell Harriman, 153; John Major, 180; Augusto Pinochet, 157

gaming, 187–98; video games (*Call of Duty*), 189, 190–94, 256n85

German Democratic Republic (GDR), 132, 139

glasnost, 170, 171

Gorbachev, Mikhail, 167–69, 178, 180, 185, 213, 218, 220; speeches by, 169, 175–77

Grudinin, Pavel, 206–7, 208

Gulag, 6, 13, 51, 219

Hariman, Robert, and John Louis Lucaites. *See under* iconic images

Hero cities, 132, 163

Hero of the Soviet Union award, 127, 166, 173

historical scholarship, 5, 8, 9, 12, 56, 60, 98, 99, 173, 183, 220; and analysis, 152, 213, 220, and film, 26, 42; writings, 3, 11, 57, 66, 134, 144, 171, 214, 217. *See also History of the Great Patriotic War of the Soviet Union, The*
history, 11–14, 124, 129, 173, 213–15, 55–60
History of the Great Patriotic War of the Soviet Union, The, 99–101, 140, 152; editorial conferences for (1960, 1961), 18, 25, 101, 103–10, 112, 124, 129, 171, 172
Hitler, Adolf, 21, 68, 78, 82, 139, 155, 176; armies of, 118, 121; in film, 115–16, 143
Hobsbawm, Eric, 8, 9
Holocaust, the, 13, 121, 155, 157–62, 180, 186; narrative of, 214–15, 219. *See also* Jews; Nazis
Hutchings, Stephen, and Natalia Rulyova, 184, 186, 187, 188

Ianukovich, Viktor, 200, 202
Iazov, Dmitrii, 172, 178
iconic images, 9, 67, 163, 197, 203; Hariman and Lucaites and, 7–8, 16, 216, 220; and Victory Banner, 120, 130, 195, 210, 211; in video games, 189, 190
Institute of Marxism-Leninism, 25, 105, 115, 124; History of the Great Patriotic War Section of the, 25, 101, 102, 105
Ivanov, Aleksei, 70–71, 78, 79

Jews, 5, 12, 85, 157–59, 180, 209; Nazis and, 121, 161, 186, 214
journalists, 8, 11, 39, 43, 162, 174; Stanislav Kondrashov, 181; Aleksandr Krivitskii, 56; Sergei Muratov and Georgii Fere, 188; Dmitrii Radyshevskii, 167
journals: *Novyi mir*, 101; *Ogonek*, 3, 30, 55; *Oktiabr′*, 55; *Voprosy istorii*, 99

Kaganovich, 94, 95, 97
Kantariia, Meliton, 10, 28, 36, 97, 108, 109, 124, 125; absent from Moscow, 71, 106; in film, 78–80, 111, 144, 195; given awards, 53, 71; in 1980s, 167, 168; with Konstantin Samsonov, 75, 164. *See also under* Egorov, Mikhail
Karmen, Roman, 29, 36, 113, 156, 163, 229n70; and television series, 122, 151–52, 154. *See also* films: *The Great Patriotic*
KGB (Komitet Gosudarstvennoy Bezopasnosti), 99, 138
Khaldei, Evgenii, 25, 174, 228n42, 228n48; photograph printed in *Ogonek*, 13 May 1945, 3, 30; photograph reused, 156, 175; photograph titled *The Victory Banner over the Reichstag*, 4, 10, 17, 29, 173, 209, 230n78
Khaniutin, Iurii, 137, 140
Khrushchev, Nikita, 12, 94, 111, 116, 124, 220, 234n29; era, 96–99, 109, 125; "secret speech" by, 56, 96, 98
Kiev, 155, 158
Kleinerman, Isaac, 154, 157, 160
Klimov, editor, 104, 106, 107–8
Konev, Ivan, 22, 137, 139
Kremlin, the, 47, 111, 126, 164, 188, 217, 227n36; and Stalin, 27–29; Tomb of the Unknown Soldier, 132, 133, 144
Krivonogov, Petr A.: painting titled *The Capitulation of the Fascist Armies in Berlin (Kapituliatsiia*

fashistskikh voisk v Berline, 1946), 61–65, 69, 143; painting titled *Victory* (*Pobeda*), 1948, 17–18, 62
Kulish, V. M., 56, 57, 60
Kumanev, Georgii, 172, 173, 214, 227–28n40
Kursk, battle of, 31, 120
Kuznetsov, Colonel-General V. I. (Third Strike Army), 105, 111, 142

Lancaster, Burt. *See under* actors
Lenin, 47, 89, 90, 109, 124, 147, 181, 243n131; funeral of, 94, 111
Leningrad, 97, 113, 155
Lisimenko, Aleksandr, 107, 172
literature, 55–56, 59, 66, 98, 104, 234n29, 245n159; "Defeated Berlin," poem by Samuil Marshak, 4, 24
Lobov, Vadim, 205, 206
Loznitsa, Sergei, 203–4
Lukov, Leonid, 25, 50, 230n78

Majdanek. *See under* concentration camps
Makov, Captain, 172, 173, 259n140
Maksimenkov, Leonid, 101, 125, 213
Malenkov, Georgii, 82, 94, 95, 97
massacres: Einsatzgruppen killings, 161; at Babyi Iar, 157–58; at Katyn, 159–60, 171
May Day, 17, 28, 29, 51–52, 54, 127; in 1900, 7; in 1945, 41, 42; in 1965, 126; in 1993, 178
memoirs, 8, 99, 107, 126, 129, 172, 214, 217; Brezhnev's, 161; collection of, 55–56; Neustroev's, 47; of participants in battle for Berlin, 21–22, 37, 47, 105, 171; Raizman's, 37; Samsonov's, 106, 107; television series of, 150; tightly controlled, 56, 130; used in filmmaking, 139, 148; various, 12, 37, 59, 165; of veterans, 25, 55, 100–101; war, published in the 1960s, 134, 149, 161; Zhukov's, 21, 134, 139, 171, 225n1, 228n40
Mesiatsev, Nikolai, 126, 128
Mikoian, 94, 95, 97
military hardware, 33, 138, 179, 185–86, 187, 197, 206
military historians, 138, 139, 140, 170, 227n36
military parades, 41, 44, 45, 51, 179, 184, 195, 200, 252n25; between 1965 and 1985, 131, 132; on May Day, 42, 52; in November, 134, 165; on Victory Day, 53, 125–27, 168, 174, 177, 218
Molotov, Viacheslav, 57, 82, 94, 97
Moscow, 108, 121, 129, 178–79; Patriot Park, 10, 204, 205, 257n113; Synergy University, 205; University students, 212. *See also* Victory Parades
Mosfil′m film studio, 73, 80, 147
music: Beethoven's "Ode to Joy", 44; Briskin, V., "Let Us Raise the Victory Banner over Berlin!" Za chest′ rodiny, 24 April 1945, 23; Bulat Okudzhava's "Pick up your greatcoat and go home" ("Beri shinel′, poshli domoi," 1975), 204; Glinka's *A Life for the Tsar*, 43–44, 185; national anthem, 44, 48, 164, 185; Red Army's band and orchestras, 43; Shostakovich's Thirteenth Symphony, 158; Frank Sinatra, 153; V. G. Fere, composer, 84; "Victory Day," composed by David Tukhmanov, 185; work of Vertov or Shub, 66

Nazis, 27, 64, 82, 83, 113, 155, 156, 180; atrocities of, 11, 84, 157–59,

161, 214; and banners, 47, 48, 69, 120–21
Nazism, 186, 209
Nazi-Soviet pact, 5, 57, 171
Neustroev, Stepan, 46, 47, 53, 78, 97, 105–7, 111, 141, 172
newspaper coverage, 32, 90, 95, 164, 177
newspapers: *Berlin Operation*, 58; *Der Tagesspiel*, 66; *Guardian*, 200; *Izvestiia*, 54, 132, 170, 171, 175, 181, 184; *Krasnaia zvezda*, 23, 29, 36, 112, 165; *Los Angeles Times*, 160; *Morning Star*, 209; *Neues Deutschland*, 66; *New York Times*, 154; *Rabochaia gazeta*, 171–72; *Trud*, 47. *See also Pravda*
newsreel, 36–37, 38, 46, 68, 91, 156; and documentary, 31–32, 33, 69; footage, 39, 66, 97, 110–11, 139, 150, 191; *Novosti dnia*, 110, 111; and film, 39, 110, 126, 129
Novosti Press Agency, 126, 212
Nuremberg International Military Tribunal, 113, 161

Okudzhava, Bulat, 133, 104
150th Rifle Division, Third Strike Army, 7, 45–56, 109, 173, 209; 356th Regiment, 46; 674th Rifle Regiment, 20; 756th Rifle Regiment, 20, 141, 172; in video game, 190
Ozerov, Iurii, 135–39, 142, 145, 146, 148. *See also* films: *Liberation*

parades, 44–45, 82, 131, 178, 184, 213; and television, 164, 165; on 24 June 1945, 41–43, 45, 51, 97, 127, 143, 184; on 9 May, 53, 55; in November, 68, 165; in 2000 and 2005, 183, 186. *See also* military parades; Victory Parades
Paris Commune, 17, 147
Perestroika, 176, 178
Perevertkin, Semen, 56, 105, 106, 109, 111
photography, 7, 29, 30–31, 93, 126, 129, 213, 228n44; still, 38, 74, 76, 85, 196
photojournalism, 17, 29–31, 66
Pioneers (Soviet youth organization), 35, 119, 198; Fountain of, 119
Poland, 5, 103, 153, 158–59
Politburo, 43, 167, 169
Pravda, 23, 25, 39, 53, 106, 132, 143n131; from 1945, 4, 24, 43, 47; from 1946, 52, 53, 54; from Victory Day 1947, 55; from 1953, 91, 93; from 1954, 95–96; from 1990, 172; from 1993, 179
prisoners of war (POWs), 12, 20, 65, 82, 171, 184
propaganda, 81, 86, 96, 117, 128; Soviet, 25, 153–54, 160, 173
Putin, Vladimir, 16, 18, 183, 213, 218, 219; and CPRF, 187, 199; speeches, 185, 186

Raizman, Iulii, 33, 40, 42, 121, 156, 229n61, 230n77; *Berlin* (1945) by, 27, 34–35, 38–39, 68, 81, 111, 112, 118; footage in video game,190, 191–92; memoir by, 37
Red Army, 6, 12, 13, 20, 21, 43, 45, 158, 159, 186; Central Museum of the, 17, 28, 46, 48–49, 53, 198; Day, 59, 163, 205; in film, 73–74, 84, 156; and flags, 22, 25, 48–49, 57, 190; and graffiti, 28, 156; in paintings, 62, 64; in photos, 29, 31; and the press, 23, 38; victorious, 52, 68, 81, 143; in video games, 190, 193, 196
red flag, 3–5, 11, 17–18, 21–22, 25–29, 35, 40, 48, 52, 55, 64, 73, 75, 78, 80,

82, 99, 120, 147, 179, 182, 186, 190, 195, 202, 206, 208–9, 219, 258n126
Red Square, 44, 179, 244n135; in film, 67, 68, 112; military parades on, 42, 185, 187, 200; speeches on, 178, 180, 182; on television, 126–27, 187–88; veteran reunions on, 131, 179. *See also* parades; Victory Day; Victory Parades
Reich Chancellery, 21, 39, 82, 226n9
Rolf, Malte, 43, 82
Romm, Mikhail, 27, 69
Roshchin, Colonel S. I., 100, 101, 103, 105, 106, 108–9
Russian Federation, 178, 185, 232n118; Russian Soviet Federative Socialist Republic, 17

S′ianov, Il′ia, 46, 78, 111, 173
Salisbury, Harrison, 154, 162
Samsonov, Konstantin, 46, 71, 97, 111, 124–25; given awards, 53, 70, 127; memoir by, 106, 107; with Egorov and Kantariia, 75, 164
Semin, A. G., 119, 120
Seoev, Vladimir, 171, 172
Shatalin, V. D., 103, 172
Shatilov, General V. M., 70, 105, 109, 111, 141, 172
Shtemenko, Sergei, 45, 139
Simonov, Konstantin, 56, 82, 98, 149, 150
Smirnov, Sergei, 113, 117, 122, 133, 148–49
Soviet media, 31, 36, 95, 137, 217, 232n120
Stalin, Joseph, 21, 40–41, 50, 57, 59, 82, 114–17, 214; crimes of, 121, 150; cult of, 65, 66, 89, 93, 98, 123–24, 217, 244n135; in film, 73, 79–80, 90, 92, 136; following the death of, 14, 16, 88; funeral of, 91, 92, 94, 95, 111; and “Glory,” 44; orders of, 26–27, 38, 52, 56; at parades, 43, 45, 48, 116; Prize, 33, 43, 61, 62, 64; statues of, removed, 244n135; and victory, 53, 77, 86
Stalingrad, 26, 86; battle of, 31, 97, 108, 120, 121, 207
Stalinism, 176–77, 184, 219
State Committee for Defense, 96, 97, 116
Supreme Soviet, 53, 54, 71, 106

Tarkovskii, Andrei, 12, 122, 135
Taylor, Richard, 66, 68, 78, 82
Tehran conference, 116, 139
television, 126, 127, 146–49, 164, 187, 217; American, 122, 160; commentary, 127, 177, 183, 184; coverage, 18, 188, 189; documentaries, 163, 165, 196–97; minute of silence on, 128, 132, 133, 162, 164, 211; programs, 113, 133, 174; Russian, 187, 194, 196, 203; series, 150, 155, 160–61, 165, 166, 194, 195, 196, 256n87. *See also Unknown War, The*
Thames Television, 155, 190
Third Strike Army of the First Belorussian Front, 20, 22, 101, 105, 111, 142, 229n62; 171st Division, 46, 103, 109, 172. *See also* 150th Rifle Division, Third Strike Army
Tomb of the Unknown Soldier, 5, 160–61, 132–33, 144, 155
tricolor, Russian, 178, 179, 187; of Revolution, 17
Tucker, Robert C., 90, 95
Tumarkin, Nina, 8, 62, 167, 178, 195, 213
Twenty-Eight Panfilovites, 11, 16, 56

Ukraine, 16–17, 158, 200, 206; Crimea, 201, 202, 203, 218

Unknown War, The (television series, 1978), 18, 147, 151, 159–61, 192, 196, 217; dubbed by Vasilii Lanovoi for Russian release titled *The Great Patriotic* (*Velikaia otechestvennaia*), 122, 155; reception of, 162–67

veterans, 60, 87, 103, 112, 129, 131, 133, 181; disabled, 176; gatherings of, 110, 179; interviewed, 69, 150; memoirs of, 55, 100; organization of, 198, 199; war, 102, 139, 167
Victory cult, 181, 189, 221
Victory Day, 3, 9, 55, 179, 182, 186, 193, 212; commemorations of, 128–29, 174–83; during the Putin era, 184, 218; a holiday, 199, 233n19; parades, 161–62, 126, 197, 204, 211, 215; song composed by David Tukhmanov, 185; in the 1940s, 51–52, 54, 55; on 9 May 1965, 18, 125, 126, 129, 131; on 9 May 1968, 132; during the 1970s, 164; in 2000, 184; in 2005, 187; in 2010, 196; in 2011 in Ukraine, 202; in 2017, 203
Victory Parades, 8, 41–50, 168, 178, 182, 183–89; film of 1945, 47, 69, 73, 143, 152; subtext to the, 127–28; on 24 June 1945, 5–6, 8, 40, 41, 73, 82, 198, 217. *See also under* Victory Day
Victory Park: Hall of Glory, 198; Hill of Prostrations (Poklonnaia gora), 174, 177–78, 179
video games. *See* gaming
voice-over, 33, 47, 93, 97, 121–22, 123, 139, 190; in *The Fall of Berlin*, 40, 81; in *The Great Farewell*, 94, 95; in *The Great Patriotic*, 152, 153, 166; narration, 110, 118, 183; television, 10, 127, 180, 184, 185, 188, 189
Voroshilov, Kliment, 57, 94, 97, 112

war: commemoration, 133, 153, 163, 203; cult, 12, 130, 162, 170, 210, 221; films, 86, 137, 138, 151, 194; games, 194–98
war memory, 18, 55, 64, 100, 134, 203, 215–17, 221; repetition of, 14, 184–85; Russian, 8, 220; and Soviet television, 150–51; Stalinization of, 28, 66, 97
Warsaw Uprising, the, 113, 153, 158–59
wartime, 104, 114, 162; footage, 35, 150, 152, 163; and postwar art, 60–65
Weiner, Fred, 154–55, 160, 249n86. *See also* Air Time International Company
Winter Palace, St. Petersburg, 26, 27, 69, 71
World War II, 6, 8, 89, 169, 198–99, 218

Yalta conference, 21, 68, 177
Yeltsin, Boris, 178, 179, 180–83, 185, 199, 218
Youngblood, Denise, 67, 86, 137, 140, 146, 195
YouTube, 201, 204, 257n110
Yurchak, Alexei, 10, 15, 60, 120, 167

Zhukov, Georgii, 22, 42, 44, 46, 47, 106, 137, 171; interview with, 149, 153; memoirs of, 21, 134, 139, 171, 225n1, 228n40; not mentioned, 56, 59, 78, 116; and Stalin, 45, 142
Zinchenko, Fedor, 27, 47, 70, 141, 171; in film, 75, 78, 79, 111–12